Exporting Chinese Architecture

Charlie Qiuli Xue · Guanghui Ding
Editors

Exporting Chinese Architecture

History, Issues and "One Belt One Road"

Springer

Editors
Charlie Qiuli Xue
Department of Architecture and Civil Engineering
City University of Hong Kong
Kowloon, Hong Kong

Guanghui Ding
Department of Architecture
Beijing University of Civil Engineering and Architecture
Beijing, China

ISBN 978-981-19-2785-0 ISBN 978-981-19-2786-7 (eBook)
https://doi.org/10.1007/978-981-19-2786-7

This Springer imprint is published by the registered company Springer Nature Singapore Pte Ltd.
The registered company address is: 152 Beach Road, #21-01/04 Gateway East, Singapore 189721, Singapore

Preface

In China's years of industrial development under Mao Zedong's leadership, foreign aid was mixed with the Third Front (*sanxian jianshe*) and other production activities, mainly in the hinterland mountain areas. When artistic expression gradually resurged at the end of the Cultural Revolution in the mid-1970s, a famous comic dialogue (*xiangsheng*) about the Tanzania–Zambia Railway spread throughout China via radio, providing a form of "internationalism" education through entertainment. Except for those who were directly involved in foreign aid, most people knew little about remote foreign countries and the achievements and hardship of Chinese construction overseas. In the years of the planned economy, "traveling abroad" was unthinkable for most people living in China.

In our survey of China's state-owned design institutes of the past decade, Chinese architects' overseas work gradually emerges into view. Our article "China's architectural aid: Exporting a transformational modernism" describes a brief history of China's construction aid. Thanks to the editor and reviewers, this article was published in *Habitat International*, No. 1, 2015. As one of only a few articles examining China's construction aid, it attracted attention and citations and prompted further exploration of the topic of construction aid in relation to several building types, including stadia, conference halls, schools and shopping malls, and in different regions and areas, such as the Horn of Africa and the Caucasus. These explorations are reflected in this volume.

In June 2021, we held an international symposium on the topic of "exporting Chinese architecture". Thanks to modern technology, 10 speakers from various places delivered talks that were attended by more than 300 people via Zoom despite the havoc caused by the COVID-19 pandemic. The speakers had a common desire to compile a special book based on the symposium. We are grateful that Springer organized a rigorous review of our proposal and agreed to publish and distribute our book of 13 chapters. This book stands together with our previous Springer publications "*Grand Theater Urbanism: Chinese cities in the 21st century*" (2019) and "*Hong Kong Architecture 1945–2015: from colonial to global*" (2016). Both early books received a warm welcome in the world. We heartily thank the Springer editorial team, in particular Lydia Wang, for their efforts.

The study of China's design institutes was partly inspired by Professor Jianfei Zhu. Although Charlie has written about China's building practice, including design systems since the 1990s, it was Professor Zhu who raised the theoretical bar and invited us to prepare a chapter for his spectacular magnum opus, the *Routledge Handbook of Chinese Architecture* (2022). In 2015, Charlie was invited to present in "Bauhaus and its significance today", organized by Gothe Institute in Beijing, where he met scholars who had researched socialist global architecture. In 2017, Professor Cole Roskam held a symposium on socialist design institutes after World War II in the University of Hong Kong. We were fortunate to exchange ideas with a group of scholars whose research focused on Eastern Europe and Asia. In 2018, Tongji University Architectural Design Group celebrated its 60-year anniversary in Shanghai. Thanks to Professor Hua Xiahong, we contributed talks and had discussions about design systems and firms with international scholars. In the same year, Professor Murray Fraser hosted a conference on world architectural history at UCL, London, which gathered top-tier scholars in Europe and North America. The paper we presented was published in the *Arena Journal of Architectural Research*, edited by Professor Fraser in 2019. In 2021, Professors Eunice Seng and Jiat-Hwee Chang launched the "Cosmopolitanism's Others: Transnational Architecture and Planning beyond Europe and North America" group in the European Architectural History Network (EAHN). We participated and interpreted the concept along with other speakers. Through these encounters, exchanges, presentations and publications, we have gradually approached the essence and facts of transnational architecture, especially during the Cold War.

China's construction works were scattered in five continents, some are in far-flung areas. The authors of various chapters focus on their familiar areas and works, which are duly acknowledged in their text. We particularly appreciate the assistance from Dr. Anoma Kumarasuriyar and her sister and brother-in-law during Charlie's visit in Sri Lanka; and Nguyễn Mạnh Trí, Minh Nguyen Kuang of National University of Civil Engineering and Duc Tran Cong of gmp during Charlie's investigation in Vietnam. We have drawn inspirations from reading Professor Lukasz Stanek's works and talking with him. Lukasz kindly channels us to the other sources of studying the topic of socialist foreign aid.

Chinese architects and engineers are part of the protagonists of this book. Our thankful saluting list is unexhausted: Cheng Taining of Hangzhou; Xing Tonghe, Wei Dunshan, Zhang Xingjian, Jin Peng, Ren Lizhi, Dong Yingtao, Zhu Deyao, Zhang Liping, Wu Jie and Da Hongliang of Shanghai; Zhou Qinglin, You Baoxian, Man Ning, Liu Miao, Dang Zheng, Bai Jinghua, Wang Daozheng, Huang Ximiu, Zhang Ri, Zheng Yu, Sun Zhijiu, Hou Yigang, Xiong Jun, Zhang Guangyuan and Ren Hao of Beijing; Li Fang, Li Chunfang, Gao Si, Shen Tao and Zhu Shengbo of Wuhan; Liu Yi, Wang Jinxue, Peng Yuecong of Chengdu; Huang Guangwei, Su Yuan, Sun Zhiwei of Zhengzhou and Li Zeng of Cambodia. Their design works show how passions can overcome technical and long-distant hurdles and limited resources can produce suitable space and meaningful place for people in other countries.

The study of foreign aid architecture has benefitted from discussion with and help from our colleagues: Gu Daqing, Jia Beisi, Leigh Shutter, Edward Ng, Gianni

Talamini, Giorgio Strafella, Lu Yi, Tsou Jin Yeu, Carmen Tsui, Tan Gangyi, Cui Tong, Ni Yang, Xiao Jing, Tan Zheng and Huang Zhengli. In addition to Ph.D. students who contribute to chapters of this volume, the other students assist the work in various capacities: Xiao Yingbo, Sun Cong, Liu Xin, Chan Kai Chun, Ma Kaiyue, Qiu Yue, Gu Yanqiu and Chang Wei.

This book is part of a study supported by the National Natural Science Foundation of China, Project No. 51878584. This book provides an introduction to the issue of China's architectural engagement with developing countries within the context of foreign aid. In "throwing a sprat to catch a mackerel", our hope is that more in-depth works will emerge.

Kowloon, Hong Kong
Beijing, China
Summer 2022

Charlie Qiuli Xue
Guanghui Ding

Contents

Editors and Contributors

About the Editors

Charlie Qiuli Xue has taught architecture at Shanghai Jiaotong University, University of Texas and City University of Hong Kong. An award-winning architect and writer, he has published 15 books, including "*Building a Revolution: Chinese Architecture since 1980*" (HKU Press, 2006), "*Hong Kong Architecture 1945–2015: From Colonial to Global*" (Springer, 2016), "*A History of Design Institutes in China: from Mao to Market*" (with G. Ding, Routledge, 2018) and "*Grand Theater Urbanism: Chinese cities in the 21st century*" (Springer, 2019, ed.). He has published more than 160 research papers in professional and international refereed journals and 40 book chapters. His papers are published in journals such as *Cities, Habitat International, Urban Design International, Journal of Architecture, Journal of Urban Design, Architectural Research Quarterly, Journal of Urban History, Planning Perspective, Architecture + Urbanism, Domus* and Chinese journals like *Architectural Journal, Architect, New Architecture, Time + Architecture, World Architecture* and *Taiwan Architect*. His book on Hong Kong was awarded by the International Committee of Architectural Critics (CICA) in 2017. His research interests are in Chinese architecture, transnational design and high-density environment. He is also extensively involved in design and consultant practice in Hong Kong, Chinese mainland and the US.

Guanghui Ding is Associate Professor of Architecture at the Beijing University of Civil Engineering and Architecture in China. He completed his Ph.D. in architecture from the University of Nottingham, United Kingdom in 2013 and later worked as a Postdoctoral Research Fellow at City University of Hong Kong. His research focuses on modern and contemporary Chinese architecture, including many subjects in critical architecture, architectural criticism and periodicals, design institutes and China's architectural aid in the Global South. He is the author of *Constructing a Place of Critical Architecture in China: Intermediate Criticality in the Journal* Time + Architecture (London and New York: Routledge, 2016) (Chinese edition,

《建筑批评的一朵浪花:实验性建筑》Beijing: China Architecture and Building Press, 2018) and co-author of *A History of Design Institutes in China: From Mao to Market* (London and New York: Routledge, 2018, with Charlie Qiuli Xue) (expanded Chinese edition,《中国设计院:价值与挑战》Beijing: China Architecture and Building Press, 2022). His scholarly articles have been published by *Architecture and Culture, Architectural Research Quarterly, ARENA Journal of Architectural Research, Domus, Habitat International, Histories of Post-War Architecture, Journal of Architecture, Journal of the Society of Architectural Historians, Jianzhushi/The Architect, Shidai jianzhu/Time + Architecture, Shijie jianzhu/World Architecture, Xin jianzhu/New Architecture* and other edited volumes.

Contributors

Amoah Lloyd G. Adu University of Ghana, Accra, Ghana

Amos Keith School of Architecture, Tianjin University, Tianjin, China

Ai Xia CCDI Group, Shanghai, China

Cai Xiaolei Department of Architecture and Civil Engineering, City University of Hong Kong, Kowloon, Hong Kong

Chen Yingting Department of Architecture and Civil Engineering, City University of Hong Kong, Kowloon, Hong Kong

Ding Guanghui Department of Architecture, Beijing University of Civil Engineering and Architecture, Beijing, China

Fan Qingnan Beijing University of Civil Engineering and Architecture, Beijing, China

Gao Yizhuo Department of Architecture and Civil Engineering, City University of Hong Kong, Kowloon, Hong Kong

Jaillon Lara Chu Hai College of Higher Education, Hong Kong, China

Li Yang China Electronics Engineering Design Institute Co., Ltd., Beijing, China

Li Ze School of Architecture, Tianjin University, Tianjin, China

Liu Xinyu Department of Architecture and Civil Engineering, City University of Hong Kong, Kowloon, Hong Kong

Liu Ye New School of Social Research, New York, USA

Marri Sohrab Ahmed Department of Architecture, Balochistan University of Information Technology, Engineering and Management Science, Quetta, Pakistan

Mbewe Davies Afiya Department of Buildings, Ministry of Transport and Public Works of Malawi, Lilongwe, Malawi

Song Ke School of Architecture, Harbin Institute of Technology, Shenzhen, China

Tang Shan School of Architecture, Tianjin University, Tianjin, China

Wan Yan University of Hong Kong, Pokfulam, Hong Kong

Xue Charlie Qiuli Department of Architecture and Civil Engineering, City University of Hong Kong, Kowloon, Hong Kong

Zhang Lujia Department of Architecture and Civil Engineering, City University of Hong Kong, Kowloon, Hong Kong

Zhang Tianjie Tianjin University, Tianjin, China

Zhang Yuqi Kyoto University, Kyoto, Japan

Part I
Historic Narrative

Chapter 1
Exporting Chinese Architecture: A Historical Perspective

Charlie Qiuli Xue and Guanghui Ding

Abstract China's foreign aid has involved the exchange of huge amounts of money, manpower and materials between donor and recipient countries over the past 70 years. Construction aid accounts for a large percentage of China's foreign aid and makes its aid-related activity visible in the world. This chapter provides the background to China's construction aid and explains the rationale, content, perspective and methodology of this book. This volume goes some way to filling the enormous gap in research on this topic and makes an appeal for the smoother operation of aid-funded buildings and transnational design/construction.

Colombo, the capital city of Sri Lanka, formerly Ceylon, has experienced the construction of many different modern-type buildings built by the Dutch and British colonists during the past hundred years, including hotels, a parliament house, government buildings and hospitals. On a tree-lined boulevard in the north district, the octagonal Bandaranaike Memorial International Conference Center, its roof supported by 40 slender columns, was erected in 1973 and became a much-admired conference hall in South Asia. Forty years later, a national theater called Nelum Pokuna ("lotus pond") was completed several blocks away from the Bandaranaike Hall. Both buildings were donated by the Chinese government, and designed and constructed by Chinese professionals. Since 2010, Sri Lanka has travelled a path of fast development and the capital city overlooking the Indian Ocean has been boosted by skyscraper office buildings, large-scale high-rise residential estates, a TV tower, and a new harbor district, most of which have been brought about by Chinese capital, design, construction, and technologies.

C. Q. Xue (✉)
Department of Architecture and Civil Engineering, City University of Hong Kong, Kowloon, Hong Kong
e-mail: bscqx@cityu.edu.hk

G. Ding
Department of Architecture, Beijing University of Civil Engineering and Architecture, Beijing, China

C. Q. Xue and G. Ding (eds.), *Exporting Chinese Architecture*,
https://doi.org/10.1007/978-981-19-2786-7_1

Colombo epitomizes China's construction aid in cities in the developing world, which mainly receive aid from developed countries and where new buildings are designed and constructed by foreign architects and contractors. In its narrowest definition, "exporting architecture" is the cross-border practice of designing and constructing buildings in other countries. North American, British, German, and French architects have exported the greatest number of designs to other countries since the end of World War II. Their designs spread modernist ideas to developing countries. While modernist architecture appeared in Asia, Africa, and Latin America, Chinese architects and constructors also built buildings overseas. During the 60-year period from 1958 to 2018, over 1,500 buildings were subsidized by the Chinese government and constructed by Chinese professionals in over 160 countries, including railways, stations, factories, congress and assembly halls, theaters, stadiums, schools, hospitals, and government buildings, together with other forms of economic aid for agriculture, irrigation, education, transportation, manufacturing, and health, involving investment equivalent to more than US$100 billion (Amoah, 2016; State Council of China, 2021).

In addition to the participation of state-owned design institutes, in the tide of "going out" in the twenty-first century, Chinese commercial engineering, procurement and construction projects have been achieved together with and led by many foreign-aid projects. China's earlier foreign-aid projects led the way for commercial projects that followed in the twenty-first century.

Why and under what conditions were Chinese-donated buildings initiated, designed, and constructed over more than half a century? Did they improve social progress and people's lives in developing countries? How do they compare with construction in China in the same period? How did they enrich the modern architectural movement outside Western countries? Is there any difference between donated and commercial buildings? This book addresses these unanswered questions and demystifies China's foreign-aid projects. It considers the motivations for architectural export, which are directly or indirectly associated with complicated social, political, economic, cultural, and ideological considerations. It also examines the design and construction processes in which specific knowledge, labor, capital, and goods are transferred between donor and recipient countries. Finally, it focuses on the agency of these projects, that is, "their capabilities to make a difference, to exercise some sort of power" (Giddens, 1984, p. 14).

The above questions have motivated a decade of investigation as well as the compilation of this book. The chapters examine the motivations, design and construction processes, spatial agency, and socio-political performances of Chinese-aided buildings in the developing world and provide a critical assessment of this long-overlooked transnational architectural practice.

1.1 Exporting Modernist Architecture

The struggles and efforts of people, organizations, and governments in vast developing countries after World War II can all be regarded as a movement toward modernization based on alleviating poverty and allowing people to lead a decent life and enjoying freedom and basic human rights. From this perspective, architecture and planning designed by foreign experts in developing countries have been framed as the "export of modernism" and its adaptations to the conditions of the Third World (Loeffler, 1998; Levin, 2016). The *Oxford Dictionary of English* defines "modern" as "relating to the present or recent times as opposed to the remote past, characterized by or using the most up-to-date techniques, ideas, or equipment… denoting a current or recent style or trend in art, architecture, or other cultural activity marked by a significant departure from traditional styles and values."[1]

In *Architecture and Modernity*, Hilde Heynen noted that "modernity is what gives the present the specific quality that makes it different from the past and points the way toward the future. Modernity is also described as being a break with tradition, and as typifying everything that rejects the inheritance of the past" (Heynen, 1999, p. 9). She continued:

> Modernity, then, constitutes the element that mediates between a process of socioeconomic development known as modernization and subjective responses to it in the form of modernist discourses and movements. In other words, modernity is a phenomenon with at least two different aspects: an objective aspect that is linked to socioeconomic processes, and a subjective one that is connected with personal experiences, artistic activities, or theoretical reflections…Architecture operates in both realms: it is unquestionably a cultural activity, but it is one that can be realized only within the world of power and money." (p. 10–11)

Reflected in architecture, "modernity" transits to "modern architecture." There are many descriptions and definitions of "modern architecture" (Berman, 1988). Duanfang Lu concisely summarized this social and architectural phenomenon as follows: "Originating in interwar Europe, modernist architecture—as a way of building, a knowledge product, a style of life consumer item, and above all—a symbol of modernity, has traversed national boundaries throughout the world" (Lu, 2011, p. 1). Lu further observed that although modernist architecture was extensively adopted in the Third World, history books only focus on its development in the West (Lu, 2011).

After World War II, European countries, whether victorious or defeated, were covered by ruins and debris. The U.S. led the post-war reconstruction effort in the West under the Marshall Plan and aid program to Japan and gave US$13 billion in aid with the goals of restoring production in Europe, expanding trade, and preventing the spread of communism. Through its examples of modernization, the U.S. showed its European peers that "you too can be like us" (Cohen, 1995; Fraser and Kerr, 2007; Hogben, 2012; Krieger, 2000; Cody, 2003). The U.S. government intended its aid to support developing countries in the "take-off" phase leading to industrial growth. The recipient countries were required to purchase construction materials and

[1] Oxford Dictionaries Language Matters, http://www.oxforddictionaries.com/definition/english/modern, Accessed May 26, 2015.

services from U.S. firms. The U.S. journal *Architectural Forum* summarized U.S. aid as "building up the basic welfare of other nations, creating climates unfavorable to communism, readying countries for industrialization and democratic independence, making them prosperous enough to buy more of our products" (Cody, 2003, p. 127). This expanded business for U.S. architects and construction companies. An architecture, engineering, and construction (AEC) strategy was encouraged and promoted by a significant number of U.S. professionals working on many types of construction site. The exporting of U.S. architecture, as an ideal, or simply a mass of building materials, reflected one dimension of a confusing mosaic and the superpower of U.S. technology and ideology (Gould, 1999; Cody, 2003). Perhaps in this regard nothing was more striking than the role played by the U.S. embassies buildings overseas (Robin, 2014; Loeffler, 1998). It can be argued that transnational architectural practice was bound up with global capitalism expansion and colonization (Harvey, 1989; Vernon, 2012; Wharton, 2011; Flowers, 2018). This phenomenon reached a new height after World War II and was associated with unequal power relations, political alliances, economic cooperation, and cultural exchange.

Aid projects sponsored by the U.S. and its multilateral frameworks (such as the World Bank, UNESCO, the OECD, and the Ford Foundation) were developed in Asia and Africa alongside those in Europe, forming post-colonial townscapes (Zunz, 1998; Herz, 2017; Langan, 2018; Moyo, 2009; Roskam, 2015). This has been described as the "mobility" of modern architecture, which was frequently illuminated by the famous overseas practices of Le Corbusier and Louis Kahn (Frampton, 1992).

Concurrently with the post-war reconstruction of Europe in the 1950s, a movement of independence from colonial rule engulfed Asia and Africa. The newly independent countries chose the way of capitalism or socialism, and received aid from the former suzerain countries and the Western and/or Eastern blocs. Some countries shrewdly accepted aid from all sides to increase their own power. The aid helped developing countries to develop their economies quickly and to establish national identities and confidence. Despite economic aid, many developing countries had strong desires to maintain peace, strive for independence and develop national economies. This desire was expressed in 1955 in the first Asia–Africa Conference in Bandung, Indonesia, which was a milestone of rising Non-Alliance countries. The principles raised in the conference have long been held as guidelines for international relations and development aid: mutual respect for other nations, territorial integrity and sovereignty, nonaggression, noninterference in internal affairs, equality and mutual benefits, and peaceful coexistence (see https://www.britannica.com/event/Bandung-Conference).

In the 1970s, Japan gradually recovered from its war trauma. Japanese architects actively promoted their designs and national policy in Southeast Asia. Their knowledge of urban planning and architectural design assisted the acceleration of urban modernization in Singapore and Malaysia (Xue & Xiao, 2014). The architectural projects exported to developing countries tended to follow modernist principles of design and aesthetics, complementing the development of modernist architecture, and have been labeled "Third World modernism" and "tropical modernism" (Levin, 2016; Pieris, 2011; Lu, 2011; Uduku, 2006).

Scholarship on the export of design and construction from the socialist Second World to the Third World began to emerge in 2010. Second World architecture in the Third World can be regarded as an extension of socialist architecture (Leach, 1999; Xue & Ding, 2018) and "global" Cold War design (Siamphukdee, 2014a, b; Beeckmans, 2018; Stanek, 2020). The Soviet Union and Eastern European countries sent infrastructure and architectural "gifts" to countries in the Middle East, Africa, Latin America and other areas. These cross-border architectural design practices have been considered by some scholars to be an extension of socialist architecture abroad under specific international conditions (Stanek, 2020; Pratt, 1991; Kulić, 2019; Mëhilli, 2017).

The encounter of Eastern European professionals with African and Middle Eastern countries was motivated by the desire of recipient countries when they turned to the socialist role model, and later "marketing socialist" before the end of the Cold War. These professionals presented their designs through socialist design institutes or as individual consultants. Some of them were employed by African local governments on planning committees and in design agencies. Stanek (2020) described this as "socialist world making" or, as the title of his book implies, "global socialism" through the exchange of tangible architectural resources.

As most imported planning and architecture projects were implemented via governments and imposed in a top-down manner, impressive man-made townscapes arose to declare the coming of a new age. In the late 1970s, to help Vietnam reemerge from the destruction of the war, East German architects planned futuristic metropolitan and residential areas for Vinh, a rural town in northern Vietnam, and transformed a largely rural population into an urban proletariat. Schwekel (2020) investigated the process of transformation and particularly the afterlife of the East German architecture. She found that alternative imaginaries of the future city subverted top-down planning and foreign blueprints for urban living. Tenants remade their social and material worlds according to spatial logics and cultural practices that expressed their own aspirations for urban futurity. Similar "abusive revisions" happened in other countries, including India. Schwenkel's work supplements the post-colonial urban scholarship by showing how an "ordinary" city in north central Vietnam became entwined with other forms of global connectivity to build a just and emancipated society.

Written from different angles, strata and locations, the literature cited above delineates the process of exporting architecture and its impact on the developing world. The emergence of international scholarship on transnational architectural practice is associated with two factors. First, previous architectural studies tended to focus on the noted works of celebrated architects, rather than conventional architectural practices, and more attention was paid to Western architects at the center of modernity (for example Le Corbusier and Louis Kahn), rather than Asian, African or Eastern European professionals, who have been regarded as being at the margin or periphery. Second, a new generation of academics in Europe and North America has gradually begun to examine ordinary architectural professionals in addition to the masters, and to reveal the little-known aspects of their domestic practice and their projects in Asia and Africa, which are inextricably linked to Western power, discourse, practice, or education. This trend contributes to the heterogeneous historiography of global architecture.

1.2 China's Foreign-Aided Construction

As stated above, the past 10 years have seen an increase in research into socialist Second World planning and design in Asia and Africa during the Cold War. However, China's overseas construction aid—amounting to trillions of dollars, requiring significant physical effort, and involving millions of end-users over the past 60 years—has rarely been the object of serious architectural study or even mentioned in the news. Prominent designs received awards in China and were published in Beijing's *Architectural Journal* from the 1970s onwards. However, there has been no serious study of China's foreign-aid construction similar to that prepared for this book. The challenge of studying this topic is that the buildings are scattered throughout various developing countries across five continents and most of them have not been reported by the media. Moreover, information from the donor/recipient governments and companies is fragmentary (Ding & Xue, 2015).

The People's Republic of China started to receive foreign aid from the socialist camp soon after its establishment in the form of a mass of construction projects and technical support, which helped to shape the industrial layout of the new China (Gao & He, 1995). Aid from the Soviet Union and Eastern Europe laid down the foundation for China's heavy industry, education, and culture, and launched an era of "learning from the big brother of the Soviet Union" in all trades. Visible milestones include the Sino-Soviet Union Friendship Buildings in Beijing, Shanghai, Wuhan, and Guangzhou.

Early in 1955, Chinese Premier Zhou Enlai (1898–1976) escaped an assassination attempt while on route to the Bandung Conference described above. Zhou participated in the conference despite the close call, and his moderate and conciliatory attitude, particularly his promotion of the Five Principles of Peaceful Coexistence, helped formulate a concluding declaration that allayed the doubts and fears of some anti-communist delegates about China's intentions. Shortly after the conference, China established diplomatic relations with more than 20 Asian and African countries and began to strengthen trade activity and expand foreign aid (Fig. 1.1).

In the early 1960s, ideological disputes between China and the Soviet Union led to the withdrawal of all Soviet aid (Shen, 2011). Surrounded by enemies in the Cold War, China attempted to break through the diplomatic bottleneck and donated construction aid projects to non-aligned countries in Asia and Africa. The donations reflected the philosophy of China' top leaders. Chairman Mao Zedong (1893–1976) expressed repeatedly this philosophy as follows: "Because China has a territory of 9.6 million square kilometers and 600 million people, our country should contribute more to mankind" (Mao, 1996); "We must strive to construct a strong socialist country, help the oppressed and exploited people in the world, and achieve our international duties"; "The justice struggle of people in various countries are supporting each

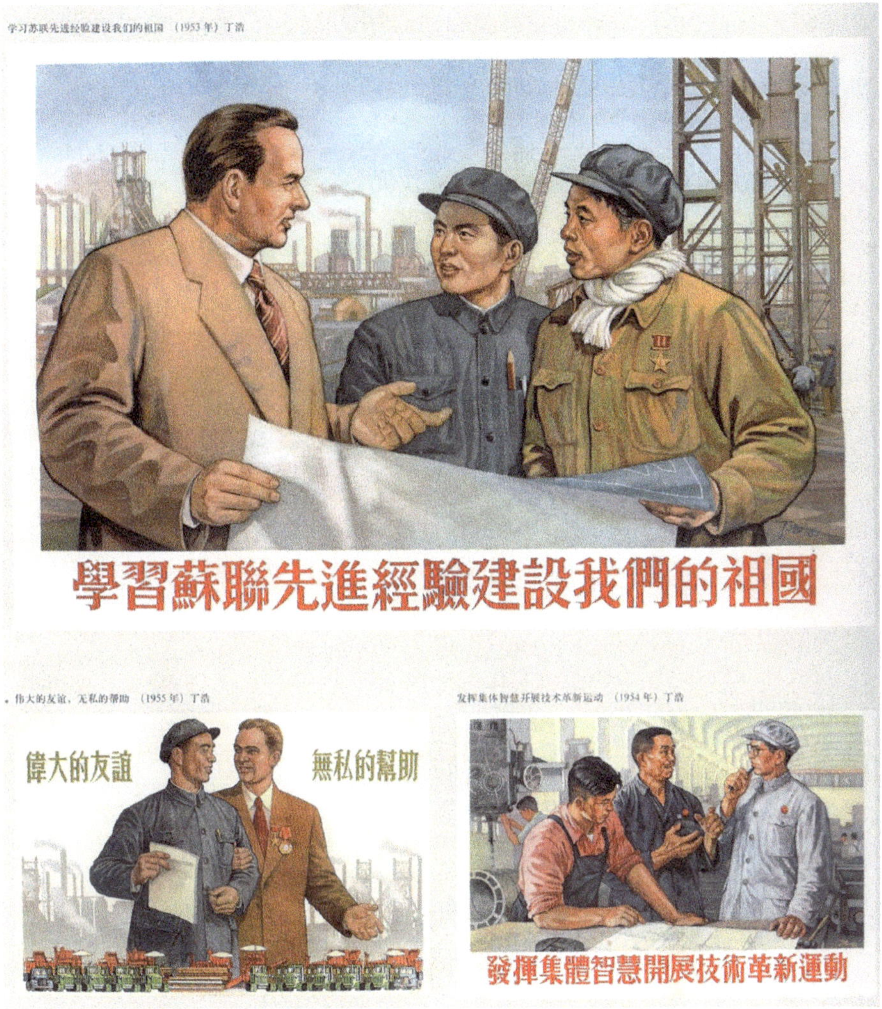

Fig. 1.1 Learning from the Soviet Union, propaganda posters, 1953–1955

other"; "Those who gained the revolutionary victory should help the other people who are still struggling for liberation. This is our international responsibility" (Mao, 1996). Mao's words described the direction of China's foreign aid in his era.

The gifts were given mainly to newly independent countries or to those holding similar socialist ideals (Amoah, 2016; Bartke, 1989; Chang et al., 2019; Taylor, 2006). The projects were all designed by Chinese architects and primarily constructed by Chinese companies. In most cases, the blueprints were written in Chinese and the construction materials, facilities, furniture, and even cutlery were shipped from China.

The 1950s and 1960s was a time of economic stringency in China. Famine ravaged the country, resulting in the deaths of millions (Dikötter, 2010). Most civil buildings at the time were constructed on a tight budget, but foreign construction aid projects were usually of a higher standard. These projects gave Chinese architects valuable opportunities to practice modernist principles and express regional tastes, which were banned in socialist China at that time (Xue, 2006; Xue & Ding, 2018; Zhu, 2009).

In the 1960s, the Chinese government decided that helping (socialist) friends was a way of weakening the (capitalist) enemy, and China should expand its circle of friends by every available means. In December 1963 and January 1964, Premier Zhou and Minister of Foreign Affairs Chen Yi (1901–1972) led a Chinese delegation to visit 14 countries in Asia, Africa, and Europe: Egypt, Algeria, Morocco, Tunisia, Ghana, Mali, Sudan, Guinea, Ethiopia, Somalia, Albania, Burma, Ceylon and Pakistan. The aims of the visits were to promote mutual understanding, inspect ongoing aid projects, and breakthrough the blockade of the U.S. and the Soviet Union. Zhou saw the "unequal" foreign aid agreements imposed by the superpowers and decided that China would provide aid in a more "equal" and friendly way. In Ghana, Zhou issued the following eight principles of Chinese foreign aid (Liu and Cao, 2018; Zhang, 2012):

(1) equality and mutual benefit;
(2) respect for sovereignty with no conditions attached;
(3) provided through interest-free or low-interest loans;
(4) promotes self-reliance, not dependency;
(5) quick results;
(6) use the highest quality Chinese manufacturing equipment;
(7) emphasize technology transfer through technical assistance; and
(8) Chinese experts dispatched overseas will have the same living standard as local experts.

These eight principles have been strongly maintained by the Chinese government since then. Zhou said, "The poor helping the poor is from the heart, without any condition attached" (Liu & Huang, 2013). Domestic construction in China was halted from 1966 to 1972. However, China's foreign aid delivered large-scale constructions every year during the Cultural Revolution (1966–1976), including the 1,860-km Tanzania–Zambia Railway in 1975. At the end of the Cultural Revolution, foreign aid accounted for 7% of China's national expenditure, which was not financially sustainable (Zhang, 2012).

In 1978, China announced the "open-door policy." There has since been an unprecedented construction boom throughout the country and an influx of overseas architectural designs (Roskam, 2021). By 2013, design competitions and invitations had resulted in over 700 landmark buildings created by foreign architects in mainland Chinese cities (Ren, 2011; Xue, 2006, 2010, 2012; Zhu, 2009). Through these projects, Chinese architects have learned design methods and technologies from their Western peers and in the twenty-first century, the pace of exporting buildings from China to Asia, Africa, and Latin America has accelerated. These projects are mainly infrastructure-based and invested in by the Chinese government, state-owned corporations, and private entrepreneurs. They are mostly the outcomes of economic rather than political considerations. China and developing countries in Asia, Africa and Latin America have embraced the market economy (Urban China, 2014, 2020; Herz, 2017; Winter, 2019; Will, 2012; Xue et al., 2019). In the trend toward "going out," many state-owned and private companies tried to find commercial opportunities overseas. Foreign-aid projects helped to lubricate China's "going out" process and to make economic exchanges win–win situations for both sides (Kong, 2011; Liu and Huang, 2013; Liu and Cao, 2018).

China's foreign aid is defined by its concessional nature and includes grants, zero-interest loans and "concessional" (low, fixed interest) loans managed by the Ministry of Commerce of China. The Chinese government's White Paper "China's Foreign-aid" (2014) lists eight forms of aid: complete projects; goods and materials; technical cooperation; human resource development cooperation; medical teams sent abroad; emergency humanitarian aid (disaster relief); volunteer programs in foreign countries; and debt relief (State Council of China, 2014). This definition is different from that of official development assistance (ODA),[2] which has been standardized for the 30 members of the OECD's Development Assistance Committee (DAC, which is effectively a donors' club). China is one of the largest emerging non-DAC countries to provide foreign aid.[3]

Completed projects financed by China's donations, interest-free loans, low-interest loans or other special aid funds to recipient countries account for approximately 40% of China's expenditure on foreign aid. Most of China's foreign-aided construction is carried out in the form of such projects. According to the Ministry of Commerce, up to 2015, China had exported over 2,700 completed projects. In recent years, local infrastructure projects in fields such as energy, health, education, sports, housing, municipal facilities, and other public buildings have accounted for a greater proportion of China's foreign-aided construction projects.

From 1960 to 2009, China constructed numerous complete projects in over 160 countries, together with other forms of assistance in the areas of health, manufacturing, agriculture, education and sports, totaling RMB256.29 billion in investment (The State Council of China, 2011). According to our database, China's foreign-aided civil constructions number over 1,500, including government offices, parliament buildings, convention and exhibition centers, stadiums, theaters, schools, hospitals, libraries, factories, railways and railway stations.[4]

---

[2] ODA is a term coined by the Development Assistance Committee (DAC) of the Organization for Economic Co-operation and Development (OECD) to measure aid. ODA is defined as flows of official financing administered with the promotion of the economic development and welfare of developing countries as the main objective and which are concessional in character with a grant element of at least 25 per cent (using a fixed 10 per cent rate of discount).

[3] The DAC, one of the dominant international aid organizations, has 30 members including the U.S., U.K., Japan, South Korea and some European countries. Some non-DAC emerging countries such as China and India now contribute considerable proportions of international aid.

[4] This number is from the authors' own collected database. Sources include government and design/construction companies' websites and news reports.

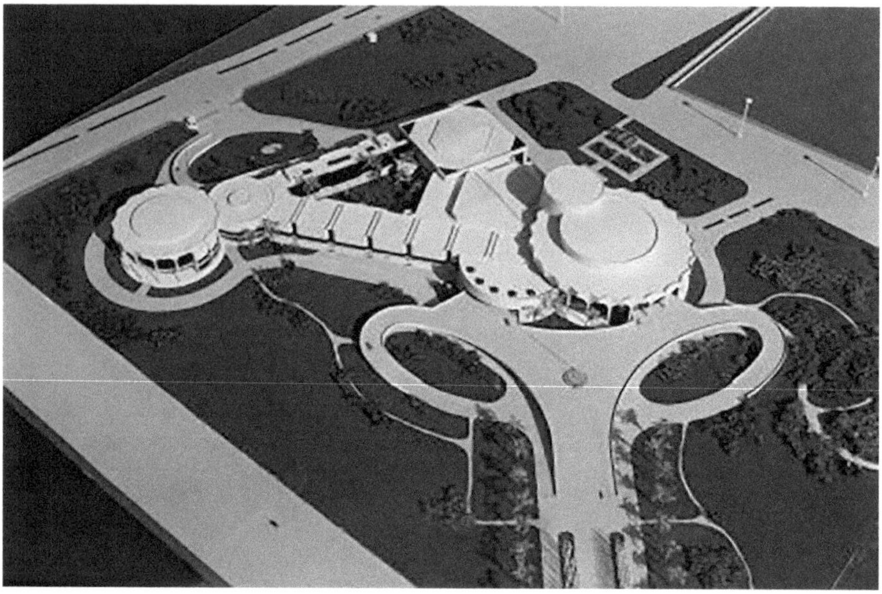

Fig. 1.2 Cairo International Convention Center, Egypt, designed by Shanghai Civil Architectural Design Institute, led by Wei Dunshan, 1991. (Courtesy of Wei Dunshan)

According to "China's International Development Cooperation in the New Era," a white paper issued by China's State Council Information Office (SCIO) on January 10, 2021, China allocated a total of RMB270.2 billion to foreign aid from 2013 to 2018 in three categories: grants, interest-free loans, and concessional loans. The aid covered 20 regional and international multilateral organizations and 122 countries (30 in Asia, 53 in Africa, 9 in Oceania, 22 in Latin America and the Caribbean, and 8 in Europe). Types of aid have also become more varied. In addition to funding complete projects, the provision of goods and materials, and technical cooperation, China set up the South–South Cooperation Assistance Fund in 2015 to launch development cooperation programs, and continues to explore new modes and methods of providing aid (Fig. 1.2).

Scholars of economics and international relations have written many books and articles analyzing China's foreign aid (e.g., Brautigam, 2011; Shimomura & Ohashi, 2013). Using relevant keywords to search the Web of Science, for the period 1970 to 2021, we find 1,782 publications.[5] Some have claimed that China's experience of moving from poverty to rapid growth is helpful for "indigenous development" (Moyo, 2009). Their work suggests that China's aid is characterized by (1) non-political conditionality, low threshold and high attraction; (2) self-reliance, encouraging the recipient side to achieve productivity by themselves; (3) infrastructure and building; and (4) implementation by state-owned companies as a political and military task

[5] The keywords contain "China's aid" or "China's foreign aid"; "aid architecture", "China's architectural aid", "China's foreign construction" or "China's architecture exportation".

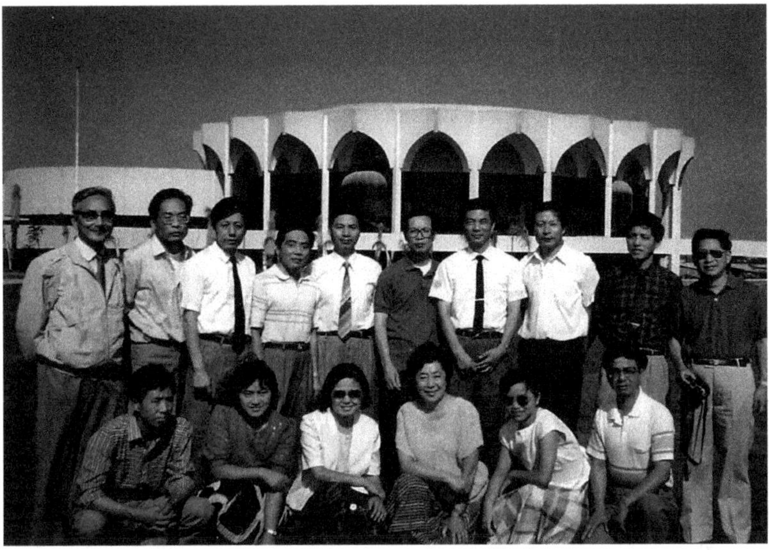

Fig. 1.3 Design team of Shanghai Institute of Architectural Design in front of Cairo International Convention Center, 1989

with quick results (Woods, 2008; Shimomura & Ohashi, 2013; Beeckmans, 2018; Xue & Ding, 2018; Liu & Huang, 2013) (Fig. 1.3).

China-aided buildings fulfil special diplomatic functions and construct delicate social relations. They have the following macro characteristics:

(1) they are the products and extensions of the upgrading of diplomatic relations between China and the recipient countries;
(2) most were built at the request of the recipient countries;
(3) they embody the collision, exchange, conflict and integration of different architectural cultures, design specifications, and construction systems;
(4) they created an equal "cultural contact zone" different from the post-colonial social spaces in which different cultures blend, conflict and struggle with each other, and have a highly asymmetric power relationship (Pratt, 1991);
(5) they were designed and implemented by China's technicians. In some cases, they were packaged in China and assembled on site to achieve a "quick" turnkey construction. These buildings are unquestionably a part of modern Chinese architecture.

1.3 From Diplomatic Maneuvers to Building Technology

Transnational architectural practice, both as a product of global interactions and as a network of international relations, complicates and enriches our inquiry into global architectural history. China's architectural aid can be described as a social relationship with three key components: the donor, the recipients, and the context in which they interact. This relationship determines the motivation, extent, program, and implications of aid. In this book, contributors seek to blur the line between donor and recipient nations, investigating the global context in which China's architectural exports happen. The authors examine the connections and competition in the production of these exported buildings and trace the particular routes of these architectural exchanges (Fig. 1.4).

This book marks the emerging scholarship on China's architectural engagement in developing countries. This previously unexplored story constitutes an important subfield within the field of contemporary Chinese architecture. Over the past six decades, China's architectural exports have had three motivations: political and ideological, economic, and cultural. China-aided building projects are characterized by several principles that deserve detailed analysis and interpretation (Fig. 1.5).

(1) Foreign aid is a component of international relations between governments. However, when programs and sites are confirmed, a construction aid project becomes just another building task. The designers will face the same problems of site, orientation, climate, plan, section, space, and volume that they habitually face in their work. This book focuses on building projects, design, construction, technology, and implementation in the context of policy, finance, economy, and international relations to provide an architectural perspective on foreign aid activity and to delineate a "Chinese construction model."

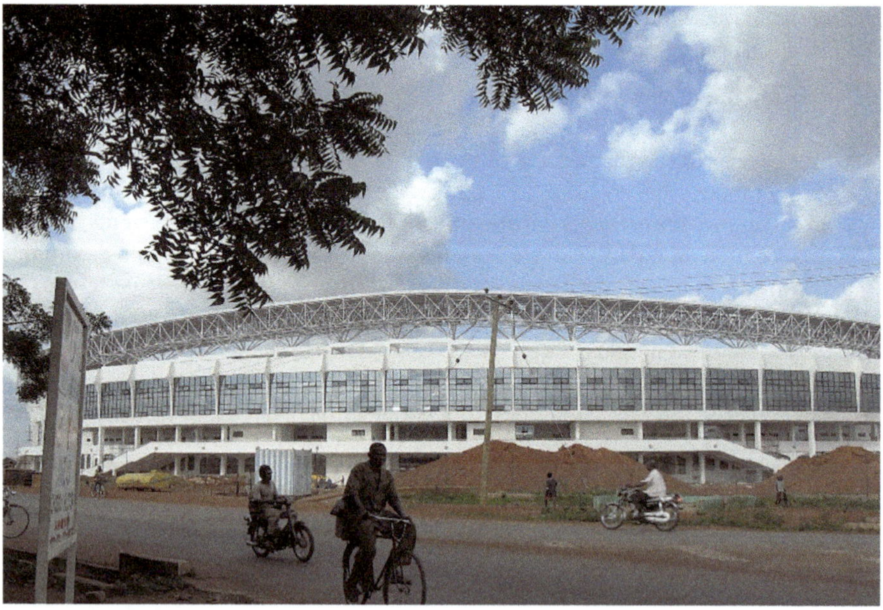

Fig. 1.4 Tamali Stadium, Ghana, 2008, designed by Tongji University Design Group (Picture courtesy of architect Dong Yingtao)

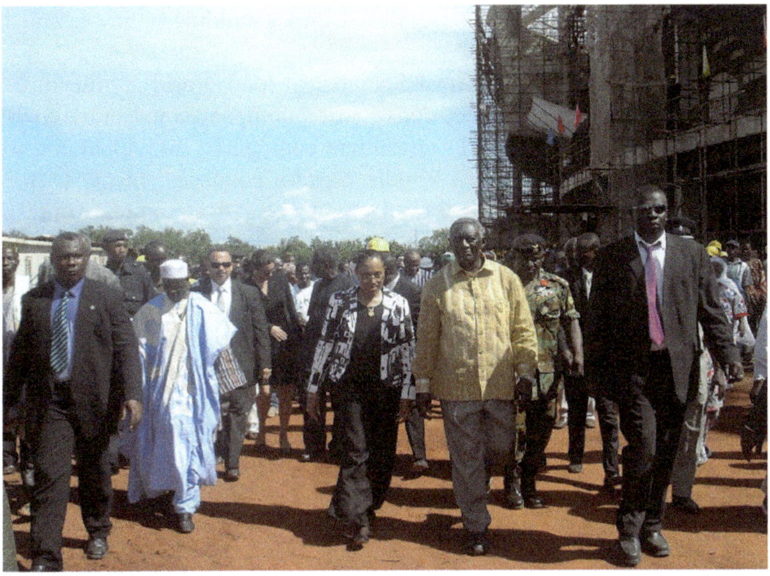

Fig. 1.5 John Agyekum Kufuor, Ghanaian President, visited the construction site of Tamali Stadium, 2008 (Picture courtesy of architect Dong Yingtao)

(2) Foreign-aid projects are negotiated between donor and recipient countries. The projects are delivered, sometimes in "turn-key" format, by Chinese design institutes and constructed by Chinese construction companies. In most cases, materials, machinery, and furniture are shipped from China. Buildings in China and abroad have been designed by the same groups of people, who have been inevitably confined by the conditions and availability of Chinese building technology and knowledge at the time of construction. Therefore, foreign-aid construction projects demonstrate Chinese architectural development over the past 60 years. Popular trends in Chinese building design, typology and technology are inevitably reflected in foreign-aid projects. This study of such projects draws attention to parallels in architectural development in China and abroad.

(3) As mentioned above, foreign aid expenditure was once a great burden on China's national economy. The country catered to demands from many Asian and African countries while most of its own people lived below the poverty line. In both prestige and civil projects, China's thrift in its own developing economy is evidenced by the use of sustainable or low-tech technologies and materials in its overseas projects. In lieu of hard currency, many types of aid were provided in the form of materials, services, transportation, and goods. In the twenty-first century, although China's national economy has considerably improved, its building projects still use limited resources to maximize social effects. Many projects are skillfully designed to be "pragmatic, economical

and delightful if the condition allows" (China's building policy established in 1960).

(4) As noted above, in the export of Socialist Second World architecture to the Third World, design institutes, construction companies and individuals from Eastern Europe participated as consultant companies, individual consultants, or employees in African and Middle Eastern countries. In the U.S. export of buildings, private architects and engineering firms were commissioned and contracted by the government. In contrast, most of China's foreign-aid projects have been undertaken by state-owned design institutes and construction companies, selected either by political assignment or commercial tender. Individual designers and their services were not directly involved in work in foreign countries and building designs and forms are closely associated with China's domestic building production mechanism namely, state-owned companies (Xue & Ding, 2018).

(5) Although this book highlights exportation, its scope includes the importation of ideas and the experiences of Chinese professionals in other nations, both capitalist and socialist. The cross-border mobility of materials, knowledge, labor, and technology constitutes a highly dynamic process. Cross-border design will inevitably attract attention to regional and indigenous features and design and is usually framed as an "encounter zone" for many different cultures and forces (Avermaete, 2012). Chinese architects have made great efforts to reflect indigenous characteristics, which were a major consideration when schemes were selected in China and by recipient countries. Nevertheless, their endeavors have been one-sided because of the "turn-key" nature of most projects. The duration of the design process and engagement of local technical forces have not always been sufficient in the twenty-first century.

(6) In the twenty-first century, the export of Chinese architecture has encompassed both foreign aid and commercial works. Under the banner of "going out", foreign aid projects and history paved the way for China's Silk Road Economic Belt and the 21st-century Maritime Silk Road ("One Belt One Road") initiative. Private developers have found opportunities in new locations and business niches, and they have engaged private designers to carry out planning and design. A few private design companies have directly acquired commissions overseas. These commercial works have merged with aid projects to form a trend of Chinese design/construction/infrastructure.

1.4 Structure of the Book

Based on the above understanding of Chinese "exportation," this book is divided into three parts. Part I traces the history of China's construction aid; Part II describes various types of aided buildings and practices; and Part III looks at the ongoing "One Belt One Road" initiative.

This chapter provides the background to China's construction aid and motivations for building in other countries. China was propelled by circumstances into the world arena, which at the time was mainly dominated by the U.S.—led West and the Eastern blocs. The strenuous road travelled by China for a period of 60 years has given Chinese foreign-aid architecture a special flavor, which is elaborated in later chapters. In this chapter, the unique traits of Chinese foreign construction aid are identified and explained.

The long journey of China's foreign aid started with the political and philosophical logic of the Mao era. In Chapter 2, Liu identifies three dimensions of that foundational period: style, type, and geography. In general, these dimensions reveal that China's foreign aid practice formed a historical mechanism that facilitated unprecedented encounters between African and Asian societies that were distant from and previously unfamiliar with each other. The style dimension shows that architectural aid was not a one-way transfer from China to the outside world but a dialectical pathway that allowed both exportation and the importation of architectural styles that supplemented China's late-Mao modernism. The type dimension highlights that most of China's aid was for productive projects that promoted economic independence: "productive" space such as factories and farms became classic spaces in the Third World that embodied (pro-)socialist and anti-colonial sensitivities. The geography dimension contextualizes China's tropical-responsive building techniques and the knowledge-mapping of foreign land that contributed to China's repositioning itself in the world and its epistemological renewal.

Chapter 3 considers China's foreign aid projects from 1964 to 1976. Amid the high tide of China's donations during its domestically turbulent and difficult years, "Maoist pragmatism" and "Chinese modernism" in architectural design matured. Song examines the multidirectional knowledge exchange between China and other countries in this period. An in-depth case study of the Tanzania–Zambia Railway (TAZARA) Terminus in Dar es Salaam, built in 1976, demonstrates the presence of a Chinese modernism in architecture as an alternative approach to the Western postwar modernist trends. This chapter raises the question of how to construct a culturally sensitive understanding of architecture, whether Chinese, African, Western or more specific, in architectural discourse.

From 1960 to 2019, 70% of China's foreign-aid constructions have been in Africa. In 1960, China and Ghana established a diplomatic relationship. President Kwame Nkrumah (1909–1972) visited China wishing to industrialize Ghana and follow China's model of self-reliance. Premier Zhou Enlai visited Ghana in 1964. Chapter 4 reviews Ghana's 60-year entanglement with China. Amoah teases out the changes and continuities of China's key construction and architectural activities in Ghana and critically analyzes the intersection of form, knowledge transfer and politics through examples of several building and infrastructure projects. The author's critique reflects the starkly different views of recipient countries.

Among many aided buildings of Mao's era, the Bandaranaike Memorial International Conference Hall (BMICH) in Colombo, Sri Lanka stood out, and was praised as a classic example of China's early aid. By focusing on China's engagement with Sri Lanka and on the BMICH and later Nelum Pokuna Theater in Colombo, and on the manifestation of appropriation in contemporary transcultural practice, Chapter 5 traces the interactions between the intention to respond to local tropical climatic conditions and the approach to appropriate Chinese, Sri Lankan, and international architectural styles. Ding and Xue argue that the appropriation, synthesis and transformation of architectural ideas from various contexts created new forms of identity that articulated political and cultural manifestations. Parallel to China's architectural aid to Colombo is the increasing popularity of Sri Lankan architect Geoffrey Bawa in the eyes of emerging Chinese architects of the twenty-first century. The juxtaposition of Sri Lankan architecture appropriated in both Colombo and in China suggests that the dual mobility of architectural ideas helps to contribute to the formation of new and urgently needed political and cultural identities.

Part II provides more examples of building design, production, and evaluation. One important item of foreign aid is medical assistance, which includes sending medical teams and building hospitals and clinics. China is a key player in both tasks. Chapter 6 provides a picture of hospitals donated by China to Africa. Tang, Li and Amos examine the social impact of Mahusekwa Hospital in Zimbabwe and evaluate its impacts on economic development, social services, social compatibility and the natural environment via interviews and questionnaires. Based on the evaluation results, they propose countermeasures and suggestions, including optimizing development policies, encouraging public participation, and strengthening departmental collaboration, to provide a reference for the better planning and implementation of China's medical aid to Africa.

As important city landmarks, administrative buildings are an important type of Chinese aid to Africa. In Chapter 7, Zhang, Zhang, and Mbewe analyze the aid modes and local feedback on Chinese-aided administrative buildings in Africa. Taking the Malawi Parliament Building as an example, they describe the multi-participatory construction process and examine the results of a questionnaire survey and in-depth interviews designed to uncover local people's satisfaction with the "turn-key" project mode, as well as their perception of its social impact. Aid projects help the beneficiary country to build a good national image and achieve some financial benefit, and they bring opportunities for urban development. However, more local involvement is expected in the aid process in the future.

Chinese philosophy emphasizes "teaching fishing" over "giving fish" when helping others. In Zhou Enlai's eight principles of foreign aid, "self-reliance" is a key concept. In the twenty-first century, the number and scale of school buildings arising from Chinese aid has increased. These include university campuses, medical schools, technical schools, and primary and middle school buildings. Education is the best way to achieve national sustainability and nurture the next generation. In Chapter 8, Chen, Xue, Ding and Gao review the trend of constructing educational buildings overseas. The authors analyze key influential factors and design features of representative cases selected from a database of 182 projects of four major types: schools for deprived groups, schools of vocational and police training, schools of politics and diplomacy, and the Confucius Institutes.

China has built three railways in Africa: from Tanzania to Zambia (1970–1975), Mombasa to Nairobi (2014–2017), and Addis Ababa to Djibouti (2012–2016). The railway in the Horn of Africa realized the dream of two countries and brought a series of business as well as hope to the area. In Chapter 9, Zhang, Wan, Liu and Xue reveal the plight of the former colonies of Djibouti and Ethiopia. A shortage of urban infrastructure and old colonial separation made development in the area fragmented and fragile. China's construction aid in the form of people's palaces, stadiums, libraries and schools, has satisfied urgent demand, defining a sense of place and boosting national confidence. Addis Ababa, the capital city of Ethiopia, is experiencing rampant expansion without order or proper management. Chinese constructors' works and aid projects quickly pushed forward the city's society and economy. However, due to their individual and sporadic nature, they cannot thoroughly transform the city (Fig. 1.6).

The "One Belt One Road" initiative was proposed in 2013. This is China's strategy of engaging more countries in trade and exchange. The early beneficiaries have been both state-owned and private design and construction companies, whose active profiles can be seen in five continents. Part III follows the business trajectories of Chinese companies (Fig. 1.7).

Chapter 10 examines Chinese projects in Pakistan in the twenty-first century. Through descriptions of the Pakistan China Friendship Center and the Gwadar Business Center, Ahmed Marri showcases a "contact zone," in which the design languages and expertise of both countries interact. The author appreciates the efforts of Chinese designers in transcultural engagement. He argues that architectural design models in

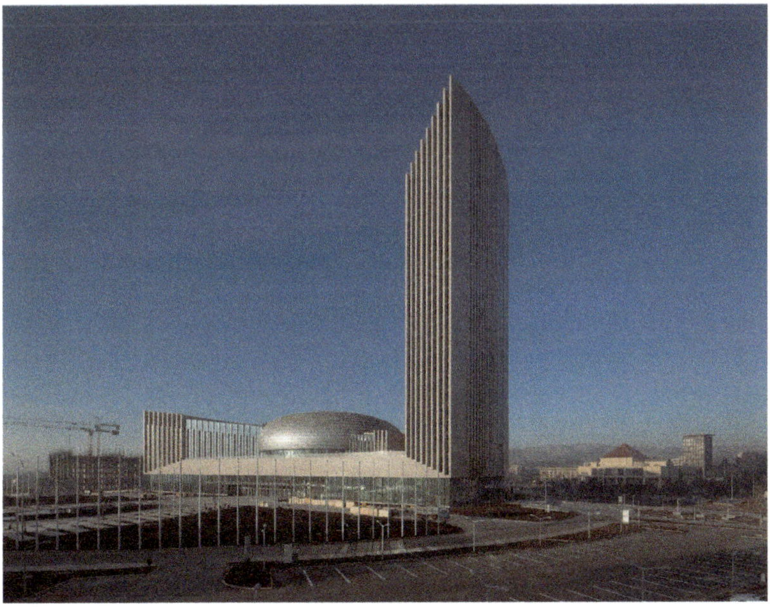

Fig. 1.6 African Union Headquarters, Addis Ababa, designed by Tongji University Design Group, led by Ren Lizhi, 2011 (courtesy of Prof. Ren Lizhi)

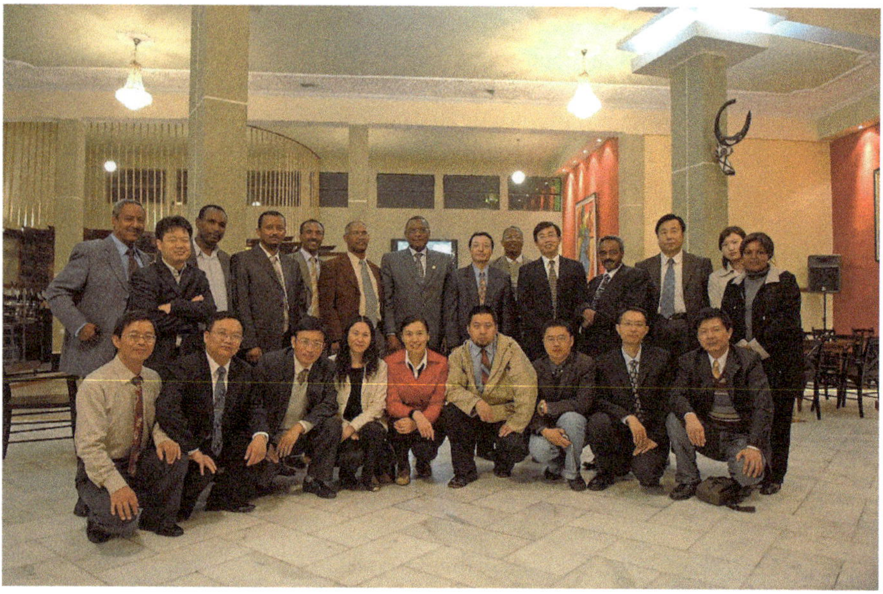

Fig. 1.7 Chinese design team, led by Professor Ren Lizhi (No. 5 from right hand side, back row), and officers of African Union and Ethiopia in the African Union Headquarters, 2008. (courtesy of Zhang Liping)

the Global South are not inadequate copies or distortions of developments in the North but have their own logics and can be considered unique and creative articulations.

During Mao's era, China's construction aid was assigned to several centrally administered design institutes in Beijing and Shanghai. Taking advantage of their momentum, these institutes won most of the commissions when a bidding method was adopted in the market economy. Some capable state-owned or private firms then started to share the pie by providing outstanding solutions to specific design tasks. CCDI (China Construction Design International Co. Ltd) is one such firm. In Chapter 11, Ai reviews its 20-year history of designing projects overseas. Some are donated works, some commercial. The Chinese design firms obtain design commitments by following the general contractors and developers. The company has acquired fully commercial design firms in the US and Australia. CCDI is a prodigious competitor both in the Chinese domestic and overseas markets, and through "going out," with its wide international network and portfolio.

The same can be said of IPPR (China IPPR International Engineering Co., Ltd). Apart from a couple of design institutes in Beijing and Shanghai, IPPR has occupied most of the market share of China's overseas building projects. Its journey started in the 1970s when the institute designed a factory in Pakistan. It has since designed more than 70 hospitals for the developing world. Chapter 12 describes its milestone works: the National Stadium of Cambodia built for the Southeast Asia Games in 2023 and the China-Cambodian Friendship Hospital. Li and colleagues' design for this large-scale stadium was selected by the Cambodian premier. IPPR's characteristic technical and symbolic approaches, balancing functional requirements, cultural expression, low maintenance costs and sustainable performance, have also been applied in several other winning schemes for stadiums, hospitals and cultural centers.

Chapter 13 examines the role of a property developer in a location that Western scholarship has largely ignored. Georgia, a former republic of the Soviet Union, experienced a faltering economy after its independence. "One Belt One Road" has provided the impetus for the construction of infrastructure because the country plays a role in linking the new Silk Road from China to Central Europe. Cai, Xue and Jaillon investigate the case of Hualing, a local property developer in Xinjiang. The company was successful in developing a shopping mall and residential areas in Tbilisi, which was in desperate need of decent buildings and planning. The company adapted China's model to the local conditions and the developments have been warmly welcomed. Chapter 13 compares two shopping malls designed by private firms and developed by Hualing, one in Urumqi, the other in Tbilisi. Some problems have occurred and are discussed; however, this is a new way of "exporting Chinese architecture."

The contributors to this volume are scholars and practitioners who are either familiar with or directly involved in design projects. They connect the disparate events, countries, buildings and people across span of 70 years. Together, they provide a rich panoramic view of how China and its professionals have engaged with the international world through architectural design and construction. Their writings demonstrate that Chinese development and architectural modernism have, in various ways, spread throughout the world during periods when China was "closed" to the world as well as when it has been "open."

(This chapter is part of a research supported by the National Natural Science Foundation of China, Project No. 51878584.)

References

Amoah, L. (2016). China, architecture and Ghana's spaces: Concrete signs of a soft Chinese imperium? *Journal of Asian and African Studies, 51*(2), 238–255.

Avermaete, T. (2012). Coda: The reflectivity of cold war architectural modernism. *The Journal of Architecture, 17*(3), 475–477.

Bartke, W. (1989). *The economic aid of the PR China to developing and socialist countries.* K.G. Saur.

Beeckmans, L. (2018). The architecture of nation-building in Africa as a development aid project: Designing the capitols of Kinshasa (Congo) and Dodoma (Tanzania) in the post-independence years. *Progress in Planning, 122*, 1–28.

Berman, M. (1988). *All that is solid melts into air: The experience of modernity* (pp. 15–36). Penguin Books.

Brautigam, D. (2011). *The dragon's gift: The real story of China in Africa.* Oxford University Press.

Chang, W., Xue, C., & Ding, G. (2019). Architecture of Diplomacy: Chinese Construction Aid in Asia, 1950–1976. *Arena Journal of Architectural Research*, 16. https://ajar.arena-architecture.eu/articles/10.5334/ajar.147/

Cody, J. W. (2003). *Exporting American Architecture, 1870–2000*. London; New York: Routledge.

Cohen, J. L. (1995). *Scenes of the world to come: European architecture and the American challenge, 1893–1960*. Paris and Montreal: Flammarion and the Canadian Centre for Architecture.

Ding, G., & Xue, C. (2015). China's architectural aid: Exporting a transformational modernism. *Habitat International, 47*(1), 136–147.

Dikötter, F. (2010). *Mao's great famine—the history of China's most devastating catastrophe, 1958–62*. London, Berlin and New York: Bloomsbury.

Flowers, B. S. (2018). *Sport and architecture*. Routledge.

Frampton, K. (1992). *Modern architecture: A critical history*. Thames and Hudson.

Fraser, M., & Kerr, J. (2007). *Architecture and the "special relationship": The American influence on post-war British architecture*. Routledge.

Gao, H. & He, L. (1995). Zhonghua renmin guoheguo shi (A history of the People's Republic of China). Beijing: zhongguo dangan chuban she.

Giddens, A. (1984). *The Constitution of Society: Outline of the Theory of Structuration* (Berkeley, Cal.: University of California Press).

Gould, K. (1999). American architects export collaboration as a mean to sustainability. *AIArchitect*, (November), 23.

Harvey, D. (1989). *The condition of postmodernity: An enquiry into the origins of cultural change*. Blackwell.

Herz, M. (2017). Nation building. *Architectural Review, 241*(1441), 55–61.

Heynen, H. (1999). *Architecture and modernity*. MIT Press.

Hogan, M. (1989). *The marshall plan: America, Britain and the reconstruction of Western Europe, 1947–1952*. Cambridge University Press.

Hogben, P. (2012). Architecture and arts' and the mediation of American architecture in post-war Australia. *Fabrications, 1*, 30.

Kong, Y. (2011). Zhongguo yu xifang dui feizhou yuanzhu de yiyuli [China and western countries' aid to Africa: responsibilities and benefits]. Ershiyi shiji shuangyuekan [*Bi-monthly 21st Century*] 孔永乐 中国与西方对非洲援助的义与利 二十一世纪双月刊, No.123, Issue 2, 27–37.

Kulić, V. (Ed.). (2019). *Second world postmodernisms: Architecture and society under late socialism*. Bloomsbury Publishing.

Krieger, P. (2000). Learning from America: Postwar urban recovery in West Germany, in: *Transactions, Transgressions, Transformations: American Culture in Western Europe and Japan*, ed. Fehrenbach, H. and Poiger, U. G. New York: Berghahn.

Langan, M. (2018). *Neo-colonialism and the poverty of 'development' in Africa*. Palgrave Macmillan.

Leach, N. (Ed.) (1999). *Architecture and revolution: contemporary perspectives on Central and Eastern Europe*. London: Routledge.

Loeffler, J. C. (1998). *The architecture of diplomacy: Building America's embassies*. Princeton Architectural Press.

Liu, F., & Cao, Y. (2018). Gaige kaifang sishinian: zhongguo duiwai yuanzhu lichen yu zhanwang [40 years of open door and reform: the history and prospect of China's foreign aid], Gaige [*Reform*]. 刘方平, 曹亚雄 (2018) . 改革开放40年中国对外援助历程与展望. 改革, 10, 52–59.

Levin, A. (2016). Haile Selassie's imperial modernity: Expatriate architects and the shaping of Addis Ababa. *Journal of the Society of Architectural Historians, 75*(4), 447–468.

Liu, H & Huang, M. (2013). Zhongguo duiwai yuanzhu yu guoji zeren de zhanlue yanjiu [The strategy of China's foreign aid and international responsibility]. Beijing: China Social Science Press. 刘鸿武、黄梅波 (2013) 中国对外援助与国际责任的战略研究. 中国社会科学出版社.

Lu, D. (Ed.). (2011). *Third world modernism: Architecture*. Routledge.

Mao, Z. (1996). *Selected works of Mao Zedong* (Vol. 7). People's Press.

Mëhilli, E. (2017). *From Stalin to Mao: Albania and the socialist world*. Cornell University Press.

Moyo, D. (2009). *Dead aid: Why aid is not working and how there is a better way for Africa*. Farrar, Straus and Giroux.

Pieris, A. (2011). "Tropical" Cosmopolitanism? The untoward legacy of the American style in post-independence Ceylon/Sri Lanka. *Singapore Journal of Tropical Geography, 32*(3), 332–349.
Pratt, M. L. (1991). Arts of the contact zone. *Profession*, 33–40.
Ren, X. (2011). *Building globalization: Transnational architecture production in urban China*. The University of Chicago Press.
Robin, R. T. (2014). *Enclaves of America: The Rhetoric of American political architecture abroad, 1900–1965*. Princeton University Press.
Roskam, C. (2015). Non-aligned architecture: China's design on and in Ghana and Guinea 1955–92. *Architectural History, 58*(1), 261–291.
Roskam, C. (2021). *Designing reform: Architecture in the People's Republic of China, 1970–1992*. Yale University Press.
Siamphukdee, C. (2014a). Introduction: "Export architecture" and the Cold War. *Journal of Export Architecture: A War of the Worlds—Cold War Projects abroad*. Deakin: Deakin University, 1–2.
Siamphukdee, C. (2014b). What have you done? Typologies of export architecture. Journal of Export Architecture: A War of the Worlds—Cold War Projects Abroad. Deakin: Deakin University, 6–8.
Schwekel, C. (2020). *Building Socialism: The afterlife of East German architecture in urban Vietnam*. Duke University Press.
Shen, Z. (2011). *After leaning to one side: China and its allies in the Cold War*. Stanford University Press.
Shimomura, Y., & Ohashi, H. (2013). *A study of China's foreign Aid: An Asian perspective*. Palgrave McMillan.
Stanek, L. (2020). *Architecture in global socialism: Eastern Europe, West African, and the Middle East in the Cold War*. Princeton University Press.
State Council. (2011). White Book on China's Foreign Aid. Beijing: State Council of China.
State Council. (2021). *China's International Development Cooperation in the New Era*. Beijing: State Council.
State Council of China. (2014). *China's foreign aid*. Beijing: Government White Paper.
Taylor, I. (2006). *China and Africa: Engagement and compromise*. Routledge.
Uduku, O. (2006). Modernist architecture and "the tropical" in the West Africa: The tropical architecture movement in West Africa—1948-1970. *Habitat International, 30*(6), 396–411.
Urban China. (2014). Special issue "China on Africa".
Urban China (2020). Special issue "Overseas Chinese industrial park".
Vernon, P. (2012). Shopping towns Australia. *Fabrications: The Journal of the Society of Architectural Historians Australia & New Zealand,* 22(1), 102–121.
Wharton, A. J. (2011). Building the cold war—Hilton international hotels and modern architecture. University of Chicago Press.
Winter, T. (2019). Geocultural power—China's quest to revive the silk roads for the twenty-first century. University of Chicago Press.
Will, R. (2012). China's stadium diplomacy. *World Policy Journal, 29*(2), 36–43.
Woods, N. (2008). Whose aid? Whose influence? China, emerging donors and the silent revolution in development assistance. *International Affairs., 84*(6), 1205–1221.
Xue, C. Q. L. (2006). *Building a revolution: Chinese architecture since 1980* (p. 2006). Hong Kong University Press.
Xue, C. Q. L. (2010). *World architecture in China*. Joint Publishing Ltd. Co.
Xue, C. Q. L. (2012). Western Architectural Design in China (1978–2010), *New Architecture*, No. 2, 18–25.
Xue, C., & Ding, G. (2018). *A history of design institutes in China: From Mao to market*. Routledge.
Xue, C., Ding, G., Chang, W., & Wan, Y. (2019). Architecture of "Stadium diplomacy"—China-aid sport buildings in Africa, *Habitat International*, Volume 90, Aug. 101985.
Xue, C., & Xiao, J. (2014). Japanese modernity deviated: its importation and legacy in the Southeast Asian architecture since the 1970s. *Habitat International, 44*, 227–236.

Zhang, Y. (2012). Zhongguo duiwai yuanzhu yanjiu 1950–2010 [Research of China Foreign Aid 1950–2010]. Beijing: Jiuzhou Press. 张郁慧 (2012).中国对外援助研究1950–2010. 北京: 九州出版社.

Zhu, J. (2009). *Architecture of modern China: A historical critique.* Routledge.

Zunz, O. (1998). *Why the American Century?* University of Chicago Press.

Charlie Qiuli Xue has taught architecture at Shanghai Jiaotong University, University of Texas and City University of Hong Kong. An award-winning architect and writer, he has published 15 books, including '*Building a Revolution: Chinese Architecture since 1980*' (HKU Press, 2006), '*Hong Kong Architecture 1945–2015: From Colonial to Global*' (Springer, 2016), '*A History of Design Institutes in China: from Mao to Market*' (with G. Ding, Routledge, 2018) and '*Grand Theater Urbanism: Chinese cities in the 21st century*' (Springer, 2019, ed.). He has published more than 160 research papers in professional and international refereed journals and 40 book chapters. His papers are published in such journals as *Cities, Habitat International, Urban Design International, Journal of Architecture, Journal of Urban Design, Architectural Research Quarterly, Journal of Urban History, Planning Perspective, Architecture + Urbanism, Domus* and Chinese journals like *Architectural Journal, Architect, New Architecture, Time + Architecture, World Architecture* and *Taiwan Architect*. His book on Hong Kong was awarded by the International Committee of Architectural Critics (CICA) in 2017. Xue's research interests are in Chinese architecture, transnational design and high-density environment. Xue is also extensively involved in design and consultant practice in Hong Kong, Chinese mainland and the US.

Guanghui Ding is Associate Professor of Architecture at the Beijing University of Civil Engineering and Architecture in China. He completed his Ph.D. in architecture from the University of Nottingham, United Kingdom in 2013 and later worked as a Postdoctoral Research Fellow at City University of Hong Kong. His research focuses on modern and contemporary Chinese architecture, including many subjects in critical architecture, architectural criticism and periodicals, design institutes and China's architectural aid in the Global South. He is the author of *Constructing a Place of Critical Architecture in China: Intermediate Criticality in the Journal* Time + Architecture (London and New York: Routledge, 2016) (Chinese edition,《建筑批评的一朵浪花: 实验性建筑》Beijing: China Architecture and Building Press, 2018) and co-author of *A History of Design Institutes in China: From Mao to Market* (London and New York: Routledge, 2018, with Charlie Qiuli Xue) (expanded Chinese edition,《中国设计院: 价值与挑战》Beijing: China Architecture and Building Press, 2022). His scholarly articles have been published by *Architecture and Culture, Architectural Research Quarterly, ARENA Journal of Architectural Research, Domus, Habitat International, Histories of Post-War Architecture, Journal of Architecture, Journal of the Society of Architectural Historians, Jianzhushi/The Architect, Shidai jianzhu/Time + Architecture, Shijie jianzhu/World Architecture, Xin jianzhu/New Architecture* and other edited volumes.

Chapter 2
New China and the New World: Three Lines to Understand China's Early Architectural Foreign Aid

Ye Liu

Abstract This research situates the architectural aid in early PRC history (the Maoist period) into the context of socialist world-Third World political solidarity. The author theorizes such historical practice with three lines, namely, the exportation and importation of styles, the materialist formation of the productive space, and the natural geographic question raised by the tropical-responsive designs. The chapter points out that the Chinese construction aid in the Third World was not a linear transfer of resources and information from China to the foreign land, but also a reflection of China's internalization of the information feedback made from the overseas circumstances. This helps us better understand the dialectic inside-outside relation between China and the World. The perspective from a global framework in which China embeds itself can also provide historical reference for a more appropriate self-position and self-reflex of the ongoing Belt and Road Initiative.

The Belt and Road Initiative (BRI) has pushed China to rethink its relation with the outside world after the country's three decades' focus on economic development after the Cold War. Based on the planet-scale investment, development, and construction projects, the practice of BRI inevitably involves a retrospective reassessment of the history of China's overseas construction especially in the form of aid in the Mao Zedong period (1950s–70s). In its early stage, People's Republic of China was long embedded in the resonance of the global communist and internationalist movements. China's foreign aid almost started at the same pace with the founding of the republic. With the industrial foundation being laid by the "156 Projects" aided by the Soviet Union and the completion of the first five-year plan (1953–1957), engineering and technical projects had also become an important category of Chinese aid.

Around 1960, the Sino-Soviet cleavage became increasingly irreversible, and the split between the two sides finally came. China gradually faded out from the socialist bloc thereafter and began to independently practice its revolutionary foreign policy and blueprint for the Third World politics. The progress of Chinese foreign aid had

Y. Liu (✉)
New School of Social Research, New York, USA
e-mail: liuye@newschool.edu

C. Q. Xue and G. Ding (eds.), *Exporting Chinese Architecture*,
https://doi.org/10.1007/978-981-19-2786-7_2

accelerated significantly. In 1960, the "Foreign Construction Bureau" (*duiwai jianzhu shigongju*) and "Construction Corporation of China"(*zhongguo jianzhu gongcheng gongsi*) to supplement foreign aid works were established; at the same time, the Ministry of Construction held the first foreign aid affairs conference to establish a special research office and related institutional arrangements. By 1965, up to 8 specialized foreign engineering and foreign building material supply companies had been established. The foreign construction aid had gradually grown into a professional system with multi-layered structures of institutions and personnel (Ye et al., 2008). Despite of the differences (or even rivalry and antagonism in the end) of both sides, China and the Soviet-Eastern European bloc had jointly shaped the grand history of the large-scale, long-term, and in-depth assistance took place between the socialist world and the vast Asia-Africa-Latin America regions during the 1950s to the 1980s. This socialist collective action was not only a strong support for the anti-imperialist and anti-colonial movements of the Third World, but also an attempt to provide an alternative "modernization" path different from capitalism for the vast areas that have not yet been "modernized".

In the early 1990s, with the collapse of the Soviet Union and Eastern European bloc and the marketization reform of China, the United States and its capitalist allies declared victory from the Cold War that took nearly half a century. In the illusion of "the end of history", socialist civilization has been through a rapid dismantling, landfill and oblivion. The material relics such as socialist architecture was not exceptional in this process of ruination. Only in recent years did a few (East) European-origin scholars based in Western institutions begin to salvage this part of the global heritage (Stanek, 2012, 2014, 2020; Mark, 2020; Schwenkel, 2020). Fields beyond the academia also partially joined this new trend.[1] China was an important participant to this section of the history of global socialism. But due to its special positionality and the limitations of the global intellectual mapping of socialism, China's role has been largely missing in current literature even those produced by postsocialist eastern European authors. In fact, the study of China's overseas aid construction in the Third World has just began among Chinese or China-based scholars (Ding & Xue, 2015; Roskam, 2015; Song, 2017; Ding, Xue & Chang, 2018; Liu, 2020). How to map out this complicated history of transcontinental exchanges poses substantial challenges both empirically and theoretically. It requires a full comprehension of the profound tension between common features of socialist socieities and the individual characters embodied in China during that period. As a specific hub of global history in which China habited, the architectural foreign aid discovers and implies the temporal and spatial clues that give shape to the basic political characteristics and political body

[1] The most typical cases should be "Concrete Utopia" on the architectural heritage of socialist Yugoslavia in 2018 fall, Museum of Modern Art (MoMA) which has aroused heated discussion. Similar cases included "The Lost Vanguard: Soviet Modernist Architecture", 1922–1932, MoMA, 2007. At the centenary of the October Revolution of Russia, a series of exhibitions were staged included "Red Star Over Russia: A Revolution in Visual Culture, 1905–55" (Tate Modern, 2017); "A Revolutionary Impulse: The Rise of the Russian Avant-Garde (MoMA, 2017); "Chagall, Lissitzky, Malevitch: L'Avant-Garde Russe Vitebsk, 1918–1922" (Centre Pompidou, 2018).

of socialist China, as well as to the specific world of meaning in which China had situated itself.

This chapter attempts to construct three juxtaposed but interrelated lines from the interlaced relationship, namely (1) style: the perspective of architectural symbols, representations, aesthetics and their design to explore the bidirectional and even multidirectional transnational mobility of such knowledge; (2) material: industrial architecture and built environment can best represent the fundamental materialist logic of China's socialist aid in the Third World; (3) Geography: the technical challenges faced by overseas aid construction especially the tropical natural/social conditions and its corresponsive knowledge production. Of course, these lines do not delineate the "full picture" of the history. The reason to select such clues is due to their potential to communicate between the architectural field and its exterior on different levels. These relations help to identify the characteristics of China's construction aid practices, allowing us to discern the meaning of the complicated historical situation.

2.1 Style: Export Versus Import

It is generally believed that China was largely absent from the global modernist architectural movement during the postwar period especially the 1950s to the 1970s.[2] What makes people confused is that why the style of modernism, which has obvious affinities to socialist ideology,[3] had been marginalized and even suppressed to various degrees in different socialist countries (while periods vary) including China. Chinese architectural (or building) industry has become one of the earliest cases that a professional field had been involved in political campaign. The close relationship between the Soviet Union and early avant-garde art was severely damaged in the Stalin era, and "socialist content + national form" became a common aesthetic principle for the post-war socialist countries.[4] Hua Lanhong pointed out in 1957 that the biggest problem of current construction is "the problem of standards", that is, "in order to determine the proportion of various types of architecture and the content of buildings in urban construction and then studying the form of architecture, we have to depart from current availability and requirements of our country, and to depart from our

[2] In the early 1950s, there were still modernist works done such as Children's Hospital in Beijing and Wenyuan Building in Tongji University, Shanghai. Xia Changshi's architectural experiment in response to the hot and humid climate in Guangzhou took place almost at the same time with the plans of Le Corbusier, Jean-Pierre, Fry & Drew in Chandigarh, India. Both sides shared substantial technical similarities. Both were different variants of the localization of the principles of modernism practiced in two new Asian countries. In addition, in 1956, Jiang Weihong and Jin Zhiqiang published "We Want Modern Architecture" in *Journal of Architecture* and sparked a small circle debate before the trend was soon interrupted.

[3] For instance, the characteristics of standardization, prefabrication, collectivization, mass production, and low cost for a mass society.

[4] China abandoned this term after since the Sino-Soviet split and instead proposed new principles: revolutionary realism and revolutionary romanticism.

economic conditions and people's actual living standards. Without this, to talk about art forms is like putting the cart before the horse" (Hua & Liu, 1957). Today, when we discuss the restrictions and taboos on architectural styles in the Mao era, we should pay attention to the key reasons behind such conflicts in symbols and discourses. It includes the state's intense control over extremely scarce material resources, the limitation imposed on the elite culture under the principle of radical equality, and the aesthetic anxiety in a highly symbolic and rhetorical world during the Cold War.

But this does not mean that China has ever been isolated from the world. The period of China's confrontation with the West also witnessed a history that China was open to the Third World, or Asia, Africa, and Latin America. In an era when foreign aid work "must firmly hold the concept of serving the people of the world", [5]China itself was less a normative self-sustained entity than a conjuncture of a series of dialectical relations intertwined between internal and external elements. In the 1980s, Gong Deshun who led the review of Chinese modern architectural history recognized the necessity to reserve a place for the Chinese foreign aid architecture (Gong et al., 1989). This idea was carried on by scholars like Zou Denong (Zou et al., 2010) who argues that the road to modern architecture that was blocked in domestic environment has been worked out in foreign aid construction. Therefore, can we say that the composition of Chinese modernist architecture should include an overseas dimension in a transnational manner during that particular period? Had China's practice abroad in the Maoist period developed new styles and techniques that had never been theorized? These are important problems that should have more attention (Ding & Xue, 2015; Lu, 2010; Roskam, 2015; Song, 2017).

The reevaluation of overseas architecture is not simply to bring back a missing part. This overlooked foreign dimension is not only an outward extension or "exportation" of Chinese architecture, but it also organically constitutes the overall condition of the latter. In other words, between China and the Third World, exportation and importation actually coexisted. The interaction between the Chinese and the overseas architecture was by no means limited to that between China and the West or the Soviet bloc. We should bring the deep communication and certain sharing features between China and the Third World back to the analyses. The Third World has never been a blank slate, but a land filled with Western architectural heritage due to prolonged colonialization. This existing architecture provided a convenient reference for later Chinese experts who were totally unfamiliar to local conditions, and also difficulties and challenges to them at the same time. After all, no matter how fierce the ideological confrontation between socialism and capitalism could be, it could not replace the comparison of technoscientific advancement. Therefore, the Chinese state required foreign aid design to "stand up to imperialism": on the one hand, it hoped to narrow

[5] From a speech by Fang Yi, Director of the Foreign Economic and Trade Commission, at the Meeting of the Diplomatic Envoys of the Ministry of Foreign Affairs, January 1, 1966, *Biography of Fang Yi*.

the gap with the West, on the other hand, it called to maintain the distinction from the West.[6]

In 1961, Chen Dengao, the Chief expert of China's Ministry of Construction, visited Guinea and focused on the tropical modernist architecture built by the French in the late colonial period, which were new to Chinese architects at the time. He and his team made a preliminary summary of typical architectural elements such as shading boards, screen walls, and verandas.[7] If the eye-catching monumental architecture could be undertaken by a small number of famous Chinese architects, then huge amount of industrial buildings were faced with the severe shortage of designers.[8] Since then, dispatching experts to the Third World to learn and investigate "in order to obtain information and make foreign aid design more adaptable to local conditions" had become an important task of the Chinese foreign aid system.

Meanwhile, important journals such as *Journal of Architecture* (*jianzhu xuebao*) has consecutively published specific articles focusing on Africa such as "Introduction to African Tropical Architecture", "Architecture in Guinea" and "Architecture in Ghana" during 1962–64 (see Chen, 1962; Ren, 1964; Wei, 1964). At the end of 1964, when Chinese Premier Zhou Enlai met with the Vice Prime Minister of Egypt (then named "United Arab Republic"), Aziz Sedki, Zhou mentioned that China's foreign aid projects "could not be designed in a closed studio, but should be designed according to your situation… We must first learn from you and understand you, otherwise the aid will fall into subjectivism" (Ye et al., 2008). An idea of inspiring and pushing domestic technical progress through overseas work experience was quickly formulated in China's foreign economic system in the name of "insisting foreign aid and promoting domestic work" (*zhua yuanwai, cu guonei*). All of this reminds us that early China's overseas architectural practice was not a one-way movement. The socialist politics need to transcend the scope of a single country. The connection between home and abroad for a socialist country should be embodied in the long-distance exportation/importation relation woven by personnel, capital, technology, standards, and knowledge installed by architecture.

The Third World, with its multi-layered architectural scenes, provided China with another lens for understanding the world. It enabled the Chinese workers in architectural aid to gain valuable reference for the self-reflex and self-positioning with the new knowledge and information. Roughly speaking, China's foreign aid architecture in the 1960s and 1970s already showed a certain recognizable trend of stylization. Taking public architecture as an example, the cases of the 1960s were mainly based on imitating the tropical modernist paradigm that prevailed in postcolonial areas which took shape in the 1940s and 1950s. People's Palace in Guinea (1967) (Fig. 2.1),

[6] "Documents and Regulations of the National Basic Construction Commission, the Bureau of Foreign Economic Liaison, etc. on the Foreign Aid Design Work Conference" (1965.2–1965.8), Shanghai Municipal Archives (B 32-2-1-121).

[7] In his late years, Chen Dengao published *Tropical Architecture* (*redai jianzhu*) based on his long-term survey and design practice in tropical regions such as Africa and the Middle East (China Construction Industry Press, 1989).

[8] Report of Shanghai Textile Industry Bureau on Re-requesting Help to Solve the issues of Foreign Aid Design Cadres" (1963.2.25), Shanghai Municipal Archives (A36-2-629-48).

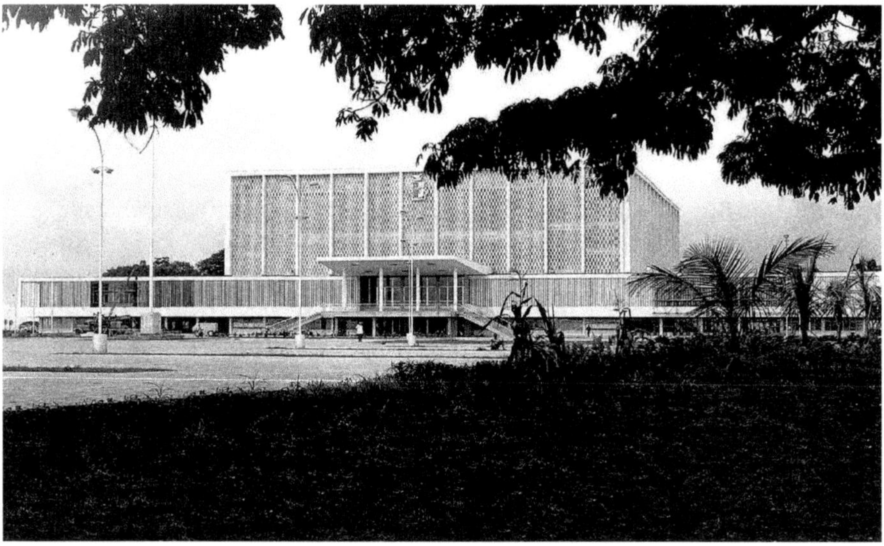

Fig. 2.1 People's Palace, Conakry, Guinea. *Source World Architecture (shijie jianzhu)* 2015(1):43

National Theatre in Somali (1967), Bandaranaike Memorial International Conference Hall in Sri Lanka (1973)[9] are the typical cases. These buildings basically have no obvious "socialist features" in ordinary Chinese views. These practices may illustrate two points: First, China hopes to prove to recipient countries that China has the ability to understand regionalism and its construction techniques is not infeiror to those of former colonizers. This was the demonstration of "socialist superiority". Second, China was not certain in what kind of message of itself should be expressed through architecture. But in the 1970s, some important projects, such as the Federal Government Building in Sierra Leone (i.e. the Youyi [Friendship] Building, 1982[10]) (Fig. 2.2) and the People's Palace in Zaire (1979) began to have a different look. They included an architectural tropical-responsive language but also reflected simplicity, solemnness, and symmetry of Chinese socialist public architecture accompanied by simplified traditional Chinese aesthetical symbols overall.

This is even more apparent for some important stations and office buildings of the Tanzania-Zambia Railway built between 1970 and 1976: "modern" is their primary impression for the locals which forms a stark contrast with (Fig. 2.3) a somewhat tropical variant of the Bavarian style in the Central Railway left by German colonial rule from the 1910s.[11] In the Dar es Salaam Terminal (Fig. 2.4), the large-size

[9] The design was already completed by 1965 led by chief architect Dai Nianci. However, due to the turmoil of Sri Lanka's political situation, the construction only began in 1970.

[10] The design was completed in 1975 by the Design Institute of the Construction and Research Institute of the National Basic Construction Commission.

[11] From my interview with Kironde Lusugga, a retired engineer in Tanzania, July 2019, Dar es Salaam, Tanzania

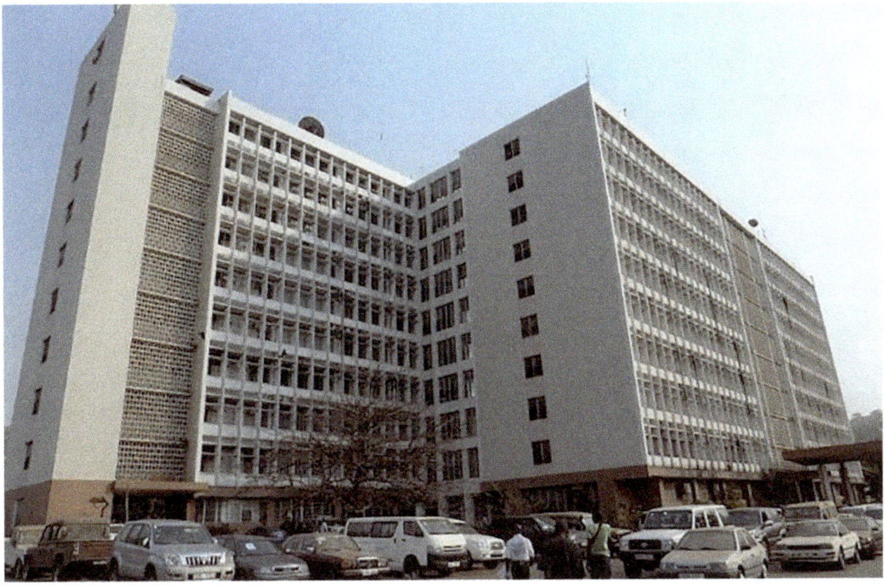

Fig. 2.2 Youyi Building, Freetown, Sierra Leone. *Source* https://commons.wikimedia.org/wiki/File:Youyi_Building.jpg

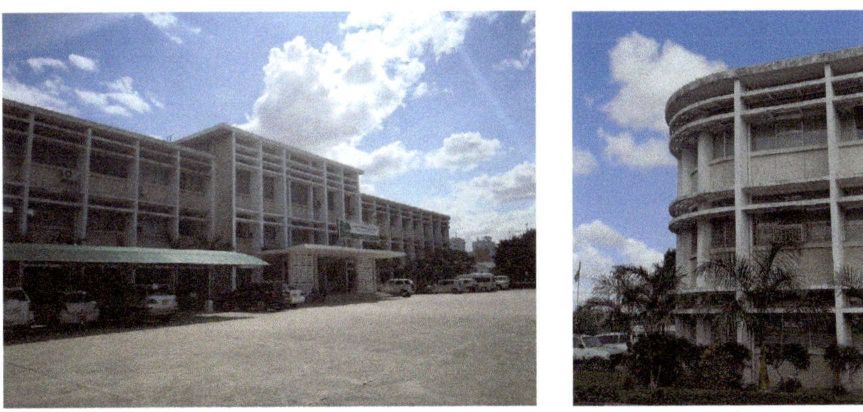

(a) Front view of the office building **(b)** The details of the building corner

Fig. 2.3 Headquarter Office of the Tazara (Tan-Zam Railway) [photo by the author, 2019]

windows are clearly adapted to tropical conditions, and the interior of the main structure of the building resembles the Beijing Railway Station completed in 1959. Nearly half century past after its completion, the Terminal is still one of the most spectacular public architecture in local area. Additionally, some small stations are also noteworthy (Fig. 2.5). They explicitly reveal the characteristics of simplicity,

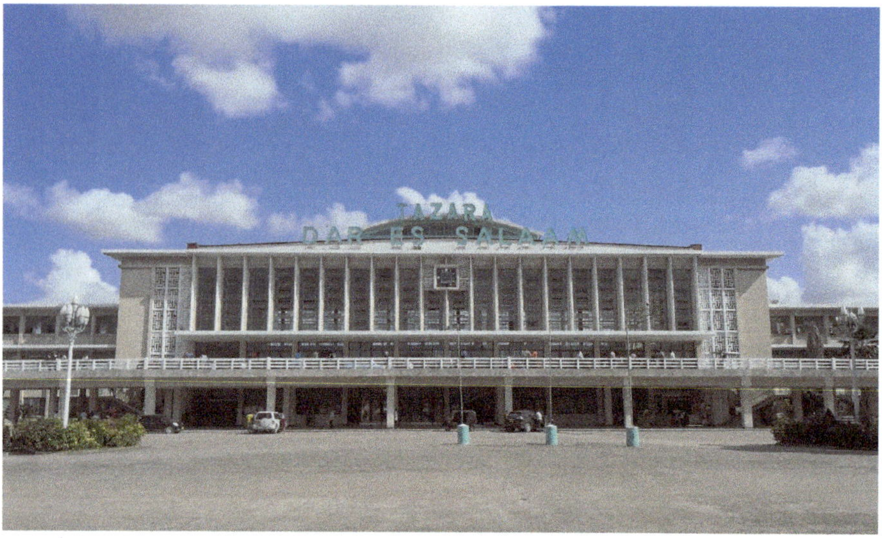

Fig. 2.4 Terminal of Dar es Salaam of the Tazara [photo by the author, 2019]

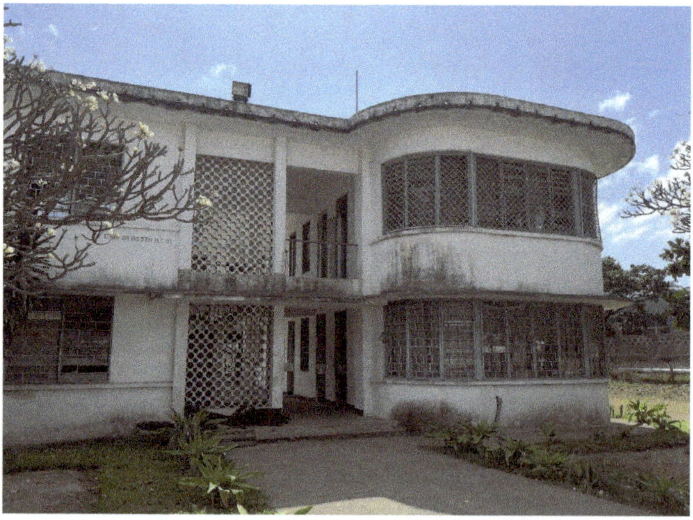

Fig. 2.5 Kurasini Transfer Station of the Tazara [photo by the author, 2019]

clarity and lightness on the one hand, but still maintain a restraint in aesthetics and an avoidance of exuberant symbolization on the other hand.[12]

[12] As the largest single foreign aid project in Chinese history, the Tanzania-Zambia Railway (TAZARA) has once again received greater attention in recent years under the background of BRI projects and research. Most commentators, however, still understand it in terms of infrastructure or

During the same period, new buildings with obvious modernist style in China especially in Beijing and Guangzhou began to appear sporadically, which were generally used for foreign affairs, commerce and entertainment (such as Beijing International Club, Guangzhou Baiyun Hotel, etc.). Research points out that this breakthrough was made possible due to the relatively relaxed environment after the restoration of limited contacts between China and the United States since 1972. It was the result of the renewal of design ideas brought about by the exchange of thoughts and personnel visits between the architect delegations of the two sides (Song, 2017; Song & Zhu, 2016). However, if we pay attention to African modern architecture and related practice that Chinese architects started working on since the early 1960s, it should be reasonable to conclude that this context of the Chinese mastery of modernist knowledge can be mapped through a wider picture beyond Europe and America.

2.2 Material: Politics of Productive Space

If the discussion in the previous section takes public architecture as the main context, then there are a series of questions to be answered: Why the practice of China is ignored while the counterpart works of other socialist countries in the Third World have re-entered the horizon of the field? Why China did not offer architectural works that could become legacy and be memorize in either the industry or the public realm? The answer is probably related to the type classification and nature of China's overseas projects at that time. Projects categorized as construction or building projects are generally large-scale monumental and public architecture with symbolic meanings. Their supervision was often taken by the Ministry of Construction (later the National Basic Construction Commission, now the Ministry of Housing and Urban–Rural Construction). Differently, almost productive projects (especially light industry), including the design and construction process of the entire factory area (workshops, office buildings, residential buildings), were counted as "industrial projects". Indeed, due to the obvious restrictions on spatial arrangement and configuration, as well as the rigid requirements of production equipment and working flow, industrial architecture is more like a relatively independent field with less popular attention.

Therefore, when we discuss architectural "exportation" of China during the Cold War, we need to recognize this blind spot. This is not only because these projects account for the largest proportion in number, but also because the "exportation" of industrial architecture reflects the specific spatial and technological politics of China during the socialist revolution and construction period. Communism requires the complete mastery of the production process centered by the proletariat and the

development projects in a broad sense, ignoring that it has 93 stations in total (including the Dar es Salaam Terminal) of great architectural significance. In fact, modern transportation architecture such as railway stations was a specific symbol of modernity in the early stage of industrialization.

working people which functions as the foundation of social liberation.[13] In the early days of the People's Republic of China, in order to ensure that the industrialization that started with difficulty would not be interrupted, the proletariat state forcibly lowered the collective consumption standards of urban and rural residents, and used the surplus to expand reproduction. In such a production-over-consumption policy, being productive or non-productive became the most fundamental categorization for architecture. Productive space has become the most legitimized socialist space.

This productive space was generally absent in the Third World at that time. Before the independence, important colonial cities and ports in the Afro-asian world were often highly cosmopolitan enclaves. Taking Dar es Salaam, the largest city in Tanzania as an example. As early as the period from the 1920s to the 1940s, the city had witnessed the first emergence of architecture with traditional Gujarat regional characters, the Art Deco style, and even the International style with horizontal windows and cantilevered structures. That was a material manifestation of "colonial modernity".[14] When it came to the 1960s, in the documents of Chinese experts working in Tanzania, they wrote: "In order to meet their own needs, the colonialists stepped up their plunder of Tanzania's resources and wealth, and gradually constructed buildings, ports and major transportation and roads in large and small cities. Many cities have western-style modern buildings, such as theaters, churches, banks, hotels, shops, and some high-level residences. However, industrial architecture is very poor. Except some substantial industrial enterprises set up in the mining industry and cash crop processing industry controlled by foreign monopoly capital, there are only simple assembly and repair factories for the locals. The abnormal development of urban construction in that period … has a distinctive colonialist feature."[15]

At that time, the revolutionaries in the national liberation waves in the Third World had already reached a consensus that if they could not get rid of their economic and technical dependence on the former colonizers or capitalist powers, the anti-colonial struggle would easily fall into an indirect "neocolonial" rule. Political independence can turn out nothing but a piece of certificate.[16] Zhou Enlai's "Eight Principles of China's Foreign Aid" (1964) clearly pointed out that the purpose of aid is to "enable

---

[13] In the tradition of critical theory, whether this production politics has reproduced alienation or essentially repeated the capitalist logic has been a subject of ongoing debate. This debate cannot be clear without a concrete and historical settings which is not contained by this article.

[14] From my visit to the Dar Es Salaam Architectural Heritage Centre (DARCH) and my interview with Aida Mulokozi, the director of the Centre, July 2019. In the interview, we talked about the industrial architectural heritage of Tanzania's early days of decolonization. Aida told me that their current protection plan of architectural heritage can only cover the colonial period, and there was only one post-independence architecture listed as heritage (which is the brutalist Kariakoo Market by B.J. Amuli).

[15] From the reference book *Basic Data Collection on Design of Foreign Aid Complete Projects* (Volume 2 of Tanzania) edited by the Ministry of Foreign Economic Relations in 1976; also from my interview of Mr. Shu Xiansui, a former Beijing textile expert, August 2019, Beijing, China

[16] Ghana's President Kwame Nkrumah was among the earliest to theorize neocolonialism. His work *Neocolonialism - The Last Stage of Imperialism* (1965) is a classic literature of this thought which directly inspired Samir Amin and other thinkers of Dependence Theory.

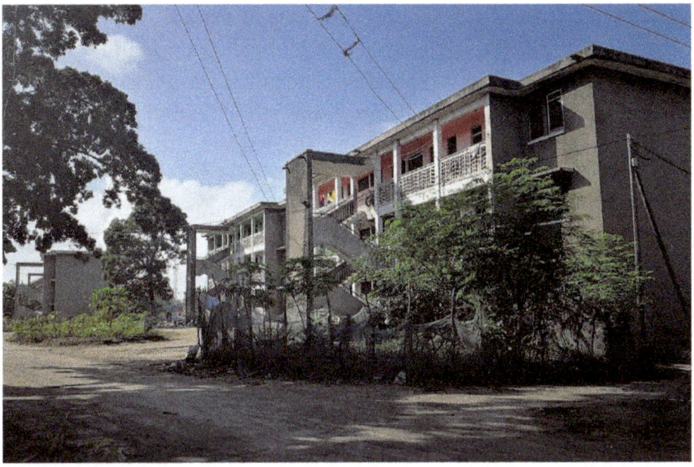

Fig. 2.6 Collective Dormitory (two-room style), Friendship Textile Factory. There are three types of them (one-room for bachelors, two-room for couples, and three-room for big families or cadres) [photo by the author, 2019]

the government of the recipient country to increase its income and accumulate funds" and "gradually embark on the road of self-reliance and economic independence".

The tension between production and consumption is an enduring and structural issue to the Third World . China always suggested aid recipient countries to insist on production which would be the cornerstone of economic independence (Zhou et al., 2014). An important legacy of China's early practice in Africa might be such an understanding of production politics in which productive architecture, production activities, and producers were prioritized, and the space was formed to support certain political and economic arrangements. The Friendship Textile Mill in Tanzania, built during 1966–68, was the largest factory in East Africa in the last century. It was located 7 km west of Dar es Salaam city center. At its peak, there were about 5,000 workers producing cloth such as Konga which had the highest quality in that region.

The project was originally included 1,500 apartment units with schools, shops, hospitals and more. But soon, considering the limitation of funding, the Chinese ambassador had finally persuaded the Tanzania government to reduce the number of apartments in order to guarantee the investment in the production sector. Even after being compressed (with only 500 apartment units left), Friendship Textile Factory, as a major model project, has to a large extent resembled the classic socialist space in which work, living, and welfare facilities were integrated. This case was also the birthplace of the first "workers' collective residential unit" in Tanzania (Fig. 2.6). Following that, several state or public sector employers intended to copy it, attempting to build similar welfare apartments for their own employees.[17]

[17] I interviewed three veteran workers of Friendship Textile Factory, Dar es Salaam, Tanzania, July 2019. Two of them joined the factory in 1968 and the other one in 1970. All of them are currently working in factory management board (re-employment after retirement).

Except this, many other Chinese aid projects that I have visited such as the agricultural tool factory, the cigarette factory, the leather factory, and many other kinds of factories did not have living quarters.[18] Production-over-consumption policy in aid projects also differentiated China from other socialist countries that have achieved industrialization to varying degrees. In contrast, during the period of 1964–72, the three major projects aided by the GDR (East Germany) in Zanzibar (a semi-autonomous region of Tanzania) were large-scale and high-standard collective housing, many apartment units of which were as spacious as 100 square meters (including some duplex structures). Even the bathroom facilities including bathtubs were completely shipped from Germany.[19] Such an approach was unimaginable for China where frugal life was a part of the revolutionary spirit.

The Friendship Textile Factory (Fig. 2.7) displayed a scale that was rare in Africa at that time, leaving a shocking impression to the young workers: "The first day I came to the factory to register, it felt like walking into a palace". The construction progress of the factory has been repeatedly reported in Tanzania's national newspapers. Tanzanian President Julius Nyerere had also visited the construction site many times (Fig. 2.8). The giant factory has become a symbol of the new country's independence from colonialism and its pursuit to be modern. After the factory's completion, the front area of it has often function as a stage for politicians to give speeches and mobilize workers (Fig. 2.9).[20] As time goes by, the word "friendship" (Swahili: Urafiki) for the Friendship Textile Factory has become a name for that area (e.g. the bus stop is named "Urafiki").

After the 1980s, Africa had experienced a long and painful history of falling into an economic trap caused by privatization and the decomposition of state-owned property initiated by the global wave of neoliberal policies started in the United Kingdom and the United States (Tomlinson, 2003). The history is also recorded and reflected in this group of industrial architecture. Mass numbers of factories aided by China in those years were immersed in the tide of loss of state-owned assets in Tanzania - now almost all of them are either vacant, abandoned, or appropriated for other purposes. The former Ubungo Agricultural Tool Factory adjacent to the Friendship Textile Factory is such a case. The Mang'ula Machinery Factory in the inner-land area, as a supplement in the Tazara Railway construction, is even more derelict. It was a rare heavy industrial base in Africa which could produce motorcycles in the 1980s. But at present, its workshop, office building, and ancillary buildings are all empty shells. The satellite map shows that the non-construction area of the factory has been covered by farmland or weeds again. The formation and deformation of this series of productive spaces fully bear witness to the political and economic upheavals of

[18] Based on my limited observation, there are two exceptions. One is the dormitory at some train stations of Tazara for workers must be on duty at all times; the other one is state farms for people have no possibility for daily commute in rural areas.

[19] From my interview with resident, Mr. Ali Mussa, August 2019, Zanzibar, Tanzania.

[20] For example, Tanzania's newspaper *The Nationalist* reported on May 6, 1967, that President Nyerere inspected the textile factory; on July 24, 1969, *Nationalist* reported Tanzanian revolutionaries, Minister of Commerce and Industry, A.M. Babu's speech to workers in front of the main office building, with Chinese technical representatives in the factory sat at his side.

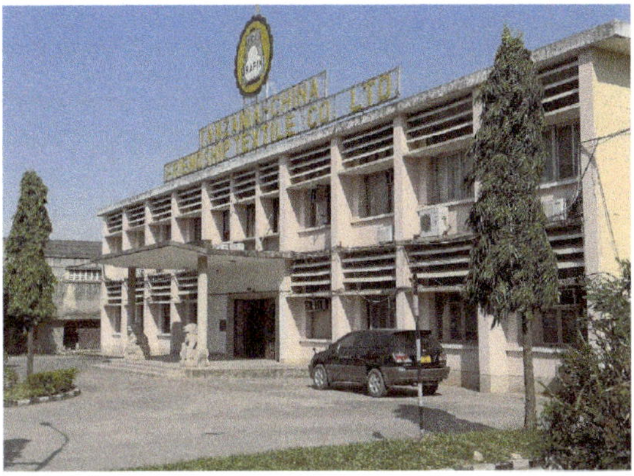

(a) Main Office, Friendship Textile Factory, the pair of lions in the entrance were not there until 1997 when the factory turned to a Tanzania-China joint factory

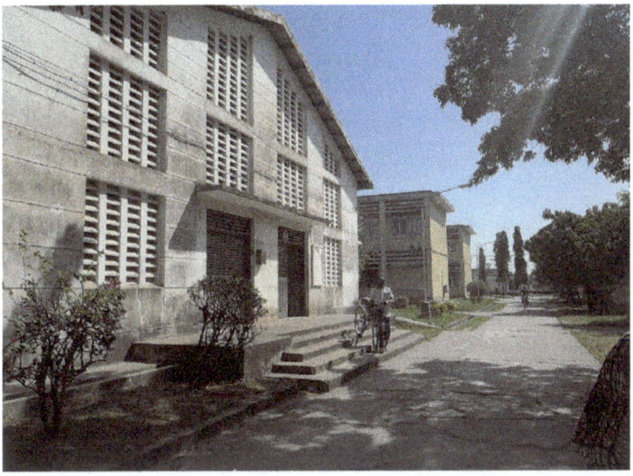

(b) Living Quarter. The dining hall is on the left side.

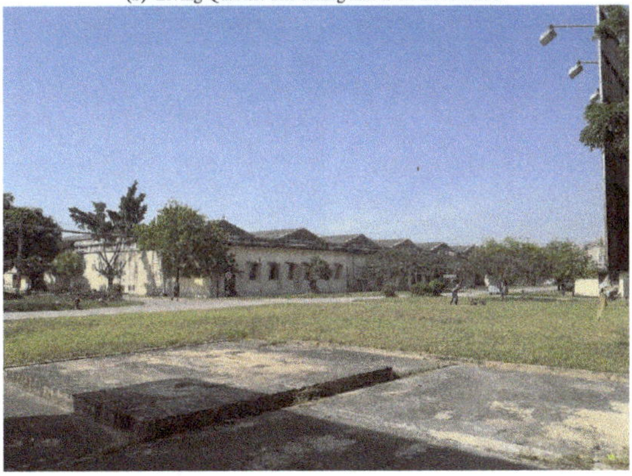

(c) Production Quarter. This is one of the workshops.

Fig. 2.7 Friendship textile factory. [Photo by the author, 2019]

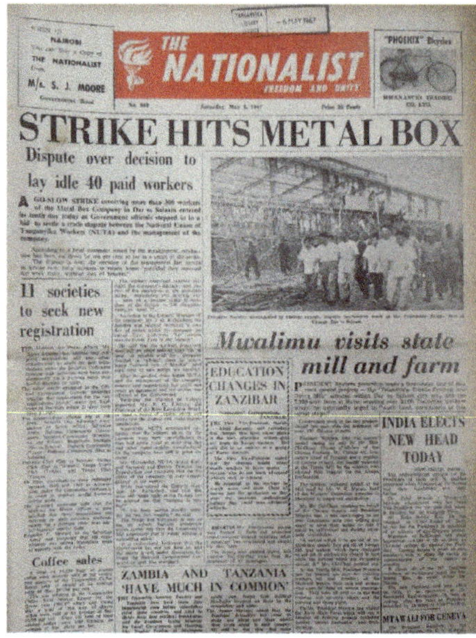
THE NATIONALIST

FREEDOM AND UNITY

STRIKE HITS METAL BOX

Dispute over decision to lay idle 40 paid workers

11 societies to seek new registration

Mwalimu visits state mill and farm

EDUCATION CHANGES IN ZANZIBAR

INDIA ELECTS NEW HEAD TODAY

Coffee sales

ZAMBIA AND TANZANIA 'HAVE MUCH IN COMMON'

Fig. 2.8 "Mwalimu Visits State Mill and Farm", *Nationalist,* May 6, 1967. "Mwalimu" means teacher or tutor in Swahili which is the honorific title of President Julius Nyerere. [photo by the author, and Courtesy of East African Special Collection, University of Dar es Salaam, 2019]

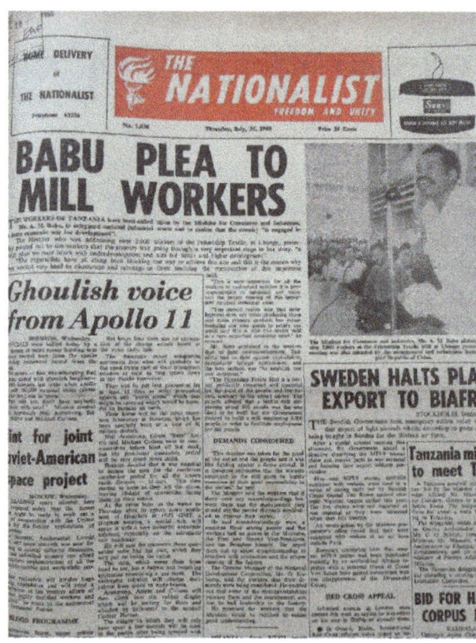
THE NATIONALIST

FREEDOM AND UNITY

BABU PLEA TO MILL WORKERS

Ghoulish voice from Apollo 11

SWEDEN HALTS PLAN EXPORT TO BIAFRA

Fig. 2.9 "Babu Plea To Mill Worker Tanzanian", *Nationalist,* July 24, 1969. Babu is the head of Ministry of Commerce and Industry. In this picture, he was promoting workers to workhard and be vigilant in protecting state assets. [photo by the author and the courtesy of East African Special Collection, Univeristy of Dar es Salaam, 2019]

Africa since independence. Since 2015, new Tanzanian government has put forward the goal of "re-industrialization". The Friendship Textile Factory which is more than half a century old has been taken as a living fossil of China-Africa friendship in the context. In short, we should pay more attention to the productive architecture scattered in many African countries.

2.3 Geography: The Tropical and the Regional Issues

Similar to the technicians from the Soviet Union and Eastern Europe, the most basic problem facing Chinese architects and engineers who had just arrived Africa was the tropical climate in various (sub)types that occupies almost the entire continent. The tropical climate zone was rarely studied or even experienced in most part of China. Whether among the professionals who returned from studying in Europe, America or Japan in the early days, or in the knowledge and technical standards transplanted from the Soviet Union in the 1950s, the tropical area was a missing piece of the puzzle in Chinese knowledge map.[21] With the absence of ready-made data and the lack of technical standards in recipient countries that were newly independent, China's aid construction had to be accompanied by systematic research on local natural and geographical conditions, and then to explore design solutions accordingly (You, 2012). In 1961, Shanghai Light Industry Design Institute began to prepare for the master plan of the match-cigarette joint factory in Conakry, the capital city of Guinea. In order to make up for the absence of knowledge about Guinea as much as possible, the Shanghai designers even contacted the Chinese Acrobatic Art Troupe delegates who went to perform in Guinea to learn about their impressions of the streetscape in Conakry.[22] Striving to overcome the insufficient mastery of tropical architecture, the design completed in 1962 was once too exaggerated with "excessive consideration of tropical characteristics".[23] It was out of joint with the production process and the budget went extremely high. As a result, the blueprints that had already arrived Guinea were recalled to be revised substantially.

In response to China's rapidly expanding contact with the outside world, the study of tropical climatic characteristics and its construction technical response gradually grew from the early 1960s into an independent category of overseas knowledge. As Fang Yi, the head of the foreign aid system, said in 1966, "foreign aid work faces the world and faces many areas that we have not yet known". "In every cycle of the work, it is necessary to accumulate data and establish and improve technical archivization.

[21] It can be a good question that did Xia Changshi's experimental passive cooling architecture in Guangzhou in the 1950s and the establishment of the Institute of Subtropical Architecture Research in South China play a role in foreign aid project in Africa in the following two decades. But my preliminary research found no evidence of this knowledge transfer path (Interview with Professors Peng Changxin and Xiao Yiqiang from South China University of Science and Technology, July 2018, Guangzhou). I was also benefited from the discussion with Prof Feng Jiang from the same institute in 2017.

[22] "Some Experiences of Shanghai Light Industry Design Institute of the Ministry of Light Industry on Implementing Foreign Aid Design Guidelines". Shanghai Municipal Archives (B 163-2-1562-107).

[23] *Ditto.*

The basic data collected abroad must be sorted and compiled into books timely. And major problems that occur during construction and pilot production must be recorded with special itemization and included in the list of technical archives".[24] This was the beginning of China's large-scale establishment of its own knowledge system as a whole about the nature and geography of the Third World. The Technical Information Bureau of the Ministry of Construction had accelerated the collection and study of overseas tropical-responsive design cases. The cases selected included Cuba, Nigeria, Tanzania, Guinea, Senegal, Brazil, Kenya, Ghana, Ivory Coast (Côte d'Ivoire), etc.[25] Although cases were analyzed briefly, the question awareness of the analysis was very clear.

During the construction of the Guinean match-cigarette joint factory from 1963 to 1964, Zhou Enlai and Fang Yi inspected the construction site in Guinea. They found it convincing that the architectural structure, form and material adopted by the Chinese could not be adapted to local conditions and the tropical climate. Zhou soon promoted the development of tropical knowledge-producing clusters by having two National Foreign Aid Design Work Series Conferences in 1964 and 1965. The breakthrough in tropical architectural techniques was regarded as a nation-wide top scientific research project. For instance, five institutes including Tsinghua University and Tongji University had collaborated to carry out experiments on light building materials for tropical climates; Institute of Geophysics of the Chinese Academy of Sciences, the Research Institute of the Ministry of Construction, and the Guangzhou Institute of Humid Tropical Electrical Appliances worked together to solve the quantification and standardization of tropical climates. Meanwhile, designs for Mali Cigarette Factory, Mali Textile Factory, and the Ghana Pencil Factory that were done by 1964–65 had also gone through a modification accordingly. In addition to domestic scientific research, experts also travelled abroad (mainly Africa) to investigate, survey, or collect information about climate and geology[26] which included properties of various possible local building materials (such as wood, stone, sand, soil).

The tropical issues for Chinese were first and foremost about how to ensure shading, ventilation, cooling, and moisture-proof through architectural design, all of which had to be done within a limited budget and the anxiety of style. This included an examination and limited reference to the classical African "tropical modernism". "The tropics" was also a problem for early European empires in their conquest of colonies. In order to alleviate the physical and mental discomfort caused by the high temperature and humidity, the imperial engineers launched a series of microclimate modification experiments to ensure the human in-door thermal comfort as much as possible. This architectural paradigm, which was later condensed into "tropical modernism" during 1940s–50s (Chang, 2016; Crison, 2003; Roux, 2003).

---

[24] "Notice of the State Capital Construction Committee and the Foreign Economic Liaison Committee" Issued "Regulations on Several Issues Concerning Foreign Aid Design Work (Draft)" (1965.5.28) Shanghai Municipal Archives (B 32-2-121).

[25] *Architectural Translation Series-Architectural Design* 1964, No. 3, 4, 8, 10, 11, 12.

[26] Climate and geological data are listed as "necessary data" for foreign aid project practitioners.

The tropical modernism has undoubtedly inspired Chinese architects working in African countries since the 1960s.[27] But obviously, the architectural design in a specific climatic environment was not only about forms and styles. With the extension of time and space, another problem had gradually emerged for the Chinese: the cycle of dry and rainy seasons brought about immersion and erosion of the foundation which caused base bulge or wall crack. Unfortunately, it usually costed one or two years after a project was completed to be sensed which was always late. In 1973, the Chinese State Council sent various expert teams to Africa to conduct a six-month inspection on more than 300 buildings in more than 50 projects. The base problem was especially examined. The key was to explore the changes of different types of soil under different temperature, humidity and other conditions, which also involved the research of type, composition and ratio of building and engineering materials. In a report written by the foreign aid system to the State Council in 1975, the tropical architecture was still listed as one of the three major problems in China's aid to Africa.[28]

It was until later when the continuous improvement of data source had reached to another level that the tropical issues became less urgent. This series of changes in building technical standards reflects the efforts of Chinese technicians to organize the distant geographical and climatic conditions into China's internal knowledge system. Based on the technical challenges of foreign aid projects and the overcoming of them, a unique epistemology of China's understanding of the world was formed in the 1960s and 1970s. Techniques becomes a sensor and translator of overseas geography. Likewise, architecture becomes the intermediary between the body and the wider outside world for which climate zones function as scales, just as discussed in the classics of humanistic geography or phenomenological architecture phenomenon (Tuan, 1976; Nober-Schulz, 1980; Cresswell, 2013).

"Foreign aid projects are distributed in four continents of Asia, Africa, Latin America and Europe, in the three climate zones of frigid, temperate, and tropical, in dozens of countries, and with different situations."[29] In the modern history of China, it was the first time that large-scale amount of people were dispatched to a foreign continent to assist the construction of the local societies, until those unfamiliar places became gradually concrete in the eyes of the Chinese. It was through these surveys, designs, constructions, and operations in hundreds of concrete projects that China has established a recognizable technological map and woven a global network of knowledge production for the vast overseas world. Led by the Chinese foreign aid system, this huge scientific research of the overseas world had turn into a nationwide systematic information collection between 1975 and 1979.

[27] It can be found from the papers of Chen Dengao and others aforementioned.

[28] In the report from the circular inspection team, 1973, it was stated that, strictly speaking, the damaged condition of most buildings was light (*Biography of Fang Yi*). In my interview with Mr. Shu Xiansui, he also mentioned that many recipient countries did not care about those issues that much but it was the Chinese side that insisted to find out an explanation.

[29] "Notice of the State Basic Construction Committee and the Foreign Economic Liaison Committee Issued "Regulations on Several Issues Concerning Foreign Aid Design Work (Draft)" (1965.5.28) Shanghai Municipal Archives (B32-2-121).

It had constructed a massive series of reference books with standardized and operational knowledge base to serve all the working sectors and personals with overseas projects. These books were even seen as the unintentional origin of regional geography study in China according to *Chinese Academic Encyclopedia of the 20th Century: Geography* (Wu et al., 2002). The consecutive projects conducted abroad have brought to China new categories of knowledge beyond traditional East Asian cosmic order and the classical Marxist-Leninist theory. This not only enables socialist China to understand and change the world as an active and modern epistemological subject, but also promotes the knowledge production about the Third World to move beyond the rule of the former colonial empires.

2.4 Closing

Overseas aid for construction is not only a historical method for China to participate in understanding and engaging with the world. It in turn facilitates China to understand itself and deal with the relationship between itself and others, which is one of the major historical clues that make up today's China. As an intermediary for China to be deeply involved in the process of world history, foreign aid projects deserve to be sorted out in a broader and more connected vision. The foreign aid construction in the Maoist period not only directly affected the early stage of the People's Republic of China, but also indirectly and unexpectedly laid the material, technical, organizational and knowledge foundation for the deep interaction between China and the world in the later marketized form.

China's construction in the Third World had once declined during the 1980s–1990s. In line with a series of changes in China's domestic and diplomatic affairs, China's international perspective was increasingly receding. The 1990s was especially a low point (Zhou et al., 2014). After entering the twenty-first century, China's contact with the Third World, typically Africa, has become much more active. The number of commercial, development, and aid projects in the form of investment has experienced an unprecedentedly eruption. A seldom-noticed fact is that among the earliest four giant state-owned enterprises of China that entered the international engineering contracting market (namely, China Civil Engineering, China Harbor, China Communications Construction, and AVIC), the first three were all born in the background of Maoist foreign aid history.

After many years of working and experience accumulation in Africa, the Middle East, and the Mediterranean region, these previous aid systems eventually turned into marketized players around 1979–80 in the reform led by Deng Xiaoping.[30] Today, when China plays a role with much more weight in the construction of the Third

[30] In fact, as early as 1973, Nigeria, with better economic conditions due to oil trade, had accepted technical support from China but was covered the Nigerian funding. That is to say, before the reform of 1979, China had preliminarily experienced a quasi-market contracting service overseas. But it was only a special case of course.

World which also carries various controversies, a comprehension of China's early architectural construction aid will give us a long-time reference to better understand the reality.

References

Chang, J. (2016). *A genealogy of tropical architecture: Colonial networks, nature and technoscience*. Routledge.

Chen, D. (1962) feizhou redai jianzhu jieshao [An Introduction to African Tropical Architecture]. *Jianzhu xuebao*, [Journal of Architecture], 10: 15–20 陈登鳌. 非洲热带建筑介绍[J]. 建筑学报 1962(10): 15–20.

Cresswell, T. (2013). *Place: An introduction*. Wiley.

Crison, M. (2003). *Modern architecture and the end of empire*. Ashgate.

Ding, G., & Xue, C. Q. L. (2015). China's architectural aid: Exporting a transformational modernism. *Habitat International, 4*, 136–147.

Gong, D., et al, (1989) zhongguo xiandai jianzhu shigang [*The Historical Outline of Chinese Modern Architecture*]. Tianjin: Tianjin Science and Technology Press 龚德顺、邹德侬、窦以德. 中国现代建筑史纲, 天津: 天津科学技术出版社. 1989.

Hua, L., & Liu, G. (1957) buneng zai guangguzhe gai gaolou dasha le [We Should No Longer Only Focus on Grand Buildings]. *Jianzhu xuebao* [Journal of Architecture] (9) 华揽洪、刘光采. "不能再光顾着盖高楼大厦了" 建筑学报 1957(9).

Liu, Y. 2020 Refunctioning "Tropical Modernism": Anticolonial constructions in Chinese-built Architecturein Africa, 1960s–70s, *Mediapolis: A Journal of Cities and Culture* (5) https://www.mediapolisjournal.com/2020/03/refunctioning-tropical-architecture/.

Lu, D. (2010). Introduction: Architecture, modernity and identity in the third world. In Lu. Duanfang (Ed.), *Third world modernism: Architecture, development and identity* (pp. 1–28). Routledge.

Mark, J., et al. (2020). *Alternative globalizations: Eastern Europe and the postcolonial world*. Indiana University Press.

Norber-Schulz, C. (1980). *Genius loci: Towards a phenomenology of architecture*. Rizzoli.

Ren, G. (1964). jineiya jianzhu [Architecture in Guinea]. *jianzhu xuebao* [Journal of Architecture], 8: 29–33 任国允. 几内亚建筑. 建筑学报 1964(8): 29–33.

Roskam, C. (2015). Non-aligned architecture: China's design on and in Ghana and Guinea, 1955–92. *Architectural History, 58*, 261–291.

Roux, L. (2003). The networks of tropical architecture. *The Journal of Architecture, 8*, 337–354.

Schwenkel, C. (2020). *Building socialism: The afterlife of East German Architecture in Urban Vietnam*. Duke University Press.

Stanek, L. (2012). Cold war transfer: Architecture and Planning from socialist countries in the 'Third World' [J]. *Journal of Architecture, 3*, 299–307.

Stanek, L. (2014) Socialist networks and the internationalization of building culture after 1945, *ABE Journal*, 6.

Stanek, L. (2020). *Architecture in global socialism: Eastern Europe, West Africa, and the Middle East in the Cold War*. Princeton University Press.

Song, K. (2017). Modernism in Late-Mao China: A Critical Analysis on State-sponsored Buildings inBeijing, Guangzhou and Overseas, 1969–1976. (dissertation), Melbourne University of Melbourne.

Song, K., & Zhu, J. (2016). The architectural influence of the United States in Mao's China (1949–1976). *Fabrication, 26*, 337–356.

Tomlinson, B. (2003). What was the third world. *Journal of Contemporary History, 38*, 307–321.

Tuan, Y. (1976). Humanistic Geography[J]. *Annals of the Association of American Geographers* 266–276

Wei, Z. (1964). jiana jianzhu [Architecture in Ghana]. *Jianzhu xuebao* [Journal of Architecture], 5: 30–33 魏志达. 加纳建筑. 建筑学报 1964(5): 30–33.

Wu, et al. (2002). 20 shiji zhongguo xueshu dadian dilixue [*Chinese Academic Encyclopedia of the 20th Century: Geography*]. Fuzhou: Fujian Education Press 吴传均. 20世纪中国学术大典 地理学. 福州 福建教育出版社, 2002.

Xue, et al. (2018). yuanwai jianzhu: zhongguo shejiyuan zai haiwai de lichen [Architectural Export from China's Design Institutes]. *Shidai jianzhu*, [Times+Architecture] (163), 50–57 薛求理、丁光辉、常威等. 援外建筑: 中国设计院在海外的历程. 时代建筑, 2018(163).

Ye, et al. (2008). Biograpy of Fang Yi. Beijing: People's Press. 叶如根等, 方毅传. 北京, 人民出版社, 2008.

You et al. (2012) *Jianzhu zhongsi youyi zhi mingzhu: jinian banda la naike guoji huiyi dasha yuanjian jishi* [Building the Pearl of Sino-Sri Lanka Friendship: Documentary of the China-aided Bandaranaike Memorial International Conference Building]. Beijing: China Architecture and Building Press. 由宝贤等编著. 建筑中斯友谊之明珠: 纪念班达拉奈克国际会议大厦援建纪实. 北京: 中国建筑工业出版社, 2012.

Zhou, H., et al. (2014). *China's forign aid: 60 years in retrospect*. Springer.

Zou, et al. (2010). zhongguo xiandai jianzhushi [*The History of Chinese Modern Architecture*]. Beijing: China Construction Industry Press 邹德侬、戴路、张向炜. 中国现代建筑史, 北京: 中国建筑工业出版社, 2010.

Ye Liu is a Ph.D. candidate in sociology/social theory at the New School for Social Research, New York. He has a wide interest in architecture, geography, Third World decolonial politics, the Cold War/global sixties, socialist modernity, and radical theory in general. His dissertation project is devoted to a theoretical reconstruction to historicize socialism by reviewing China's climate-responsive building practice and its epistemological politics in African tropical areas during the 1960s–70s. Ye Liu's projects have been supported by programs including the Andrew W. Mellon Integrative Ph.D. Fellowship.

Chapter 3
Aesthetics and Politics of China's Foreign Aid Buildings from the 1950s to 1970s

Ke Song

Abstract This chapter reviews the development of China's foreign aid and foreign aid architecture from the 1950s to the 1970s, focusing on the relationship between the aesthetics of foreign aid architecture and its political implications. It aims to interpret the connotation and meaning of the "Chinese model" in foreign aid through architectural lens. From the perspective of history of knowledge, it analyses the development and evolution of the design knowledge of China's foreign aid architecture and the transnational knowledge flows, focusing on the influence of Western modernist architectural trends on Chinese foreign aid architecture from 1964 to 1976. Taking the Tanzania-Zambia Railway Terminus in Dar es Salaam as the primary example, it reveals the "Chineseness" of Chinese foreign aid architecture in the aspects of both aesthetics and politics, and discusses the contemporary value of Chinese foreign aid architecture of that period as an intellectual heritage.

3.1 Introduction

China's foreign aid increased dramatically in recent years, which attracted divergent academic responses from the fields of political science, international relations and global economics (Brautigam, 2009; Moyo, 2009; Shimomura & Ohashi, 2013). Architectural scholars also made significant contribution to this topic by scrutinizing China's foreign aid architecture (Ding & Xue, 2015; Roskam, 2015).

The white paper published by the Information Office of the State Council (IOSC) of China, titled *China's Foreign Aid* (2011) has systematically reviewed China's foreign aid since the 1950s. According to the white paper, China's foreign aid is often provided in the form of complete project, in a wide range of sectors including agriculture, industry, education, medicine, energy, infrastructure of transportation, electricity, and telecommunications, and public buildings. Among these, public building is closest to what is known as foreign aid architecture. It is regarded as a "feature area" of China's foreign aid, including conference and exhibition halls, stadia, schools,

K. Song (✉)
School of Architecture, Harbin Institute of Technology, Shenzhen, China
e-mail: songke@hit.edu.cn

C. Q. Xue and G. Ding (eds.), *Exporting Chinese Architecture*,
https://doi.org/10.1007/978-981-19-2786-7_3

museums, government buildings, parliament buildings, government building, and housing, among others. Many of these buildings have become the “icons of the city and centres for local social, political and cultural activities”, as stated by the white paper (IOSC, 2011).

Scholars proposed a concept “Chinese model”, as an alternative approach to the Western approaches, to identify the Chinese characteristics in the operation and organization of foreign aid in the global arena, including: strong state leadership, emphasis on economic development without political strings, diverse forms of aid both official and unofficial, and the preference for high-profile buildings (Söderberg, 2010; Zhang & Smith, 2017; Brautigam, 2011).

Both Chinese government’s white paper and international scholars’ researches and observations confirmed the significance of architectural aid as an important form of foreign aid by China. In particular, the material, visible and iconic buildings, with strong architectural ambition, are emphatically used as a political and diplomatic gift.

These high-profile buildings inevitably concern with the issues of design, form and aesthetics, which are all at the core of architectural discipline. Also, these architectural issues, were often intersected and intertwined with the non-architectural issues, in particular, the geopolitical, economic and ideological forces. To analyse foreign aid architecture, one need to think beyond architecture, treating architecture as a multidisciplinary and interdisciplinary subject that discusses aesthetics and politics at the same time. French philosopher Jacques Rancière’s research on aesthetics and politics provides an important theoretical framework (Ranciere, 2004). Rancière critically reviewed the art history in relation to the socio-political history of the West, and discovered the simultaneity of the changing paradigms of both art and politics throughout history. He further explained this simultaneity by introducing a concept “the distribution of the sensible”, which reveals the similarity of the inner structure between art and politics, both of which are structured based on “what can or cannot be seen, be said, and be known”. Therefore, an art intrinsically points to a politics, and vice versa, no matter whether this correspondence is acknowledged or not.

From this perspective, foreign aid architecture can be better analysed to unpack its entangled relationship between art and politics. For example, African Union Conference Centre and Office Complex, built in 2012, is one of the most significant and iconic buildings aided by China in recent years. It is a gift promised by then Chinese president Hu Jintao at the Beijing Summit of the Forum on China-Africa Cooperation (FOCAC). Its sleek and shiny facade demonstrated African leaders’ ambition to modernize Africa, but many details in the building disclosed Chinese omnipresent influence, for example, the Chinese artworks, Chinese labels on the fire distinguishers and even the Chinese voice in the elevators (Hulshof & Roggeveen, 2014).

Between aesthetics and politics, knowledge is an important mediator. Inspired by Michel Foucault’s methodology of history of knowledge (Dreyfus & Rabinow, 1982: xx–xxii), this paper proposes to focus on the evolution of architectural design knowledge system to reinterpret the history of Chinese foreign aid architecture since the 1950s. We can have some initial observations. First, Chinese foreign aid architecture is based on the knowledge accumulated by Chinese architects both inside and outside China, which is intrinsically marked with Chinese identity or Chineseness, in both aesthetic and political dimensions, either straightforward or obscure. Second, Chinese foreign aid architecture is also based on successive absorption of Western influences, particularly the Western modernist trends in the post-WWII decades, although in the Cold War context, Western influence was not openly discussed in China due to the ideological confrontation between China and the West. Third, Chinese foreign aid architecture also adapted to the local conditions of the recipient countries, in which process Chinese architects also absorbed new knowledge. Therefore, Chinese foreign aid architecture, as a node of transnational flows of knowledge, is deeply embedded in a complex global knowledge network that has been constantly changing. To understand the Chineseness, especially the aesthetics and politics behind it, one needs to adopt a comparative perspective, particularly focusing on the difference between Chinese modernism and Western modernism.

Based on Ranciere's theory of "aesthetics and politics" and Foucault's methodology of "history of knowledge", this paper aims to review and rethink China's foreign aid and foreign aid architecture since the 1950s. It analyses the aesthetics and politics of Chinese foreign aid architecture, and reflects on its Chineseness. In doing so, it aims to demystify the concept of "Chinese model" from an architectural perspective, by selectively discussing a few cases, including the Bandaranaike Memorial International Conference Hall (1973), Sri Lanka, and the TAZARA Railway Terminus (1976), Dar es Salaam, Tanzania.

3.2 China's Foreign Aid and Foreign Aid Architecture, 1950s–70s

From the 1950s to the 1970s, China in the Mao era executed extensive foreign aid programs, behind the decision-making of which, the ideological and political strategies, surpassing the economic interests, played dominant roles (Brautigam, 2009: 17–18). China's foreign aid in the Mao era needs to be studied against the backdrop of global Cold War politics. In the early 1950s, even though the new government of People's Republic of China was newly established, China began to provide the earliest foreign aid to the socialist neighbours, including North Vietnam and North Korea, in the form of both economic and military aid. By supporting the socialist neighbours, China aimed to strengthen its own security in the hostile international environment. Since then, China increasingly used foreign aid as important diplomatic tools to fulfill its long-term strategies in international relations. China's foreign aid increased dramatically in the 1960s, accounting for 1% of the Gross Domestic Product (GDP) each year, twice of the 1950s (Zhang, 2006: 165–67). This generosity contrasted with China's extremely stringent economic situation caused by the Great Leap Forward (1958–1960) and the Cultural Revolution (1966–1969).[1]

[1] Cultural Revolution, according to the CCP's official periodization of political history approved in 1978, lasted ten years from 1966 to 1976. Nevertheless, the heights of the Cultural Revolution,

China continued to increase foreign aid despite the huge lost during the great famine (1959–1961), largely because of the looming threats from both the Soviet Union and the United States . China therefore had to rely more on the Third World brothers for political support in the international environment. The huge investment in foreign aid eventually paid off when China replaced Taiwan under the rule of Kuomintang party to become one of the five Permanent membership of the United Nations (UN) Security Council.

From the 1950s to the early 1960s, China's foreign policy put the ideological confrontation at the centre, and China's foreign aid was part of the larger aim of exporting communist revolution. In many cases, China's foreign aid took form of exporting "armed struggle" to support the anti-government revolution in the African countries ruled by white governments.[2] But this radical approach suffered serious failure, leading to the lapse of the Second Asia-Afro Conference.[3]

To cope with the unfavourable situation, Chinese Premier Zhou Enlai led a fourteen-day visit to Asia and Africa in 1964. During his visit, Zhou declared the "Eight Principles for Economic Aid and Technical Assistance to Other Countries" ("Eight Principles"), which later became the guiding principles for China's foreign aid. The "Eight Principles" emphasizes such core values as equality, mutual benefit, no attached political conditions, and the objectives of fostering self-reliance and privileging low-investment, rapid-yield projects. Zhou Enlai's 1964 trip marked a crucial shift of China's foreign aid strategy, which terminated the export of "armed struggle" and emphasized the material and physical projects (Xie, 1988: 393–404). This trend was further confirmed in the 1970s, when China began to adopt a more pragmatic attitude to foreign relations and foreign aid by emphasizing "peaceful development" instead of ideological struggle (Armstrong, 1977: 236). China's foreign aid peaked in 1973, with the total expense of foreign aid accounting for more than 2% of the GDP of that year. After the opening up and reform, China's total expense on foreign aid gradually decreased to around 0.05% of the GDP each year till now. By the end of 2009, China had delivered more than 2000 building projects, including 687 public buildings and facilities of various kinds: 85 conference buildings, 85 sports facilities, 12 theatres & cinemas and 236 science, education and health care facilities (IOSC, 2011). Among these buildings, the iconic, high-profile buildings with political significance were increasingly used as an effective diplomatic tool.

---

the deepest turmoil, lasted from 1966 to 1969. Since 1969, Mao and state government began to cope with the economic disorder and the deterioration of international relations, by re-emphasizing economic development and restoring the relations with the West.

[2] For examples, in the 1960s, China provided military supports to Algeria, Mozambique and Congo for their "anti-imperialist movements". See (Jiang, 2014: 75–77).

[3] The Second Asia-Afro Conference was scheduled in 1965 but lapsed due to the division among the countries.

3.3 Absorbing Post-War Modernism

Chinese architects and design institutes began to practice overseas from 1956 onwards. From 1956 to 1960, Lin Leyi and Gong Deshun, the architects from Beijing Industrial Design Institute (BIDI)[4], designed fourteen aid projects in Mongolia, including such types as bridge, factory, hospital, hotel and department stores (Zou, 2001: 285). In these years, Mongolia was the largest recipient of China's aid, for geo-political reason. After Nikita Khrushchev denounced Stalin in 1956, China began to lose the mutual trust with the Soviet Union . Mongolia as a barrier between China and the Soviet Union was considered as an important country to win over at the time.

The aid projects overseas offered Chinese architects fresh opportunities to experiment with new architectural approaches. Notably, Gong Deshun's experimentation with modernism, exemplified by Ulan Bator Department Store (1961), Choibalsan International Hotel (1961) (Fig. 3.1) and the guesthouses (1962), formed a contrast to the prevailing National Style within China (Zhang, 2009).[5] The International Style actually conveyed an internationalism as a political gesture, by reputing signs and symbols of any culture or political regime and displaying a "neutral" modern guise. Gong's modernist experiment in the 1950s laid down a foundation for the design of later aid projects in the 1960s and 1970s in Africa and Southeast Asia. Most buildings overseas in these years were in line with the International Style as defined by Henry-Russell Hitchcock and Philip Johnson (Hitchcock & Johnson, 1996), characterised by light volumes, overhanging eaves, the composition of horizontal and vertical lines on façade, and the symmetry of plan and façade.

Although the International Style and other pre-World War II modernist trends were introduced to China as early as in the 1930s, the post-World War II Western modernist trends remained distant to most Chinese architects. It was largely because of China's ideological confrontation with the West after the 1950s in the context of the Cold War confrontation. In this context, the aid projects overseas provided Chinese architects precious opportunities to go abroad to see, experience and study Western contemporary architecture.

In 1961, for the design of a series of projects in Ghana and Guinea, including the People's Palace in Conakry, Guinea, built in 1967, a group of Chinese architects led by Chen Deng'ao from Beijing Institute of Architectural Design (BIAD) conducted a field work there (Roskam, 2015: 261–91). Chinese architects actively absorbed new knowledge of tropical modernism there. They noticed the latest architectural innovations and building technologies, including the sun-shading devices called brise-soleil

[4] Most of the aid projects in the 1950s were designed by Beijing Industrial Design Institute under the Ministry of Construction (Zou, 2001: 285). This design institute as the precursor of China Architectural Design and Research Group (CAG) today, was one of the most important design institutes in the Mao era.

[5] Gong Deshun (1923–1994) graduated from Institut des Hautes Etudes et Commerciales in Tianjin in 1945. This university put more emphasis on technical and practical knowledge of architecture compared to other universities that promoted Beaux-Arts education. (Zhang, 2009: 8).

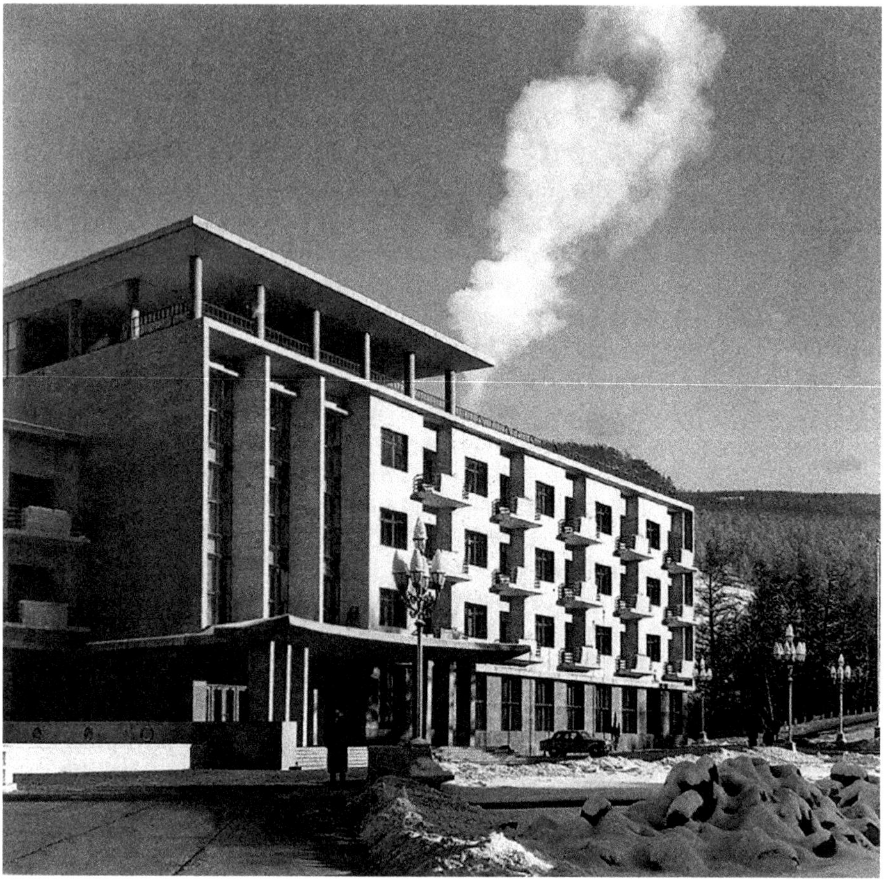

Fig. 3.1 Choibalsan International Hotel, Ulan Bator, Mongolia, 1961. Architect: Gong Deshun

(Ren, 1964). They also collected reference books on design methodology in tropical climate, including *Housing and Building in Hot-Humid and Hot-Dry Climates,* published in the United States and *Tropical Architecture in the Humid Zone,* written by British architects Fry and Drew (Chen, 1962).[6] Later in 1964, Chinese architect Dai Nianci from BIDI led a design team to Ceylon (Sri Lanka after 1972) for the design of Bandaranaike Memorial International Conference Hall (BMICH) (Zhang, 2000), where they collected climate data and surveyed local vernacular architecture. They were also believed to have noticed the American Embassy in India by Edward Stone which is an exemplary work of American formalism (Song & Zhu, 2016).

In the 1960–70s, Chinese architects consciously referenced two specific trends of Western postwar modernism, namely, European tropical modernism and American formalism (also known as American populism). The two approaches are different

[6] Chen (1962).

but related to each other. Tropical modernism was developed by a group of European architects working in Africa and South Asia from the 1930s onwards. It aimed to adapt orthodox modernism, the so-called International Style, to the hot and humid climate in the tropics, by innovating architectural devices and tectonics for heat proof, ventilation, and sun-shading, while at the same time maintaining a low-cost strategy. American formalism on the contrary originated in the postwar United States, where American architects revitalized classic Beaux-Arts composition in the modernist framework to create a new architectural expression with monumentality, elegance, and delicacy to please both government and the middle class (Hunting, 2013; Loeffler, 1998). Chinese architects referenced these two postwar modernist trends at the same time, in order to find new solutions to a series of architectural problems in the unfamiliar context of Africa and Southeast Asia, particularly the expression of monumentality and the response to tropical climate.

By absorbing Western postwar modernism, Chinese foreign aid architecture conveyed the political messages of modernization and internationalization. For most design cases, the expression of Chinese identity was intentionally downplayed, not just out of a political requirement,[7] but also due to the lack of the relevant knowledge to combine Chineseness and modernism. The conundrum about the relationship between Chineseness and modernism had been haunting Chinese architects since the inception of Chinese modernism in the 1930s. But it was only in the 1970s that this conundrum was solved both in China and overseas by Chinese architects (Song, 2016).

3.4 Chinese Modernism and Its Aesthetics and Politics

The TAZARA Terminus, built in Dar es Salaam in 1976, was a prominent example in this aspect, which could offer some insights for us to reflect on the knowledge of Chinese modernism and its aesthetics and politics (Fig. 3.2).

TAZARA project was the largest complete project aided by China to date. Its construction lasted from the late 1960s to the late 1970s, including 320 bridges, 22 tunnels, and 2225 culverts along the railway.[8] The railway connected the inland city Kapiri Mposhi in Zambia to the port city Dar es Salaam in Tanzania, stretching 1860 kms long. It was of crucial geopolitical value for Africa and the two countries in particular, being "indispensable for the safety of Tanzania and Zambia and for

[7] Zhou Enlai once indicated that the design of the BMICH in Sri Lanka should represent the local tradition and tropical climate. See (You, 2012: 6).

[8] At the height of the construction, 38,000 Tanzanian and Zambian workers and 13,500 Chinese technical and engineering personnel were on the construction site. Over 160 workers including 64 Chinese, died during the construction of the railway. For the project, China also helped to expand the port of Dar es Salaam and build schools to train local railway talents, and even helped to establish farms and provide medical service for the local communities along the railway. See "Our History," TAZARA. Accessed Sep 4, 2016. http://tazarasite.com/?page_id=131.

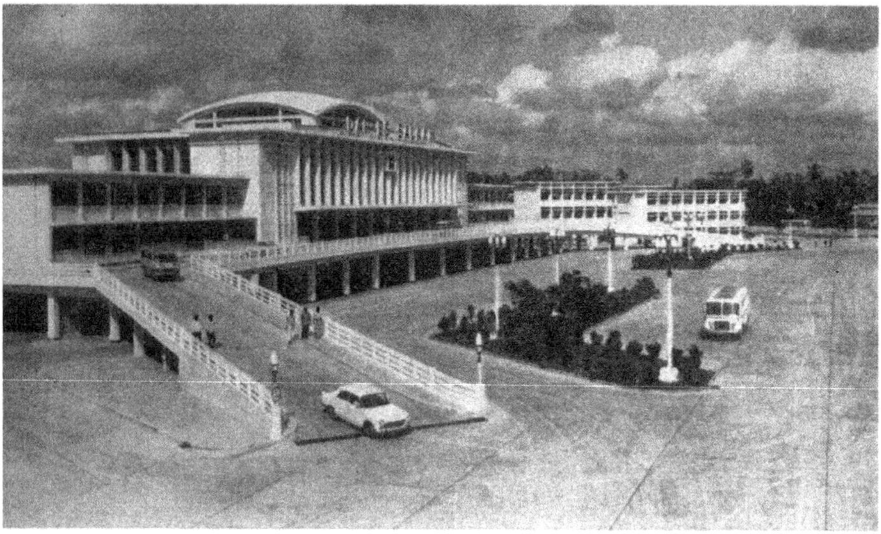

Fig. 3.2 TAZARA Terminus, Dar es Salaam, Tanzania, 1976. Designed by The Third Design Institute of Ministry of Railway (TRSDI, 1976)

the future unification of Arica" as explained by Tanzanian President Julius Nyerere (1969, 1973).

The Third Railway Survey and Design Institute (TRSDI) was responsible for the survey and design of the TAZARA project (TRSDI, 1976). In the design process, president Nyerere was particularly concerned with the architectural design of the Dar es Salaam terminus, the largest station and the headquarter of the railway. To strengthen the architectural design team, a team of architects including Wu Jinghuan, Ling Weixin and Xu Qifan from Beijing Institute of Architectural Design (BIAD) were temporarily transferred to TRSDI (Xue & Ding, 2018; Wu, 2016: 69–74). Nyerere paid particular attention to Chinese railway stations during his visit in China. He proposed to combine Beijing station's dome and Dalian station's ramp in the design of the terminus in Dar es Salaam, which was realized by the architects.

After the completion of the TAZARA terminus in 1976, a German architect Georg Lippsmeier working in East Africa applauded its "pragmatic approach", although some of his Western colleagues mocked its dull composition and banal details. He criticised Western aided architecture in Africa as mostly idealistic, with extensive use of sophisticated technology and imported materials, which often caused the building hard to build and maintain (Folkers, 2010: 183–186).[9] While on the contrary, the Chinese designs were more suitable and adaptive to African local conditions. This observation came from the architect's own experience of designing the Faculty of Engineering (FOE) building for the University of Dar es Salaam (Fig. 3.3),[10] which

[9] The concept of "pragmatic architecture" was firstly proposed by the German architect Hans Demeter in the 1960s who also worked in Dar es Salaam. See (Folkers, 2010: 183).

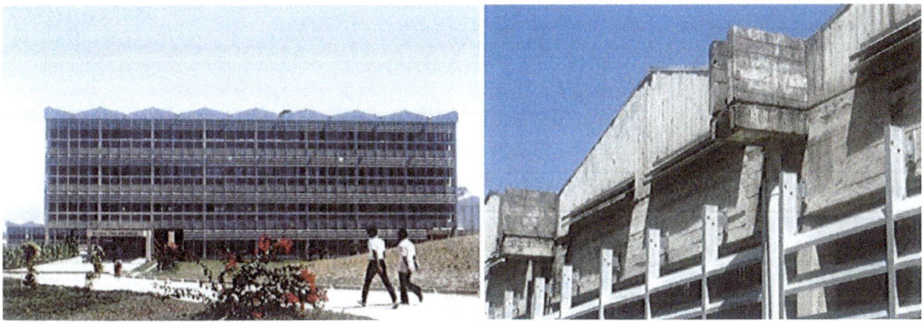

Fig. 3.3 Faculty of engineering

was completed in 1974, slightly before the completion of TAZARA Terminus. He designed sophisticated façade and roof details for shading, ventilation and drainage. However, due to the limited budget, many details including the reversed roof canopy couldn't be realized, which caused a serious leaking problem.[11]

In the design of TAZARA Terminus, modernist aesthetics and technology was adapted to the local condition and Chinese practical experience and specific cultural-political preference shared by both China and Africa. The fast and low-cost construction and the minimization of the maintenance cost, demonstrated the effectiveness of this specific Chinese version of modernism. The pragmatic approach and the Chineseness of the TAZARA Terminus can be further demystified by analysing its façade, floor plan, and the site plan.

First, to compare the facades of the terminus and the FOE building, we can see the difference between Chinese modernism and European modernism. Chinese design absorbed the abstraction of European modernism, while rejecting the quest for tectonic articulation. For example, the FOE building featured a contrast between the brutalist concrete structure and the exquisite steel components, with a straightforward and honest expression of materiality and rigorous articulation of tectonics. The articulation of tectonics is based on both functional logics of heat proofing, drainage and load bearing, and formal logics of proportion, connection, and contrast. Comparatively, the Chinese design emphasized formal composition of vertical and horizontal lines on the façade, with an ambiguous expression of tectonic relation. For example, the overhanging roof of the Chinese building not only served for functional-technological purpose of shading, but also for the formal-compositional purpose to emphasize the horizontal lines on the façade. The modernist aesthetics in the Chinese

[10] The University of Dar es Salaam (UDSM) was aided by Western countries in the 1960s. The English firm Norman & Dawbarn, designed the master plan in line with pure modernist principles. Architects from West Germany were also involved in the design of this university. See (Folkers, 2010: 171–74).

[11] The leaking problem persisted and further caused a dispute between the faculty and the architect in 1985. The faculty accused the architect of using import-dependent components and materials, which made maintenance work difficult. See (Folkers, 2010: 184–86).

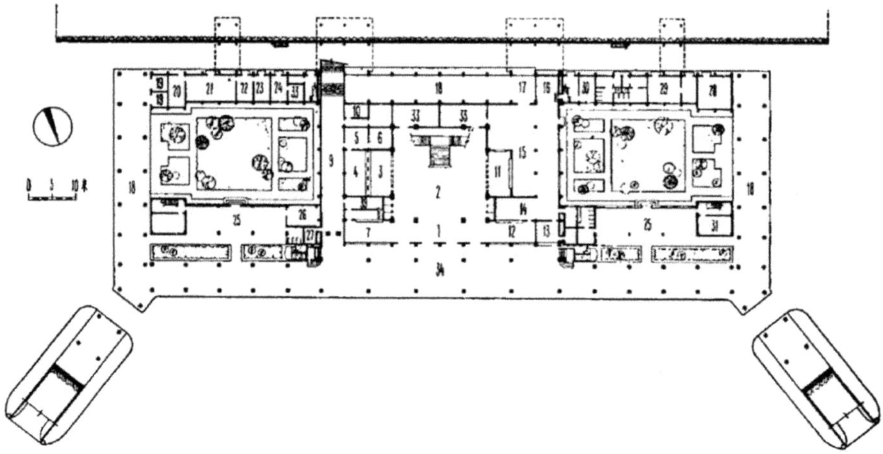

Fig. 3.4 First-level plan and section, TAZARA Terminus (TRSDI, 1976)

design was mainly manifested at the level of composition, particularly in the simplification and abstraction of formal elements, not at the level of tectonics. Even the composition is still based on the classic Beaux-Arts tradition. In this regard, it was similar to American formalism, both of which were aimed at achieving a monumentality through the combination of modernist elements and classical composition (Fig. 3.4).

Second, the floor plans of TAZARA terminus disclosed a manipulation of building scale which was not entirely congruent with Chinese building standards. According to the Chinese standards[12], the design capacity of TAZARA Terminus, which is to serve 500 people at the peak, is only a middle size station (TRSDI, 1976: 32–34), equivalent to the county-level small cities in China. A typical middle-size station is only one storey with an asymmetrical floor plan, around 1,000–2,000 square meters. But the actual size of TAZARA Terminus reached 63,000 square meters, with a floor plan layout comparable with the super-large stations in China such as Beijing and Guangzhou stations.[13] These three stations all adopted symmetrical plan layouts, with multiple storeys and two courtyards at both sides. In particular, Beijing Railway Station as one of the Ten Great Buildings in Beijing in 1959 served as a prototype for TAZARA Terminus. Even the iconic shell structure was used at the top of the entrance hall in both cases, as required by Tanzanian president Nyerere (Fig. 3.5). Interestingly,

[12] An official reference book published in 1977, written by the TRSDI, with Nanjing Institute of Technology and Tianjin University, summarized the types and standards of railway stations including a bunch of examples in China built from the 1950s to the 1970s. Railway stations were categorized into four grades of size in relation to its "capacity" (the maximum number of people staying in the station): "super-large" for more than 4,000 people, "large" for 1,500–4,000, "middle" for 400–1,500, and "small" for less than 400 people.

[13] The actual dimensions of the three stations were similar: Beijing Station was 220 m for the main façade, Guangzhou was 185 m wide, and Dar es Salaam was 140 m excluding the two ramps.

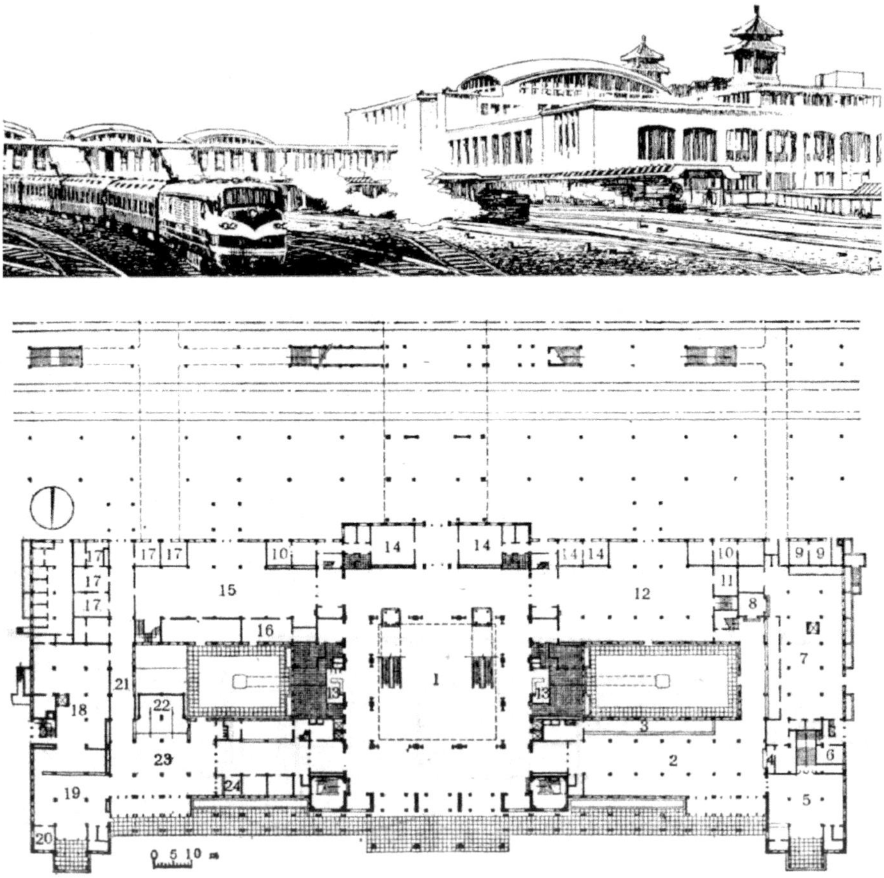

Fig. 3.5 Beijing Railway Station, Beijing, 1959

Wu Jinghuan, the architect of TAZARA Terminus was once a student and assistant of renowned Chinese architect Yang Tingbao, who designed Beijing Station following a Beaux-Arts tradition. This lineage further explained the continuation of Beaux-Arts composition in the design of TAZARA Terminus.

Third, the site plan further demonstrated the combination of tropical modernism and Beaux-Arts tradition (Fig. 3.6). The elevated semi-outdoor veranda not only provided shaded resting space but also effectively enlarged the building volume. The two ramps leading up to the departure hall at the second level and the two office buildings that flanked the main building further elongated the façade. A spacious plaza in front of the building, and a wide road leading to the city provided enough space and distance to appreciate the monumental façade.

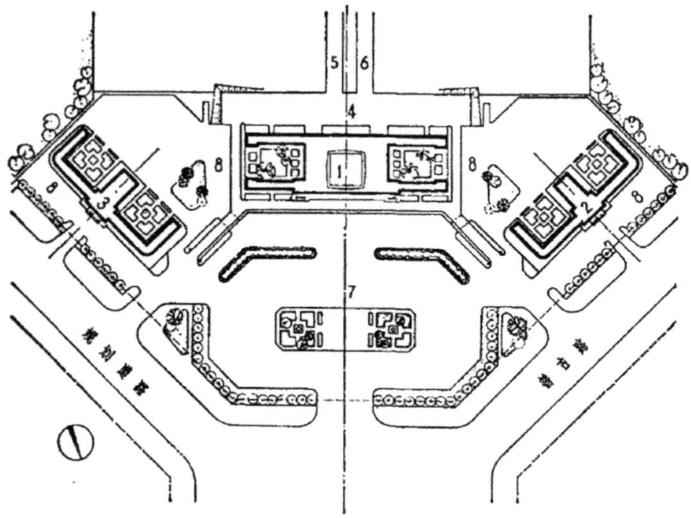

Fig. 3.6 Master plan, TAZARA Terminus (TRSDI, 1976)

Compared to European modernist architects, who mostly privileged asymmetrical composition and light volume, Chinese architects made every effort to emphasize the monumentality in architectural expression. Its legitimacy was based on a tacit requirement of the expression of political authority through architecture, which was prevalent in both China and Africa. For this aim, Chinese architects adapted Chinese building standards and referenced both Chinese precedents and tropical modernism. In particular, an unconscious continuation of Beaux-arts tradition in the framework of modernism played a key role to achieve monumentality.

3.5 Conclusion

This chapter argues that the relationship between aesthetics and politics is the key to understanding Chinese foreign aid architecture and its "Chineseness", and it also provides a unique architectural perspective for understanding the "Chinese model" of foreign aid. It reviews the history of foreign aid architecture in Mao's China from the perspective of history of knowledge, and analyses the relationship between the aesthetics and politics in architectural design in the three historical stages, and reveals the evolution of the knowledge system of architectural design. First, in the late 1950s and early 1960s, Chinese architects experimented with a modernism based on the International Style, in which modernist aesthetics and political internationalism overlapped. This experiment laid down a modernist line for China's subsequent design of foreign aid architecture. Second, in the 1960s, Chinese architects actively absorbed new trends of Western post-war modernism, especially tropical modernism and American formalism, to achieve unique design innovation by responding to specific aesthetic and geopolitical demands. Third, in the 1970s, based on the output of Chinese experience and standards, the design of TAZARA Terminus demonstrated a distinctive "Chineseness" in both aspects of aesthetics and politics, as an alternative to Western modernism.

China's foreign aid from the 1950s to the 1970s provided an opportunity for Chinese architects to learn from Western architecture, and also provided a testing ground for them to explore new forms and new methods. In the design of foreign aid architecture, Chinese architects integrated two sets of knowledge systems, Western modernism and Chinese local experience, and creatively responded to local conditions. There is a complex knowledge flow network encompassing China, the Third World and the West. The knowledge flow between China and the Third World is not China's one-way knowledge output, but a two-way knowledge flow that occurs simultaneously with both the export and import of architectural knowledge.

China's foreign aid architecture in the Mao era should be regarded as a valuable knowledge heritage, which has important significance today. It continues to inspire contemporary Chinese architects to reflect on such issues: in the design of foreign aid architecture, how to export China's native knowledge system while continuously absorbing advanced Western knowledge and technology? How to adapt the knowledge of both China and the West to local economic and technical conditions? How to create an aesthetic form that respects multicultural traditions, so that it is both modern-universal and cultural-specific at the same time?

References

Armstrong, J. D. (1977). *Revolutionary diplomacy: Chinese foreign policy and the united front doctrine*. University of California Press.

Brautigam, D. (2009). *The dragon's gift: The real story of China in Africa*. Oxford University Press.

Brautigam, D. (2011). Aid 'with Chinese characteristics': Chinese foreign aid and development finance meet the OECD-DAC aid regime. *Journal of International Development, 23*, 752–764.

Chen, D. (1962). Feizhou Redai Jianzhu Jieshao [introduction to tropical architecture in africa]. *Jianzhu Xuebao [Architectural Journal]* (10), 17–22. 陈登鳌 (1989). 热带建筑. 北京: 中国建筑工业出版社.

Ding, G., & Xue, C. Q. L. (2015). China's architectural aid: Exporting a transformational modernism. *Habitat International, 47*, 136–147.

Dreyfus, H. L., & Rabinow, P. (1982). *Michel Foucault: Beyond structuralism and hermeneutics*. Taylor and Francis.

Folkers, A. (2010). *Modern architecture in Africa*. Sun.

Hitchcock, H. R., & Johnson, P. (1996[1932]). *The international style*. W.W. Norton.

Hulshof, M., & Roggeveen, D. (2014). Eight characteristics of the African Union Headquater. *Urban China, 63*:60–65. Hulshof, M. & Roggeveen, D. (2014). 非盟大楼八大特征. 城市中国, 63:60–65.

Hunting, M. A. (2013). *Edward Durell Stone: Modernism's populist architect*. W.W. Norton & Company.

Information Office of the State Council (IOSC). (2011). *China's Foreign Aid (2011)*, Information Office of the State Council of the PRC. http://english.www.gov.cn/archive/white_paper/2014/09/09/content_281474986284620.htm

Jiang, H. (2014). *Lengzhan Shiqi Zhongguo dui Feizhou Guojia de Yuanzhu Yanjiu (1960–1978)* [China's aid to African countries in the Cold War period, 1960–1978]. PhD. Diss., China East Normal University. 蒋华杰 (2014). 冷战时期中国对非洲国家的援助研究 (1960–1978). 博士, 华东师范大学.

Loeffler, J. C. (1998). *The architecture of diplomacy: Building America's embassies.* Princeton Architectural Press.

Moyo, D. (2009). *Dead aid: Why aid is not working and how there is a better way for Africa.* Macmillan.

Nyerere, J. (1969). *Ujamaa: Essays on socialism.* Oxfor University Press.

Nyerere, J. (1973). *Freedom and development: Uhuru na Maendeleo, a selection from writings and speeches, 1968–1973.* Oxford University Press.

Ranciere, J. (2004[2000]). *The politics of aesthetics: The distribution of the sensible.* Continuum.

Ren, G. (1964). Jineiya Jianzhu [Guinea architecture]. *Jianzhu Xuebao [Architectural Journal]*, 31–35. 任国允 (1964). 几内亚建筑. 建筑学报, 31–35.

Roskam, C. (2015). Non-aligned architecture: China's designs on and in Ghana and Guinea, 1955–92. *Architectural History, 58*, 261–291.

Shimomura, Y., & Ohashi, H. (2013). *A study of china's foreign aid: An asian perspective.* Palgrave Macmillan.

Söderberg, M. (2010). Challenges or Complements for the West: Is there an 'Asian' Model of Aid Emerging? In: Sorensen, J. S. (ed.) *Challenging the aid paradigm: Western currents and asian alternatives.* Palgrave Macmillan.

Song, K. (2016). A forgotten golden era: Modernism in late-Mao China, 1969–76. In: Brennan, A. & Goad, P. (Eds.) *Proceedings of the society of architectural historians, Australia and New Zealand: 33*, Gold (pp. 637–647). Sahanz.

Song, K., & Zhu, J. (2016). The Architectural Influence of the United States in Mao's China (1949–1976). *Fabrications: The Journal of the Society of Architectural Historians Australia & New Zealand, 26*, 337–356.

Third Railway Survey and Design Institute (TRSDI). (1976). *Tanzan Tielu Da Aisi Salamu Kezhan-Jianzhu* [Dar es Salaam Railway Station of TAZARA]. *Jianzhu Xuebao [Architectural Journal]*, 32–34.

Third Railway Survey and Design Institute (TRSDI). (1977). *The architectural design of railway station.* Beijing: Zhongguo Jianzhu Gongye Chubanshe. 铁道部第三设计院等 (1977). 铁路旅客站建筑设计. 北京: 中国建筑工业出版社.

Wu, J. (2016). *Jianzhu Yiran zai Gechang: Yi Jianzhushi Wu Jinghuan Zhang Qiyun* [Architecture is still singing: remembering architects Wu Jinghuan and Zhang Qiyun], Beijing, Zhongguo Jianzhu Gongye Chubanshe. 巫加郁 (2016). 建筑依然在歌唱: 忆建筑师巫敬桓、张琦云. 北京: 中国建筑工业出版社.

Xie, Y. (1988). *Zhongguo Waijiao Shi, 1949–1979* [A Diplomatic History of China, 1949–1979]. Zhengzhou: Henan Renmin Chubanshe. 谢益显 (1988). 中国外交史, 1949–1979. 郑州: 河南人民出版社.

Xue, C. Q., & Ding, G. (2018). *A history of design institutes in China: From Mao to market.* Routledge.

You, B. (2012). *Zhujian Zhongsi Youyi zhi Mingzhu* [Build the Friendship of China and Sri Lanka], Beijing, Zhongguo Jianzhu Gongye Chubanshe. 由宝贤 (2012). 筑建中斯友谊之明珠. 北京: 中国建筑工业出版社.

Zhang, Y. (2006). *Zhongguo Duiwai Yuanzhu Yanjiu* [Research on China's Foreign Aid]. PhD. Diss., Party School of the Central Committee of CPC. 张郁慧 (2006). 中国对外援助研究. 博士, 中共中央党校.

Zhang, Z. (2000). *Dangdai Zhongguo Jianzhu Dashi: Dainianci* [Contemporary Chinese master architects: Dai Nianci. Zhongguo Jianzhu Gongye Chubanshe. 张祖刚 (2000). 当代中国建筑大师: 戴念慈. 北京: 中国建筑工业出版社.

Zhang, Z. (2009). *Jianzhu shi Gong Deshun* [Architect Gong Deshun]. Beijing, Qinghua Daxue Chubanshe. 张祖刚 (2009). 建筑师龚德顺. 北京: 清华大学出版社.

Zhang, D., & Smith, G. (2017). China's foreign aid system: Structure, agencies, and identities. *Third World Quarterly, 38*, 2330–2346.

Zou, D. (2001). *Zhongguo Xiandai Jianzhu Shi [A history of modern Chinese architecture]*. Tianjin, Tianjin Kexue Jishu Chubanshe. 邹德侬 (2001). 中国现代建筑史. 天津: 天津科学技术出版社.

Ke Song is an Associate Professor at School of Architecture, Harbin Institute of Technology, Shenzhen. His research is centred on architectural history of modern China and the urban history of Shenzhen, with a focus on the period after 1949. He received his bachelor's (2011) and master's (2013) degrees from Tsinghua University in Beijing and his PhD (2017) from the University of Melbourne. He has published papers in prestigious journals, including *Architectural Histories*, *ABE Journal: Architecture beyond Europe*, *Fabrications* and Architectural Journal (Chinese). He has teaching experience of both design studios and theory subjects in China and Australia and practical experience at several architectural design firms, including CPG Corporation (Singapore), Teamminus (Beijing) and Lab Architects (Melbourne).

Chapter 4
Diplomacy of Architecture: Ghana, China and 60 Years of Spatial Engagement

Lloyd G. Adu Amoah

Abstract Africa- Asia relations entered upon a particularly intense and mutually entangling phase in the last two decades of the twentieth century; this process continues apace in this century. To be sure these relations have a long temporal sweep. Understanding holistically contemporary Ghana-China relations, and in particular the ways in which the manipulation of space has intervened upon and shaped the interaction must be located within this temporal sweep. Methodologically this work will engage discursively with the historical and contemporary information on some of China's key construction and architectural activities in Ghana over the last six decades with the central aim of teasing out the changes and continuities (ideological, institutional, ideational and strategic) that have marked such undertakings. This work introduces in the process the idea of diplomacy of architecture as a useful analytic lens for exploring Africa-China relations.

4.1 Ghana-China Relations: Historical Background in Outline

Amoah (2016) argues that Africa-China relations in contemporary times have been marked by two distinct but connected phases. The first phase (spanning the 1940s to the mid-1960s) was driven by an ideological-developmental rationale. The two partners considered themselves victims of Western imperialist predation escape from which required the guiding hand and inspiration of revolutionary Marxist praxis. This ideological choice was no mere expression of fanciful theorizing for this was expected to undergird the rapid industrialization of Africa and China. The construction of the Tazara Railway was the most concrete expression of this (Monson, 2009). It is worth noting how at the very beginning construction backgrounded Africa-China relations. It is within this first phase that Ghana established diplomatic relations with China on July 5, 1960. Under the Nkrumah Administration (1957–1966) a left leaning

L. G. A. Amoah (✉)
University of Ghana, Accra, Ghana
e-mail: lgamoah@ug.edu.gh

C. Q. Xue and G. Ding (eds.), *Exporting Chinese Architecture*,
https://doi.org/10.1007/978-981-19-2786-7_4

Ghana deepened trade, economic, diplomatic, security, commercial and other ties with China (marking arguably the halcyon years of the relationship and conditioning enduringly this tie). Nkrumah, by his own admission, was in a hurry to industrialize Ghana and China served as a self-reliant and independent exemplar.

The second phase of Africa-China relations has seen a scaling down of the ideological rationale or at least its muting. The developmentalist rationale will remain though overlain by the mutually interlinked resources and power rationales (Amoah, 2016, p. 241):

> With regard to the rationale of power, on the Africa side there does not appear to be an actively expressed logic of global power in the engagement of China, even though the emergent preference of some African countries for China's aid regime over that of Western countries in particular suggests this, albeit subtly. The question of resources is related to the power component of the rationale argument being canvassed here with which it subsists reciprocally. For China this is expressed in both pecuniary (investments in the financial, telecommunications, infrastructure and manufacturing sectors in Africa) and physical terms (a focused interest in Africa's extractive sectors, especially oil). For African countries, China serves as a resource provider in terms of aid in the form of technical expertise and concessionary loans and grants.

On the power rationale, Africa becomes critical for China as it increases its influence across the world in its scarcely disguised bid to be a super power. This second phase, is in temporal terms, tied to the adoption of many African countries of free market economics (at the behest of World Bank [WB] and International Monetary Fund [IMF]) in the 1980s and the beginnings (1978–1980) of China's reform and opening up period to the present. Ghanaian statecraft will be called upon to confront these changing logics of Africa-China relations. This confrontation will be mediated by factors such as the Ghana's turn to the WB/IMF, democratic governance and China's miraculously rapid rise as a formidable global economic power.

4.2 Nkrumah's Statecraft, China and the Emergence of Construction and the Diplomacy of Architecture

Nkrumah's statecraft was wily (even if on occasion rather forceful and grating) and pragmatic and all this reflected in the service of Ghana's development. I will argue that the building blocks of Nkrumah's statecraft relative to his engagement with China became manifest as he began to fully engage that country. Kwame Nkrumah visited China (Beijing and Shanghai) during August 14–19, 1961 and met Chairman Mao in the process. Premier Zhou Enlai paid a reciprocal visit (in spite of security concerns after the assassination attempt on Nkrumah on January 2, 1964) in January 1964 to Ghana with foreign minister Chen Yi as part of a high-powered delegation. These visits cemented China's place in Nkrumah's Pan-African Developmentalist Statecraft (PDS) directed at China. Four key agreements were signed during Nkrumah's trip to China: Treaty of Ghana-China Friendship; Agreement between Ghana and China on Economic and Technical Co-operation; Agreement between Ghana and China on Trade Payments; and Agreement between Ghana and China on Cultural Co-operation.

By 1966 China's construction footprints in Ghana were just beginning to emerge if only inchoately. The Juapong Textile and Knitting Factory was one of the major Chinese structural undertakings in Ghana during Nkrumah's governance at the time. It is useful to quote Kwame Nkrumah (2001) himself fully on this:

> The Juapong Textile and Knitting Factory near Akosombo in the Volta Region, was one of the many vital development projects…… This factory, half completed when the army and police traitors seized power, was to offer employment to over 800 people and to make use of 400,000 tonnes of locally produced cotton from the Abutia, Chinderi and Zongo Mancheri state farms. The factory when completed, was expected to produce over 80,000 tons of textiles of various kinds annually, and about 3,000 tons of knitwear.

This project was obviously abandoned under a new military junta, the National Liberation Council (NLC) which broke diplomatic ties with China on October 20, 1966. The National Redemption Council (NRC) restored Ghana's diplomatic ties with China when a new Chinese envoy, Mr. Ke Hua presented his credentials to Ghanaian leader Col. Ignatius Kutu Acheampong on September 29, 1972.

The Chinese got involved once again in construction related projects in a manner reminiscent, albeit cautious, of the Nkrumah era. The NRC (Government of Ghana, n.d., p. 309) provided details on two such projects involving the Chinese in a report titled *Investment, Trade and Self Reliance for Growth*: (i) a ten-member team of Chinese irrigation experts worked on a dam at Afife in the Volta Region. The dam was expected to irrigate 5,000 acres of rice and vegetable farms when completed; (ii) a four-man Chinese team arrived to undertake feasibility studies on a clinker project in Nauli in the Western Region. China's construction interactions with Ghana in the 1970s were at best emergent. It was driven in the main by what I have described above as the ideologic-developmental rationale. This changed beginning in the 1980s as China's rationale for engaging countries like Ghana came to be more trenchantly marked by the logics of the market (Hui, 2003). The Chinese began to frame their engagement with other countries in ways that was concerned less with class struggle and more with economic advantage pursued in multiform ways (Zhang, 2011). This phase coincided uncannily with Ghana's own neoliberalization drawing the West African country tighter than ever before into China's economic orbit. The upshot of this was that the inchoate construction imprint of China will morph into what I describe as the "diplomacy of architecture." Amoah (2016) was one of the first scholarly works that looked at this switch relative to Ghana-China relations specifically and Africa-China relations generally and the links between architecture and space. To be sure the Chinese have long been aware of the entanglements of the manipulation of space and diplomacy and with it the rhetorical and practical power of architecture first at the receiving end and now as dutiful purveyors. Amoah draws attention to this thus (Ibid, p. 245):

> Given the history of the Chinese Communist Party with regard to architecture and space as instruments of power, it is perhaps not far-fetched to posit the utilization of architectural projects in Ghana as an opportunity for China's geo-strategists to project China's growing influence in Africa.

Song and Zhu (2017) articulate a similar view using the construction of diplomatic buildings in Beijing in the 1970s as their discursive frame of reference. Ding and Xue (2015) engage with this problematic as well. A triptych of themes namely formal expression, knowledge transfer and power marks the analysis of the literature on China, architecture and space albeit in varying modes and geographical contexts. Song and Zhu train their focus on China as an object of American architectural influence; in other words, China at the receiving end. For Amoah and Xue, Africa is the object of China's architectural imprints. It is on the theme of formal expression that this work departs from Ding and Xue's overall tone and tenor. Ding and Xue construe formal expression in terms of an economistic conduit of export of "a transformational modernism" in a way that is particularly benign and therefore shorn of any complications and real challenges to African countries (Ding & Xue, 2015, p. 136):

> Within the framework of architectural export, Chinese architects endeavoured to deliver a 'transformational modernism' that integrated efficiency, affordability, accessibility and creativity. This progressive modern project was both a product of social transformation in China and a positive engagement with the recipient nations' local conditions.

Xue et al., (2019, p. 1) consolidate this rather overly optimistic view when they aver that China's building of stadia in Africa "revealed a soft, and ultimately progressive mode of cultural engagement in transnational architectural practice." It is my view that this focus on modernism while useful need not be overplayed nor simplified in ways that mask the problematic political-economy dynamics at play. It is for this reason that the work presents a diplomacy of architecture lens through which the morphological and architectural manifestations of diplomacy and with it the political and economic fall outs (i.e. realities and results) can be more critically examined and interrogated. Loeffler (1990) has pointed in that direction in her seminal work which focused specifically on US embassy buildings in some capital cities around the world. Two recent works (Levin, 2016; Gameren & Tola, 2017) follow this mode by emphasizing the role of foreign architects, architecture and diplomacy in shaping the Ethiopian capital, Addis Ababa. To be sure for this diplomacy of architecture lens, the discursive field is more extensive in its focus on the national context instead of just the capitals and the architectural objects in this particular reading. The architectural objects are not just buildings but encompass other construction like roads and dams. A carefully selected number of cases will be utilized to unpack the diplomacy of architecture of Ghana-China relations with a focus on the political-economy dynamics. My interest in this regard is to sketch out China's growing power ensemble encapsulated in the manipulation of space in Africa as reflected in Ghana (beginning in the 1990s) and the ways in which Ghana has been responding to this.

4.3 China's Power Designs in Ghana: Soft or Sharp?

Traditional soft power influence tactics is construed as utilizing the allure of culture and values to enhance a country's strength while sharp power is about puncturing the political and information environments in the targeted countries. On balance then China's key mode of influence (under Ghana's Fourth Republic generation) is through subtle, measured, soft rather than sharp power. While it may be hard to pinpoint clear examples of Chinese sharp power deployed in Ghana consistently and of any significance to constitute a pattern worthy of policy value, it can be argued that China learnt some bitter lessons from the 1960s concerning overplaying her influence in Ghana and has been following a subtle soft power route as a consequence.

Amoah provides four key nodes of China's soft power designs in her interactions with Ghana which are logically distinct but operationally deeply intertwined (Amoah, 2018a, 2018b). These are Capacity Developmentalism (CD), Infrastructural Symbology (IS), Philanthropic Gestures (PG) and Information Space Penetration (ISP) Nodes. These nodes have become deployable in the Ghanaian space because of the organizational and ideational path breaking that have long been set in place by China. The organizational prong is the Forum on China-Africa Co-operation (FOCAC) while the ideational one is the China Africa Policy Document (released in 2006 and then revised in 2015). These two prongs have kept the two sides in regular physical, organizational and ideational contact (at the bi-multilateral levels) thereby softening the ground for strategic moves depending on the will and strategic foresight of the partners. I adopt all these nodes for my analysis here. In my view they are entangled in the ways in which they frame the diplomacy of architecture of Ghana-China relations in recent times.

China has cleverly appropriated and adapted the developmentalist discourse and practice of Western donor institutions and countries led in the main by the WB (Rist, 2014). This discourse and practice are a familiar register for Africa's elites including Ghana's: advanced countries (at the bi-and multilateral levels) are models and facilitators of development through aid, loans and technical support. China has appropriated the capacity building (CD) aspect of developmentalism in ways that fit its current world view which is arguably Marxist, Confucian and neo-developmentalist (Loureiro & Saad-Filho, 2019). China in this vein has cast itself as the altruistic nation (capacity building simultaneously projects the China model of development which is construed as self-reliant and independent) teaching countries like Ghana to fish rather providing the proverbial fish (I will interrogate this in subsequent sections). Through scholarships (some of which are financially supported partially by the Government of Ghana), China has provided academic opportunities for significant numbers of Ghanaian students in Chinese universities. Recent reports indicate that Ghana has the largest number of students (over 7,000 students including the self-sponsored and those on scholarships) as at September 2018 from Africa in China. China also provides a range of short term fully funded study tours and visits for Ghana's bureaucrats, policymakers and politicians from the center right down to the local level (Ghana Web, 2018). To all these must be added the construction of Chinese institutions of learning in Ghana notably the Confucius Institutes at the University of Ghana, Legon, the University of Cape-Coast (Confucius Institute at UCC, 2021) and the funding of the University of Health and Allied Sciences (UHAS) at Ho, 180 km northeast of the capital, Accra.

It is being asserted that China has been actively using Infrastructural Symbology (IS) as part of its soft power arsenal in Ghana. By IS I mean the utilization of infrastructure construction opportunities (encompassing Horizontal and Vertical Spatiality) to project Chinese benevolence, know-how, emergent globality and power. I will explicate Horizontal Spatiality (HS) by means of an analogy. A road is a typical example of an embodiment of the idea of HS because it is less about height and reaching into the skies than spread. This should incorporate for example factories and bridges. Vertical Spatiality (VS) refers to the contrary of the HS in terms of height but shares the concern with spread as well but obviously less so. Here I invoke Jaffé (1964):

> The history of symbolism shows that everything can assume symbolic significance: natural objects (like stones, plants, animals, men, mountains and valleys, sun and moon, wind, water, and fire), or ***man-made things*** (like houses, boats, or cars), or even abstract forms (like numbers, or the triangle, the square, and the circle). In fact, the whole cosmos is a potential symbol.

With regards to VS, China has constructed as already alluded, to some of Ghana's most sensitive and strategically located public buildings among them the National Theater, Ministries of Foreign Affairs and Defense and the 34 Court-room Complex for the Judicial Service.

In terms of the HS China has positioned itself in Ghana as one of the most reliable master builders of roads, railways (Embassy of the People's Republic of China in the Republic of Ghana, 2021), bridges and ports (Tema Expansion Project & GHANA GOV, 2019) and other sophisticated marine related facilities. On roads, China's construction of the National Highway, N4, burnished her credentials as a capable builder and development model. The stretch was built by China Water Engineering with funding by the Government of Ghana. The author has been using that mountain pass from the age of 5 and the change the construction of the route has brought in terms of socio-economic activity is tangible and visible. One example is that the new road has become a route for many people from all over Accra who want to keep in shape. They congregate in their numbers on weekends for walks and other exercises up and down the mountain. Real estate is booming and colleges and businesses have been set up.

China has consciously focused on PG in Ghana which present her in a positive light to the Ghanaian public; a key node of her soft power in her dealings with Ghana. There has emerged as consequence what I describe as the "Beggary Spectacle" with roots in the 1980s when many donor projects became the vogue. The "Beggary Spectacle" is the textual, sonic and visual record of all manner of "gifts" presented to either the Government of Ghana through its institutions and assigns or to a community/organization/individual(s). These records are conspicuously placed in the media for effect; the benefactor providing succor to hapless and helpless indigents. The

Chinese Government acting through the Chinese Embassy in Accra has been riding on this to garner influence. In fact Chinese companies, associations and individuals in Ghana have also taken a cue (Figs. 4.1 and 4.2). The last Chinese Ambassador to Ghana, Sun Baohong, seems to have made such philanthropic gestures central to her duties. These philanthropic gestures are usually tailored to respond to pressing needs of the recipients at either the deepest grassroots levels or targeted at key institutions at the center of power for maximum optic value.

One of the key institutions under the State Council in the Chinese administrative infrastructure is the General Administration of Press and Publication (GAPP). The GAPP is responsible for projecting a deliberately crafted image of China to the Chinese and to the world. Indeed information management is central to how the Chinese Communist Party wants to be perceived both at home (see Fig. 4.3) and abroad. In Ghana the ISP is a key node for deploying Chinese influence. This Chinese exploitation of the information space is effected along two primary axes. One axis taps into CD as explicated above to cultivate key media outlets, associations and personalities. Study tours of China and Chinese scholarships have been offered to personnel from leading media houses ensuring access to key gatekeepers who at the very least will have some exposure to, if not sympathy for the Chinese perspective on issues. The other axis is the deployment of superior Chinese know-how in digital television technology to penetrate and establish a foothold in Ghana's information space; to be sure this is nascent and cannot constitute a reflection of sharp power. This axis reflects both Capacity Developmentalism and Philanthropic Gestures at play (Amoah, 2014). One

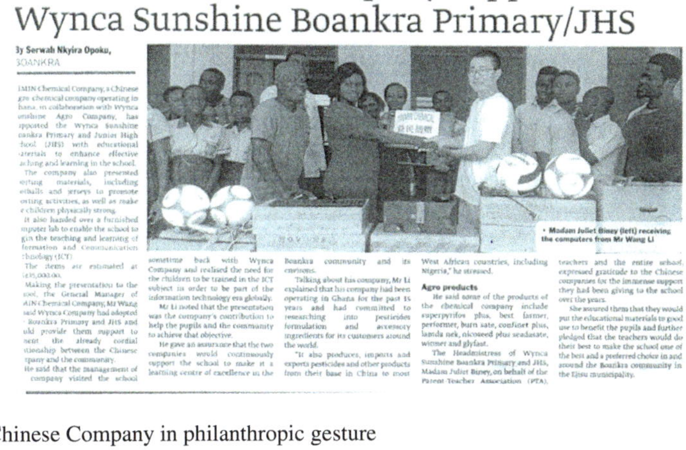

No. 20836

Daily Graphic, Monday, November 23, 2015. 23

Regional

YIMIN Chemical Company supports Wynca Sunshine Boankra Primary/JHS

By Serwah Nkyira Opoku, BOANKRA

• Madam Juliet Biney (left) receiving the computers from Mr Wang Li

IMIN Chemical Company, a Chinese gro chemical company operating in hana, in collaboration with Wynca unshine Agro Company, has upported the Wynca Sunshine oankra Primary and Junior High chool (JHS) with educational aterials to enhance effective aching and learning in the school.

The company also presented orting materials, including otballs and jerseys to promote orting activities, as well as make e children physically strong.

It also handed over a furnished mputer lab to enable the school to gin the teaching and learning of formation and Communication chnology (ICT).

The items are estimated at ¢15,000.00.

Making the presentation to the ool, the General Manager of MIN Chemical Company, Mr Wang said Wynca Company had adopted Boankra Primary and JHS and uld provide them support to nent the already cordial tionship between the Chinese pany and the community.

He said that the management of company visited the school sometime back with Wynca Company and realised the need for the children to be trained in the ICT subject in order to be part of the information technology era globally.

Mr Li noted that the presentation was the company's contribution to help the pupils and the community to achieve that objective.

He gave an assurance that the two companies would continuously support the school to make it a learning centre of excellence in the Boankra community and its environs.

Talking about his company, Mr Li explained that his company had been operating in Ghana for the past 15 years and had committed to researching into pesticides formulation and accessory ingredients for its customers around the world.

"It also produces, imports and exports pesticides and other products from their base in China to most West African countries, including Nigeria," he stressed.

Agro products

He said some of the products of the chemical company include superpyrifos plus, best farmer, performer, burn sate, confinet plus, lamda nek, nicoseed plus seadastate, winner and glyfast.

The Headmistress of Wynca Sunshine Boankra Primary and JHS, Madam Juliet Biney, on behalf of the Parent-Teacher Association (PTA), teachers and the entire school, expressed gratitude to the Chinese companies for the immense support they had been giving to the school over the years.

She assured them that they would put the educational materials to good use to benefit the pupils and further pledged that the teachers would do their best to make the school one of the best and a preferred choice in and around the Boankra community in the Ejisu municipality.

Fig. 4.1 Chinese Company in philanthropic gesture

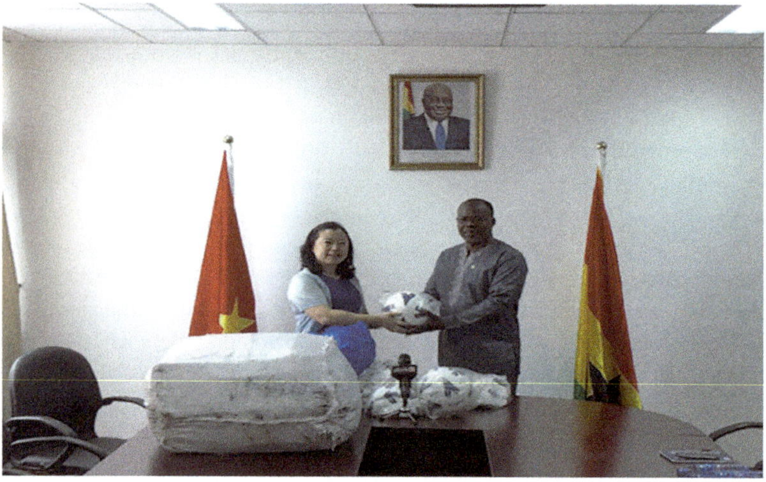

Fig. 4.2 Ambassador Sun making a presentation at Ghana's Foreign Ministry. *Source* http://gh.china-embassy.org/eng/sgxw/t1507867.htm

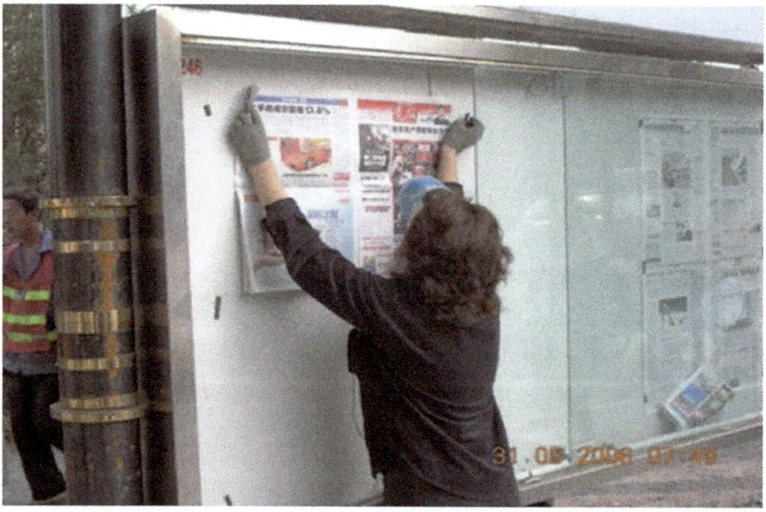

Fig. 4.3 A Grass root News Bulletin Board in Beijing, China, 2006. Author's archives

of the telling examples of this is Ghana's Ministry of Communications-StarTimes Project aimed at providing 300 Ghanaian rural communities access to satellite television. At the core of this initiative is exploiting communal viewing of television in these communities (in places such as town halls and schools) (Ghana News Agency, 2018). Acting through StarTimes the Chinese Government will be able to lock into the channel offerings the programming of a global Chinese network such as China Global Television Network (CGTN) to shape and mold Ghanaian views on China.

4.4 The Ghanaian Establishment and Chinese Soft Power Tactics

The explications thus far point clearly to a Ghana in which China does not ride roughshod in diplomatic, trade, economic, commercial and other dealings with Ghana. Given the economy of space I will unpack succinctly my claim above with two case studies involving state connected and non-state linked Chinese actors in Ghana . Ghana contracted a USD 3 billion (final signing took place on December 16, 2011) loan from the CDB under the Mills Administration "to undertake various infrastructure projects in the country" (Confidential Parliamentary Document). The terms (repayment schedule, commitment fees etc.) of the loan was subjected to blistering critique in the Ghanaian Parliament. Indeed the Master Facility Agreement (MFA) had to go back to Parliament because it conflicted with Ghana's laws on petroleum (Petroleum Revenue Management Act, 2011, Act 815). Civil society groups such as the Africa Center for Energy Policy (ACEP) led calls for more transparency on the CDB loan (Chen, 2016), provided options on how to utilize the loan and insisted on environmental globally benchmarked practices.

The other example is the campaign against illegal small scale mining in Ghana popularly known as "Galamsey." Chinese nationals became heavily involved (and thereby naturally drew in the Chinese Government) and introduced revolutionary technology in dredging auriferous river basins in the South of Ghana leading to increase in productivity but egregious damage to the Ghana's key water bodies. Public outcry on the devastation wrought on the environment led to Presidential action in the Mahama Administration and also under President Akufo-Addo (Amoah, 2018a, 2018b). In the latter case a Media Coalition Against Galamsey (set up in April 2017) that was led by Ghana's most widely circulated newspaper *Daily Graphic* had played a key role in mobilizing public opinion and forcing politicians to act. It must be added here that public intellectuals with a deep knowledge of Asian and Chinese Affairs had long added their voices as well to shape public opinion on this matter (Allotey & Abu-Baidu, 2017). Ultimately under Operation Vanguard, Aisha Huang, the Chinese national alleged to be in charge of some nefarious Galamsey Chinese rings was arrested, arraigned before court and deported. In both instances involving different "faces" (public and private) of the Chinese presence and influence the Ghanaian establishment exhibited some appreciable level of resilience. The state was not immobilized from taking drastic and robust action even though ties with China are deepening. Indeed the Chinese Government publicly (acknowledgment of Ghana's resilience) declared its support for the Government of Ghana's actions. This resilience however is complicated when the architectural variable is introduced into the power dynamic. I will demonstrate this by using carefully selected Chinese constructions in Ghana made up of the National Theater, N4, UHAS, and the Essipon Stadium.

4.5 Ghana's Resilience to China's Soft Power in the Maw of the Diplomacy of Architecture

As already indicated the idea for the construction of a National Theater (NT) for Ghana was mooted when Rawlings first visited China in 1985. But this idea had a far longer provenance tied to the career and vision of one of Ghana's pioneer theatrists and cultural icons, Efua Sutherland. She founded the Experimental Theater Players in Accra in 1958 which morphed in 1960 into the Ghana Drama Studio. Plays were produced and staged at the Ghana Drama Studio until 1990 when the building was demolished for the National Theater to be built. As Fig. 4.4 shows the NT is located on one of the choicest lands in the capital, Accra, right in the heart of Ministries' Enclave (Fig. 4.5).

The NT sits on the Independence Avenue which is an extension of the Liberation Road along which can be found the Jubilee House (the Seat of Government from where the president works and lives), the Ministry of Foreign Affairs and Regional

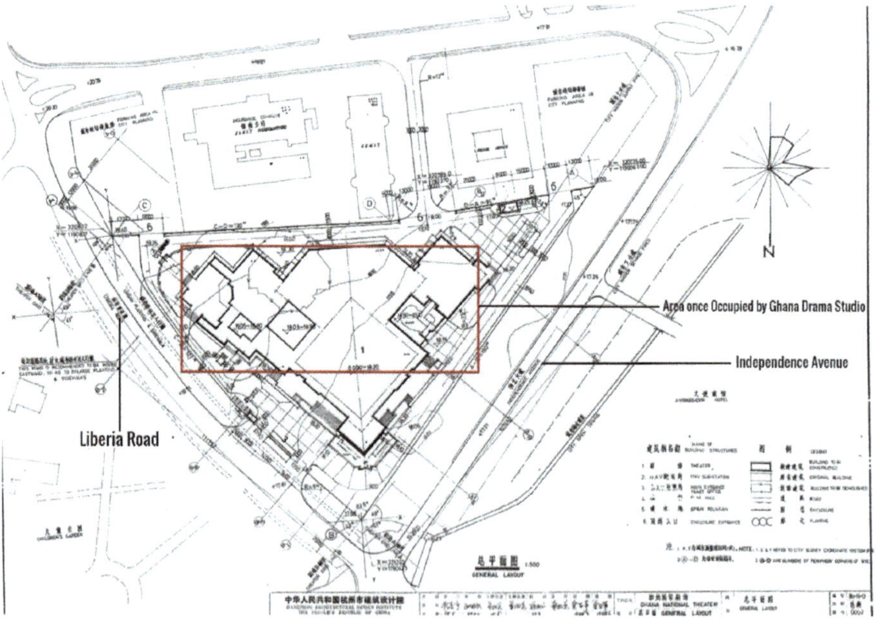

Fig. 4.4 General area of former location of Ghana Drama Studio in downtown Accra, with Author's annotations (Courtesy of Cheng Taining)

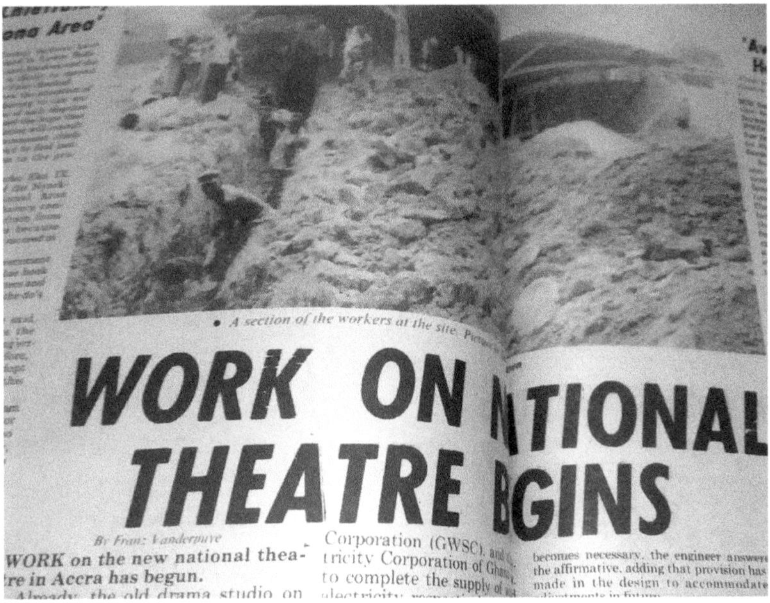

Fig. 4.5 Report in *People's Daily Graphic* on the start of construction of the Ghana National Theatre, December 19, 1989 (Courtesy Institute of African Studies Archives, University of Ghana.)

Integration and Ghana's only Military Hospital. The main entrance of the NT is on Liberia Road which dovetails into the 28th February Road on which sits the Black Star Square built to commemorate Ghana's independence. In 1985 the Chinese promised US$10 million to build the NT. In 1989 when the project took off the *People's Daily Graphic* reports that the Chinese offered a grant of US$15 million (4.05 billion cedis) for building the NT in the Agreement that was signed that year (Figs. 4.6, 4.7 and 4.8).

If this project was about knowledge transfer, "transformational modernism" as Ding and Xue claimed, subsequent events depict in part a "deformational modernism" in which China through its monetary power managed to allow its architects to plant Chinese architectural inscriptions onto the most symbolic part of Accra (Ding & Xue, 2015). It may well be that the Ghanaian authorities did not drive a hard bargain during the negotiations. That is a possibility that cannot be discounted giving the obvious asymmetry of power between the parties. I can only speculate though. What the empirics indicate however, is what I can work with. Once the agreement was signed, a national competition was organized in mainland China for designs of the NT. In effect no Ghanaian architects were involved; at least the available records do not so indicate. This same format was replicated with the African Union Building, the design of which was acquired through a national competition in China. Chinese architect, Cheng Taining, working from Hangzhou Institute of Architectural Design won the competition and had a rare opportunity to insert the first major Chinese architectural inscription on Ghana. The irony is that Cheng Taining had long been

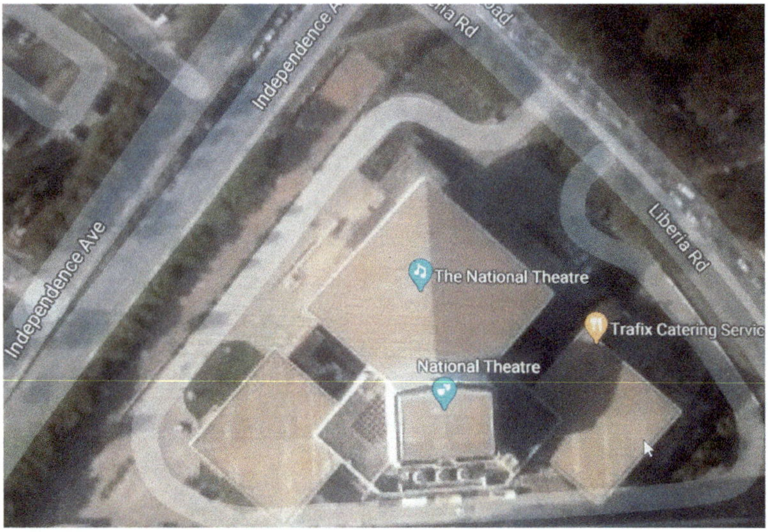

Fig. 4.6 The NT abutted by the Independence Avenue and Liberia Road, Accra (Google Satellite Maps)

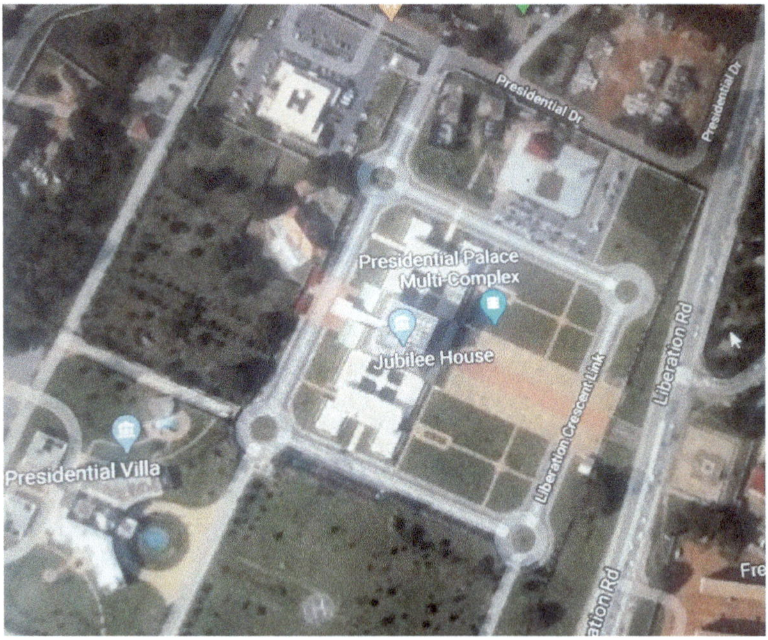

Fig. 4.7 Jubilee house on liberation road, Accra (Google Satellite Maps)

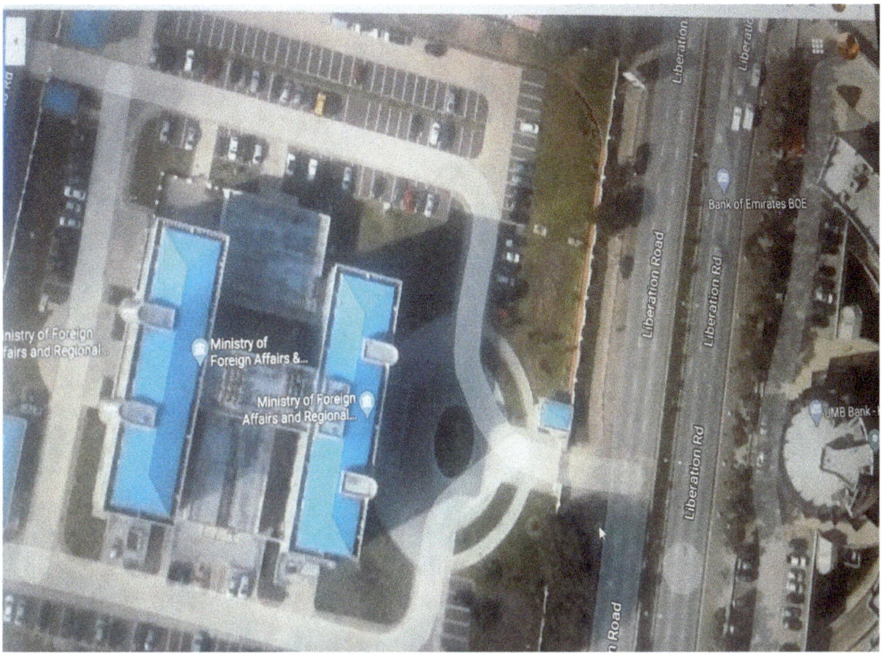

Fig. 4.8 Ghana's Foreign Ministry on liberation road, Accra (Google Satellite Maps)

averse to the influence of foreign architects on his country's major cities and had argued that China's "…buildings should speak Mandarin and be designed according to the tenets of Chinese culture" (Yu, 2011). Cheng reportedly insisted paradoxically that "It is really painful to see the characteristics of ancient China's architectural style losing out" (Ibid). This is exactly what happened to Ghana's architectural vernacular with the monopoly of design passed on to a Chinese architect. To be sure, Cheng was aware of this and tried to blunt it by introducing some Ghanaian cultural motifs into the exterior and interior of the NT. Commendable and even sensitive as this may be it scarcely ameliorated the reality that the overall form of the NT was Chinese through and through. It is instructive that Ghanaian artist Ibrahim Mahama tried to aesthetically reclaim the NT by draping it in his jute sack installation given his interest "in how crisis and failure are absorbed into this material with a strong reference to global[1] transaction….." Ghana was at the wrong end of this peculiar global architectural transaction and the artist sought to engage the liminality this monument constantly evokes (Amoah, 2016) (Figs. 4.9 and 4.10).

This "deformational modernism" is brought home further by the deterioration that the NT suffered after it was constructed requiring the Chinese to bring in their own technicians to rehabilitate it at a cost of over USD 2 million. In a real sense, the politics seemed to have trumped all other considerations. The NT had been built; it was easy

[1] https://whitecube.com/artists/artist/ibrahim_mahama.

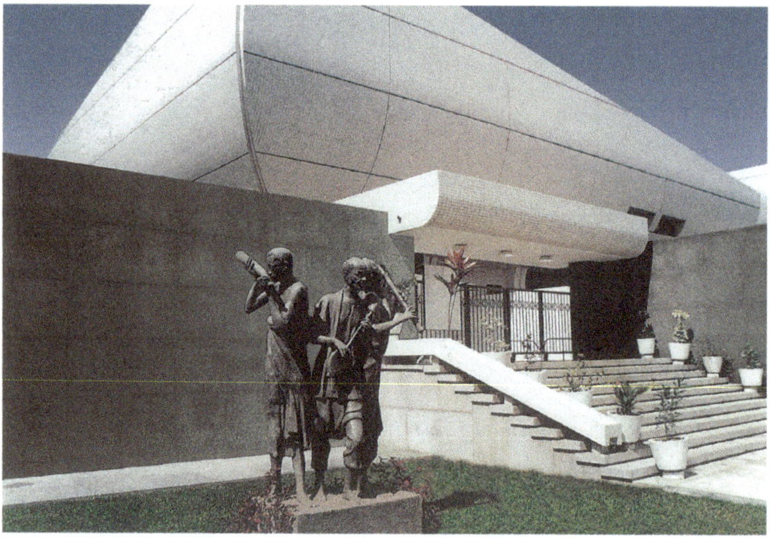

Fig. 4.9 Part of exterior of NT with Ghanaian sculpture (Courtesy of CCTN Architectural Design)

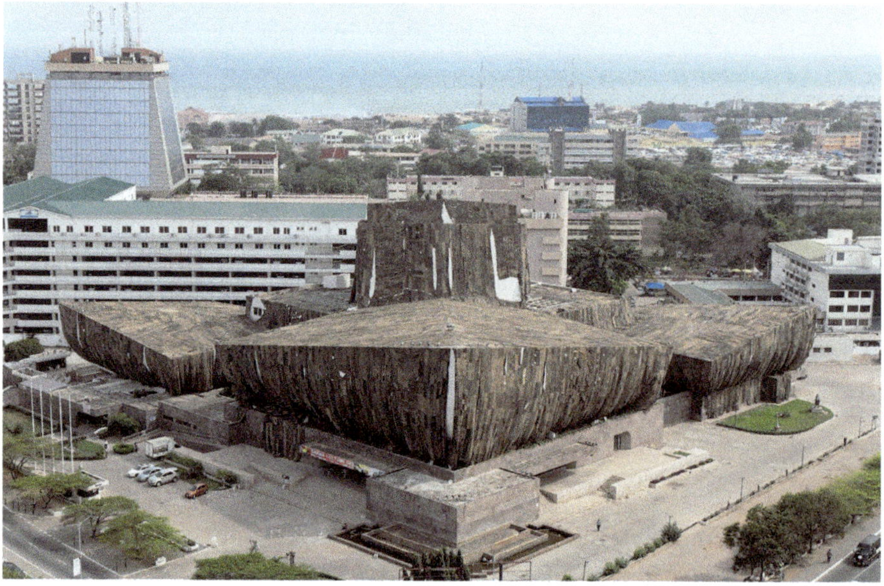

Fig. 4.10 Mahama's jute installation over NT, 2016 (Courtesy https://publicdelivery.org/ibrahim-mahama-jute-sacks/)

to check that box. But checking other boxes on technology and skill transfer, cultural sensitivity among others is proving far tricky and less straight forward. This reality is replicated in the other cases in this work. The Essipon Stadium was one of the two stadia built by China as part of preparations for the 2008 Africa Cup of Nations. The Essipon Stadium (built by the Shanghai Construction Company Ltd) can seat 20,000 fans and is equipped with athletics track, fully covered stands, 40 hotel rooms and VIP boxes. This stadium together with the Tamale Stadium cost USD 39 million (2010 dollars) financed via a soft loan from China with Barclays Bank serving as the financial intermediary (Dreher et al., 2021). The Essipon Stadium has fallen into absolute disrepair as at 2020 causing the Nana Akufo-Addo administration to seek funds for rehabilitation in just 12 short years (Ashanti Today, 2015). The Cape-Coast Stadium has fallen into disrepair as well and renovation works on it begun in 2019 (Mandela, 2021). The stadium was built in 2012 (designed by Chinese architect Zhou Ju; it cost USD 33.5 million of which USD 30 million was borne by the China) and in just six years was rotting away. President Akufo-Addo on his first visit to China in 2018 signed a renovation agreement with China for the Cape-Coast Stadium. It is instructive that the renovation agreement expressly asked for capacity training so Ghanaians can maintain the facility. Xue argues that China's stadia building serves as "Chinese economic, cultural and intellectual intervention" (Xue et al., 2019) (Figs. 4.11 and 4.12).

Purely at the level of the physical and symbolic this may be true but over time the reality makes such claims rather hollow especially given the shocking disrepair Ghana's Chinese built stadia have experienced.

The N4 (constructed by China Water Engineering and funded by the Government of Ghana) comes in for interrogation in respect of the cultural losses Ghana has suffered on account of China linked impact on her space. The N4 snakes through what is known as the Mampong Ridge in the Eastern Region of Ghana. This Mampong

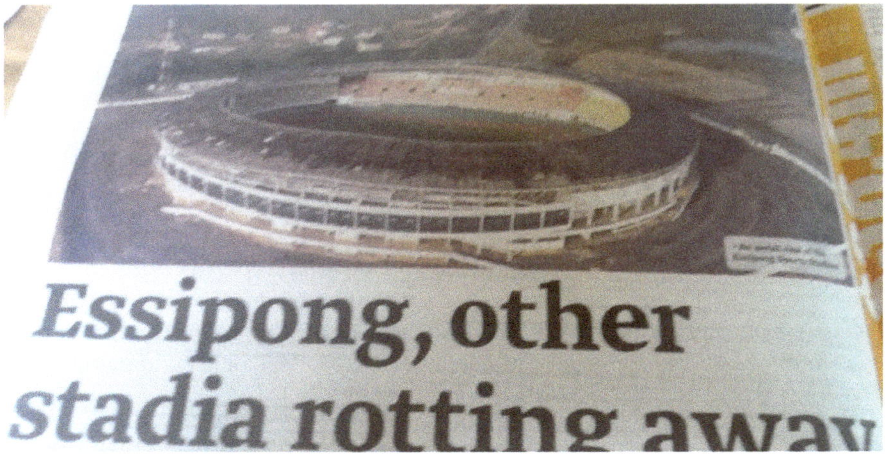

Fig. 4.11 Daily graphic report (March, 2019)

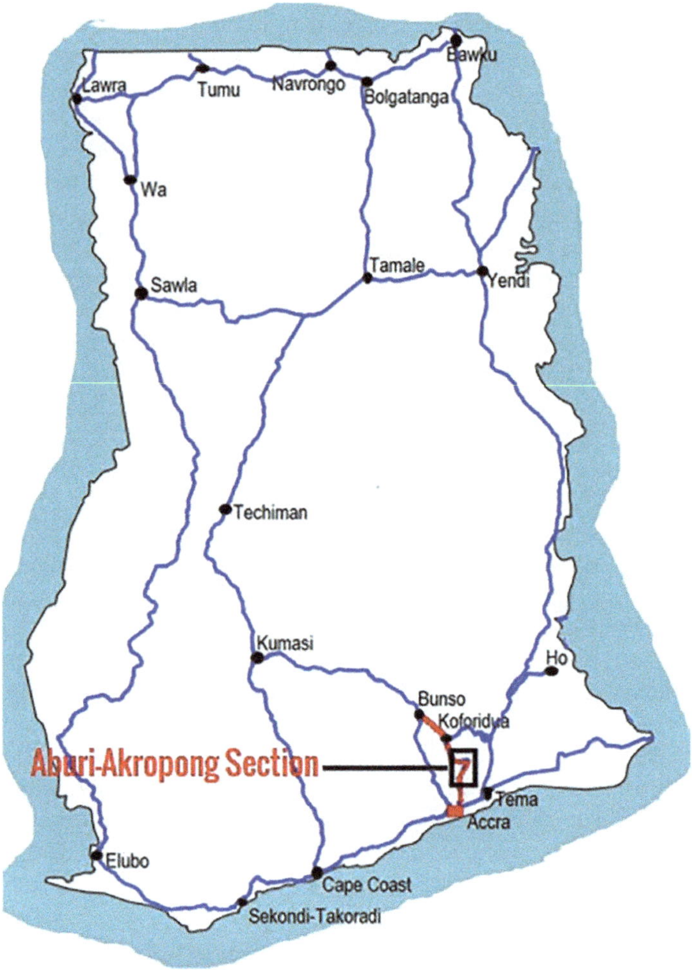

Fig. 4.12 The N4 showing the Aburi-Akropong Section, annoted by author (*Credit* https://commons.wikimedia.org/wiki/File:GH_N4_highway_route.png)

Ridge has great historical and cultural value because it is linked to a great agricultural revolution of global consequence. It was in this space that cocoa was finally successfully cultivated and turned into a global industrial crop. All efforts elsewhere on the globe had failed. The process was led by Nana John Kwame Ayew of the Akyepere Kotoku Quarter in Mampong (Boahen, 1985[2]). As a consequence certain key cultural sites became linked to Mampong. One of such iconic buildings (Jacobs,

[2] On his role as Chief Farmer of the Gold Coast (Ghana's name in the colonial era) because of his pioneering status in cocoa cultivation and his activities in the fight against British colonialism see Boahen (1985).

2016[3]) was the one purchased by Peter Botwe (a cocoa farmer and merchant) from a Dutch trader. In front of the building he put up a sign with the inscription: ***Honesty is the Best Policy. Softly, Softly, Catch Monkey. Peter Botwe, Mampong-Akuapem***. The sign symbolized the long wait he had to endure for payment after selling his cocoa seeds to the Basel Trading Company. The building became a notable place for weighing cocoa. In his short history of Mampong, Kwame Fosu described the building as "monumental" (Fosu, n.d., p. 1). This building was demolished during the construction of the N4 to make way for the Mampong By-Pass. In interviews with Kojo Ayew (uncle of this author and one of the Akyepere Clan elders), he lamented the loss of such a historic and iconic building; a huge loss not just for Ghana and Mampong but for the world as well given Mampong's role in the whole global chocolate industry worth an estimated USD103 billion in November 2017 and expected to reach USD 161.56 billion by 2024 (Zion Market Research, 2018). What is evident here is a classic case of "deformational modernism" which snuffs out the heritage, cultural, touristic and economic future of a place instead of securing it. One can compare this to taking out a section of the Great Wall of China to make way for a road. The N4 has been built and box duly checked. Its sleek presence embodied in the shiny bitumen and white markings cannot be doubted but these mask the cultural loss it has wrought and which hardly is reckoned with in official narratives Ghanaian or Chinese (Figs. 4.13 and 4.14).

UHAS represents one of the major architectural inscriptions of the VS type after the NT. The NT covers a total area of 11, 896 square meters. UHAS arguably comes in second with a total area of 10,386 square meters after it was handed over to the Government of Ghana in September 2015. UHAS consists of equipment for the school of basic and biomedical science, lecture halls, libraries, student housing facilities and senior staff residential area. In January 2019 both governments signed a note to expand UHAS. This will bring the total area occupied by UHAS to 39,586 square meter which is approximately 40.3% of the expanse of the Black Star Square. When completed the UHAS campus will represent the most extensive representation of Chinese architectural form on Ghana's soil. This form is expressed in the use of tiles, the dour grey and white hues, and in this particular case, the signature tower and roof. It is not difficult to observe the aesthetics of the Wuhan University School of Economics and Management and Law School buildings which reflect these signatures and those of UHAS. UHAS which has been handed to Ghana seems to have some unfinished critical business that are in the main infrastructural. The Vice-Chancellor, Professor Gyapong, in January 2020 made a call for funds to "complete the laboratory complex, the classrooms as well as the work on campus because we need the laboratory to do our training and research and would see how we can increase the admission number" (ABC News, 2020) (Figs. 4.15 and 4.16).

[3] For a fascinating account of why old buildings matter see in particular pp. 126–133.

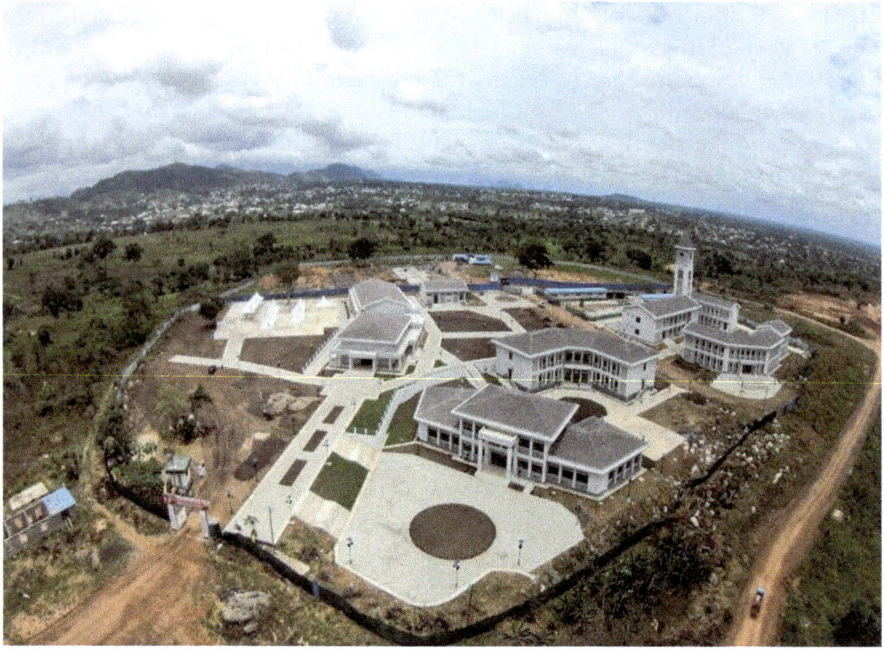

Fig. 4.13 Aerial shots of UHAS buildings. *Source* https://twitter.com/search?q=%23DearPrezMahama%20UHAS&src=typeahead_click

4.6 A Conclusion Cast as an Appeal

This chapter has been concerned to expose the ways in which architectural form masks the complexity that attends Ghana-China relations which raises questions about the lofty ideals embedded in official narratives. Using the diplomacy of architecture frame, I have attempted to analyze the intersection between form, knowledge transfer and politics. As I have argued, the neoliberal turn in the 1980s attenuated the ideology driven foundations of the interactions and accentuated a market driven developmentalist orientation. China termed this a win–win interaction with developing countries which lay at the core of its "going out strategy" (*zouchuqu zhanlue*). Construction and with it architecture has come to underline this developmentalist interaction. What architecture has done with its representational power is to serve as a convenient conduit to make tangible a superficial realization of developmentalism in which Chinese and Ghanaian political elites gain transactionally because they can check outcome boxes. What a diplomacy of architecture lens offers is a means to probe deeper the cultural, intellectual, aesthetic and even financial costs that may not be interrogated because of the elation and satisfaction the tangible architectural forms inspire.

The diplomacy of architecture lens allows the power dynamics at play to be highlighted by going behind the seducing power of stone and masonry. This Ghana case

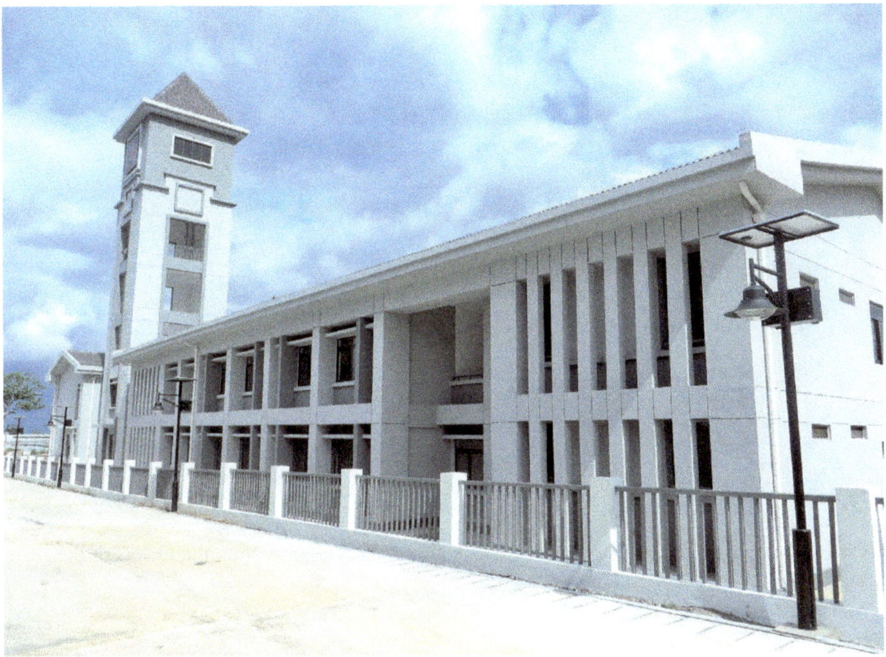

Fig. 4.14 UHAS buildings. Note roof style, the grey and white hues and tower *Source* https://twitter.com/search?q=%23DearPrezMahama%20UHAS&src=typeahead_click

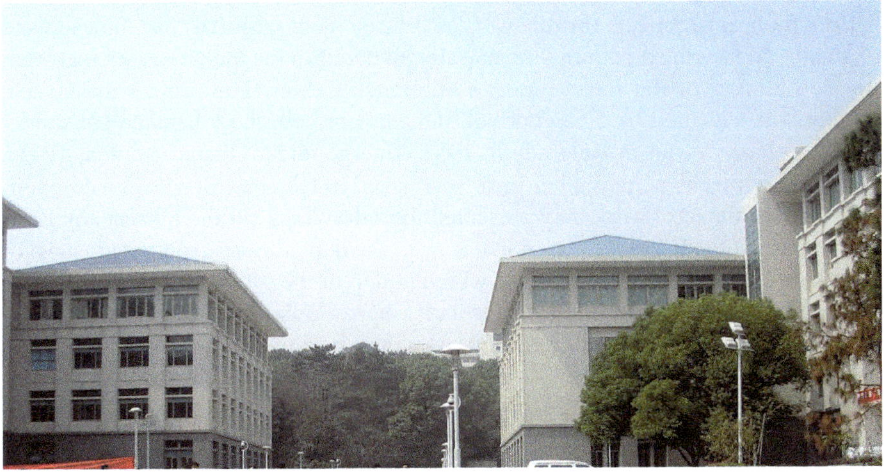

Fig. 4.15 Wuhan School of Law buildings. Note roof style and hues. (*Credit* Author's archives)

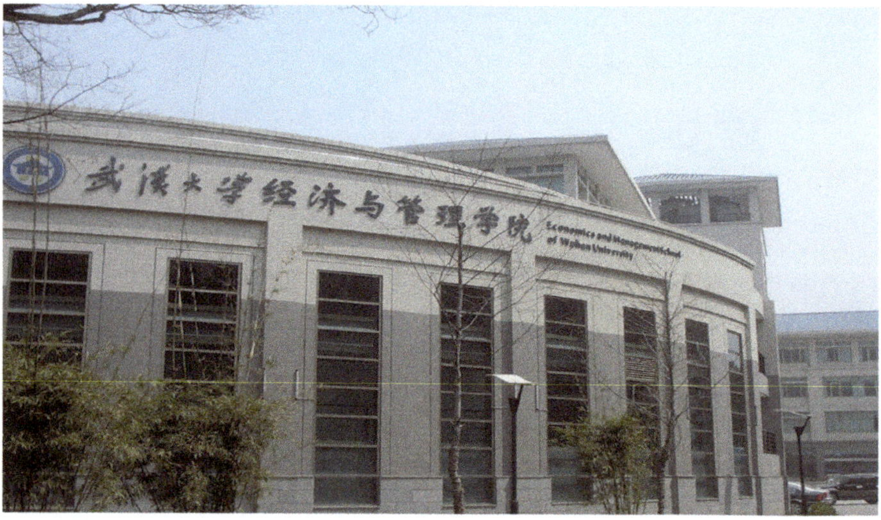

Fig. 4.16 Wuhan School of Economics and Management buildings. Note the towers to the right. (*Credit* Author's archives)

study has shown, for example, that Ghanaian architects have been sidelined and with it opportunities for strengthening their capacity and know-how thereby undermining the flourishing of a self-conscious vernacular tried by the fire of practice. In a sense, China has usurped Ghanaian architectural exertion by stealth. I interviewed one of Ghana's pioneer architects for this work and her lament was that the Chinese were essentially continuing a pattern. She narrated in detail to me the processes that went into the building of the International Conference Center. The project design and building was executed by Energoprojekt Ghana Limited, the Ghanaian subsidiary of the company set up in Belgrade in 1951 (Energopojekt Ghana Limited, 1991). Ghanaian architects including her firm were asked to take part in a design competition. After all the hard work they presented their drawings but did not get any feedback from the organizers. I have shown as well the dependence generated instead of self-reliance after these constructions which undercut the often rosy picture painted by official narratives. The NT provides a classic example. This dependence is also reflected in the disrepair after construction evident in some of the cases. To be sure, some of these complications may very well stem from incompetence (poor negotiations, poor maintenance culture, corruption etc.) on the Ghanaian side. This raises formidable questions about how the long term objectives of these interactions will truly be realized without casting China as a shrewd powerful player manipulating developing countries like Ghana. What this chapter has attempted to do using one of the longest relations between China and another developing country (6 decades as at 2020) is to suggest a critical path for unpacking China's engagement of Africa. Such a critical path can only benefit Africa-China relations as long hoped and envisioned.

References

ABC News. (2020). UHAS Management pleads with government to release funds for stalled projects. https://www.abcnewsgh.com/uhas-management-pleads-with-govt-to-release-funds-for-completion-of-stalled-projects/.

Allotey, G. A., & Abu-Baidu, Z. (2017). Be firm on Chinese illegal miners–Lloyd Amoah to gov't. http://citifmonline.com/2017/03/28/be-firm-on-chinese-illegal-miners-lloyd-amoah-to-govt/.

Amoah, L. G. A. (Ed.). (2014). *Impacts of the Knowledge Society on Economic and Social Growth in Africa*. IGI Global.

Amoah, L. G. A. (2016). China, architecture and Ghana's spaces: Concrete signs of a soft Chinese imperium? *Journal of Asian and African Studies, 51*(2), 238–255.

Amoah, L. G. A. (2018a). Ghana, China's Presence and Resilience-An IRI BRIDGE Research Project Report. A Research Commissioned on Contract by the International Republican Institute.

Amoah, L. G. A. (2018b). *Five Ghanaian Presidents and China: Patterns, Pitfalls and Possibilities*. Accra: University of Ghana Press.

Ashanti Today. (2015). Kumasi Youth Centre left to Rot. http://ashantitoday.blogspot.com/2015/03/kumasi-youth-centre-left-to-rot.html.

Boahen, A. A. (1985). Politics and nationalism in West Africa, 1919–3. In A. A. Boahen (Ed.), *General History of Africa, VII: Africa Under Colonial Domination, 1880–1935* (pp. 641–642). Paris and California: UNESCO and Heinemann.

Chen, T. (2016). *What Happened to China Development Bank's $3 Billion Loan to Ghana? SAIS-CARI Policy Brief* (Vol. 10, pp. 1–4). Washington D.C.: John Hopkins University. https://static1.squarespace.com/static/5652847de4b033f56d2bdc29/t/56fab64ecf80a125ba5f4f5a/1459271482280/SAIS-CARI+Brief+%2310+-+Chen+V.8_NEW.pdf. Accessed 2 June 2017.

Confidential Parliamentary Document.

Confucius Institute at UCC. (2021). *Chinese Ambassador's Scholarship at Ciucc*. http://confuciusucc.com/.

Ding, G., & Xue, C. Q. (2015). China's architectural aid: Exporting a transformational modernism. *Habitat International, 47*, 136–147.

Dreher, A., Fuchs, A., Parks, B., Strange, A., & Tierney, M. J. (2021). Aid, China, and growth: Evidence from a new global development finance dataset. *American Economic Journal: Economic Policy, 13*(2), 135–174.

Embassy of the people's Republic of China in the republic of China. (2021). *Ghana Receives ¢ 22.2bn Chinese Support*. http://gh.china-embassy.org/eng/xwdt/t210792.htm.

Energopojekt Ghana Limited. (1991). International Conference center, Accra, Ghana. https://energoprojektghana.com/references/international-conference-centre.

Fosu, K. (n.d). *A Short History of Mampong Akuapem: 1730–2012* (p. 10). Self Published.

Ghana News Agency (GNA). (2018). *StarTimes; Ministry of Communication Launch Satellite TV Project*. https://www.modernghana.com/news/885674/startimes-ministry-of-communication-launch-satellite-tv-pro.html.

Ghana Web. (2018). *Ghana tops African students in China*. https://www.ghanaweb.com/GhanaHomePage/NewsArchive/Ghana-tops-African-students-in-China-687116.

Government of Ghana (n.d.). *Fourth Year in Office of Colonel Ignatius Kutu Acheampong*. Accra, Office of the Press Secretary to the National Redemption Council.

Hui, W. (2003). The historical origin of Chinese Neoliberalism: Another discussion on the ideological situation in contemporary mainland China and the issue of modernity. *Chinese Economy, 36*(4), 3–42.

Jacobs, J. (2016). *The Death and Life of Great American cities*. Vintage.

Jaffé, A. (1964). Symbolism in the visual arts. In C. Jung (Ed.), *Man and his Symbols* (p. 232). New York: Anchor Press/Double Day.

Levin, A. (2016). Haile Selassie's imperial modernity: Expatriate architects and the shaping of addis ababa. *Journal of the Society of Architectural Historians, 75*(4), 447–468.

Loeffler, J. C. (1990). The architecture of diplomacy: Heyday of the United States embassy-building program, 1954–1960. *The Journal of the Society of Architectural Historians, 49*(3), 251–278.
Loureiro, P. M., & Saad-Filho, A. (2019). The limits of pragmatism: The rise and fall of the Brazilian Workers' Party (2002–2016). *Latin American Perspectives, 46*(1), 66–84.
Mandela, D. (2021). *Ghana Begins Renovation Works on Cape Coast Sports Stadium*. https://constructionreviewonline.com/2019/08/ghana-begins-renovation-works-on-cape-coast-sports-stadium/.
Monson, J. (2009). *Africa's Freedom Railway: How a Chinese development project changed lives and livelihoods in Tanzania*. Indiana University Press.
Nkrumah, K. (2001). *Dark days in Ghana* (pp. 100–101). Panaf.
Rist, G. (2014). *The History of Development: From Western Origins to Global Faith*. Bloomsbury Publishing.
Song, K., & Zhu, J. (2017). Architecture at a political turning point: Diplomatic buildings in 1970s Beijing. *ABE Journal. Architecture beyond Europe, 12*.
Tema Expansion Project & GHANA GOV. (2019). *The Ghana Western Corridor Gas Infrastructure Development Project involves Chinese companies, China Habour Engineering Company and Sinopec respectively*. https://www.aecom.com/projects/tema-port-expansion/, http://www.ghana.gov.gh/index.php/media-center/news/1417-phase-two-of-gas-infrastructure-project-ongoing-sinopec.
Van Gameren, D., & Tola, A. T. (2017). A city shaped by diplomacy. The case of Ethiopia's capital Addis Ababa. *ABE Journal Architecture beyond Europe, 12*.
Wikipedia, Operation Vanguard. https://en.wikipedia.org/wiki/Operation_Vanguard.
Xue, C. Q., Ding, G., Chang, W., & Wan, Y. (2019). Architecture of "Stadium diplomacy"-China-aid sport buildings in Africa. *Habitat International, 90*, 101985.
Yu, T. (2011). *Buildings that Speak Volumes*. http://www.chinadaily.com.cn/cndy/2011-06/29/content_12797648.htm.
Zhang, Y. (2011). *Research on China's foreign Aid(1950–2010) 中国对外援助研究 (1950–2010)*. Jiuzhou Press Institute.
Zion Market Research. (2018). Global Chocolate Market Expected to Reach USD 161.56 Billion By 2024". https://www.globenewswire.com/news-release/2018/10/22/1624439/0/en/Global-Chocolate-Market-Expected-to-Reach-USD-161-56-Billion-By-2024-Zion-Market-Research.html.

Lloyd G. Adu Amoah is a Senior Lecturer at the Dept. of Political Science and is founding Director of the Centre for Asian Studies at the University of Ghana, Legon. He was just recently acting Director of the Centre for European Studies, University of Ghana. Legon. He is a fellow of the African Studies Centre (ASC) and the International Institute of Asian Studies (where he did his postdoctoral work) both in Leiden, the Netherlands. Dr. Amoah is a member of the Ghana Studies Association, World Economics Association, Association for Heterodox Economics and the African Urban Planning Research Network. He served on the editorial board of *Pacific Affairs*. His research focuses on public policy formation theory, strategy in government, Africa-Asia-China relations, public administration and philosophy, e-governance and ICT policy in developing countries and the political-economy of space in developing polities. His recently published books include *Five Ghanaian Presidents and China: Patterns, Pitfalls and Possibilities* (2020) and *Sixty Years of Ghana China Relations: Friendship, Friction, and the Future* (2021).

Chapter 5
Traveling Ideas: Appropriation and Identity in the China-Sri Lanka Architectural Exchanges

Guanghui Ding and Charlie Qiuli Xue

Abstract Drawing upon the concept of "appropriation", this chapter seeks to understand the processes by which Chinese architectural professionals incorporated and synthesized various aesthetic and intellectual sources in the transnational practice of China's architectural exports to the Global South. By focusing on China's engagement with Sri Lanka and on the work of the Bandaranaike Memorial International Conference Hall (BMICH) and later Nelum Pokuna Theater in Colombo and on the manifestation of appropriation in contemporary transcultural practice, this chapter traces the interactions between an intention to respond to local tropical climatic condition and an approach to appropriate Chinese, Sri Lankan, and international architectural culture. It argues that the appropriation, synthesis and transformation of architectural ideas from various contexts created new forms of identity which articulated political and cultural manifestations. Formally and technically, the Chinese architects' attempt to adopt an appropriate aesthetics of tropics away from a domestic kind of socialist realism was premised upon an effort to create building able to reflect Sri Lanka's environmental and cultural identity. The juxtaposition of appropriating Sri Lankan architecture in both Colombo and in China suggests that the dual mobility of architectural ideas helped contribute to forming new political and cultural identities urgently needed both by the Bandaranaike administration and by a group of emerging Chinese architects.

5.1 Introduction

In the last decade, there has been an important change in the historiography of modern Chinese architecture. While the field was for a long time dominated by domestic

---

G. Ding (✉)
Department of Architecture, Beijing University of Civil Engineering and Architecture, Beijing, China
e-mail: tin_tin0504@hotmail.com

C. Q. Xue
Department of Architecture and Civil Engineering, City University of Hong Kong, Kowloon, Hong Kong

C. Q. Xue and G. Ding (eds.), *Exporting Chinese Architecture*,
https://doi.org/10.1007/978-981-19-2786-7_5

visions of architectural production, recent scholarships have paid much attention to China's overseas architectural practices, including comprehensive historical reviews, in-depth case studies within a certain historical period, and monographic analysis on specific architectural types (Chang, 2020; Ding & Xue, 2015; Roskam, 2015; Verri, 2020; Xue et al., 2019). With the gradual expansion of research scope, an unresolved question remains to be explored: In the transnational practice of architecture, how did Chinese architects respond to the request of cultural, political, and environmental identity by the recipient country through formal expression and spatial articulation? This issue is a long lasting challenge faced by architects being involved of cross-cultural practice.

China's architectural exports to the Global South, as part of the country's developmental aid, is a transnational practice that was jointly shaped by geopolitics, power contest, competition and collaboration, knowledge transfer and the mobility of people, capital, goods and ideas. Since its beginning in the 1950s, architectural aid was not a purely technical activity, but was entangled with the purpose of gaining international influence, promoting political trust, economic exchange and cultural engagement. The aid program initiated by the People's Republic of China emerged within the context of the Cold War (the political and military tension between the powers in the Western and Eastern blocs) and played an essential role in reinforcing its international legitimacy while competing with the capitalist and the socialist blocs.

China's foreign aid in general was not operated in a vacuum environment but a product of interactions at multi-level associated with the donor, the recipients, and the historical circumstance. Simultaneously, the realization of specific architecture also epitomized the complex social, cultural and ideological interactions, exhibiting the intricate and intertwined connections of design knowledge and idea sources. In the Mao era (1949–1976), the Chinese had very limited geographical and cultural knowledge of Asian and African countries, and only a very small number of architectural professionals had the opportunity to travel abroad. What impact did this limited knowledge have on the transnational architectural practice? How did Chinese architects investigate and understand Asian and African architectural culture? Considering that countries receiving China's economic aid and technical assistance are mainly located in the tropical regions, how did Chinese architects interpret tropical architecture? What are the implications of this creative process and aesthetic expression for contemporary practice in the context of the Belt and Road Initiative?

In his seminal article "Traveling Theory," Edward Said (1983) claimed that theory had impact not only in the period and place where it was produced, but also can travel to a new context—in most cases, from Western nations to developing countries, as the latter desperately needed such theories—and give rise to new meanings. Similar to Said's observation, architecture ideas can also be travelling or disseminated trans-regionally through publication, discussion and discursive and material reinterpretation. During the process of cross-cultural exchange, architectural ideas might be appropriated, synthesized and transformed into new forms of narrative in a new cultural context. In cultural studies, appropriation is often seen as bound up with the oppression of minority cultures and usually adopts a posture of critique and even assault; therefore it was in many respects controversial (Young, 2008). However, in transcultural architecture practice, how to express regional identity is an important issue considered by many architects and clients, and formal "appropriation" is a very common tactics and usually an effective countermeasure.

Architectural appropriation is by no means a new notion; it is a process that has been undertaken for centuries and which has manifested itself across many cultures. In recent years, scholars began to examine the interdependence between new architecture and historical precedents, interrogating the issue of copyright, originality, right and the transfer of ideas (Lawrence & Miljački, 2018). Appropriation has gained a particular significance in the context of transnational architectural production, which has been dependent on aesthetic interpretation involved in any interaction with existent architectural forms. While appropriation should not be seen as a thing in itself but rather as a process embedded in an array of social practices, identity formation is not static but constructed in specific historical context (Vives-Ferrándiz, 2010; Zubrzycki, 2017). Architecture as a material object better reveals the dynamics and complexity of this construction process.

To better understand how Chinese architects deal with domestic, foreign and international cultures in transnational architecture production, this chapter examines the architectural exchange between China and Sri Lanka (formerly known as Ceylon). There are two main reasons behind this selection of case study. First, among the Chinese architecture exported to the developing countries during the Mao's time, the Bandaranaike Memorial International Conference Hall (BMICH), located in Colombo, Sri Lanka, typically demonstrated Chinese architects' skill at integrating modern vocabularies with local tradition and climate. The project was widely recognized as an exemplar and highest quality of China's architectural aid by top-level Chinese and Sri Lankan officials and admired by international leaders (You, 2012; Lu, 2012).

Second, whereas China's architectural aid to the developing nations was largely a one-way process, its architectural engagement with Sri Lanka was a remarkable two-way mobility, if not a two-way dialogue. China tended to provide complete package of assistance including funding, design, materials, construction, maintenance and even reconstruction after many years' operation, while local architects and engineers would normally work as project consultants and local builders would participate into construction process. This is true for the case the BMICH. What made the case of Sri Lanka however unique is that Chinese architectural community had also "imported" design ideas from Sri Lankan architects. This notion was an exception not a rule, as Chinese architects were inclined to draw inspirations from the Soviet architects in the 1950s and from their Western peers since the 1980s onwards. In other words, few Chinese architectural professionals paid enough attention to either the Asian and African architectural culture or the China-aided projects there.

In spite of being critically acclaimed by Chinese architectural professionals and briefly mentioned in a few articles, the BMICH did not receive detailed scholarly examination on its singular role in the context of China's architectural engagement with the rest of the world. The BMICH, as a single building, is somehow connected to a network of existing architecture, as it displays a combination of various formal sources including Chinese, Sri Lankan, Soviet and Western influences. As the works of historical and modern culture converged into the project, it was characterized with a kind of "appropriation", embodying a complex process of re-interpretation and re-composition of existing elements. We use the term "appropriation" precisely because the BMICH project transformed various "informing sources into a wholly new cultural product" (Sanders, 2006, p. 26).[1]

Understood in the conventional sense, appropriation refers to the simple copy or duplication of existing design with an intention to confuse authorship and originality. American architect Philip Johnson in his long career had noticeably practiced this approach. Consider, for instance, the copy of Claude-Nicolas Ledoux's drawing of the House of Education project (1773–1779) into his work, the College of Architecture building at the University of Houston (1985) (Bjone, 2014). In this chapter, however, we define the term "appropriation" as a subtle transformation or abstraction of existing buildings as a basis of new design in a new context. In this regard, it is more close to the term "bricolage or collage" or "inspiration" that draws incomplete elements and motifs of existing design, with that new part keeping its own unique identity. Architects tend to take as their own to use styles, motifs, formal languages, spatial compositions, material articulations, and other architectural elements. Almost all architects engage in some sort of "appropriation" in that they borrow ideas, formal, spatial, and technical solutions, and so forth from other buildings and architects.

While novelists and artists from many cultures are constantly engaging in appropriation, architects are also doing the same thing, exemplified, for example, by the fact that the majority of China-aided buildings in the Global South tended to adopt the approach of appropriation, albeit in a less innovative way. What made the BMICH project striking is that both architects and various stakeholders jointly experimented with new ideas that resourcefully combined local, national and global cultures, challenging the conventional imagination of both Chinese architectural community and of local political elites. The Nelum Pokuna theater followed the similar route later. Interestingly, Sri Lankan architecture, particularly the work of Geoffrey Bawa, were also introduced and reinterpreted by contemporary Chinese architects, in an attempt to formulate differential narratives and positions. The appropriation, synthesis and transformation of architectural ideas from various contexts created new forms of identity which articulated political and cultural manifestations.

5.2 Geopolitics and China-Sri Lanka Relations

The relationship between China and Sri Lanka can be dated back to the fifth century when Faxian, a Buddhist monk who had traveled to Sri Lanka and played a crucial role in promoting cultural exchange through writing and translation of ancient Buddhist texts. This civil contacts and relationships lasted for more than a dozen centuries

[1] In terms of the difference between appropriation and adaption, Julie Sanders argues that, the latter implies an ostensible relationship with an original work, albeit achieved in alternative temporal and generic modes. Consider, for instance, a cinematic version of Shakespeare's *Hamlet*.

and continued to exist in modern history. In 1948, Sri Lanka received its political independence from the British Empire. By then, the nascent nation was governed by political elites who were sympathetic to colonial values and practiced colonial rules (Wijetunge, 2013). When the Solomon Bandaranaike-led party came to power in 1956, he adopted a strong socialist agenda, reacted against the bitter memories and promoted new national identity. It was in this ideological context that the People's Republic of China and Sri Lanka established diplomatic relations in 1957.

Before the establishment of formal diplomatic relations, China and Sri Lanka had signed the noticeable "China-Ceylon Five-Year Trade Agreement on Rubber and Rice" (commonly known as the "Rice Rubber Agreement") in 1952. While rubber is an important strategic material announced by the US-led United Nations Paris Coordination Committee to impose an embargo on the People's Republic of China, Sri Lanka in the early 1950s was facing a severe shortage of rice and struggling for buying it from the US market at a higher price with limited foreign exchange resources (Chang, 1953). Despite the pressure from the US and the opposition from domestic officials, Sri Lanka Prime Minister, Dudley Senanayake, however, fully backed his Minister of Commerce, R. G. Senanayake and was prepared to exchange with Communist China rubber for rice (Kelegama, 2002). He insisted that the benefits to Sri Lanka from the agreement far outweighed losses consequent to the cutting-off of American aid.[2]

The burgeoning China-Sri Lanka relation was initially manifested in Chinese Premier Zhou Enlai's first visit to Colombo in 1957, when he attended the people's assembly at the Independence Square in Colombo to celebrate the ninth anniversary of Sri Lanka's independence. This official visit was later paralleled by more civil contacts of commerce and exhibition. For instance, on March 18, 1958, the China Commodity Fair was held at Victoria Park in Colombo. The exhibition showcased more than 3,000 pieces of China-made exhibits, including both daily commodities and manufacturing products, demonstrating the progress that the People's Republic achieved without US aid, attracting hundreds of thousands of audiences, including Prime Minister Solomon Bandaranaike, United Nations staff and local and regional citizens (Ji, 1958).

In 1964, Chinese Premier Zhou Enlai visited Sri Lanka again, where the world's first female Prime Minister, Mrs. Sirimavo Bandaranaike, requested China's aid in a project in memory of her husband, the assassinated former Prime Minister Solomon Bandaranaike. However, the proposal to build a memorial hall with Chinese assistance also caused domestic criticism within Sri Lanka. One critic with strong nationalist attitude claimed that:

> It is in the first place completely shameless for Ceylon to have a foreign country donate a local memorial to a Ceylonese politician and even though the Ceylon Government is very friendly with Red China, the whole schema is an unworthy slight to Mr. Bandaranaike. If this country wants a memorial, in addition to the one at Horagolla, let it build it itself with

[2] The agreement lasted for 30 years from 1952 to 1982. The implementation of the Rice Rubber Agreement not only provided China with much-needed rubber and supported the resistance to US aggression and aid to Korea, but also played a positive role in breaking the blockade and embargo imposed by Western capitalist countries.

> its own money and its own design and expertise and labour. The Chinese Government would laugh at us if we offered to erect a memorial in Peking to some Chinese national leader. What self-respect can Ceylon have if it permits the Red Chinese to erect a memorial, here in Colombo, to one of our own Prime Ministers? (You, et al., 2012).[3]

Despite domestic criticism, the Bandaranaike Administration still decided to start this project. It is worth noting that Sri Lanka was not the first nation requesting and receiving China's architectural assistance. Prior to this, China has assisted Mongolia, North Korea, Vietnam, Laos, Cambodia, Indonesia, and Guinea in creating factories and buildings (Liu, 2015). The architectural aid program was part of China's efforts to expand its global influence, combat the Washington-led isolation and sanction, compete with the Soviet Union and help developing nations to seek for national independence and economic development.

The initial direction of Chinese aid was bound up with neighbor nations sharing similar ideologies and historical experience with China (Zhongyang wenxian yanjiushi, 1992). This economic and technical assistance primarily included the design and construction of civil projects and industrial factories, including the support of labor, materials, technologies and complete sets of equipment. As the central government acknowledged that foreign assistance was a complex and arduous project, a few special institutions, including the Central Foreign Affairs Group, the State Planning Commission, and the Ministry of Finance, were responsible for organization and coordination. The Ministry of Building Engineering, like other industrial ministries, was one of the principal sectors of procurement and delivery. The Beijing Industrial Architecture Design Institute, affiliated to the Ministry of Building Engineering was the primary force of implementing design task, establishing two internal design offices specialized in foreign-aid project design, while each department had hundreds of design professionals (You et al., 2012).

To better understand China's architectural aid to Sri Lanka, two significant background facts should be mentioned. First, due to the countries' shared consistent ideology of non-intervention, bilateral relations have maintained an upward trajectory since 1957. Sri Lanka's strategic location in the Indian Ocean was crucial for China's commerce and competition with India. Second, just weeks before Zhou's visit to Colombo, he had proposed China's eight principles of economic and technical assistance in Ghana, highlighting aid based on mutuality and equality, respect for sovereignty, interest-free credits, provision of top-quality equipment, training of local technical cadres, and living standards for Chinese experts not to exceed their local counter parts (Zhonghua renmin gongheguo waijiaobu, Zhongyang wenxian yanjiushi, 1990). This announcement marked a fundamental difference from the aid model of other countries in West Africa, such as the Soviet Union and East European nations.[4]

[3] This passage appeared in an unidentified Ceylonese newspaper collected in the 2012 book by You et al.

[4] While some principles presented a contrast to the existing model from the Socialist Bloc that had been practiced in West Africa in the early 1960s, the origin of others can be dated back to the 1950s when China began to aid Vietnam.

5.3 Initial Encounter with Sri Lanka

There are two important factors determining China's promise to assist Sri Lanka: one is the need to compete with the Soviet Union who had also provided funding to Colombo; the other is the hope that Sri Lanka would mediate the Sino-Indian conflict. Immediately after Zhou agreed to his counterpart's request, the Chinese Ministry of Building Engineering designated the Beijing Industrial Architecture Design Institute to offer design solutions. In 1964, a project team consisting of the Head of the Institute, Yuan Jingshen, Chief Architect Dai Nianci, senior architect Yang Yun, structural engineer You Baoxian and other professionals flew to Colombo. Before going, these professionals were not familiar with the territory. It can be said that the Chinese at that time had very limited knowledge of Sri Lanka. In one of the earliest descriptions of Sri Lanka published in a domestic magazine *Shijie zhishi* [World Knowledge] in (1953), the author wrote that,

> Colombo is the capital of Ceylon. In terms of maritime traffic, it is the concentrated point of various routes in the Indian Ocean. The city has towering architectures, tall colonial buildings, and damp simple houses covered with palm branches. The former are the locations of British colonial trade, the Governor's House and Ceylon government offices. The latter is the residence of the general Ceylonese and Tamils. Ships of various countries are anchored in the port, and flags of different colors are flying, which shows that Colombo is a typical semi-colonial city and Ceylon is a typical semi-colonial country (Chong, 1953).

It is conceivable that when the Chinese architects arrived at Colombo in 1964, what they perceived of the local urban landscape was not dramatically different from the above-mentioned description (Fig. 5.1). The sharp contrast between the monumental, institutional architecture in the forms of Colonial and Indic styles and

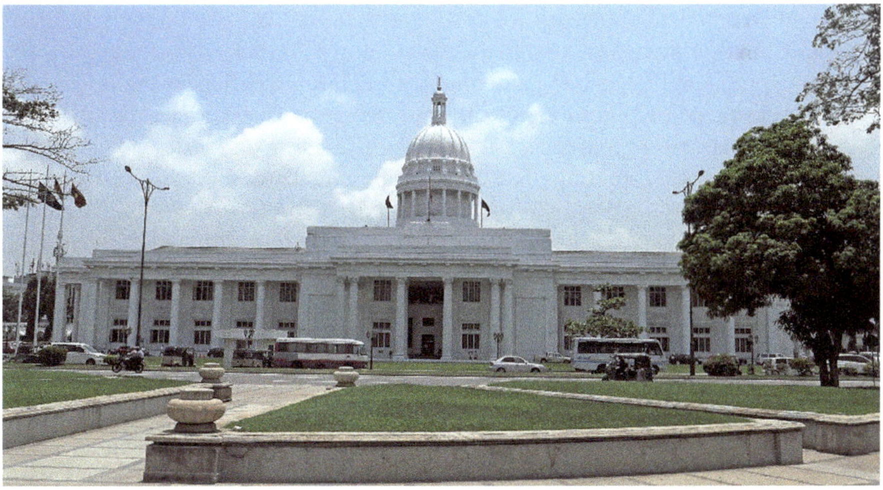

Fig. 5.1 City hall of Colombo, at the edge of Independent Square, photo taken in 2017

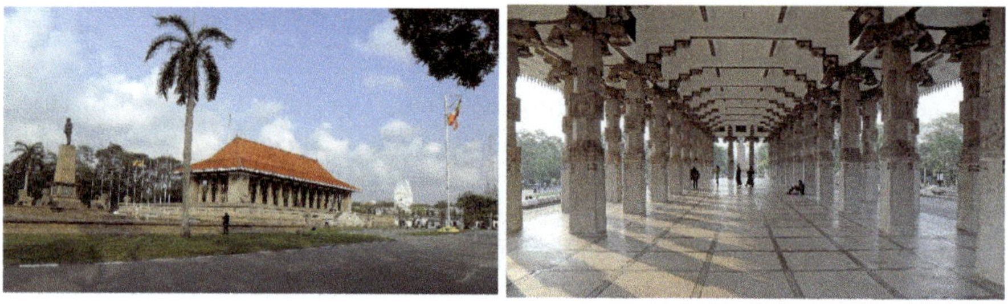

Fig. 5.2 Pavilion at the center of Independent Square, Colombo, built for celebrating 10-year anniversary of independence, 1958. Its beam structure adopted the form of Temple of Teeth in Kandy, photos taken in 2017

the local, domestic buildings in the forms of bungalow-influenced Tropical style created by the Public Works Department still existed (Fig. 5.2).

By then, the profession and education of architecture in Sri Lanka were still nascent. The handful number of local architects educated in the Architecture Association School of Architecture in 1950s London just started their junior professional career. Consider, for instance, Minnette de Silva (1918–1998), the first female architect in Sri Lanka, who adopted a synthesis between the vernacular and Tropical Modernism ; Geoffery Bawa (1919–2003) and Valentine Gunasekara (1931–2017) who had been working for Edwards, Reid and Begg and began to design small scale domestic projects for elite clients. In sharp contrast, these Chinese architects and engineers had gained sufficient experience in designing large-scale urban architecture, such as the Ten Great Buildings in Beijing produced to celebrate the tenth anniversary of the People's Republic in 1959. Equally significant, by the mid-1960s, professionals from the Beijing Industrial Architecture Design Institute had also accumulated much practical knowledge of designing factories and buildings overseas, as a form of China's architectural aid to the developing countries.

These Chinese architects had gained both successful experiences and lessons of failure. Domestically, Chinese architects were struggling to mediate the representation of national culture and the performance of function and efficiency. The fact that some institutional buildings built within the context of national in form and socialist in content (socialist realism) were criticized for their excessive scale and lavish waste implied the overt debate on aesthetics and politics. Internationally, some Chinese professionals were also struggling to address tropical climate and foreign culture in the China-aided projects in Southeast Asia and West Africa. Some buildings were initially created with problems of ventilation, rain-proof, moisture-proof, and the inappropriate selection of structures and materials. Premier Zhou, officials in charge of foreign aid projects such as Fang Yi, and professionals from the Beijing Industrial Architecture Design Institute such as Jin Oubo, Yuan Jingshen and Dai Nianci should be very clear about the above design issues, because they have participated in, inspected, and coordinated the design and construction process of these aided projects. For example, during his visit to Guinea in 1964, Premier Zhou had inspected the China-aided match-cigarette factory buildings, remarking critically that the projects' cumbersome appearance costed a lot of materials, required more investment, and took a longer time for construction (Fang Yi Zhuan Bianxiezu, 2008, p. 314).

As the first large scale culture building that China aided to the developing world, the Bandaranaike Memorial International Conference Hall (BMICH) received special instructions from Premier Zhou, who, together with design professionals, established ideological consensus and identified three principles: (1) being appropriate in scale and volume; (2) taking the tropical climate and local culture into account; and (3) using state-of-the-art technology and facilities (Yuan et al., 2002; You et al., 2012). Clearly, these guidelines were in consonance with the eight principles previously declared by the Chinese government.

During their four-month stay in Sri Lanka, it is probable that the Chinese professionals did not meet these emerging local architects, but what is certain is that they visited important historical buildings and towns, such as Anuradhapura, Polonnaruwa and Kandy (Fig. 5.3). They were impressed by the rich Buddhist architecture heritages such as the Temple of the Tooth (Sri Dalada Maligawa), particularly Paththirippuwa (Pattirippuwa). This octagonal pavilion was a significant icon of Sri Lankan culture, enjoyed a supreme status and brought inspirations for Chinese architects. Aside from these traditional heritages, the Chinese might also visit some newly-built projects erected in Colombo, presumably, the Lionel Wendt Theatre and Gallery designed in the 1950s, a major art center and theater with white appearance and modest volume, although they did not leave a note on such experience.[5]

5.4 The Bandaranaike Memorial International Conference Hall

Based on historical surveys and site observations, architects Dai Nianci and Yang Yun sketched two preliminary proposals.[6] The biggest difference between the two options lay in the shape of the main conference hall: one was octagonal and the other circular. During internal discussions among the Chinese design team, the octagonal schema was questioned, as it was quite bold and novel, and completely different from domestic conference halls which were either square or round. In this regards, Dai was under great pressure and his colleagues were worried that it would be difficult to get project approval from Beijing. When the two schemes were presented to the

[5] The Lionel Wendt Gallery was a project demonstrating the design combination of collective contributions. The plans of the gallery were drawn by Edward, Reid & Begg, based on the drawings provided by artist W. J. G. Beling who was a close friend of Lionel Wendt and architect Jane Drew who offered technical expertise, particularly with regard to lighting, with Geoffrey Bawa as the principal consultant architect. Chinese architects from the design institutes had known the works of Fry and Drew, as they were cited in several articles published in 1958 and 1963.

[6] According to Yuan Jingshen, the design team had made initial proposal before arriving at Colombo. Dai's proposal was a refined one based on initial schema.

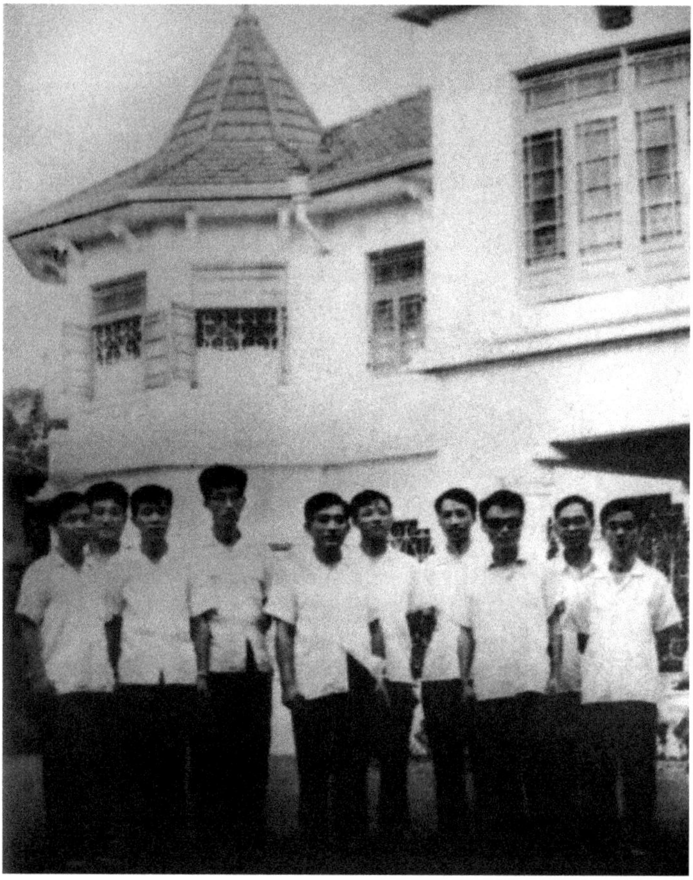

Fig. 5.3 Group photo of the Chinese Design Team in Colombo, 1964 (Courtesy of China Architecture Design and Research Group)

Sri Lankan leaders, however, Mrs. Bandaranaike selected the first option. Given her cultural background, it is no coincidence that Mrs. Bandaranaike appreciated the octagonal one, as the proposal was reminiscent of the octagonal pavilion in the Temple of the Tooth in Kandy. Mrs. Bandaranaike was born in a prominent Sinhalese family in the Kandyan hill country and would recognize the bold modern reinterpretation of traditional Sinhalese architectural culture (Peebles, 2006). The selection of the octagonal scheme implied that the Sri Lanka leader intended to search for national identity through architectural expression.

Occupying a 13-acre site previously used as a golf court, the 30,000 square meters BMICH was divided into two visually separated yet interconnected parts, the main conference hall able to accommodate 1,500 people and an three-story building with courtyards housing small and middle-size conference rooms, offices, staff canteen, and other program facilities (Figs. 5.4 and 5.5). A close comparative reading of the

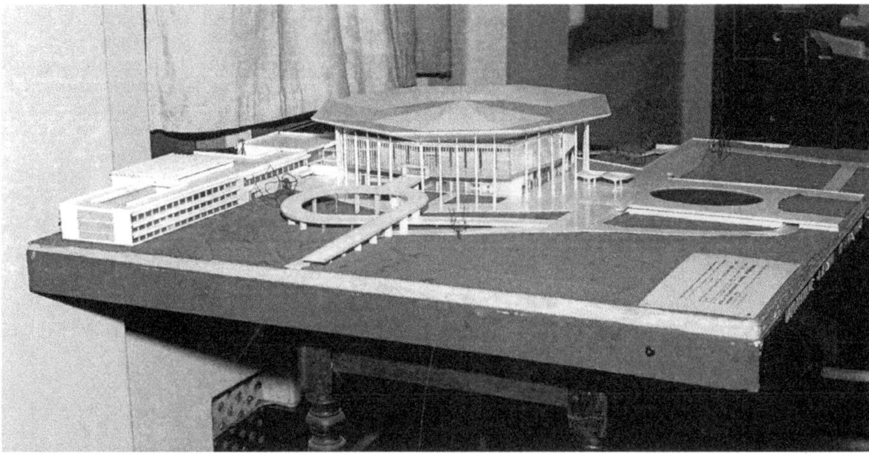

Fig. 5.4 The model of the BMICH, 1964 (Courtesy of China Architecture Design and Research Group)

original model and the final layout reveals some changes of formal composition during the process of project development. First, in the original model, the octagonal hall maintained two entrances; the main entrance was a ceremonial one without central staircase, the other was a spiral car ramp located on the east side. In the final layout, the car ramp was integrated with the central staircase. The original proposal that highlighted the principle of separation of people and vehicles was following the then international trend while almost never seen in domestic projects in 1960s China. While it was not clear why the change of entrance happened, one possible reason might be that the integrated scheme helped facilitate construction and strengthen the monumentality of the entrance, which was also a common practice in China.

Second, the auxiliary building had been changed from a linear volume directly behind the main hall to an unsymmetrical U-shaped one located at the southeast corner of the main building. This significant change is understandable, as the project's program had been slightly amended during the design process, demonstrated by the fact that members of a delegation led by V. C. de Silva, Director of the Public Works Department had conveyed Sri Lankan Government's suggestions during their visiting to Beijing (You et al., 2012). In terms of the auxiliary building, the staff canteen located at the end of the shorter wing deserves special attention. The one-story volume consists of four 12 m x 12 m quadrilateral umbrella-shaped shells, creating a simple and straightforward interior space without normal ceiling decoration (Fig. 5.6). This bold reinforced concrete structure had been rarely seen in Chinese architecture at that time and its design sources may be traced back to Frank Lloyd Wright's Johnson Wax building, although in a different form.

The overall layout displayed that the architects aimed to achieve prudent balance between representation and pragmatism. The monolithic, octagonal hall surrounded by an expansive marble colonnade of 40 columns (five columns on each side of the

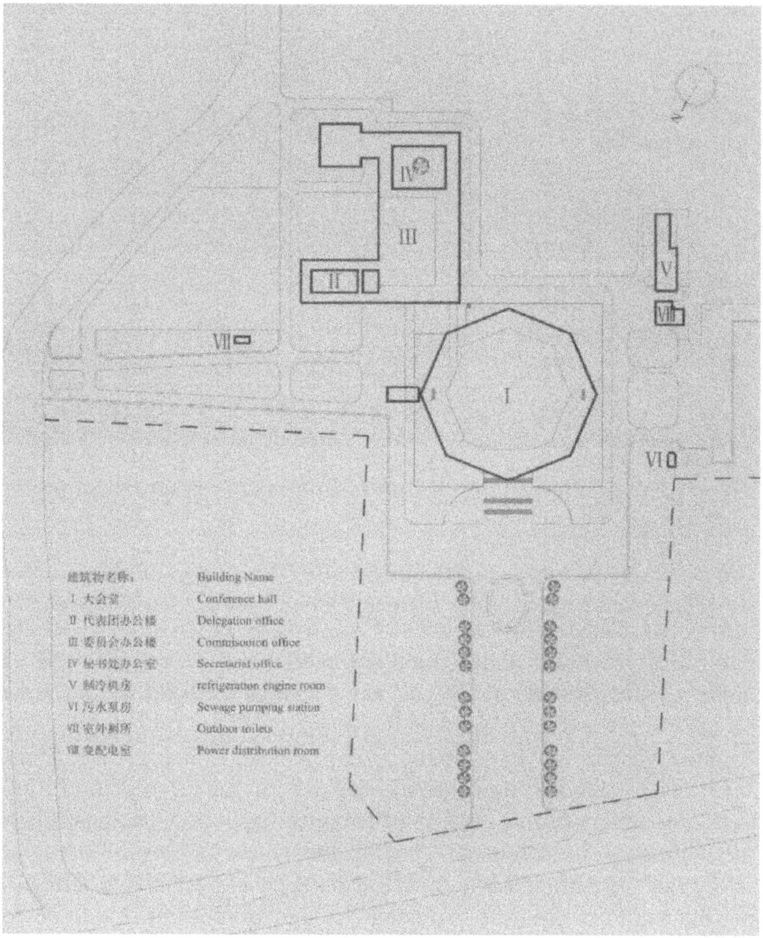

Fig. 5.5 The layout of the BMICH (Courtesy of China Architecture Design and Research Group)

octagon) demonstrated a sense of monumentality. This Beaux-Arts style symmetry rendered the solemnity and order of institutional architecture, a remarkable continuity of the formal characteristic of China's domestic conference halls. This 28-m-tall hall behind a formal reflecting pool rested atop a podium (Fig. 5.7). A centrally located ceremonial staircase led directly to the main entrance. White columns decorated with golden patterns supported the gently pitched steel roof, which cantilevered from the structure to provide shade for the glass envelope (Fig. 5.8).

The auxiliary building incorporates three internal courtyards into the building, a common motif that was prominent in local and Chinese and international architecture. These open courtyards located within the heart of the building enable rooms to open directly into a secure interior outdoor space, and promote natural ventilation.

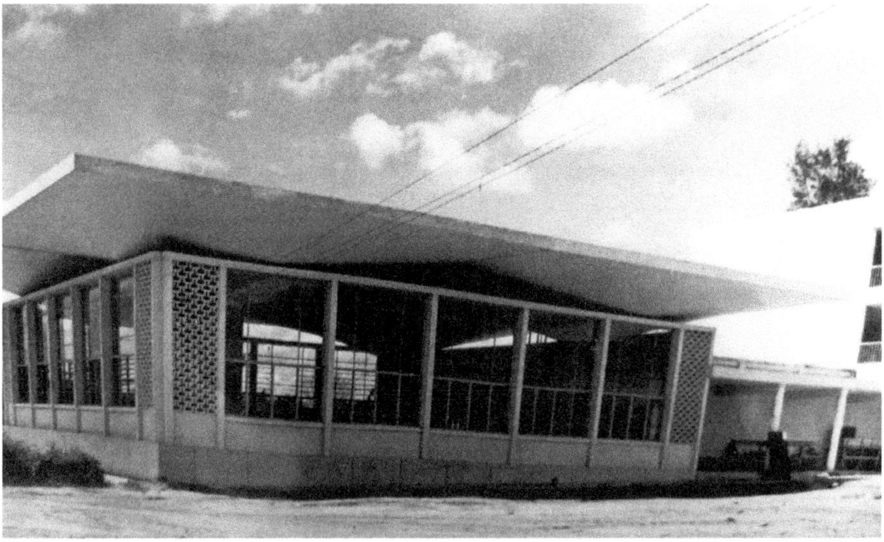

Fig. 5.6 The staff canteen of the BMICH (Courtesy of China Architecture Design and Research Group)

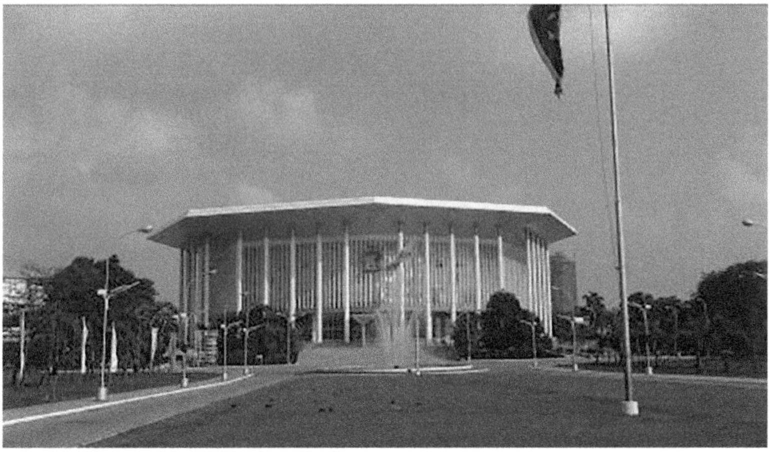

Fig. 5.7 The front view of the BMICH, photo taken in 2017

The spatial consideration on environmental feature was also paralleled by the characteristics of formal articulation, where exterior pierced grille, or screen made of precast cement bricks that wrap around the west façade, helps reduce the intensity of solar radiation while maintaining natural ventilation. Another feature of *brises-soleil* devices was the horizontal, cantilevered concrete panels outside the wall, which also provided a certain shading effect and visual privacy, reduced heat and glare (Fig. 5.9).

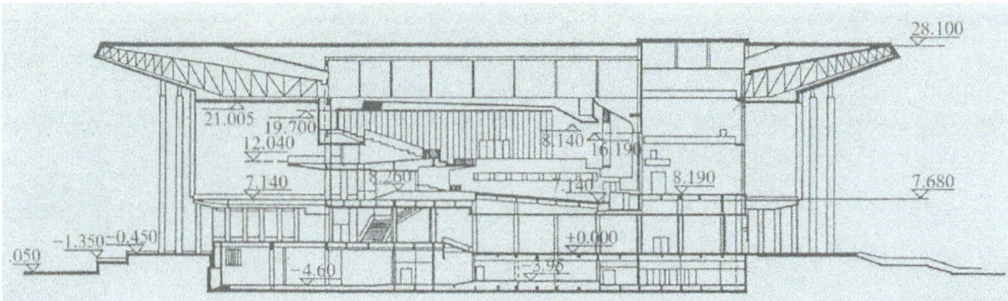

Fig. 5.8 Section of the auditorium of BMICH (Courtesy of China Architecture Design and Research Group)

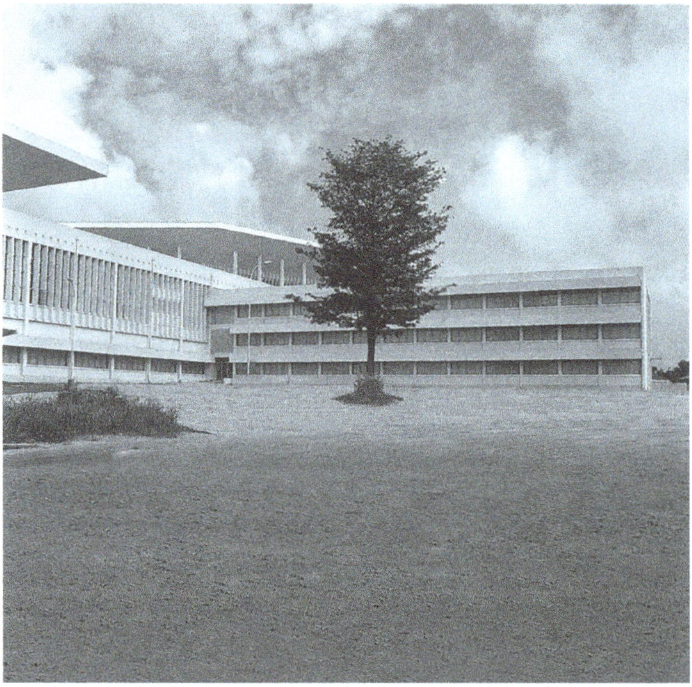

Fig. 5.9 Horizontal, cantilevered concrete panels outside the wall (Courtesy of China Architecture Design and Research Group)

After returning to China, the design institute immediately organized and established a design team of more than 50 people to carry out in-depth design, including 17 interns from the Civil Engineering Department of Tianjin University (You et al., 2012). The technical design of the BMICH was suspended however, when Mrs. Bandaranaike ended her first term as Prime Minister in 1965, but after winning the 1970 election and regaining power she requested that China continue the project.

At that time, however, China was embroiled in the turbulence of the Cultural Revolution (1966–1976). In the same year, the architects and engineers for this project, including Dai Nianci and You Baoxian, who had been sent to labor camps to reform their "bourgeois" ideologies, were summoned back to Beijing to restart work.

5.5 The Ideas of "Appropriation"

In the process of design review, Sri Lankan architects from the Public Works Department were concerned that the building's design did not fully express local cultural identity and once suggested that an iconic towering roof should be added on the top (Yuan, 1991).

While expressing design intentions to their Sri Lankan counterparts, Chinese architects were also inclined to accept some suggestions, such as adopting the motifs and elements of traditional architecture. To be more specific, the four square pillars on the entrance level imitated the pillars of local temple buildings, with engraved pattern decoration and cross-sectional changes, reminiscent of the local Buddhist architecture. The interior was equipped with a statue of Prime Minister Bandaranaike located at the end of the central concourse, behind which a large-scale oil painting depicting the landscape of Sri Lanka and created by noted Chinese painter Ai Zhongxin was hung on the wall, as a gesture to represent and respect native Sri Lankan culture (Fig. 5.10).

Aside from the appropriation of local culture, the BMICH also incorporated many international influences. In many aspects, the project was reminiscent of American

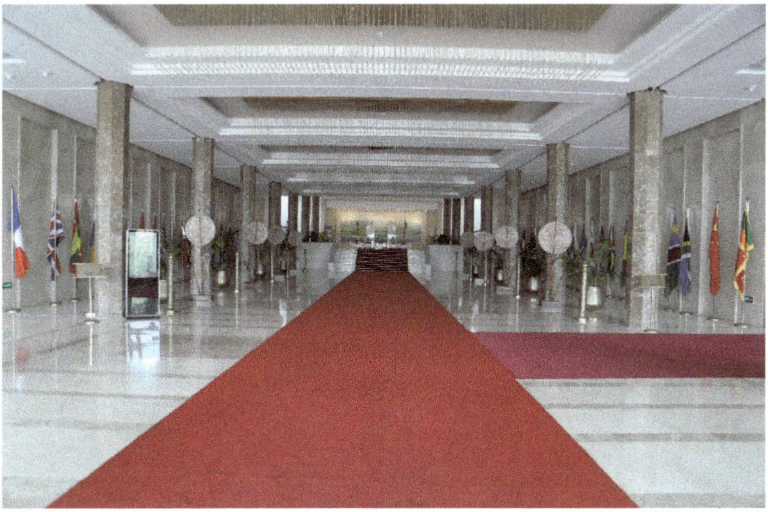

Fig. 5.10 Ground floor entrance, BMICH, photo taken in 2017

architect Edward Durell Stone's US Embassy in New Delhi, India, completed in 1959. The Chinese architects would be familiar with Stone's projects which had been widely published in the *Architectural Record* magazine in the late 1950s (Fig. 5.11). Both the conference hall and the US Embassy shared a sense of lightness and monumentality, which were resulted from the creation of colonnade. Whereas the Embassy's flat roof was supported by golden-leafed steel structure, the conference hall's inward sloping roof was held by octagonal concrete columns covered by white marble (Fig. 5.12). Both buildings' cantilevered roofs were able to protect their main bodies from the sun. In terms of façade behind the colonnades, what is different among the two buildings is that Stone in the Embassy employed a layer of screening with abstract geometric pattern closely following Muslim decoration to cover the air-conditioned office rooms behind, while the conference hall's exterior appearance was featured by glass louvres being able to enhance natural ventilation and only the auditorium space in the central was air-conditioned (Hunting, 2007).

The Bandaranaike Memorial International Conference Hall illustrated a series of inspirations and appropriations. The climatic responsive design, as the most noteworthy feature of tropical architecture, had been widely used by Le Corbusier in Brazil, by Maxwell Fry and Jane Drew in West Africa, by Edward Stone in India, by Minnette de Silva in Sri Lanka and also embodied in domestic buildings erected in Guangzhou, southern China. The BMICH, together with other China-aided buildings in Africa, such as the People's Palace in Conakry, Guinea (1964–1967), the National Theater in Mogadishu, Somalia (1964–1967), and the Friendship Hall in Khartoum,

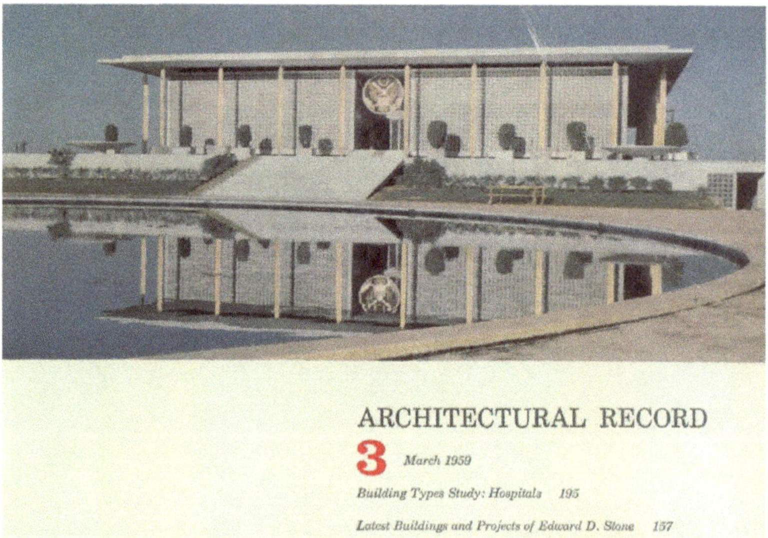

Fig. 5.11 Edward Durell Stone's US Embassy in New Delhi, India, published in the *Architectural Record* magazine, 1959

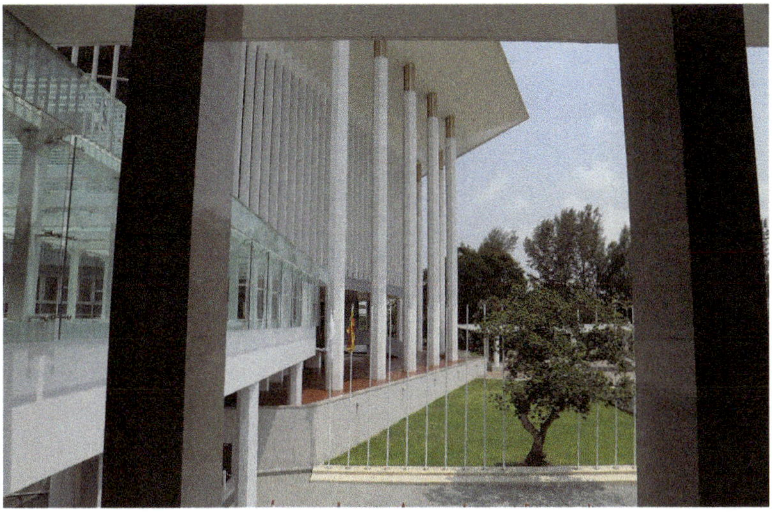

Fig. 5.12 Connection between the hall and auxiliary building, BMICH, photo taken in 2017

Sudan (1971–1976), among others, aligned themselves with the global trend of tropical architecture. The expression of tropical architectural features embodied in these buildings was not only a simply aesthetic consideration, but also associated with both the politics of decolonization in these newly independent nations and the consideration of economic rationality from the perspective of Chinese decision-makers (Chee et al., 2011).

Within the context of Sri Lanka in the 1960s and early 1970s, the adoption of modernist languages embodied in the BMICH was not an exception, as pavilions built in the Colombo Industrial Exhibition of 1965 also followed the principles of the tropical modernist approach (Pieris, 2012). During the same period, both Geoffrey Bawa and Valentine Gunasekara had also built modernist hotels and private villas, albeit their different aesthetic tastes and serving different clients (the former designed for elite clients while the latter for working middle class) (Pieris, 2007). However, this tropical modernist tendency was gradually fading since the late 1970s, as the widespread availability of air-conditioning equipment enabled architects to rely on mechanical techniques to ensure bodily comforts within the interior. As a result, in the renovation of BMICH in 2013, the louvres were replaced by window wall, and the lobby part was fully air-conditioned (Fig. 5.13).

5.6 The Materiality of "Appropriation"

The design and construction of the BMICH not only involved the contribution and creativity of architects, engineers, and builders from China's leading state-owned

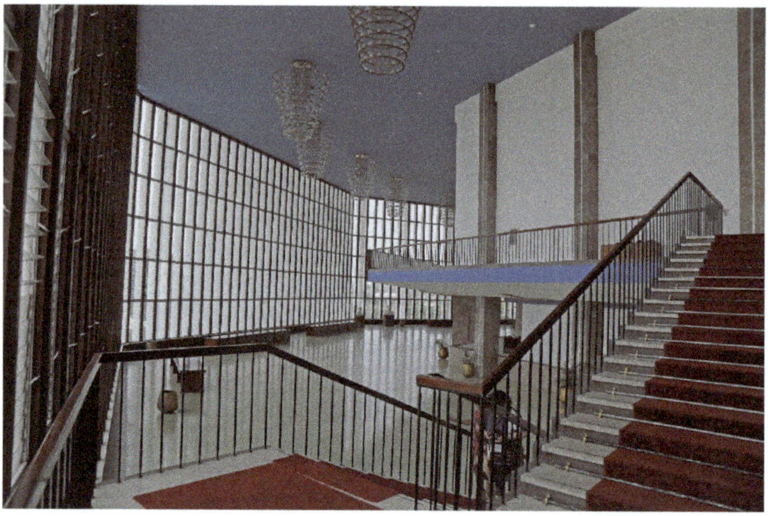

Fig. 5.13 Lobby of BMICH, the cladding was once louvre, changed to glass wall in 2013, photo taken in 2017

design institute and construction companies, but also appropriated and used the best quality of building materials produced in China, such as the white marble and state-of-the-art air-conditioning equipment (Fig. 5.14). In the early 1970s, the air-conditioned auditoriums in China might be less than 10 in number. The project illustrated Chinese government's generosity, commitment and dedication to selflessly

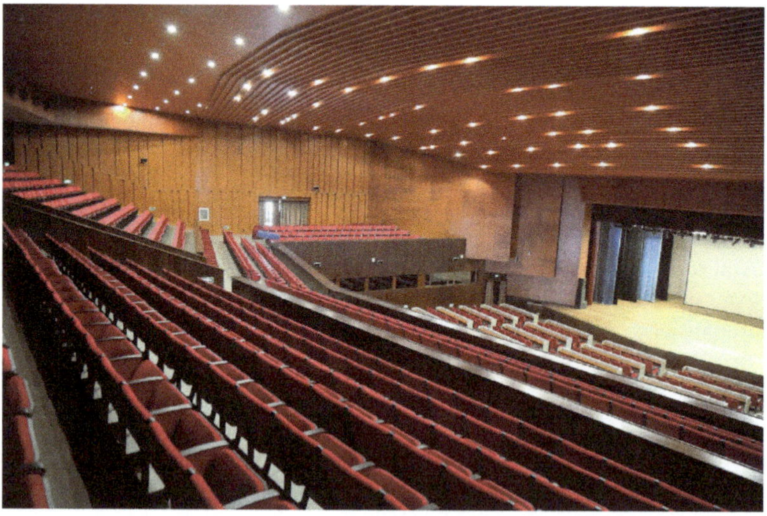

Fig. 5.14 Auditorium of BMICH, instant translation facilities were installed in 1973, photo taken in 2017

helping other developing nations, despite its weak economic condition at that time. To fulfill its commitment, China had from late 1970 to early 1973 sent around 450 technicians and builders who, together with 900 Sri Lankans, were involved in the labor-intensive construction.

As one of the 50 Chinese carpenters working for the BMICH, Tao Jinbiao had taught his Sri Lankan counterparts to use woodworking machinery and tools, thus helped elevate their carpenter skills, cultivate talents and speed up construction (You et al., 2012). While the language differences between Chinese and Sinhalese builders created some communication barriers, they quickly found ways and techniques to work together. It is worth noting that many Chinese builders were largely confined to the specific area of construction site and had little interaction with locals except some organized surrounding trips. A few senior leaders had opportunities to be invited to visit the house of local engineers and to attend party activities. The construction site had also become a crucial venue for social exchange and cultural interactions. The Chinese had showed some war-related films such as *Tunnel Warfare*, and *Landmine Warfare*. When the Chinese sports delegations visited Colombo, they were invited to the construction site and to demonstrate their skills and to share some domestic news.

The majority of materials and equipment, including gold, marble, steel, silver tableware, generators, and sofas were donated by China (You, 2007). Due to a severe shortage of foreign exchange, Sri Lanka was unable to buy the large machinery necessary for construction, but offering basic equipment and raw materials (sand, cement, wood and stone) (Fig. 5.15). The wooded panels used in the interior decoration were produced locally, but the exquisite details, including the wooden railings of the grand staircase, were all hand-made by highly skilled Chinese woodworkers. In order to decorate the interior space, China shipped more than 3,000 pieces of furniture and

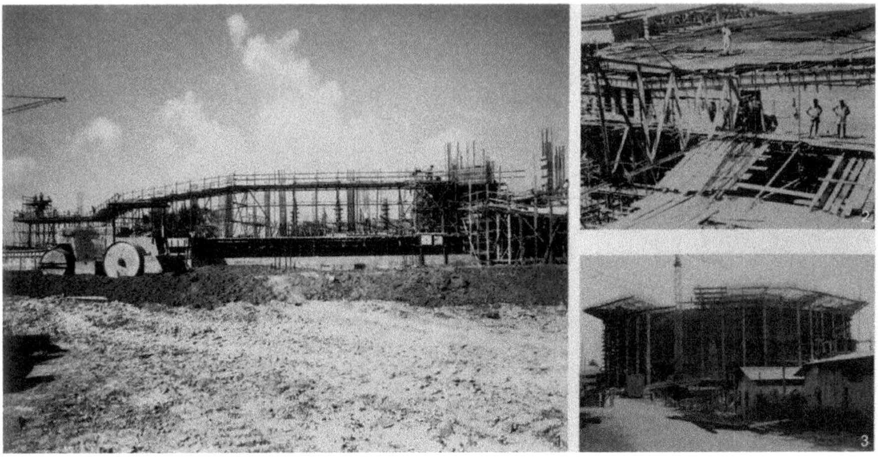

Fig. 5.15 Construction process of the BMICH, 1970s (Courtesy of China Architecture Design and Research Group)

used 1.5 tons of silver to cast more than 50,000 pieces of shiny silver alloy tableware. Structural engineer You Baoxian, who has been working on site for nearly 3 years, handed over the tableware and furniture to the local management.

The project using Chinese and Sri Lankan materials, skills and knowledge was described by Sri Lankan authorities as symbolic of the robust relationship between the two nations. The building has become a remarkable material presence of modern Chinese architecture beyond the nation, demonstrating unique cultural memory, identity and meaning. The building materials it used and the architectural skills required to carefully combine these materials convey a special material culture. For example, the slim concrete colonnade around the building is veneered with white marble produced and shipped from China's Shandong Province, while the white color conveyed a sense of coolness in a hot and humid environment. Similarly, the indoor terrazzo floor, mosaic floor, wooden wall skirt and red clay tile floor appeared hardly novel and luxurious, but they showed high-quality construction skills and craftsmanship.

5.7 The Continuity of "Appropriation"

While China continued to deliver aided projects to Sri Lanka after completing the BMICH, the formal expression of identity in the subsequently erected new buildings had greatly changed. For instance, the China-aided Colombo Higher Court project (1986–1989), created by Anhui Provincial Architectural Design Institute, adopted a combination of geometric volume as functional body and tented roofs as symbolic requirement (Yu, 1991) (Fig. 5.16). The expression of tropical architectural features, such as *brises-soleil* devices, the sense of lightness and the preoccupation with natural ventilation, was rarely seen. Rather, the Kandyan style octagonal and square roofs with red tiles and towering gestures showcased a more tangle, direct appropriation of historical buildings, which was dramatically different from the subtle, abstract transformation of the BMICH. Perhaps, the post-modernist approach of appropriation

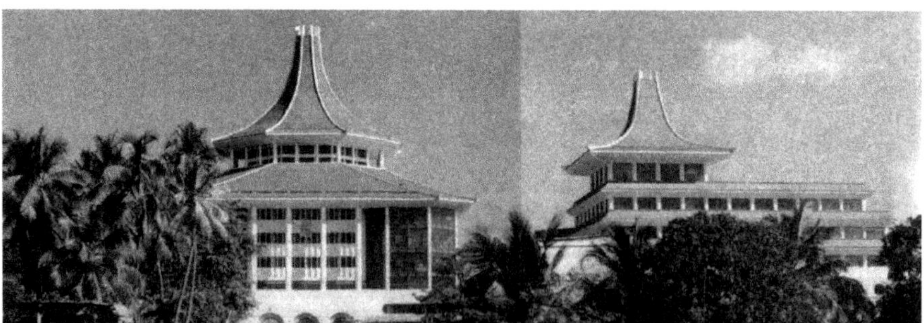

Fig. 5.16 The China-aided Colombo Higher Court, 1989 (Reprinted with permission from the Journal *Jianzhu xuebao*, 1991)

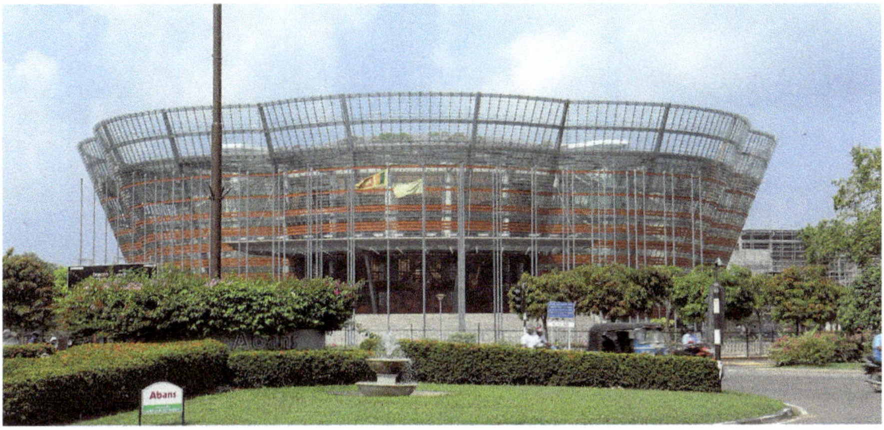

Fig. 5.17 "Nelum Pokuna" Mahinda Rajapaksa Theatre, photo taken in 2017

of historical motifs and elements was more powerful, for architects and officials, to form a recognizable identity.

In the last quarter of the 20th century, Sri Lanka was turbulent by turmoil of Tamil Tiger, and its economy was hence stagnant. In the beginning of the 21th century, the government army got a series of victory and the aurora of ceasefire appeared. After years of legislative and opposition career, Mahinda Rajapaksa came to power, first as Prime Minister in April 2004, and then President in 2005. His aspirations of initiating large-scale infrastructure coincided with China's policy of "going out". The first project of this intention is Colombo National Performing Arts Theater, which was unwaveringly supported by the Chinese government (Fig. 5.17). The agreement was signed on July 8, 2004, in which Chinese government provided support equivalent to US$ 17 million, accounting to 2/3 of the investment.

The site of national theater was around 1 km south to the BMICH. It was jointly designed by Kahawita De Silva & Associates of Colombo and Beijing Institute of Architectural Design (BIAD). When the Colombo Theater was designed in 2005, a movement of constructing grand theater and other cultural mega-structure was heated in China. Several high-profile grand theaters had stood in the Chinese cities, for example, Shanghai Grand Theater designed by Jean-Marie Charpentier (1939–2010) of France in 1998; Dongguan grand theater and Hangzhou grand theater both designed by Carlos Ott of Canada, 2005 and Oriental Art Center of Shanghai, designed by Paul Andreu (1938–2018) of France in 2005. The controversial national theater of Beijing, designed by Paul Andreu, was in the interior fitting out. BIAD was the local architect of national theater, and the company was ready technically to design theater anywhere.

The auditorium of 1,288 seats is in the center, surrounded by lobby and auxiliary rooms (Fig. 5.18). The building plate is basically a circle made of eight petals, inspired by the 12th century Nelum Pokuna (Lotus Pond) in Polonnaruwa. The slanting cladding was made of steel and glass louvres like a net, which gives interior

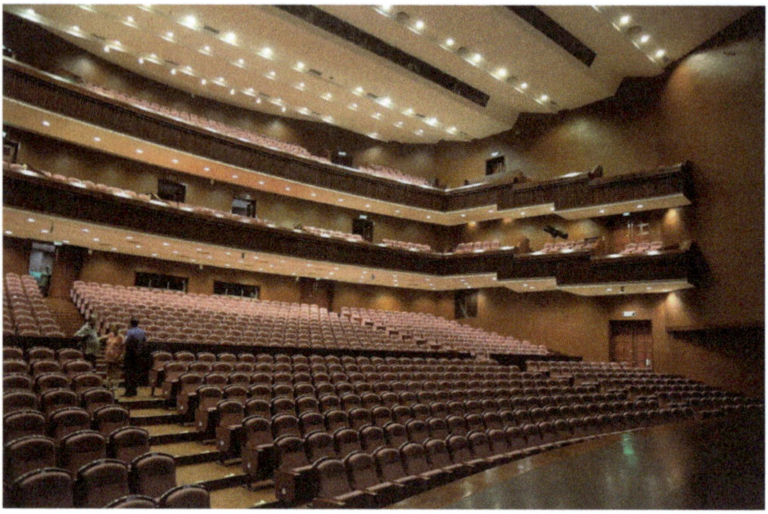

Fig. 5.18 Auditorium of Nelum Pokuna Theater, photo taken in 2017

natural lighting and ventilation. Natural ventilation in the shade, instead of enclosed air-con, is a good convention of tropical architecture found everywhere in Sri Lanka. Together with high skylight, the light-weight wall makes the interior of lobby vital (Fig. 5.19). Green grass and bushes grow on the floor of angular shaped balcony, they face upwards towards open sky. The white column capital was wrapped by traditional Lankan wooden decoration, punctuating the location. The auditorium is equipped with upholstered chair, wood floor and acoustic wall, while the roof garden accommodates an open amphitheater. The main stage of 36 m × 30 m is mechanically controlled, where modules of stage floor can be elevated or sunken to facilitate various performances from vernacular dancing to philharmonic orchestra.

The Nelum Pokuna Theater was constructed by Yantai Construction Ltd of Shandong Province, China, from 2006 to 2011. The company has undertaken many overseas projects. In the peak time, there were more than 1,000 Chinese and Lankan workers on site. Most Chinese technicians were born in the 1980s, long after the BMICH was completed. These young technicians were brought up in cities after China's open-door policy. The living and working conditions contrasted sharply with those in China. In the tropical weather of more than 30 or 40 degree Celsius, workers operated under the sunshine, facing the vapored concrete and welding sparkling. During the construction, the final battle between the government military forces and Tamil Tiger took place in Colombo. The Chinese technicians spent a hard and unforgettable time.

The theater was completed in November 2011, and was named after the president, "Nelum Pokuna" Mahinda Rajapaksa Theatre. It has accommodated many international events. Both the BMICH and Nelum Pokuna Theater serve the country's

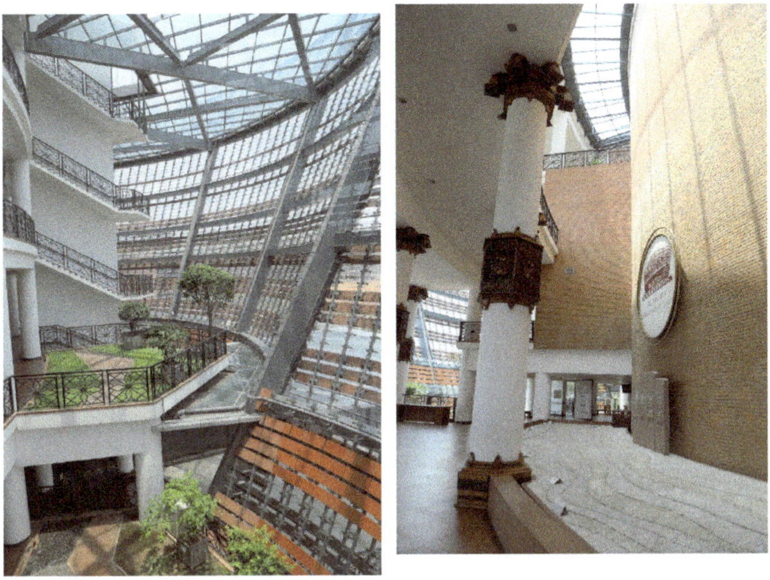

Fig. 5.19 Lobby of the Nelum Pokuna Theater. The external wall can breathe, photos taken in 2017

mission and vision, and play a visible role of nation building. The practice of tropical modernism was usually in small scale buildings, like a coffee shop, restaurant or house. At most, the method was used in hotel building, like Bawa's design as discussed below. Nelum Pokuna is a cultural mega-structure which resolutely embodies the characteristics of Sri Lankan culture and climate. If BMICH is the early step Chinese architects experimented tropical modernism, Nelum Pokuna was a matured exchange of Chinese and Lankan architectural knowledge. The theater ushers a series of infrastructure and civil projects in the country. Chinese construction companies undertook the tasks of building a highway, port, and TV tower and a brand new city development (Port City Colombo) in Sri Lanka and became principal shareholders in the Hambantota International Port Services Company (HIPS) in the 21th century.

5.8 A Reversed "Appropriation"

The top-down exportation of Chinese architecture to Sri Lanka was also paralleled by the bottom-up importation of Sri Lankan architecture culture by the Chinese architectural professionals. Among them, the work of Bawa undoubtedly dominated this exchange process. Chinese architects first came to know Bawa's architecture through Western architectural publications. Since the early 1980s they paid increasingly more attention to modern Western architecture, and the limited publications on

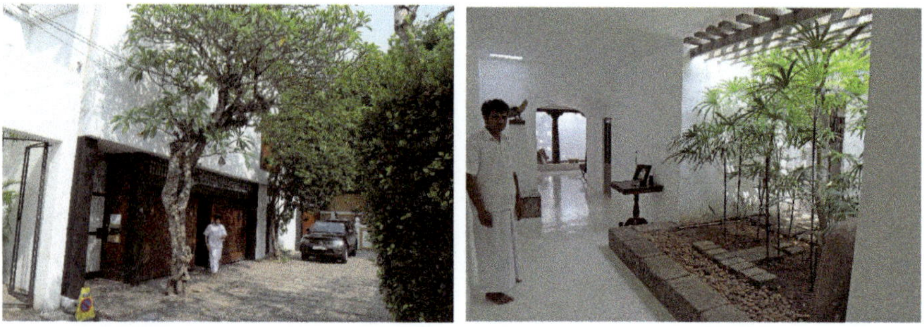

Fig. 5.20 Bawa's house in Colombo, photos taken in 2017

Bawa's buildings that appeared in 1980s China were largely translated from Western architectural magazines. The introduction of Bawa's Parliamentary Complex and the University of Ruhunu projects, published in the Chinese journal *Shijie jianzhu* [World Architecture] in 1982 and 1989 respectively, did not give rise to scholarly response (Guan, 1982; Luo, 1989).

It was reported that a number of architects had traveled to Sri Lanka since the late 1990s and been touched by the characteristics of simplicity, nature, local (foreign) culture and poetry manifested in Bawa's work (Wang, 2008; Yang, 2001) (Fig. 5.20). However, the Chinese architectural community at the turn of the millennium was largely preoccupied with formal novelty of contemporary Western architecture. It seemed that Bawa's buildings lack unique formal identity and experimental languages, and thus can hardly provide immediate formal inspirations. In the booming design market at the early 2000s, even some architects appropriated Bawa's formal languages, they would be reluctant to acknowledge this aesthetic appropriation.

What made Bawa's reputation sudden resurgence in recent years is that a younger generation of Chinese architects and academics tried to highlight an alternative experience through reading, experiencing and discussing his work. The bodily experience they gained from Bawa's tropical buildings was quite different from that of modern architecture massively produced in China's urban process and became a refreshing complement to the works of international star-architects. Under the organization of cultural intermediaries such as the Shenzhen-based *Youfang-Position*, a private architectural agent and media platform, several groups of architects traveled to Sri Lanka to visit Bawa's buildings.[7] The organized trips, seminars and various publications associated with Bawa's work written by international authors and domestic architects

[7] For the organizer of *Youfang-Position*, Sri Lanka was one destination of their many planned travel routes. Other similar destinations include India, Japan, the United States, Western Europe, Latin America and other places. During each tour a scholar or architect was invited to serve as the academic leader, and the group members included professional architects and/or architecture students. Given the relatively lower level of consumption and architects' stable economic foundation, the study tour to Sri Lanka has become affordable and popular. Once finishing the tour, participating members will be encouraged to write essays to be published on social media.

profoundly promoted the dissemination of his ideas among the Chinese architectural community.

The purposeful promotion of Bawa's work both reinforces some traditions and obscures some facts. For example, in October 2016, the Beijing-based journal *Jianzhu xuebao* [Architectural Journal], the Institute of Architecture Criticism of the Beijing University of Civil Engineering and Architecture, and the Guangzhou Fei Architects jointly organized a Geoffrey Bawa symposium themed "Accessing Tradition, Accessing Modernity" (*Pingshi chuantong, shiyong xiandai*). Held at the Bawa-designed Bentota Hotel near Colombo, the symposium invited about ten Chinese architects and scholars, whose speech notes and essays were later published in *Jianzhu xuebao*'s special issue on Bawa's work. A close reading of both these published articles and other associated papers reveal the following characteristics:

Firstly, the Chinese architects' interpretation perspective on Bawa's work implied their own long-term preoccupation with specific design issues. Consider, for instance, Jin Qiuye's closely reading of the plan evolution of Bawa's house design (Jin & Chang, 2020), Ge Ming's interest in Bawa's section design (Ge & Chen, 2017) and Dong Yugan's focus on Bawa's courtyards and staircase design (Dong, 2017). These architect-academics shared an interest in transforming the heritage of Chinese traditional scholarly gardens into languages of contemporary design, while Bawa's approaches to dealing with topography, landscape, and courtyard spaces seemed to provide a contemporary exemplar. To put this differently, Bawa's architecture that echoed the construction methods and space creation of traditional Chinese gardens offered a formal, spatial and intellectual benchmark upon which contemporary Chinese architects might draw certain inspirations (Fig. 5.21).

Secondly, while it is less clear that these architects directly appropriate Bawa's formal languages, Bawa's design method, particularly his approach of "bricolage", had a subtle influence on their creative works. The way in which Bawa carefully arranged combinations of diverse domestic objects and things in his house in 33rd Lane, Colombo, could also been seen in Jin Qiuye's interior designs in Beijing. Like Bawa, the various objects in Jin's projects "allowed for the articulation of different narratives" (Jones, 2012). They re-arranged what was already there and created new meanings and experience.

Similarly, in the eyes of Zhuang and Hua (2014), Bawa's approach of "bricolage" created hybrid forms and spaces that cannot be easily classified, categorized or identified, something they called a system of the unrecognizable. For them, the unrecognizable system incorporated the marginal, the hybrid, the everyday and the less creative buildings, which were normally excluded from the modernist canon. Interestingly enough, it is no accident that Zhuang's recent practices tended to focus on the abandoned spaces and inconspicuous urban territories, trying to rebuild a kind of spatial and structural order, for example, in his recently completed Pocket Plaza at the Yongjia Road in Shanghai. In this regard, one can also add the case of Dong Yugan who was fascinated by Bawa's courtyard design. Although it is hard to say that his courtyard construction directly benefited from Bawa, he at least saw and would probably be moved by these familiar scenes in Bawa's work.

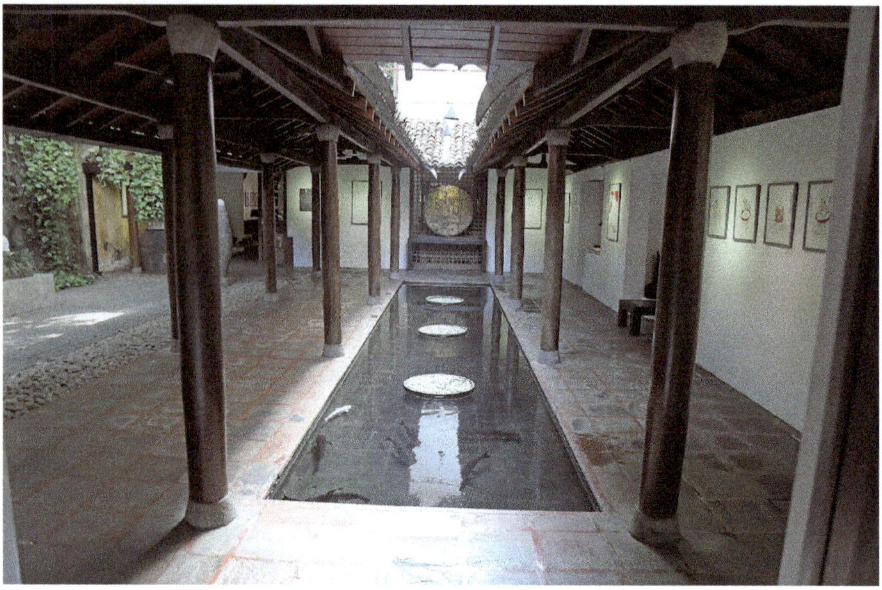

Fig. 5.21 Bawa's design studio in the 1980s, now used as a coffee shop, photo taken in 2017

Thirdly, while the abovementioned architect-academics promoted and reinterpreted contemporary Sri Lankan architecture culture, their "appropriation" was highly selective and intellectually instrumental. The focus of these discussions is on the buildings themselves, confined to the architect Bawa alone (without mentioning the work of Minnette de Silva and Valentine Gunasekara, let alone their connections and differences), particularly his elite villas and boutique hotels, and did not involve the social context of contemporary Sri Lanka. Behind this climate-sensitive, hospitality-oriented, and indigenizing practice, a common identity that Sri Lanka architecture has presented globally, both international scholars and Chinese architects overlooked the humane responses required of professionals during conflict and post-tsunami reconstruction (Pieris, 2020). The Chinese architects seemed to have seen their long-awaited "ideal world" (*lixiang shijie*) and "spiritual home" (*jingshen jiayuan*) in Bawa's architecture.

These architect-academics ignored the huge social and wealthy differences between noble and rich family-inherited Bawa and majority grassroots Lankans who live in poverty. These Chinese scholars turned back to the context for which Bawa was once working. Even in the capital city of Sri Lanka, there are very few traffic lights in the city center in the 21st century. The best-quality highway, from Colombo to the international airport, was built by the Chinese companies. In many respects, Bawa represents the perfect fantasy of Chinese architectural circles for an architect, as he came from a nobleman, received elite education, traveled around the world, fully expressed his self-awareness, and created an ideal world and aesthetic paradise in his own land and house while ignoring the surrounding chaotic world. This subjective projection towards an "exotic" world is mostly a one-sided impression, and it is also a deliberate avoidance of the reality in which we live today.

5.9 Conclusion

By focusing on the architectural exchange between China and Sri Lanka, this chapter investigates the process, method and value of the mobility of ideas, materials and labor. While appropriation has played a significant role in the transnational and transcultural architectural practice, the purpose of traveling ideas was to formulate new knowledge and establish unique identities. Sri Lanka's tropical modern architecture, as Tariq Jazeel (2017) has argued, can never be considered simply "art for art's sake." This statement is convincing not only for the works of architects like Minnette de Silva, and Geoffrey Bawa, but also meaningful for the BMICH and Nelum Pokuna theater, despite their architects from China. The projects were deeply entangled with national and international politics and the architects' appropriation of a wide range of forms and sources contributed to the formation of national and international identity of Sri Lanka.

To be more specific, considering the 1960s ethnic conflict between the Sinhalese majority and the Tamil minority in terms of political rights and languages, the remarkable octagonal form of the BMICH demonstrated Sinhalese Buddhist nationalism and became their explicit political manifestations, on the one hand. As Sri Lanka intended to build the BMICH to host the Asian-African International Conference and later held the fifth Summit Conference of Heads of State or Government of the Non-Aligned Movement in 1976, the conference hall completed the reception and display tasks of the event, marking the peak of its international influence, on the other hand. In addition to the formal political assembly, the BMICH and Nelum Pokuna Theater frequently serve for civic usages like company annual dinner, college graduation ceremony and performance by foreign artist troupes.

Behind the process of identity formation, the BMICH also epitomized the mobility and assembly of Chinese labor, materials, technologies, craftsmanship and vision. Despite little scholarly discussion on the project, the building can be considered one of the most remarkable representatives of Chinese modernist architecture produced in the 1960s and 70s. Its completion and quality were indispensable from the Chinese government's efforts to mobilize the best resources available, both human and material, to fulfill its promise. For architect Dai Nianci, the experimentation with elements of modernist architecture and local tradition explicitly manifested in his intention of integrating traditional Sri Lankan architectural decoration with a modern concept. Thanks to the opportunity of architectural aid and the vision of Sri Lankan leaders, his pro-modernist ideas were materialized better in Colombo than in any of his projects in China. As the architectural historian (Zou, 2001) noted, compared with the complex domestic circumstances, the reduced restrictions on aid projects allowed architects to experiment with a critical modernist approach. The Nelum Pokuna Theater was a continuity and reflection of China's heat of constructing grand theaters in the 21st century. In the socialist and revolutionary years, China mainly built congress buildings like the Great Hall of the People in 1959 Beijing. Its technical experiences were used in China's foreign aid projects and crystalized in around 20 conference buildings – "People's palace" in some countries and BMICH in Sri Lanka. When the economic development replaced revolution, grand theaters for performance were suitable for middle class consumption, children education, cultural production and city's brand. This transition also resulted more than 10 grand theaters overseas (Xue, 2019).

China's architectural aid to Sri Lanka was not a one-way exportation. Conversely, Sri Lankan modernist architecture had a subtle influence on the Chinese architectural community. Since the 1960s onwards, China continued to provide Sri Lanka with its expertise, materials, capital and labors that were desperately needed for large-scale architectural construction and urban expansion. In recent decades, a number of Chinese architects were fascinated by the tropical atmosphere, spatial and temporal experience within contemporary Sri Lankan architecture, particularly demonstrated in Bawa's works. If there are any limitations in this exchange process, it is that Chinese architects were more active, whether they went out to carry out oversea design or introduced Sri Lankan architectural culture to domestic audiences. On the contrary, owing to some practical reasons, Sri Lankan architects has neither substantively participated in the China-aided projects nor extensively practiced in the Chinese design market, as many Western architects have done over the past two decades.

Acknowledgements The authors heartily thank the kind help from Dr. Anoma Kumarasuriyar, Chandra and Lal. Unless noted, all photos were taken by the authors. This chapter is part of a research supported by the National Natural Science Foundation of China, Project No. 51878584.

References

Bjone, C. (2014). *Philip Johnson and His Mischief: Appropriation in Art and Architecture.* Images Publishing.

Chang, L. (1953). Ceylon's trade with communist China. *Far Eastern Survey, 22*(6), 70–72.

Chang, W. (2020). *Aid, Sport and Architectural Exportation–A Study of China's Foreign-aided Stadiums from the 1950s to the 21st Century.* City University of Hong Kong.

Chee, L., Chang, J. H., & Wong, B. C. T. (2011). Introduction–tropicality-inmotion: Situating tropical architecture. *Singapore Journal of Tropical Geography, 32*, 277–282.

Chong, B. (1953). Silan jiqi xiangjiao [Ceylon and its rubber]. *Shijie zhishi [World Knowledge], (01)*, 16–17. 崇宾. 锡兰及其橡胶. 世界知识, 1953 (01), 16–17.

Ding, G., & Xue, C. Q. L. (2015). China's architectural aid: Exporting a transformational modernism. *Habitat International, 47*, 136–147.

Dong, Y. (2017). Bawa zhi ting [Bawa's Courtyards]. *Jianzhu xuebao [Architectural Journal], (03)*, 6–12. 董豫赣.巴瓦之庭.建筑学报, 2017(03), 6–12.

Fang Yi Zhuan Bianxiezu. (2008). *Fang Yi Zhuan* [Bibliography of Fang Yi]. Beijing: People's Press. 方毅传编写组. 方毅传. 北京: 人民出版社, 2008.

Ge, M., Chen, J. (2017). Jiefoli bawa poumian yanjiu [Research on Jeffrey Bawa's Section]. *Jianzhu xuebao [Architectural Journal], (03)*, 13–18. 葛明,陈洁萍. 杰弗里·巴瓦剖面研究.建筑学报, 2017 (03), 13–18.

Guan, D. (1982) Sili lanka xin guohui dasha [Sri Lanka's New Parliament Building Colombo]. *Shijie jianzhu [World Architecture], (05)*, 34–36. 杰夫里·巴万, 关道询.科伦坡,斯里兰卡新国会大厦. 世界建筑, 1982 (05), 34–36.

Hunting, M. A. (2007). *Edward Durell Stone: Perception and Criticism*. City University of New York.

Jazeel, T. (2017). Tropical Modernism/Environmental Nationalism: The Politics of Built Space in Postcolonial Sri Lanka. *Fabrications, 27*(2), 134–152.

Ji, Y. (1958). Youyi yu maoyi: Ji zhongguo shangpin zhanlanhui zai kelunpo [Friendship and Trade: The Chinese Commodity Exhibition in Colombo]. *Shijie zhishi [World Knowledge], (09)*, 28–29. 吉茵.友谊与贸易: 记中国商品展览会在科伦坡.世界知识, 1958 (09), 28–29.

Jin, Q., Chang, T. (2020) Bawa jianzhu de kongjian fuzaxing: fangxiang, dengji he guishu [The Spatial Complexity of Bawa's Architecture: Direction, Hierarchy and Attribution]. *Jianzhu xuebao [Architectural Journal], (02)*, 16–22. 金秋野,常涛.巴瓦建筑的空间复杂性: 方向、归属和等级. 建筑学报, 2020 (02), 16–22.

Jones, R. D. (2012). 'Thinking' the domestic interior in postcolonial South Asia: The home of geoffrey bawa in Sri Lanka, 1960 to 1998. *Interiors, 3*(3), 203–226.

Kelegama, J. B. (2002) Significance of Ceylon-China Trade Agreement of 1952. Keynote Address at the Fiftieth Anniversary Celebrations of the historic "Rubber-Rice Pact" between Sri Lanka and China at the BMICH. https://island.lk/significance-of-ceylon-china-trade-agreement-of-1952/. Accessed 15 June 2021.

Lawrence, A. R., & Miljački, A. (Eds.). (2018). *Terms of Appropriation: Modern Architecture and Global Exchange*. Routledge.

Liu, F. (2015) Wo suo jingli de yuanwai gongcheng sheji deng gongzuo [My Experience of Foreign-aid Project Design and Other Work]. In Book Editorial Committee (Eds.), *Suiyue qinghuai: yuan jiangongbu beijing gongye jianzhu shejiyuan tongren huiyi* [Feelings of Time: Memories of Colleagues from the Beijing Industrial Architectural Design Institute, Ministry of Architectural Engineering]. Shanghai: Tongji University Press, pp. 150–157. 刘福顺. "我所经历的援外工程设计等工作"//岁月情怀: 原建工部北京工业建筑设计院同仁回忆. 本书编委会编.上海: 同济大学出版社, 2015, 150–157.

Lu, D. (2012). Introduction: Architecture, modernity and identity in the third world. In D. Lu (Ed.), *Third World Modernism: Architecture* (pp. 1–28). Routledge.

Luo, S. (1989). Luhunu daxue, sili lanka [Ruhunu University, Sri Lanka]. *Shijie jianzhu [World Architecture], (02)*, 52. 罗森.鲁呼奴大学, 斯里兰卡. 世界建筑. (02), 52.

Peebles, P. (2006). *The History of Sri Lanka Westport*. Greenwood Press.

Pieris, A. (2007). Modernism at the margins of the vernacular: Considering valentine gunasekara. *Grey Room., 28*, 56–85.

Pieris, A. (2012). Modernity and Revolution: The Architecture of Ceylon's Twentieth-century Exhibitions. In D. Lu (Ed.), *Third World Modernism: Architecture* (pp. 141–164). Routledge.

Pieris, A. (2020). Defensive alterity in contemporary Sri Lankan architecture. In S. Chattopadhyay & J. White (Eds.), *The Routledge Companion to Critical Approaches to Contemporary Architecture* (pp. 200–214). Routledge.

Roskam, C. (2015). Non-aligned architecture: China's designs on and in Ghana and Guinea, 1955–92. *Architectural History, 58*, 261–291.

Sanders, J. (2006). *Adaptation and Appropriation*. Routledge.

Said, E. W. (1983). Traveling theory. *The World, the Text, and the Critic* (pp. 226–247). Harvard University Press.

Verri, V. G. (2020). Gifting architecture: China and the national stadium in Costa Rica, 2007–2011. *Architectural History, 63*, 283–311.

Vives-Ferrándiz, J. (2010). Mobility, Materiality and Identities in Iron Age East Iberia: On the Appropriation of Material Culture and the Question of Judgement. In P. Dommelen & A. B.

Knapp (Eds.), *Material Connections in the Ancient Mediterranean: Mobility, Materiality and Identity* (pp. 190–209). Routledge.

Wang, X. (2008) "Sililanka yiyun: jiefuli bawa yu diyu jianzhu de shijian" [The Legacy of Sri Lanka: Geoffrey Bawa and the Practice of Regional Architecture]. *Nanfang jianzhu [Southern Architecture], (01)*, 30–36. 王小东. 斯里兰卡遗韵:杰弗里·巴瓦与地域建筑的实践.南方建筑, 2008 (01), 30–36.

Wijetunge, N. R. (2013). Unearthing what underlies elite domestic works of geoffrey bawa and valentine gunasekara. *Journal of the Royal Asiatic Society of Sri Lanka, New Series, 58*(1), 67–88.

Xue, C. Q. L. (Ed.). (2019). *Grand Theater Urbanism: Chinese Cities in the 21st Century*. Springer.

Xue, C. Q. L., Ding, G., Chang, W., & Wan, Y. (2019). Architecture of "Stadium Diplomacy": China-aid Sport Buildings in Africa. *Habitat International, 90*, 1–11.

Yang, T. (2001) Dangdai difangxing yu sililanka jianzhushi jiefoli bawa: ping jiefoli bawa de sanjian zuopin [Contemporary Locality and Sri Lankan Architect Geoffrey Bawa: Comment on the Three Works of Geoffrey Bawa], *Shijie jianzhu [World Architecture], (12)*, 76–79. 杨滔.当代地方性与斯里兰卡建筑师杰佛里·巴瓦——评杰佛里·巴瓦的三件作品.世界建筑,2001 (12), 76–79.

Yu, Z. (1991) Sili lanka gaoji fayuan zonghe gongcheng de chuangzuo gousi ji shijian [The Design Conception and Practice of the Comprehensive Project of Sri Lanka High Court]. *Jianzhu xuebao [Architectural Journal], (06)*, 43–48. 俞祖彭. 斯里兰卡高级法院综合工程的创作构思及实践. 建筑学报, 1991 (06), 43–48.

Yuan, J. (1991) *Jianzhu manji* [Notes on Architecture]. Beijing: China Architecture and Building Press. 袁镜身. 记班达拉奈克国际会议大厦的落成//建筑漫记. 北京: 中国建筑工业出版社, 1991.

Yuan, J. et al. (2002) *Jianyuan, fazhan, zhuangda* [The Establishment of the Institute, Development and Expanding]. In J. Wang, et al. (Eds.), *Zhongguo jianzhu sheji yanjiuyuan chengli wushi zhounian jinian congshu: licheng pian* [The 50th Anniversary Album of China Architecture Design and Research Group: History]. Beijing: Tsinghua University Press, pp. 14–26. 袁镜身, 建院、发展、壮大//中国建筑设计研究院五十周年纪念丛书:历程篇. 北京:清华大学出版社, 2002, 14–26.

You, B. et al. (2012) *Jianzhu zhongsi youyi zhi mingzhu: jinian banda la naike guoji huiyi dasha yuanjian jishi* [Building the Pearl of Sino-Sri Lanka Friendship: Documentary of the China-aided Bandaranaike Memorial International Conference Building]. Beijing: China Architecture and Building Press. 由宝贤等编著. 建筑中斯友谊之明珠: 纪念班达拉奈克国际会议大厦援建纪实. 北京: 中国建筑工业出版社, 2012.

You, B. (2007) *Yi bandalanaike guoji huiyi dasha de sheji* [Recalling the Design of Bandaranaike Memorial International Conference Hall]. In Zhongguo jianzhu sheji yanjiuyuan (Eds.), *Jianzhushi zhaji* [Architect's Notes] Beijing: Tsinghua University Press, pp. 290–295. 由宝贤. 忆班达拉奈克国际会议大厦的设计//中国建筑设计研究院主编, 建筑师札记. 北京: 清华大学出版社, 2007, 290–295.

Young, J. O. (2008) *Cultural Appropriation and the Arts*. Wiley-Blackwell.

Zhonghua renmin gongheguo waijiaobu, Zhongyang wenxian yanjiushi (Eds.). (1990). *Zhou enlai waijiao wenxuan* [The Diplomatic Documents of Zhou Enlai] Beijing: The Central Committee of the Chinese Communist Party Literature Press. 中华人民共和国外交部、中央文献研究室 周恩来外交文选 北京: 中央文献出版社, 1990.

Zhongyang wenxian yanjiushi (Eds.). (1992). *Selected Important Documents since 1949*, Vol. 11. Beijing: The Central Committee of the Chinese Communist Party Literature Press. 中央文献研究室编, 建国以来重要文献选编第11卷. 北京: 中央文献出版社, 1992.

Zhuang, S., & Hua, X. (2014) Fei shibie tixi de yizhong gaodu: jiefuli bawa de jianzhu shijie [An Altitude of Unrecognizable System: The Architectural World of Geoffrey]. *Jianzhu xuebao [Architectural Journal], (11)*, 27–35. 庄慎, 华霞虹. 非识别体系的一种高度——杰弗里·巴瓦的建筑世界.建筑学报,2014 (11), 27–35.

Zou, D. (2001) *Zhongguo jianzhushi tushuo: xiandaijuan* [A Pictorial History of Modern Chinese Architecture]. Beijing: China Architecture and Building Press. 邹德侬. 中国建筑史图说. 北京: 中国建筑工业出版社, 2001.

Zubrzycki, G. (Ed.). (2017). *National Matters: Materiality, Culture, and Nationalism.* Stanford University Press.

Guanghui Ding is Associate Professor of Architecture at the Beijing University of Civil Engineering and Architecture in China. He completed his Ph.D. in architecture from the University of Nottingham, United Kingdom in 2013 and later worked as a Postdoctoral Research Fellow at City University of Hong Kong. His research focuses on modern and contemporary Chinese architecture, including many subjects in critical architecture, architectural criticism and periodicals, design institutes and China's architectural aid in the Global South. He is the author of *Constructing a Place of Critical Architecture in China: Intermediate Criticality in the Journal* Time + Architecture (London and New York: Routledge, 2016) (Chinese edition,《建筑批评的一朵浪花: 实验性建筑》Beijing: China Architecture and Building Press, 2018) and co-author of *A History of Design Institutes in China: From Mao to Market* (London and New York: Routledge, 2018, with Charlie Qiuli Xue) (expanded Chinese edition,《中国设计院: 价值与挑战》Beijing: China Architecture and Building Press, 2022). His scholarly articles have been published by *Architecture and Culture, Architectural Research Quarterly, ARENA Journal of Architectural Research, Domus, Habitat International, Histories of Post-War Architecture, Journal of Architecture, Journal of the Society of Architectural Historians, Jianzhushi/The Architect, Shidai jianzhu/Time + Architecture, Shijie jianzhu/World Architecture, Xin jianzhu/New Architecture* and other edited volumes.

Charlie Qiuli Xue has taught architecture at Shanghai Jiaotong University, University of Texas and City University of Hong Kong. An award-winning architect and writer, he has published 15 books, including '*Building a Revolution: Chinese Architecture since 1980*' (HKU Press, 2006), '*Hong Kong Architecture 1945–2015: From Colonial to Global*' (Springer, 2016), '*A History of Design Institutes in China: from Mao to Market*' (with G. Ding, Routledge, 2018) and '*Grand Theater Urbanism: Chinese cities in the 21st century*' (Springer, 2019, ed.). He has published more than 160 research papers in professional and international refereed journals and 40 book chapters. His papers are published in such journals as *Cities, Habitat International, Urban Design International, Journal of Architecture, Journal of Urban Design, Architectural Research Quarterly, Journal of Urban History, Planning Perspective, Architecture + Urbanism, Domus and Chinese journals like Architectural Journal, Architect, New Architecture, Time + Architecture, World Architecture and Taiwan Architect*. His book on Hong Kong was awarded by the International Committee of Architectural Critics (CICA) in 2017. Xue's research interests are in Chinese architecture, transnational design and high-density environment. Xue is also extensively involved in design and consultant practice in Hong Kong, Chinese mainland and the US.

Part II
Cross-Border Practice of Design and Construction

Chapter 6
Chinese Medical Projects in Africa: A Case Study of Mahusekwa Hospital in Zimbabwe

Shan Tang, Ze Li, and Keith Amos

Abstract Under the framework of the Belt and Road Initiative, developing cooperation with African countries in the form of medical and health assistance has become an important part of China's foreign policy. The aid mode and social impact of China's aid medical architecture projects to Africa is in urgent need of research. The chapter traces the timeline of China's medical aid projects in Africa, analyzes the construction contexts, and divides the project development process into a sequence of phases. Based on general investigations, the chapter further focuses on Mahusekwa hospital in Zimbabwe as a case, and evaluates its social impacts on economic development, social services, social compatibility and the natural environment via interviews and questionnaires. According to the research results, the chapter brings forward suggestions, like optimizing development policies, encouraging public participation and strengthening departmental collaboration, which could be a reference for the planning and implementation of China's aid construction projects to Africa.

In recent years, China has reshaped the landscape of global aid and emerged as the biggest aid contributor to African countries. Chinese investment in Africa skyrocketed from a mere \$210 million in 2000 to over \$3 billion in 2011 and has since continued to grow. By the end of 2009, Africa became the largest recipient of Chinese foreign aid, accepting 45.7% of China's ¥256.29 billion total foreign aid (IOSC 2011). Chinese aid is subdivided into eight categories: medical teams sent abroad, goods and materials, technical cooperation, complete projects, emergency humanitarian aid, cooperation in human resource development, volunteer programmes in foreign countries and debt relief (Brautigam, 2010; Shimomura & Ohashi, 2013). The white paper on "China's foreign aid" reports that China has provided aid to Africa in the form of thousands of projects that were completed by the end of 2009. These projects have been closely related to the livelihood of Africa's people in areas such as culture and education, electricity, communications, energy industry and health (IOSC 2011). Medical projects, as important public supporting facilities for regional development,

S. Tang · Z. Li (✉) · K. Amos
School of Architecture, Tianjin University, Tianjin, China
e-mail: 53060111@qq.com

C. Q. Xue and G. Ding (eds.), *Exporting Chinese Architecture*,
https://doi.org/10.1007/978-981-19-2786-7_6

with strong public welfare, have extensive and far-reaching social benefits to recipient countries, and become an important component of Chinese foreign aid system.

6.1 Chinese Medical Projects in Africa

With the evolution of international development and China's comprehensive strength in international politics, the scope, mode, management mechanisms and policies of Chinese aid to Africa are also constantly changing (Armstrong, 1977). The characteristics of Chinese aid to Africa have changed extensively over time and can be divided into three developmental stages: free aid to Africa (1956–1978), rational aid to Africa (1979–1995) and institutionalised aid to Africa (1996–2021) (Brautigam, 2009; Samy, 2010; Song, 2021).

6.1.1 Free Aid to Africa (1956–1978)

China began to distribute aid to Africa in 1956 following the Bandung Conference. From 1956 to 1977, China provided more than $2.476 billion in economic aid to African countries, accounting for 58% of China's total foreign aid. During this period, China unilaterally contributed projects, technologies, materials and cash to African countries. The projects focused on the construction of large-scale infrastructure such as transportation, dams and hydropower, and agricultural irrigation facilities. Because of China's relatively weak medical and economic infrastructure, its unilateral medical aid to African countries mainly involved medical assistance teams (Davies & Cao, 2008; Li, 2011). A relatively small number of African medical projects have resulted from Chinese aid. These projects have been fully managed by the Chinese government using a "general delivery department system[1]" and a "contractor department responsible system[2]".

6.1.2 Rational Aid to Africa (1979–1995)

Since the reform and opening-up, China's assistance to Africa has explored a new path of "South–South cooperation". It shifted from unilateral assistance to a new model of cooperative project assistance that included multiple modes, such as

[1] The "general delivery system" refers to a management system used to ensure the timely completion of high-quality foreign aid projects, which, based on the professional nature of the projects, appoints relevant departments to serve as the "general delivery systems".

[2] The "contractor department responsible system" refers to a management system in which the contractor is involved in the whole process from the start of a project to the acceptance and delivery of the project.

escrow and leasing and joint ventures. The cooperative project assistance model solved many problems encountered during the subsequent operation of construction projects. The newer aid projects were small and medium-sized projects that addressed people's livelihoods, such as schools, hospitals, farms and water conservancy facilities (Wang & Elliot, 2014; Zhang & Smith, 2017). Consequently, Chinese assistance in the medical and health sectors intensified, and the number of Chinese-assisted medical projects in Africa increased rapidly. Under the guidance of China's government—enterprise cooperation, the Chinese government's previous "turnkey" approach to project management made way for newer approaches emphasising mutual benefits. These developments saw implementation of the "investment contract system[3]" and the "contract responsibility system[4]".

6.1.3 Institutionalised Aid to Africa (1996–2021)

In 1995, China carried out reforms to diversify the types of aid it provided and the channels of funds used. It also set up special policy banks, such as the Export-Import Bank of China and China Development Bank, and increased the joint construction of multi-field projects. In 2000, the Forum on China–Africa Cooperation[5] (FOCAC) was introduced, formally establishing an institutionalised multilateral consultation and dialogue mechanism between China and Africa . At the third and fourth FOCAC, the Chinese government proposed to build 60 new hospitals in Africa. This saw medical projects become a core focus of China's aid to Africa. In the construction of medical projects, economic benefits and sustainability became the main principles, and project management was transformed from a government-led approach to more government-guided and enterprise-participating approaches (Ding & Xue, 2015; Huang & Ren, 2012).

Over the course of China's 60 year-long provision of aid to Africa, medical projects have become an important means for maintaining a China–Africa partnership based on principles of equality, mutual benefit and win-win cooperation (Chen, 2014; Xue et al., 2019). Since the beginning of the 21st century, China has helped to complete

[3] The "investment contract system" refers to an operation and management system combining responsibility, power and interest, in which relevant departments and units guarantee the scale of construction, total investment, construction period, project quality and material consumption of state-determined construction projects under specified conditions.

[4] The "contract responsibility system" refers to an operation and management system whereby, on the basis of socialist public ownership and in accordance with the principle of proper separation of ownership and management rights, the relationship of responsibility, power and interest between the state and the enterprise is determined through a contract so that the enterprise can implement independent operations and be responsible for its own profits and losses.

[5] The Forum on China–Africa Cooperation (FOCAC), established in 2000, is a mechanism for collective dialogue between the People's Republic of China and African countries within the framework of South-South cooperation. Its members include the People's Republic of China, the 53 African countries that have established diplomatic relations with China, and the African Union Commission.

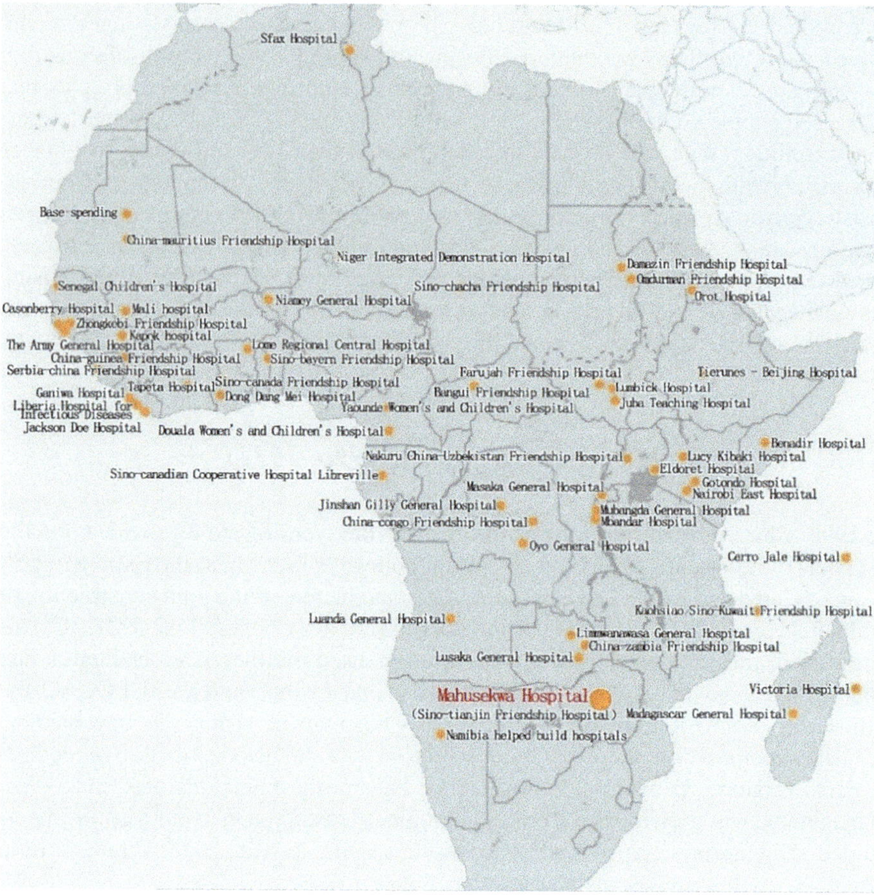

Fig. 6.1 Distribution of part of Chinese medical projects in Africa. Drawn by Shan Tang

more than 60 medical projects in 39 countries and regions in Africa[6] (Fig. 6.1). As important supporting facilities for public services, medical projects promote the development of local public health and meet the health needs of residents (Ban et al., 2016; Zou et al., 2014). They are key to the realisation of many goals of social development and are essential to the coordinated development of the economy, society and the ecological environment.

[6] Information on the number of Chinese medical projects in Africa was retrieved and summarised from the website of the Forum on China–Africa Cooperation: https://www.focac.org/chn/.

6.2 Construction Background

The government of Zimbabwe normally spends a mere 6.2% of its gross expenditure on capital expenditure, a great deal of which (42%) is channelled into agriculture while other critical sectors such as health, energy, and transport receive little to no attention (Chivanga & Monyai, 2020). The African Development Bank conducted a comprehensive study of Zimbabwe's infrastructure development for the period 2011–2020 and concluded that Zimbabwe would need to spend an estimated $14 billion on infrastructure to bring it to a modern threshold. Receiving foreign aid has therefore become an important means for Zimbabwe to improve its infrastructure. Critical to the China–Africa engagement are diplomatic relations between Zimbabwe and China, which have witnessed aid in the implementation of numerous infrastructure projects (Auret, 1990; Shamu et al., 2010).

China and Zimbabwe formally established diplomatic relations in 1980. At the beginning of these diplomatic relations, China provided substantial assistance to Zimbabwe in the fields of agriculture, mining and infrastructure construction through trade, direct investment and developmental cooperation. It also assisted in the construction of the Zimbabwe National Stadium and other public service facilities under the guidance of the rational aid model. In 2002, Zimbabwe put forward the "Look East" policy framework; in the same period, China's government actively promoted the "Go Global" strategy to Chinese enterprises. China and Zimbabwe actively carried out cooperation and exchanges through the FOCAC. Under the guidance of the institutionalised aid model, the two countries further promoted the development of bilateral strategic cooperative partnerships and increased the scale of assistance for infrastructure projects (Palmer, 1990; Vhumbunu, 2017; Zhang, 2014). From 2000 to 2017, China provided $1.7 billion in special loans for infrastructure to Zimbabwe. Chinese foreign aid companies directly participated in the construction of hospitals, schools, roads, railways, water and power supply systems, as well as other public service facilities and infrastructure projects, such as Zimbabwe's new parliament building, Mahusekwa Hospital, the Mazowe orphan school and the Victoria Falls Airport expansion project. China has also stepped up its medical assistance to Zimbabwe in recent years (Sun, 2019). In addition to sending medical teams and providing medical equipment and resources, China's construction of medical projects has played an important role in its aid system to Africa.

Mahusekwa Hospital, also known as "China–Zimbabwe Friendship Hospital", is the first hospital built by China in Zimbabwe after the FOCAC Summit. During the 2006 FOCAC Summit in Beijing, the Chinese government agreed in principle to construct a China–Zimbabwe friendship hospital in the Mahusekwa district of the east province of Mashonaland. In 2009, the Chinese government and the government of Zimbabwe signed a ¥70 million grant agreement for the first phase of construction for the China–Zimbabwe Friendship Hospital. Hunan Architectural Design Institute Group Co. Ltd. assumed responsibility for the control of the project's architectural effect and developed the schematic designs (Fig. 6.2). Nantong Construction Group Co. Ltd. was the contractor responsible for implementing the first phase of the project,

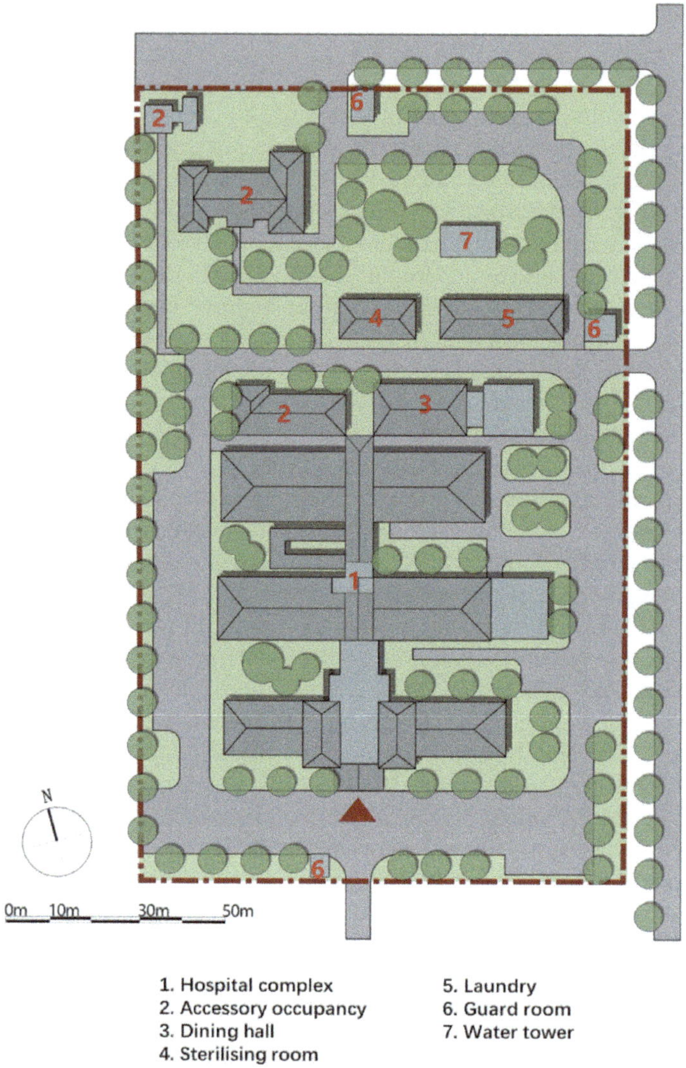

Fig. 6.2 The general layout of Mahusekwa Hospital. Drawn by Shan Tang

and China Railway Sixth Group Co. Ltd was the contractor responsible for implementing the second phase of the project (Table 6.1). The first phase of the project included the construction and furnishing of a 17,000 square-metre hospital with 129 beds, which was completed in 2011 and put into operation in 2013. It also involved the construction of one block of two-storey outpatient and emergency treatment facilities, two blocks of two-storey buildings for inpatient treatment, and the installation of a hospital canteen, a substation and a generator room. In 2017, the governments of

Table 6.1 Main stages of construction for Mahusekwa Hospital

Main stage	Activities	Participants
Project application	The government of Zimbabwe applies for hospital projects to the Chinese government through the Zimbabwe Ministry of Health and Child Welfare	Chinese government, Zimbabwe government, the Zimbabwe Ministry of Health and Child Welfare
Project funding	The Chinese government provides a grant through the export–import bank of China	Chinese government, the export–import bank of China
Project approval	The local government and the community approve the planning document, the construction stage vocational certificate. Environmental management agencies conduct environmental impact assessments before and after project implementation The department undertaking the construction is registered with the companies registry of Zimbabwe The quality of the project is certified by the Zimbabwe Standards Association	Mahusekwa government and local community, Investment Authority of Zimbabwe, Environment authority of Zimbabwe, Zimbabwe companies registry and various professional regulatory bodies, Zimbabwe standards association
Project construction	China's design institute and construction engineering group are responsible for the design, management and construction of the project	Hunan architectural design institute Co. Ltd, Nantong construction group Co. Ltd, China railway sixth group Co. Ltd

Sources Research findings in 2021

China and Zimbabwe signed a grant agreement for the second phase of construction for Mahusekwa Hospital, which involved the installation of a mortuary, an incinerator room, a concrete water tower, a borehole, access roads and a parking lot. The work was completed in February 2019 (Fig. 6.3).

Figure 6.3 shows the main entrance image and architectural details of the hospital.

6.3 Mahusekwa Hospital

Mahusekwa Hospital was built under a Chinese aid project to help Zimbabwe provide quality health services in the countryside, where 70% of the population lives. Mahusekwa Hospital is located in Mahusekwa, 80 km from Harare, the capital of Zimbabwe (Fig. 6.4). The hospital covers an area of 17,000 m^2 with a total floor area of 6,500 m^2. The hospital is composed of an emergency department, outpatient department, inpatient department, technical department, administrative area

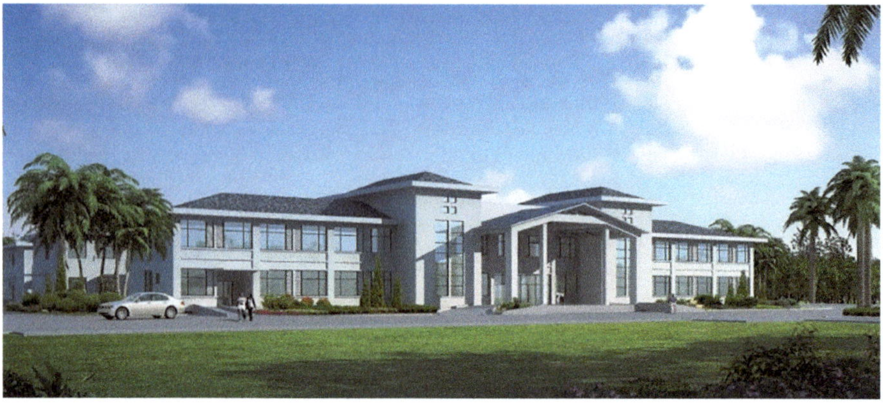

Fig. 6.3 Rendering of Mahusekwa Hospital. Courtesy of Hunan architectural design institute Co. Ltd

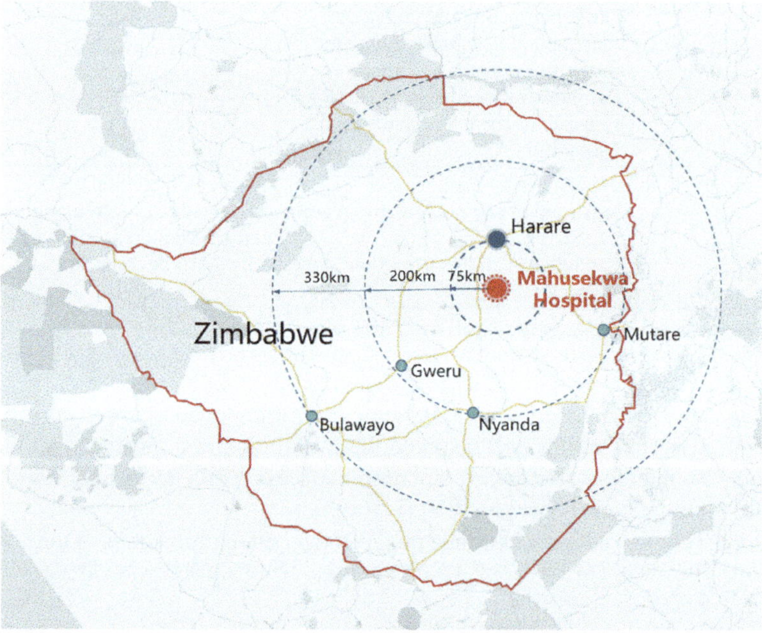

Fig. 6.4 Location of Mahusekwa Hospital and the regions it serves. Drawn by Shan Tang

and accommodation area (Figs. 6.5 and 6.6). As the only hospital in Mahusekwa, the two-storey hospital has an imposing appearance, and has become a landmark in the area. The hospital emphasizes the design principle of being "people-oriented", and it attaches importance to the ecological impact of the hospital on the premise of delivering a simple and organised flow of medical services (Liu & Huang, 2017; Zhi &

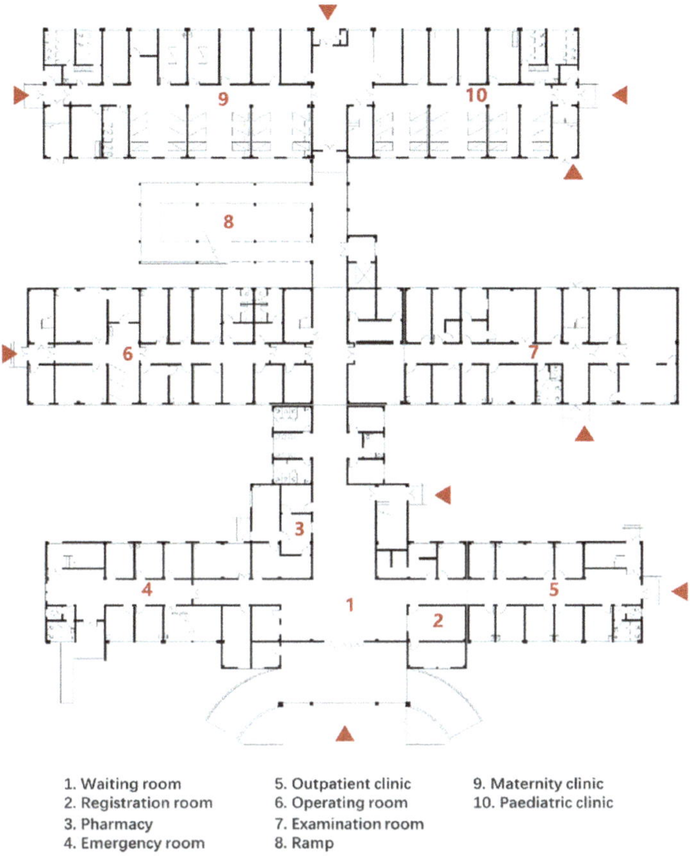

Fig. 6.5 Floor plan of the ground floor of Mahusekwa Hospital. Courtesy of Hunan Architectural Design Institute Co. Ltd

Wang, 2019). The sloping roof, abstract cornice beam and local totem composed of animals and natural elements symbolize clan identity and play a major role in Zimbabwe tradition. These main architectural elements organically combine Chinese architectural characteristics with the Zimbabwean architectural style. This creates an ecological medical treatment environment that is visible, accessible and features Chinese characteristics and natural healing power (Li, 2016; Long & Zhang, 2019).

In 2019, Zimbabwe President Emmerson Mnangagwa attended the completion ceremony of the second phase of Mahusekwa Hospital. In his speech, the president hailed Mahusekwa Hospital as a modern hospital that had promoted local economic and social development, maintaining that it bore testimony to the win-win relationship between Zimbabwe and China. At present, Mahusekwa Hospital has become the most important modern general hospital in the region, and its medical services have been

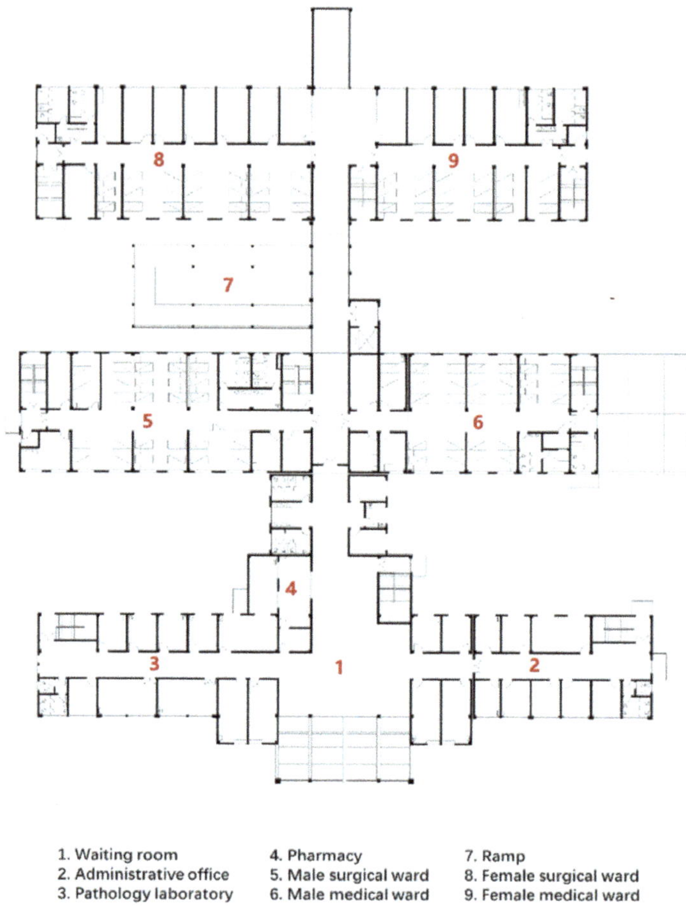

Fig. 6.6 Floor plan of the second floor of Mahusekwa Hospital. Courtesy of Hunan Architectural Design Institute Co. Ltd

extended to Gweru, Nyanda, Mutare, and other regions 200 km away. The hospital is equipped with departments of surgery, internal medicine, obstetrics and gynaecology, and paediatrics. It currently provides medical services to approximately 190,000 people in the region, significantly improving the local medical service capacity.

6.4 Social Impact of the Project

Since the inception of the National Environmental Policy Act in 1969, environmental impact assessments have been a key component of environmental planning in the

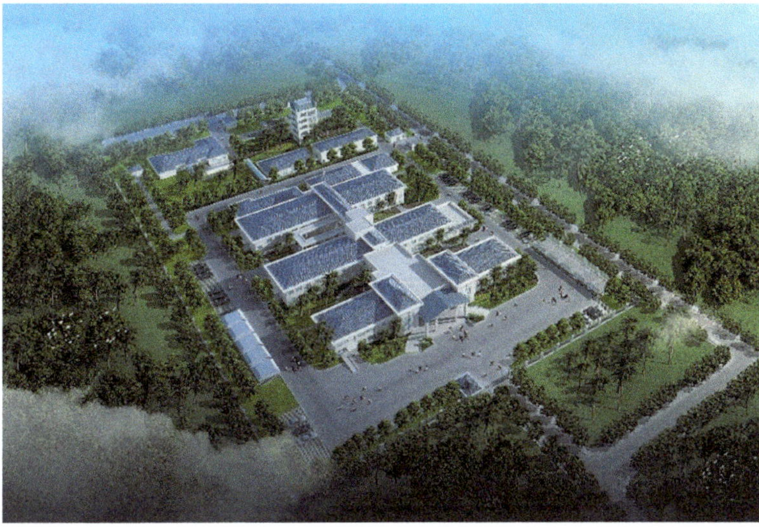

Fig. 6.7 Rendering of Mahusekwa Hospital. Courtesy of Hunan architectural design institute Co. Ltd

United States and across the globe (Freudenburg, 1986; Wolf, 1982). Recently, planners and decision makers worldwide have recognised the need for an improved understanding of the social consequences of projects, programmes and policies (Burdge, 2003; Tang & Xu, 2007; Vanclay, 2003; Vanclay et al., 2015). In line with these needs, a group of social scientists created the Inter-organisational Committee on Guidelines Principles for Social Impact Assessment (SIA), which has provided a set of major guidelines for aid projects. Although projects, programmes and policies can result in the creation of opportunities and benefits for communities, they can also cause harmful effects (Esteves et al., 2012; Teng et al., 2014). The SIA encompasses a process of detecting and addressing social issues emanating from project development. It is based on effective engagement with the affected communities, ensuring that they participate in the process of identifying, assessing and managing social impacts (Fan et al., 2013; He et al., 2020). Good SIA management is key to ensuring that the benefits of projects are fully maximised and that negative impacts are avoided or mitigated throughout the development of the project.

To fully comprehend the transformative effects that Mahusekwa Hospital has had on Zimbabwean society and communities, it is necessary to conduct a social impact assessment (Fig. 6.7). Key informant interviews were conducted with direct active stakeholders, including officials from the Zimbabwe Investment Authority, the Zimbabwe Environmental Management Agency, the Zimbabwe Ministry of Health and Child Welfare and the Mahusekwa Rural District Council[7] By soliciting the opinions of experts in related fields, the social impact of Mahusekwa Hospital was

[7] A total of 20 people from the Zimbabwe Investment Authority, Environmental Management Agency, Ministry of Health and Child Welfare and the Mahusekwa Rural District Council, were

Table 6.2 Social impacts of Mahusekwa Hospital

Main impacts	Specific social impacts
Economic development	Regional investment environment and urbanisation Regional employment Regional land values Regional industrial development
Social services	Healthcare Residents' quality of life Regional influence
Social compatibility	Adaptability of interest relevant groups Sustainability of project management
Natural environment	Natural landscape Ecological environment Resources and energy

Sources Research findings in 2021

summarised into four main impacts related to economic development, social services, social compatibility and the natural environment (Table 6.2).

6.4.1 Impact on Economic Development

Mahusekwa Hospital has promoted the development of medical-related industries and supporting service industries. It has also attracted investment projects to stimulate the appreciation of the surrounding land prices, promote regional urbanisation, stimulate regional economic growth and enhance the regional development environment (Yan & Yan, 2017). As a result of the hospital's construction, the surrounding areas have continuously witnessed increases in the numbers of developments. Commercial activities such as the opening of shops have also surged. There has also been a continuous increase in the construction of residential properties around Mahusekwa Hospital since construction of the hospital began. According to one official at the Zimbabwe Investment Authority, the significant capacity-building from research and development during the construction of Mahusekwa Hospital has not only benefited those directly involved in the project but also the wider region and even the country in general. In addition, Mahusekwa Hospital has created employment opportunities for members of the local surrounding communities during its construction, and has continued to create more employment throughout its operation. One member of the Mausekwa Rural District Council said, "The construction and operation of Mahusekwa Hospital has provided more than 200 jobs in medical care, construction, management, and service consulting to the local community and the surrounding area."

---

selected as interviewees to explore the social impact mechanism of Mahusekwa Hospital through semi-structured interviews.

6.4.2 Impact on Social Services

Chinese aid projects have generally improved the standard of living in communities in which they have been implemented. Mahusekwa Hospital has improved regional medical facilities, provided good medical health and prevention services as well as regional emergency rescue capabilities, and effectively improved regional health-care and public services. In an interview, one government official working at the Zimbabwe Ministry of Health and Child Welfare reflected that "Mahusekwa Hospital services a population of 189,994 people at the district level and 6,695 people in the locality of Mahusekwa. This has greatly improved accessibility to medical facilities, as prior to the construction of Mahusekwa Hospital, people had to travel up to 46 km to Marondera Hospital." Another official in the same ministry said, "As it is one of the few hospitals in the country equipped with state-of-the-art machinery such as a biogas system, laboratory biochemistry, fluoroscope and computerised tomography (CT) scans, Mahusekwa Hospital has become a shining beacon in the provision of medical services to its community and beyond its boundaries." In addition, one official at the Zimbabwe Investment Authority noted the opportunities that Mahusekwa Hospital has created through spillover effects or secondary benefits: "With the construction of Mahusekwa Hospital, water supply, drainage and power facilities have been continuously improved, and transportation accessibility has been continuously enhanced. The population density of the surrounding area has been increasing, and the overall strength and influence of the area has been greatly enhanced."

6.4.3 Impact on Social Compatibility

The lack of infrastructure construction in Zimbabwe has led to a bottleneck in sustainable social and economic development. Consequently, foreign direct investment and assistance have become necessary means to improve economic and social development. However, the employment of Chinese workers in Zimbabwe has often proven challenging. Many of the contexts, planning laws and various rules and regulations that Chinese contractors are familiar with are different from those in Zimbabwe. In addition, the absence of a central development agency managing overseas aid projects for China makes coordination and supervision difficult. Furthermore, all foreign employees in Zimbabwe are required to apply for work permits and to have their qualifications certified by the regulatory bodies responsible for their line of work. For example, engineers must be registered with the Engineering Council of Zimbabwe and must submit these documents to the local authorities in the jurisdictions where their projects are being implemented. These challenges have been compounded by the political ties that are usually associated with Chinese aid projects, which have made it difficult to subject the projects to the maximum required regulatory scrutiny, causing the local regulatory bodies to express significant concern regarding project quality. In an interview with one official working in the Zimbabwe Investment Authority, it was noted that differences in planning laws and other regulations were major challenges encountered during the construction of Mahusekwa Hospital.

6.4.4 *Impact on the Natural Environment*

Mahusekwa hospital has enhanced the features, identifiability and quality of the local landscape. The design of the hospital is based on principles of sustainability such as adapting measures to local conditions, achieving high efficiency and energy savings, making full use of local renewable resources and emphasising passive climate design. Fixed sunshade components are used extensively in the external walls to block direct sunlight, and many open corridors are used to deal with the hot local climate. As one official of the Zimbabwe Investment Authority noted, "The unique architectural style of Mahusekwa Hospital has produced an identifiable local landscape." Nonetheless, the large scale of the project has resulted in a loss of farmland. In addition, the treatment of the hospital's medical waste—a combination of landfills and incineration, which cause air, sewage and waste pollution—has led to the destruction of the ecological environment and degradation of the natural environment. A member of the Zimbabwe Environmental Management Agency said, "Mahusekwa Hospital was designed with the concept of eco-conservation in mind, with 30% of construction materials sourced locally and being renewable. However, the hospital's lacking medical waste disposal capacity has raised environmental concerns about the natural ecosystem."

6.5 Conclusion

This chapter reviews the evolution of Chinese medical projects in Africa in different periods and focuses on the case of Mahusekwa Hospital in Zimbabwe, specifically its construction background, architectural properties and social impact mechanisms. Where Chinese aid projects such as Mahusekwa Hospital have been implemented, they have no doubt had positive impacts and transformative effects on urban environments and local communities. Chinese aid projects serve to stimulate development through attracting complimentary or related businesses and activities, leading to further development of the surrounding communities. These aid projects have improved access to facilities and service, relieved pressure on pre-existing infrastructure, provided employment opportunities during and post construction, given opportunities for training and capacity building, and increased property values. The surrounding communities have also enjoyed access to secondary benefits from the projects such as the access to paved roads, clean water and electricity, thus improving their standard of living.

With the increase in the number of Chinese medical projects in Africa, governments and scholars around the world have become increasingly aware of the great significance of the aid projects to the coordinated and sustainable development of the regional economy, society and environment. Chinese medical projects in Africa should aim to improve regional economic and social development, bring positive impacts to other projects in the region, strengthen local policy support and collaborative project management capacity, promote sustainable development and improve the overall environmental quality of the region. Several factors are key to achieving these goals, including policy formulation, public participation and departmental collaboration.

First, the projects should optimise development policies and formulate special guidance policies on land development and utilisation, industrial structure adjustment and other aspects based on the project's social impact, while giving full play to the overall benefits of medical aid projects in Africa. Second, public participation should be encouraged to improve the effectiveness of residents' participation and their recognition of aid projects. This can be achieved through the establishment of efficient communication platforms to enhance the social compatibility of the aid projects in the African context. Finally, the plans should aim to strengthen departmental coordination, improve mechanisms for project cooperation and management between donor and recipient countries, improve project review and evaluation systems, address weaknesses in planning and management services, and improve the sustainability of Chinese medical projects in Africa. The mechanisms for managing Chinese aid projects are improving constantly, and the social impacts of these projects have received extensive attention of African recipient countries. Chinese aid projects are bound to become a platform for further cooperation and the implementation of other projects between China and African countries. They are also key to building strong China–Africa cooperative relationships.

Acknowledgements The research presented in this chapter was part of a study supported by the National Natural Science Foundation of China, project No. 51778403, and the National Natural Science Foundation of China, project No. 51778406.

References

Armstrong, J. (1977). *Revolutionary diplomacy: Chinese foreign policy and the united front doctrine*. University of California Press.

Auret, D. (1990). *A decade of development, Zimbabwe 1980–1990*. Mambo Press.

Ban, Q., Chen, B., Gelun, S. S., & Phiri, M. (2016). A study on architectural design tools and sustainability assessment standards of the healthcare environment. *Architectural Journal*, (11), 99–103. 班淇超,陈冰,格伦,斯蒂芬·沙普尔斯,迈克尔·菲利 (2016). 医疗建筑环境设计辅助工具与可持续评价标准的研究.建筑学报, (11), 99–103.

Brautigam, D. (2009). *The dragon's gift: The real story of China in Africa*. Oxford University Press.

Brautigam, D. (2010). *China, Africa and the international aid architecture*. African Development Bank Group (Working Paper No. 107).

Burdge, R. (2003). Benefiting from the practice of social impact assessment. *Impact Assessment and Project Appraisal, 21*(3), 225–229.

Chen, M. (2014). Research on the African Model of China's Aid and its Influence on African Development. Shanghai International Studies University. 陈默 (2014). 中国援助的非洲模式及其对非洲发展影响的研究.上海: 上海外国语大学博士论文.

Chivanga, S., & Monyai, P. (2020). Scramble for mutual partnerships? The case of China and Zimbabwe. *Journal of African Foreign Affairs, 7*(2), 7–20.

Davies, M., & Cao, D. (2008). China's foreign aid policy toward Africa. *World Economics and Politics*, (9), 38–44+4. 马丁·戴维斯, 曹大松 中国对非洲的援助政策及评价[J].世界经济与政治, (9), 38–44+4.

Ding, G., & Xue, C. Q. L. (2015). China's architectural aid: Exporting a transformational modernism. *Habitat International, 47*, 136–147.

Esteves, A., Franks, D., & Vanclay, F. (2012). Social impact assessment: The state of the art. *Impact Assessment and Project Appraisal, 30*(1), 34–42.

Fan, S., Jiang, H., Zhong, R., & Tian, W. (2013). Study of post evaluation for social impact of old industrial buildings recycling project. *Industrial Construction, 43*(10), 11–14+32. 樊胜军,蒋红妍,钟兴润,田卫 (2013). 旧工业建筑再利用社会影响后评价研究.工业建筑, 43(10), 11–14+32.

Freudenburg, W. (1986). Social impact assessment. *Annual Review of Sociology, 12*(1), 451–478.

He, G., Chai, J., Qin, Y., Xu, Z., & Li, S. (2020). Evaluation of dam break social impact assessments based on an improved variable fuzzy set model. *Water, 12*(4), 970.

Huang, M., & Ren, P. (2012). China's foreign aid and its role in the international aid architecture. In: International development policy: Aid, emerging economies and global policies. Palgrave Macmillan, London.

IOSC (Information Office of the State Council). (2011). *China's Foreign Aid (White paper)*. 中华人民共和国国务院新闻办公室(2011).中国的对外援助白皮书. http://www.scio.gov.cn/zxbd/nd/2011/document/896471/896471.htm.

Li, A. (2011). Chinese medical cooperation in Africa: With special emphasis on the medical teams and anti-malaria campaign. Nordiska Afrikainstitutet.

Li, H. (2016). Practical logic: Tangible impacts of building modes on architectural designs in China. *Architecture Journal*, (10), 72–77. 李海清 (2016). 实践逻辑:建造模式如何深度影响中国的建筑设计.建筑学报 (10),72–77.

Liu, C., & Huang, W. (2017). Learning from Africa: The general hospital of Niger aided by China. New Architecture, (03), 56–61. 刘琛,黄薇薇 (2017). 向非洲学习——记中国援尼日尔综合医院.新建筑, (03):56–61.

Long, H., & Zhang, M. (2019). From chaotic to integrated: New research development about integrated efficiency in medical building. New Architecture, 185(4), 65–69. 龙灏,张玛璐 (2019). 无序到综合——医疗建筑综合效率研究进展. 新建筑, 185(4), 65–69.

Palmer, R. (1990). Land reform in Zimbabwe, 1980–1990. *African Affairs, 89*(355), 163–181.

Samy, Y. (2010). China's aid policies in Africa: Opportunities and challenges. *The round Table, 99*(406), 75–90.

Shamu, S., Loewenson, R., Machemedze, R., & Mabika, A. (2010). Capital flows through medical aid societies in Zimbabwe's health sector. The Regional Network for Equity in Health in East and Southern Africa (EQUINET) Discussion Paper Series, 82.

Shimomura, Y., & Ohashi, H. (2013). *A study of China's foreign aid: An Asian perspective*. Palgrave Macmillan.

Song, K. (2021). China's foreign aid architecture in a transitional period, 1964–1976. *Journal of Asian Architecture and Building Engineering*, 1–15.

Sun, C. (2019). Study on economic and trade cooperation between China and Zimbabwe (MA thesis). Shanghai Normal University. 孙灿 (2019). 中国与津巴布韦经贸合作研究 (2000–2018). 上海:上海师范大学硕士论文.

Tang, Y., & Xu, Y. (2007). Summaries on studies about social impact assessment. *Urban Planning Forum, 171*(5), 72–77. 唐勇,徐玉红(2007). 国外社会影响评价研究综述. 城市规划学刊, 171(5): 72–77.

Teng, M., Han, C., Liu, X. (2014). Index system for social impact assessment of large scale infrastructure projects in China. *China Population, Resources and Environment, 24*(9), 170–176. 滕敏敏,韩传峰,刘兴华 (2014). 中国大型基础设施项目社会影响评价指标体系构建.中国人口·资源与环境, 24(9), 170–176.

Vanclay, F. (2003). International principles for social impact assessment. *Impact Assessment and Project Appraisal, 21*(1), 5–12.

Vanclay, F., Esteves, A. M., Aucamp, I., & Franks, D. (2015). *Social impact assessment: Guidance for assessing and managing the social impacts of projects*. International Association for Impact Assessment.

Vhumbunu, C. H. (2017). Impact assessment of the China-Zimbabwe cooperation on infrastructure development from 1980 to 2016. In O. Oniwide (Ed.), Issues in China-Africa relations (pp. 123–150). College of Humanities and Social Sciences, Kampala International University, Kampala, Uganda.

Wang, F. L., & Elliot, E. A. (2014). China in Africa: Presence, perceptions and prospects. *Journal of Contemporary China, 23*(90), 1012–1032.

Wolf, C. P. (1982). Social impact assessment. *Impact Assessment, 1*(1), 9–19.

Xue, C. Q. L., Ding, G., Chang, W., & Wan, Y. (2019). Architecture of stadium diplomacy—China-aid sport buildings in Africa. *Habitat International, 90*, 101985.

Yan, R., & Yan, L. (2017). Social impact assessment research for large residential communities based on cases in Shanghai. *Tongji University Journal Social Science Section, 28*(5), 116–124. 严荣,颜莉 (2017). 大型居住社区的社会影响评价研究——以上海三个大型居住社区为例. 同济大学学报(社会科学版), 28(5), 116–124.

Zhang, C. (2014). China–Zimbabwe relations: A model of China–Africa relations? South African Institute of International Affairs (SAIIA) Occasional Paper 205.

Zhang, D., & Smith, G. (2017). China's foreign aid system: Structure, agencies, and identities. *Third World Quarterly, 38*, 2330–2346.

Zhi, W., & Wang, X. (2019). Fluid·Infinite·Future Analysis and evaluation on the design of Heydar Aliyev Center in Baku Azerbaijan. Time Architecture, (04), 102–111. 支文军,王欣蕊(2019).流动·无限·未来 阿塞拜疆巴库阿利耶夫文化中心设计解析与评价. 时代建筑, (04), 102–111.

Zou, G., McPake, B., & Wei, X. (2014). Chinese health foreign aid and policy: Beyond medical aid. *The Lancet, 383*(9927), 1461–1462.

Shan Tang is a Ph.D. candidate at the School of Architecture, Tianjin University, China, with interests in the social impact of cultural facility. She holds a master's degree in Urban Planning in Wuhan University in 2017, and participated in several design practices and projects during her study period.

Ze Li is an Associate Professor in the Department of Urban and Rural Planning at the School of Architecture, Tianjin University, China. He obtained his PhD from the National University of Singapore with full fellowship. His research interests include urban form, land economy and property institution, urban/rural planning and design, ecological planning and green city. He has published research articles in leading Chinese journals, and has received grants from the national research foundation of China. As an urban designer and planner, he also practices both domestically and internationally, and has won considerable international bids and competitions.

Keith Amos obtained a master's degree of Urban and Rural Planning from Tianjin University, China, and bachelor's degree of Urban and Regional Planning from University of Zimbabwe, Zimbabwe. He is interested in transnational spatial planning and urban design, and participated in several design practices and research projects.

Chapter 7
Implementation Mode and Impact Perception of Chinese Aid Projects in Africa—A Case Study of the Parliament Building, Malawi

Tianjie Zhang, Yuqi Zhang, and Davies Afiya Mbewe

Abstract As city landmarks, administrative buildings are often considered to be influential architectural representations of Chinese aid projects to Africa. In this chapter, the authors analyze the aid mode for and local feedback on administrative buildings in Africa developed with Chinese aid. Using Malawi's Parliament Building as a case study, the chapter investigates the multi-participatory construction process and identifies the implications of the "turnkey" mode. Through questionnaires and in-depth interviews, the research reveals the satisfaction of the local people and their perceptions of the Parliament Building's social impact. From the perspective of the local community, the Chinese aid project benefits the country's establishment of a good national image, provides some financial benefits and introduces opportunities for city development. Nonetheless, the local community expects to be more involved in the aid process.

7.1 Introduction

China's aid projects in Africa have been the subject of a great deal of attention in recent years because of their significant economic and political significance. These projects include the establishment of administrative office buildings, hospitals, schools, theaters, residential buildings, factories and infrastructure such as roads, railways and bridges. Among these, the administrative office building is an important building type, regarded as an urban landmark by local governments. As such, administrative office buildings not only shape modern African cities but also symbolise national independence. They play a role in enhancing the influence of the country and

T. Zhang
Tianjin University, Tianjin, China

Y. Zhang (✉)
Kyoto University, Kyoto, Japan
e-mail: yuqi_zhang@foxmail.com

D. A. Mbewe
Department of Buildings, Ministry of Transport and Public Works of Malawi, Lilongwe, Malawi

C. Q. Xue and G. Ding (eds.), *Exporting Chinese Architecture*,
https://doi.org/10.1007/978-981-19-2786-7_7

the city, strengthening international communication and cooperation while boosting economic development.

However, local communities' evaluations of administrative office buildings have not received due attention. This is unfortunate, as such buildings have been the subject of widespread public attention throughout the construction process, garnering both supporters and opponents along with various interpretations. Therefore, to understand the local public's feedback regarding the implementation mode and the social impact of these projects, it is necessary to conduct a post-implementation evaluation.

The present research focuses on Malawi as the target country, given its very high dependence on international aid, essential location in the corridor between southern and eastern Africa, and its relatively short history of diplomatic relations with China. Since independence, Malawi's economic structure has been rooted in agriculture, with nearly 90% of the population engaged in subsistence farming. Malawi, which borders Zambia, Tanzania and Mozambique, is closely linked to the countries of southern Africa and has important geopolitical status. While it adopted a pro-Western policy during the Cold War period, Malawi formally established diplomatic relations with China in 2007, and subsequently further adjusted its foreign policy to meet changes in international and regional politics. As a result, Chinese aid projects in Malawi have reflected China's foreign aid policy in the new era. After a decade of Chinese aid in Malawi, it is now instructive to take stock of the role and impact of Chinese aid on Malawi's objective of attaining positive urbanisation.

As China's first aid project in Malawi, Malawi's Parliament Building is considered a catalyst for diplomatic recognition. Taking this typical administrative office building as a case in point, this study attempts to uncover the implementation mode that China adopted in the aid project by means of the following questions. Is the mode suitable for the local situation, such as levels of production? Has the aid project had a positive impact? What is the degree of local satisfaction? Furthermore, this study proposes policy suggestions for the effective and sustainable development of Chinese aid projects in Africa.

7.2 Implementation Mode of Chinese Aid Projects in Africa

At present, the construction process of Chinese aid projects in Africa proceeds basically as follows (Fig. 7.1): in most cases, a formal request is presented to the Chinese Embassy by the recipient country; thereafter, the Ministry of Commerce of China and the recipient country negotiate possible cooperation in accordance with the principle of "mutual benefit and a win-win situation" (Ling, 2010), and visits are made to the locations of feasible projects. On this basis, an assistance agreement is signed, specifying the amount, purpose, duration, and repayment method of the aid project, and the Ministry of Commerce of China designates a Chinese company as the contractor for construction (Nagar & Mutasa, 2018).

The proportion of aid designated for complete projects is relatively high, constituting approximately 40% of China's foreign aid financial expenditure. At this stage,

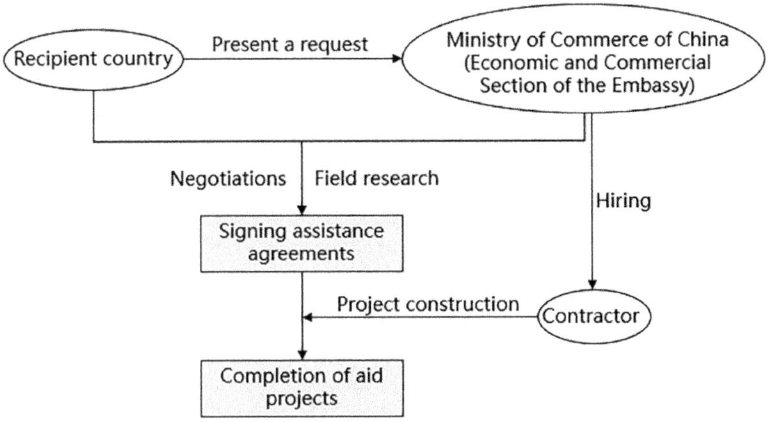

Fig. 7.1 Flow chart of the construction process of an aid project

the "turnkey" implementation mode (Fig. 7.2) has mainly been used. In this practice, a general contracting company undertakes project design, material procurement, construction and trial operations. It delivers the work within the prescribed time limit while being accountable for the overall implementation of the project's quality, safety and cost, as stipulated in the contract (Li, 2018). This special form of management contract features a long-term mutual benefit. It is widely used in construction projects for host countries by transnational corporations.

The turnkey mode is widely used in Chinese aid projects, as it is designed to address the lack of building materials, applicable technology and experienced management teams in the recipient country. This implication mode features good continuity and effectively avoids contradictions between design and construction.

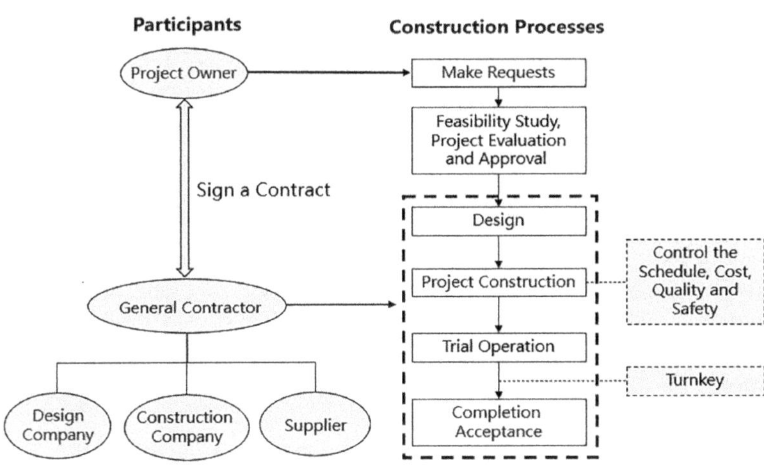

Fig. 7.2 Conceptual diagram of the turnkey implementation mode

Moreover, it has the advantages of significantly reducing project costs, shortening project durations and ensuring the high quality of the final building. The Paris Declaration on Aid Effectiveness notes that China's aid programmes have been more effective than those of Western countries, largely because they have been more expeditious and less expensive. Still, the turnkey mode has also been questioned, with some African countries fearing that China could develop a monopoly on large infrastructure projects (Shinn, 2007). The view was also expressed that although turnkey projects had assisted Africa in achieving rapid development, they fell short of providing African experts with sufficient opportunities to participate, and do not generate significant increases in local jobs in African countries (Van Dijk, 2009). In addition, as the turnkey mode does not emphasize the transfer of technology, local capacity-building has proven relatively inadequate (Liu, 2019).

Several studies have found China's aid projects to demonstrate high effectiveness since they are consistent with the urban development goals of recipient countries. Especially when African countries have faced development bottlenecks owing to poverty and social conflicts, aid projects have proven to be a powerful driver of urban development (Collier & Dollar, 2002; Sachs, 2006). In addition, aid projects can further help recipient countries to achieve their social goals (Fagernäs & Schurich, 2004). However, the 'aid fantasy' argument (McGillivray & Morrissey, 2000) put forth by several scholars emphasises that the positive impacts of aid projects on economic development have not been significant (Doucouliagos & Paldam, 2008).

7.3 An Overview of Chinese Aid Projects in Malawi

Malawi is a landlocked traditional agriculturalist country located in south-eastern Africa (Fig. 7.3) with a total land area of 118,480 square kilometres and a total population of nearly 19.71 million. Malawi became a British protectorate in 1891 and gained independence in 1964, becoming known as the Republic of Malawi. Since the 1970s, Malawi has experienced a period of rapid population growth. Malawi remains in the early stages of urbanisation at present; it had an urbanisation rate of 17.2% in 2019, well below the average urbanisation level of 38% for southern Africa. As poverty is the most serious problem Malawi faces, the country's urban development is heavily dependent on international assistance. Malawi's main donors include the United Kingdom, Germany, Norway, the United States, Japan, the European Union, the African Development Bank, the Department for International Development and the World Bank . Malawi receives more aid per capita than any other country in southern Africa, with aid projects distributed across 28 regions in the country (Dionne et al., 2013).

Following the establishment of diplomatic relations between China and Malawi in 2007, China became one of the nation's key aid donors (Table 7.1). China's aid to Malawi is based on Malawi's development goals and features a balance of "hard" and "soft" projects. The two countries identified four key areas for assistance: infrastructure, agriculture, education and public health (Thindwa, 2015). China has assisted in

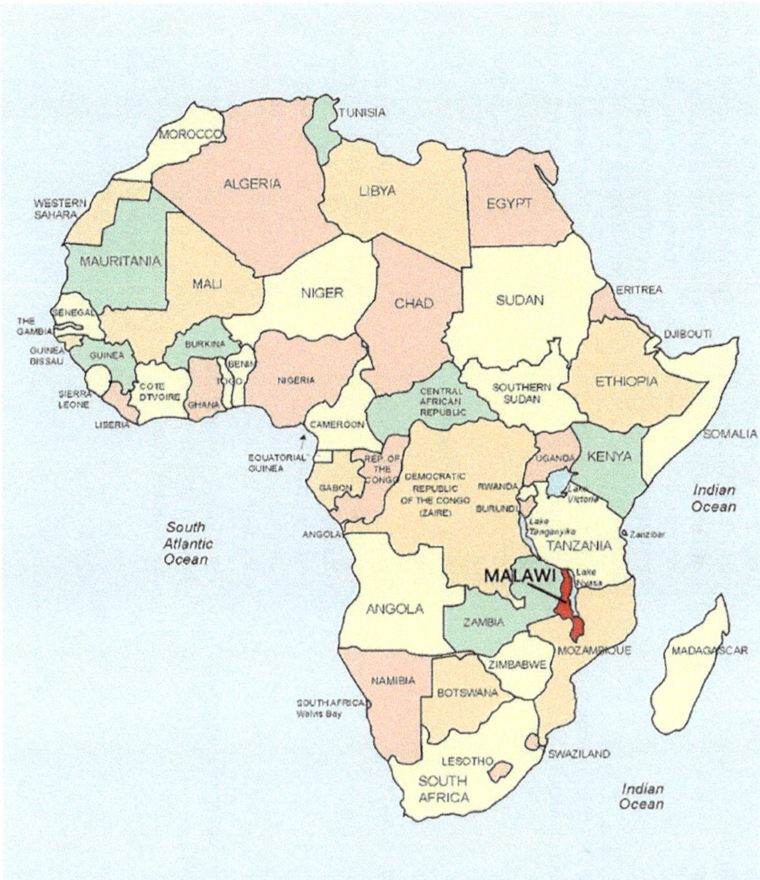

Fig. 7.3 Location of Malawi in the continent of Africa. (*Source* redrawn from http://www.map-of-africa.us/)

projects beneficial to Malawi's national image in successive fashion, including the Malawi Parliament Building, the International Conference Center and the National Stadium. In addition, projects aimed at bettering the lives of the local people have been constructed, such as the Karonga-Chitipa Road, solar streetlights and numerous wells. Technical training and education have also been the focus of assistance and aid projects, such as the Malawi Agricultural Technology Demonstration Center, the Malawi University of Science and Technology and the China–Africa Friendship Primary School.

The capital of Malawi, Lilongwe, has been a major beneficiary of Chinese aid projects in recent years. Because of economic constraints, the government of Lilongwe was unable to implement many of its planned projects, and to this end, Chinese aid projects over the last decade have assisted Lilongwe in achieving some

Table 7.1 Major Chinese aid projects in Malawi

Projects		Construction time	Overview	Social impact
Social public facilities	Malawi parliament building	February 16, 2009–May 21, 2010	The Chinese government provided US$41 million in aid. The building was constructed by Anhui Foreign Economic Construction Group Co., Ltd.	It helped Lilongwe to build the project that was planned in the master plan (1968), and is one of the national landmarks that contributing to Malawi's national image
	Malawi international convention center	2009–2012; officially put into use on May 1, 2015	The Chinese government contributed US$90 million of aid, with a concessional loan from the Export–Import Bank, and Shanghai Construction Group undertook the construction	It has enabled Malawi to hold international conferences, boost the tourism industry and increase foreign exchange earnings
	Bingu National Stadium	2012–2015	The Chinese government provided US$70 million in concessional loans and Anhui Foreign Economic Construction Group Co., Ltd. undertook the construction	It is the most modern sports facility in Malawi, with a capacity of over 40,000 spectators, and can host regional competitions
	Malawi University of Science and Technology	Handover on December 23, 2013	The Chinese government provided US$80 million in concessional loans	As the third comprehensive university and the first technology-based university in the country, it has enhanced education in Malawi

(continued)

Table 7.1 (continued)

Projects		Construction time	Overview	Social impact
	China–Africa Friendship Primary School	October 1, 2012–November 1, 2013	Identified at the Forum on China-Africa Cooperation, built by Shanghai Construction Engineering Group	It has improved educational facilities and access to education for local students
	Water well projects	November 1, 2012–November 29, 2013; handed over on March 6, 2014	Constructed by Gansu Geological Engineering Co., Ltd	A total of 600 water wells were built to provide clean drinking water to 150,000 people in six districts of Malawi, effectively improving the quality of life of the local people
Economic infrastructure	Karonga-Chitipa road	Construction started in 2009	The Chinese government provided US$55 million. The road was constructed by China communications construction company Ltd	It has significantly improved Malawi's regional transportation system
	Solar street light and mobile power project	Handed over on April 16, 2014	The project was executed by ZTE Corporation	The 533 sets of mobile solar power have effectively alleviated the problem of electricity shortages in rural hospitals and effectively demonstrated the development of solar energy

(continued)

Table 7.1 (continued)

Projects		Construction time	Overview	Social impact
	National optical fibber backbone network	Construction started on April 26, 2017	The Chinese government provided US$23 million in concessional loans and Huawei undertook the construction	Connecting 32 cities in Malawi, it has greatly improved the national communications network, increased the efficiency of government departments, promoted the development of Malawi's information industry, and created more than 300 jobs

Sources Website of the Economic and Commercial Office of the Embassy of the People's Republic of China in the Republic of Malawi; Malawi government, Ministry of Transport and Public Works; media reports

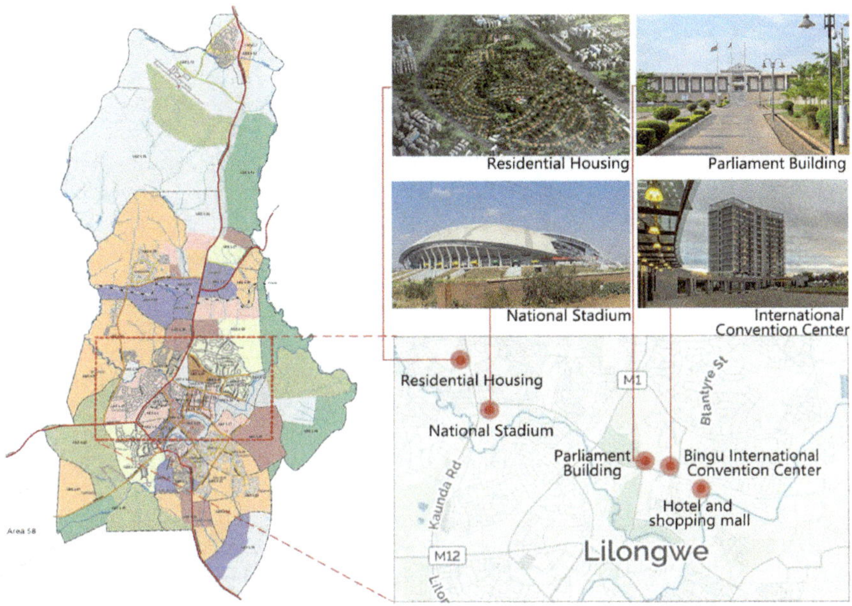

Fig. 7.4 Distribution of major Chinese aid projects in Lilongwe. (*Source* By Author, and redrawn from the website of the Malawi government and Google maps)

of its developmental goals. The construction of several landmark buildings (Fig. 7.4), such as the Parliament Building, has significantly enhanced Lilongwe's urban image. In addition, aid projects have played an active role in the provision of public services and housing in the city. For example, the Golden Peacock Shopping Center, developed using investments by Anhui Foreign Economic Construction Group Co., Ltd., is located in the center of the new city, and complements service facilities in the new city center. With the goal of increasing housing in Malawi's major cities, Malawi Housing Corporation and Henan Guoji Development Co., Ltd. have jointly established a housing complex in a high-density residential area of Lilongwe.

7.4 The Architectural Design and Implementation Mode of the Malawi Parliament Building

The Malawi Parliament Building is China's first aid project in Malawi. It features a total area of 22,365 m^2 and consists of a main house of parliament, an office of the speaker, a cafeteria, a military parade ground and Roman-style colonnades at the main entrance. The design is based on a central axis layout (Fig. 7.5), with the main entrance on the south side and the main house of parliament centrally positioned. In the open space on the south side of the main parliament building, a viewing

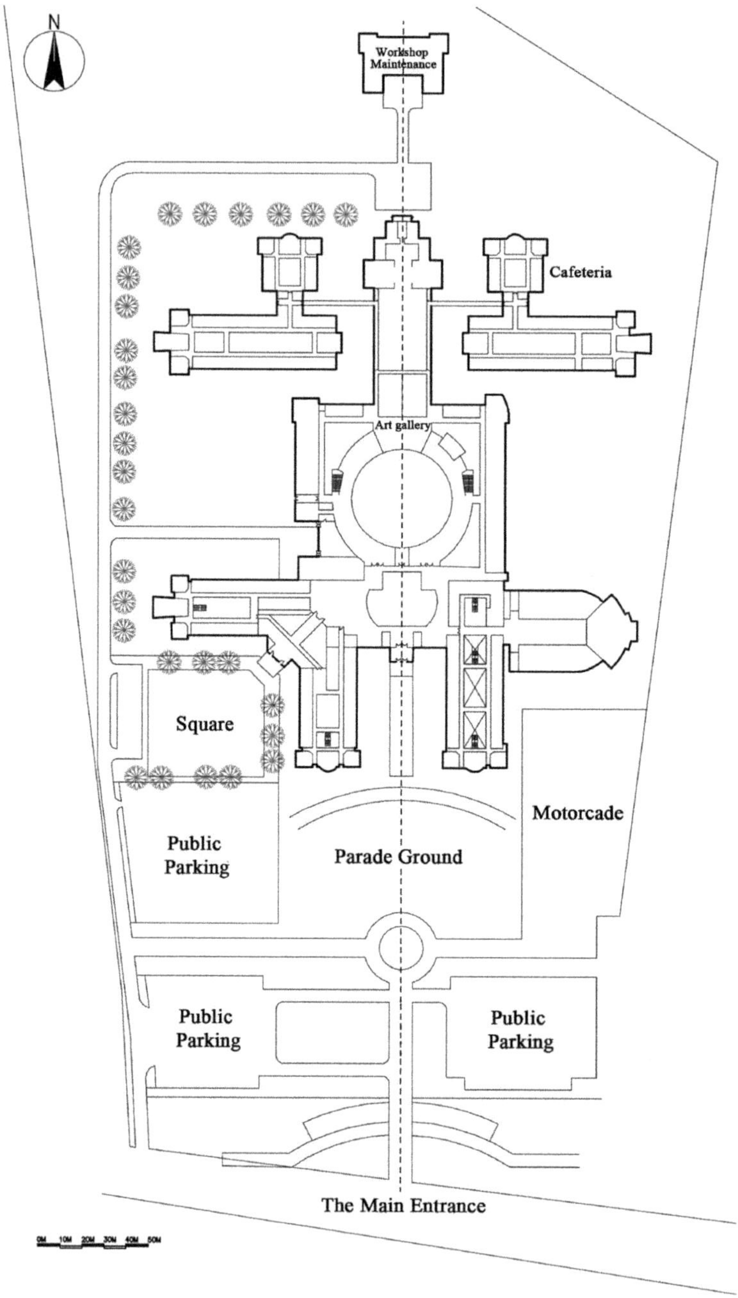

Fig. 7.5 Floor plan of the Malawi Parliament Building. (*Source* Redrawn by the author)

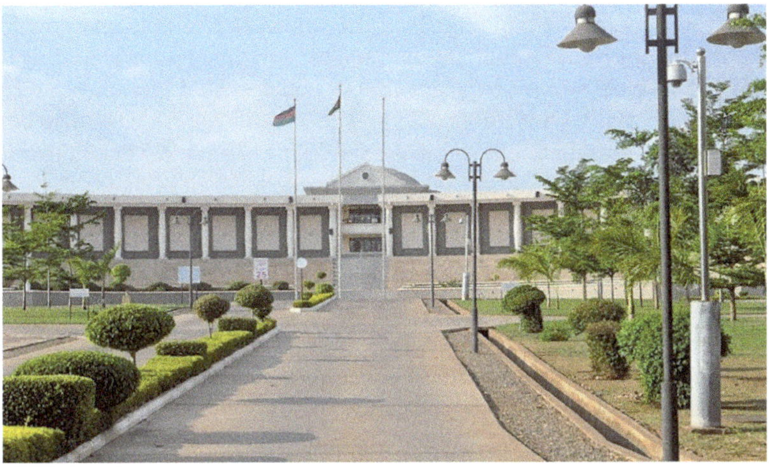

Fig. 7.6 The facade of the Malawi Parliament Building as viewed from the front (*Source* https://www.shunya.net/Pictures/Malawi/Lilongwe/Lilongwe.htm)

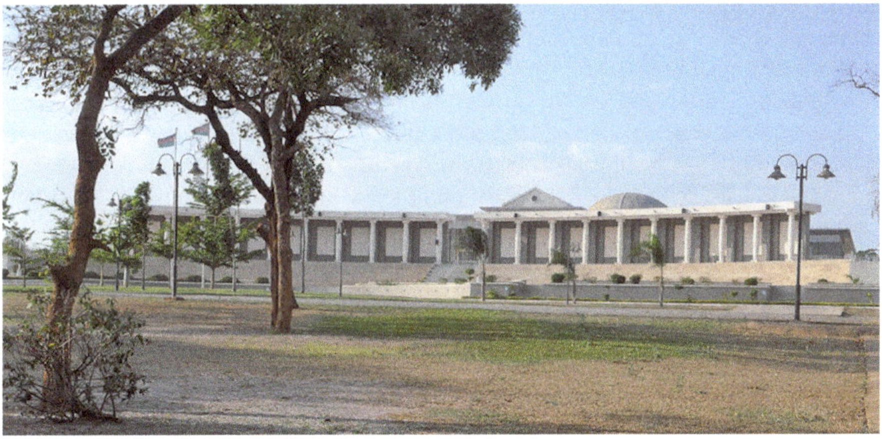

Fig. 7.7 The Malawi Parliament Building (*Source* https://www.shunya.net/Pictures/Malawi/Lilongwe/Lilongwe.htm)

platform, public square, and flowerbeds and parking lots have been constructed for public events. The area adjacent to the main parliament building is to feature four annexes housing offices, conference rooms, printing halls, etc. However, the annexes have not yet been built and are earmarked for future completion by the government of Malawi. The main house of the parliament building covers an area of 1,256 m^2, with a central conference hall that accommodates nearly 300 people, surrounded by a number of small offices and function rooms. An art gallery is on the second floor.

The overall shape of the building (Figs. 7.6 and 7.7) is simple and powerful. It primarily features the round conference hall and the horizontal square building blocks surrounding it. The design of the facade accommodates the requirements for shade and ventilation in Africa, with colonnades and observation decks. The main building features a panelled aluminium decorative dome. This is the most distinctive part of the main parliament building and is also the largest dome in Malawi. The dome is shaped like a gourd—a tribute to Malawi's indigenous culture. Malawi's Parliament Building embodies a new, thriving national image, and it has been selected as a motif for Malawi's currency.

Motivations for the construction of the Malawi Parliament Building date back to the 1960s. After gaining independence in 1964, Malawi made national construction the main objective of its development. In doing so, it launched a new plan to relocate its capital from Zomba, the economic center in the south-east of the country, to Lilongwe, which is located in the central region of Malawi. This move was symbolic of the end of colonial rule and emblematic of national independence. In 1968, the Lilongwe City Master Plan was developed by the South African company IMEX, and the relocation plan was implemented. The Lilongwe City Master Plan proposed a linear, multi-center development structure featuring a strict allocation of land use, with the administrative center located at Capital Mountain, the heart of the city. However, because of limited economic capacity, the Lilongwe City Master Plan could not be implemented.

Despite the relocation of the government to Lilongwe by 1975, Parliament continued to convene in Zomba, the old capital, because the Malawi Parliament Building had not yet been constructed. In April 2000, the Parliament relocated to Lilongwe. It was housed in the newly completed State House until 2004. When then-president, Professor Peter Mutharika, decided to use the State House for the presidential palace, Parliament was compelled to move out, with their offices scattered in disparate locations around the city center, and it used the ballroom of the New State House as a meeting location. As of 2007, China has provided $41 million for the construction of the Parliament Building in the center of the new city, under Capital Mountain. This construction has maintained the original positions of buildings laid out in the Lilongwe City Master Plan of 1967.

The construction of Malawi's Parliament Building can be divided into two phases (Fig. 7.8). In the first phase, China was not yet involved in the project; the project was under the responsibility of Malawi's local architectural design companies (i.e., MD initiative, Norman and Dawbarn and ABC Designs) and construction contractors (Terrastone co., LTD.). Little progress was made during this phase because of insufficient funding. The second phase began in 2008, when China established diplomatic relations with Malawi and the Beijing Institute of Architectural Design (Group) Co., Ltd . and Anhui Foreign Economic Construction Group Co., Ltd. took over construction of the Parliament Building. Construction using the turnkey mode began in February 2009 and was completed in May 2010.

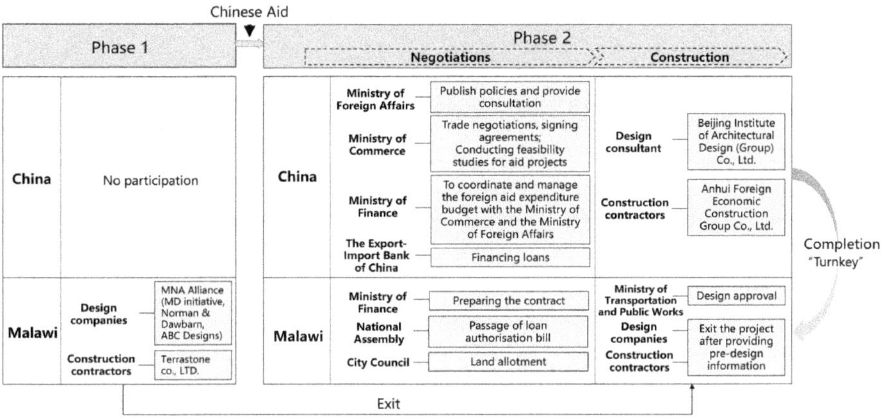

Fig. 7.8 Flow chart summarising the construction phases of the Malawi Parliament Building

7.5 Local Public Perceptions of Social Impact and the Turnkey Implementation Mode

This study was based on questionnaires delivered to the local people and interviews with key stakeholders, including staff of the Malawi Ministry of Transport and Public Works, the Ministry of Land Housing and Urban Development, and the Lilongwe City Council.

The respondents were asked to indicate their perceptions of the social impact of Parliament Building and their level of satisfaction with the turnkey mode on a questionnaire using a 5-point Likert scale. Examples of the questions included the following. "Do you agree that the Chinese-aided project addressed some of Malawi's challenges in attaining positive urbanisation?" "Do you agree that the provision of capital architectural infrastructure to an area will help transform it into a center for economic growth, due to the creation of economic opportunities?" "Do you agree that the turnkey implementation mode is good for developing architectural infrastructure projects in Malawi?"

A total of 251 valid questionnaires were collected and analysed. Out of the 251 individuals, 66.9% ($n = 168$) were males and 33.1% were females. Youths formed the majority of the respondents, as most respondents fell between the ages of 19 and 29. At least 33% of the respondents were employed by either the government or other companies, nearly 33% were business people, approximately 10% were farmers and 10% were unemployed. Respondents with a high school education or lower educational level accounted for nearly 60% of the total. The geographic locations of the respondents were relatively balanced: approximately 59% of the respondents lived in the urban areas, and 41% were from rural areas.

7.5.1 Perceptions of Social Impact

Malawi's Parliament Building is a landmark project, as it is the first building in the country built with Chinese assistance. The present study found that more than half of all respondents identified local politics as a key factor in the choice of construction projects (Fig. 7.9). They predominantly believed that Chinese aid for the construction of Malawi's Parliament Building helped Malawi to achieve the goal of building a new capital conceived at the dawning of independence. The Parliament Building and other large-scale buildings that were built using Chinese aid, such as the International Convention Center and the National Stadium, have rendered Lilongwe eligible to host international events and have greatly enhanced the city's image and influence. This has provided an important boost to Malawi's international image.

The respondents generally agreed that the construction of the Parliament Building had achieved economic benefits (Fig. 7.10). Moreover, 90% agreed that the construction of the project met Malawi's urban development goals to some extent and brought about a turnaround in urban development (Fig. 7.11). It must be noted that the cost of renting government offices in Malawi stands at $17.1 million per year, according to Malawi's national budget for 2019–2020. With the $41 million in aid funds provided by China, the construction of Parliament Building has helped Malawi to save significantly in its government expenditure, thus freeing the remaining funds for uses in other urban development projects.

In addition, nearly 60% of the respondents affirmed the momentous significance of the construction of Parliament Building (Fig. 7.12). Those who agreed asserted that the construction project played a role in promulgating Malawi's national image and

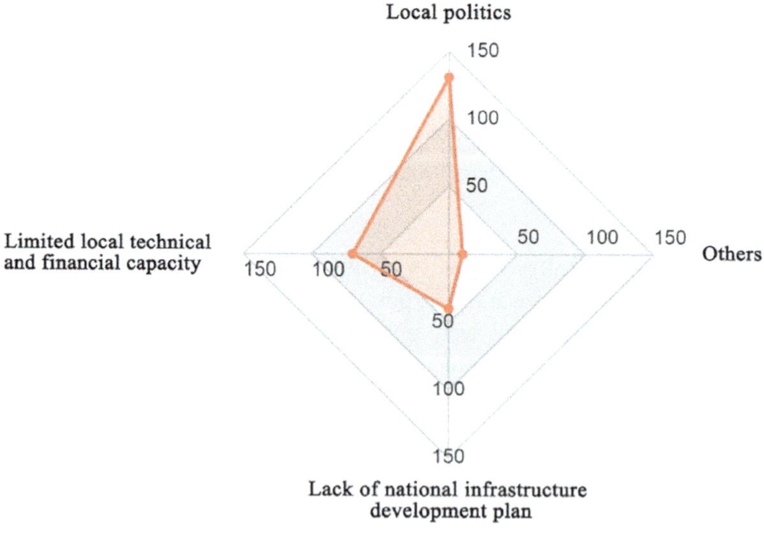

Fig. 7.9 Factors influencing the selection of aid projects

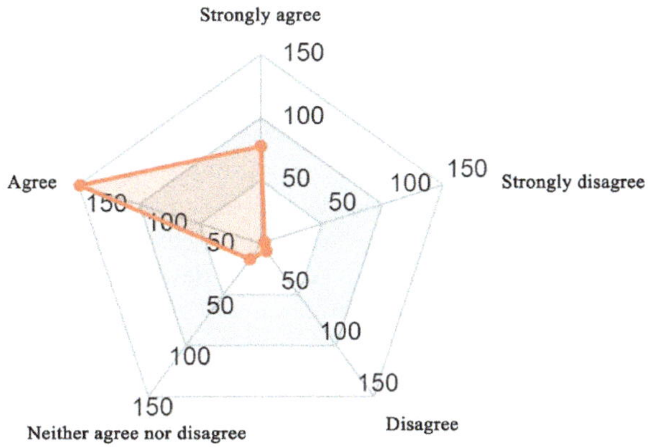

Fig. 7.10 Responses to the statement, "The aid project has brought economic benefits"

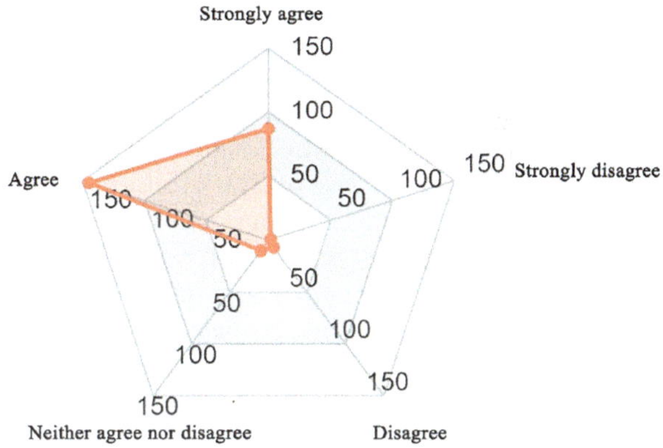

Fig. 7.11 Responses to the statement, "The aid project has promoted urban development"

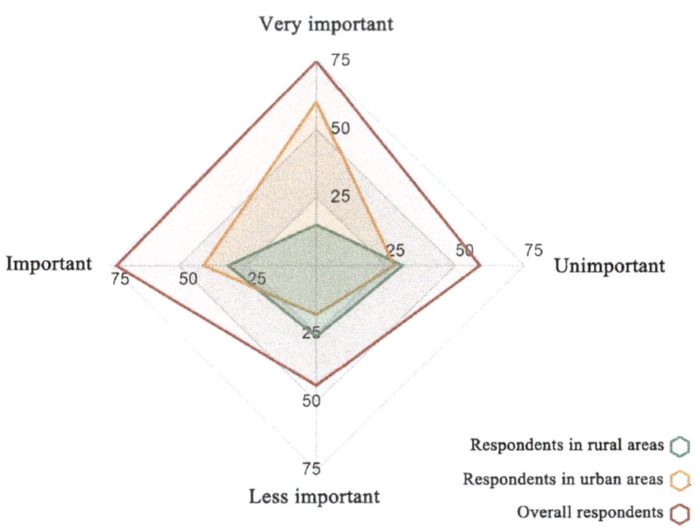

Fig. 7.12 Respondents' perceptions of importance regarding the aid project

in promoting the transformation and development of the city. In addition, respondents living in urban areas were more aware of the importance of the project than those living in rural areas. This indicated that the aid project had a more significant impact on urban areas than on rural areas.

Overall, most of the local community regarded the impact of the Parliament Building as being positive in terms of social impact. They noted that the building had contributed to improving the image of the capital city, saving on public funds and bringing new opportunities for urban development. This may have resulted from the fact that the mode of construction was tailored to the local context and the needs of the community.

7.5.2 *Satisfaction with the Turnkey Implementation Mode*

Only 27% of the respondents supported the turnkey implementation mode (Fig. 7.13). The respondents believed that under the turnkey mode, most of the construction materials and staff were from China, and they were therefore concerned that their benefits were limited because of a lack of local participation in the project.

Using a logistic regression analysis, we analysed the impact of respondents' education levels and the locations of their residences on their perceived satisfaction with the turnkey implementation mode (Table 7.2). The results demonstrated that the respondents' education levels did not have a significant effect on their satisfaction with the turnkey mode. However, the locations of the respondents' residences had a statistically significant effect on their satisfaction with the turnkey mode ($P < 0.001$).

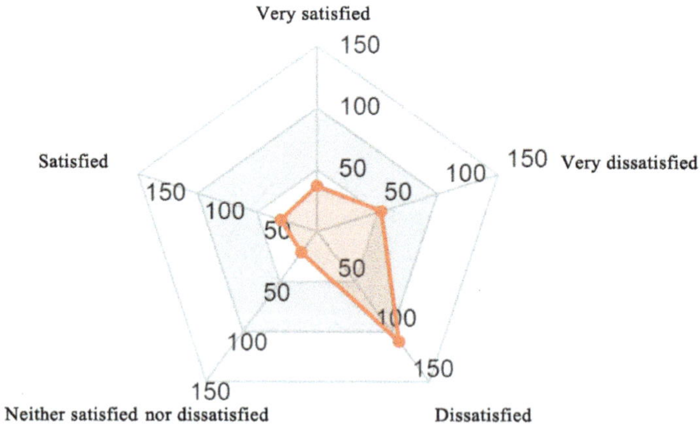

Fig. 7.13 Respondents' satisfaction with the turnkey implication mode

Table 7.2 Results of logistic regressions examining potential factors influencing respondents' satisfaction with the turnkey mode

		Estimate	Std. error	Wald	df	Sig.	95% Confidence interval	
							Lower bound	Upper bound
Constant term	[Is the turnkey mode good for Malawi = 1]	0.049	1.453	0.001	1	0.973	−2.799	2.897
	[Is the turnkey mode good for Malawi = 2]	2.286	1.462	2.445	1	0.118	−0.580	5.152
	[Is the turnkey mode good for Malawi = 3]	2.750	1.465	3.407	1	0.065	−0.167	5.577
	[Is the turnkey mode good for Malawi = 4]	3.552	1.473	5.813	1	0.016	0.665	6.440
Independent variable	[Education level of respondents = 1]	0.350	0.594	0.346	1	0.556	−0.814	1.514
	[Education level of respondents = 2]	0.233	0.700	0.110	1	0.740	−1.140	1.605
	[Education level of respondents = 3]	0.593	0.687	0.745	1	0.388	−0.754	1.940
	[Education level of respondents = 4]	−0.662	0.722	0.841	1	0.369	−2.077	0.753

(continued)

Table 7.2 (continued)

		Estimate	Std. error	Wald	df	Sig.	95% Confidence interval	
							Lower bound	Upper bound
	[Education level of respondents = 5]	0[a]	–	–	0	–	–	–
	[Place of Residence = 1]	1.175	0.347	11.444	1	0.001	0.494	1.856
	[Place of Residence 2]	0[a]	–	–	0	–	–	–

Urban residents were more satisfied with the turnkey mode than rural residents. This may have resulted from the fact that the turnkey mode offered limited opportunities for participation for people living in rural areas, whereas urban residents enjoyed more job opportunities. This showed that although most of the general public recognised that the Chinese aid project had contributed to local economic development and generated positive changes to the city's image, the benefits of the project were unequally distributed between the advantaged and vulnerable groups in society. In particular, government staff and people with higher education levels demonstrated greater positive attitudes towards the Chinese aid projects.

On the one hand, the turnkey implementation mode conforms to the "result-oriented" evaluation of aid effectiveness. It has achieved at least partial success, as the choice of aid projects have aligned with the development needs of recipient countries. One advantage of the turnkey mode is its complete management system, which ensures that the general contractor possesses high professional ability and technical skills. Moreover, effective communication is realised within the system, from design to construction, and the entire process is closely supervised and evaluated to ensure that the work of each subcontractor, along with the general quality of the work, is of high standard.

On the other hand, the turnkey implementation mode is controversial because it does not prioritise the participation of recipient countries in the construction process. Because of the tight schedule of projects and the dearth of skilled workers in the local community, turnkey projects employ more Chinese workers than locals. Although many recipient countries have imposed mandates on hiring local workers to address high unemployment, the employment of local workers is limited by practical considerations in terms of engineering efficiency and by conflicts between evaluation criteria and management systems. For example, Chinese workers are more familiar with work patterns and are thus able to work quickly to deliver urgent projects. Moreover, equipment imported from China requires Chinese operators, and experienced Chinese employees are capable of teaching local employees job skills. It must also be pointed out that because local workers enjoy relatively high welfare and strict labour protection, differing values and attitudes make it difficult for local workers to adapt to changes in standards. The above limitations make it difficult for locals to find employment in Chinese aid projects.

Nonetheless, where conditions permit, appropriate adjustments may be made to aid modes. Examples include encouraging recipient countries to participate in discussions and the planning of aid projects, increasing communication between the two sides, distributing ownership of the aid process between donors and recipients, adjusting systems and priorities through consultation, and implementing accountability measures. In the construction process, China should aim to reach a consensus with recipient countries on employment practices, understand the differences in their positions and cultures, and attain a complete understanding and respect for local laws, regulations and traditional labour practices. At the same time, recipient countries should adjust their modes of labour to meet the needs of modern production.

7.6 Conclusion and Discussion

As Malawi has a weak economic foundation and a strong dependence on foreign aid, Chinese aid projects have mainly focused on urban development. Moreover, such projects have been advantageous in showcasing Malawi's urban image, thereby attracting foreign investment. Aid projects for administrative buildings are important for reinforcing the national image, reflecting the modernisation of the city. Chinese aid projects, such as the Malawi Parliament Building, have had a positive social impact by combining local development goals with practical needs. Feedback from the local community suggests that China's aid projects have been the subject of significant recognition and that the local community hopes to continue receiving assistance.

The turnkey implementation mode has the characteristics of high efficiency, high quality, and low cost. Moreover, it is capable of meeting the requirements of the project objectives. As a result, it represents a suitable modality for project implementation in Africa, where construction capacity is weak. However, the present study found that the local people harbour some objections to this mode that mainly relate to the lack of local labour included in aid projects thus far. In view of these concerns, if conditions permit, the construction project should try to implement inclusionary measures. Through selecting high-quality subcontractors at the local level, a process carefully managed by the Chinese general contractor, construction can be both optimised and inclusive. To achieve this, Chinese contractors need to be familiar with the construction standards of the recipient country. Moreover, a standard specification needs to be established so that all stakeholders can work at the same pace. Attempts can be made to hire local employees and provide manual and technical positions, but the terms of employment should be clearly defined to effectively manage the employees. Furthermore, it is necessary to carry out job training for employees, in addition to increasing employment and completing the local talent training system, to cultivate the recipient countries' capacities for self-development.

References

Collier, P., & Dollar, D. (2002). Aid allocation and poverty reduction. *European Economic Review, 46*(8), 1475–1500.

Dionne, K. Y., Kramon, E., & Roberts, T. (2013). Aid effectiveness and allocation: Evidence from Malawi. In *Conference Research Frontiers in Foreign Aid at Princeton University*, April, 26–27.

Doucouliagos, H., & Paldam, M. (2008). Aid effectiveness on growth: A meta study. *European Journal of Political Economy, 24*(1), 1–24.

Fagernäs, S., & Schurich, C. (2004). *The fiscal effects of aid in Malawi* (Economics and Statistics Analysis Unit, Working Paper, 7). London: Overseas Development Institute (ODI).

Ling, J. (2010). Aid to Africa: What can the EU and China learn from each other? *South African Institute of International Affairs, 1*, 56.

Li, L. (2018). *Research on the influencing factors of customer satisfaction of Turnkey project*. Master's thesis, Tianjin University. 李良 (2018). 交钥匙工程客户满意度影响因素的研究. 天津: 天津大学硕士论文.

Liu, F. P. (2019). Modernization of China's foreign aid governance system in the 70 years since the founding of the People's Republic of China: Context and trend. *Journal of Shenzhen University (Humanities and Social Sciences), 36*(06), 31–40. 刘方平 (2019). 建国70年中国对外援助治理体系现代化: 脉络与走向. 深圳大学学报(人文社会科学版), 36(06), 31–40.

McGillivray, M., & Morrissey, O. (2000). Aid fungibility in assessing aid: Red herring or true concern? *Journal of International Development, 12*(3), 413–427.

Nagar, D., & Mutasa, C. (2018). *Africa and the World: Bilateral and multilateral international diplomacy*. Palgrave Macmillan.

Sachs, J. D. (2006). How aid can work. *The New York Review of Books, 53*(20), 1–3.

Shinn, D. H. (2007). An opportunistically. *Harvard International Review, 29*(2), 52.

Thindwa, T. C. (2015). China-Malawi relations: An analysis of trade patterns and development implications. *African East-Asian Affairs, 4*, 42–77.

Van Dijk, M. P. (2009). *The new presence of China in Africa*. Amsterdam University Press.

Tianjie Zhang is a professor at School of Architecture, and Deputy Director for Institute of Urban Heritage Preservation & Regeneration, Tianjin University, China. She got her PhD degree from National University of Singapore. Her main research interests include urban regeneration, transcultural landscape and emotional geographies.

Yuqi Zhang is a Ph.D. candidate at Kyoto University. She obtained her master's degree in urban planning from Tianjin University in 2020 and a bachelor's degree in urban planning from Chang'an University in 2017. She is interested in urban policy and public perception, and community development.

Davies Afiya Mbewe is a senior architect in the Department of Buildings, Ministry of Transport and Public Works, Malawi, participated in many practical projects. He obtained his master's degree in Architecture from Tianjin University in 2020.

Chapter 8
Schooling for the Future—Aided Education Buildings

Yingting Chen, Charlie Qiuli Xue, Guanghui Ding, and Yizhuo Gao

Abstract Among all types of China's foreign aid, education and construction aid are the most important in terms of proportion and influence. However, in spite of the significance and China's indisputable endeavor, researches on both disciplines are still in their infancy. While China's foreign aid has attracted much attention, it has also been controversial internationally and domestically. In contrast, the education aid is universally admired and pursued due to its internationalism and humanitarian. As a far-reaching public welfare undertaking, it is much less likely to trigger anti-sentiment and antipathy in recipient countries, and easier to win respect and praise internationally even if it is cross-regional, cross-national, cross-political, cross-cultural and cross-ideological. This chapter attempts to summarize the various types of aided school buildings through an overview and general comments. The authors analyze key influential factors and design features on representative cases selected from a database of 182 projects on four major types: schools for deprived groups, schools of vocational and police training, schools of politics and diplomacy, and the Confucius Institutes.

After the United States and the Soviet Union, China has gradually emerged as one of the major aid providers in today's international aid regime. Among all types of China's foreign aid, education and construction aid are outstanding in terms of proportion and influence. And the significance of their intersection—the design of China-aided schools—speaks for itself. Although not as grand as government buildings or stadiums, due to the advantages of less investment and faster construction, aided schools blossom everywhere and keep benefiting local people and communities persistently and extensively.

Y. Chen (✉) · C. Q. Xue · Y. Gao
Department of Architecture and Civil Engineering, City University of Hong Kong, Kowloon, Hong Kong
e-mail: ychen735-c@my.cityu.edu.hk

G. Ding
Department of Architecture, Beijing University of Civil Engineering and Architecture, Beijing, China

C. Q. Xue and G. Ding (eds.), *Exporting Chinese Architecture*,
https://doi.org/10.1007/978-981-19-2786-7_8

However, in spite of the significance and China's indisputable endeavor in education aid, or the largest proportion that construction aid has occupied in China's foreign aid, researches on both subjects are still in their infancy. Especially for construction aid, as an emerging research direction, existing studies are fragmental and unsystematic, either focus on experience sharing, introduction of engineering technology, or reports by the design institutes on their own projects. Only a couple of them have discussed architectural design from a relatively comprehensive perspective.

Compared with other types of China-aided architecture, what are the prominent features of these aided schools? What are the key factors that determine the design? How did these school projects balance endogenous and exogenous aspects, address the clash of globalism and localism, ensure respect of otherness and mutual benefit in specific natural, cultural, economic, technological, and diplomatic contexts? What are the strengths and weaknesses of the design and how can it be improved?

This chapter attempts to answer these questions through an overview of China-aided construction of schools across the world, analyzing key influential factors and design features along with detailed study on representative cases selected from a database of 182 projects on four major types of aided schools: schools for deprived groups, schools of vocational and police training, schools of politics and diplomacy, and the Confucius Institutes. This study aims to shed light on cross-border and cross-culture school design and encourage the exotic blossoming of aided school buildings.

8.1 International Education Aid: From "Hardware" Construction to "Software" Support

Education plays an important role in national construction, economic development and social progress. No matter developed countries or developing countries have always given priority to education, and education investment generally accounts for a large proportion of gross national product (GNP) and fiscal budget (Liu, 2006).

Since the end of World War II, international education development aid has practiced for more than half a century. The concept, system and mode of aid have experienced significant transformation. From focusing solely on higher and vocational education that are directly related to economic value to emphasizing basic education as one of "basic needs" and "basic rights" for human development; from project aid to institutional aid and planned aid; from accepting the inequality between the two sides of aid to advocating equal partnership; from paying attention to the effectiveness of aid to proposing the effectiveness of development (Birchler & Michaelowa, 2016). Nevertheless, no matter how the mode of aid changes and how the focus of aid shifts, school construction has always been one of the key areas of education aid.

Consistent with international aid in general, the top donors to school construction are the United States, Western Europe and Japan (Klees et al., 2019). In the 1960s, to meet the needs of increasing the rate of school access, enrollment and retention, most international education projects focused on school buildings, laboratories, educational equipment and infrastructure. While the importance has never been denied, this "hardware" construction has given way over time to a "software" support due to higher demands on the quality of education instead of quantity and coverage, consisting primarily of faculty training, strengthening of staff and institutional capacity, scholarship provision, education system building and policy reform to better perform the role of the "hardware". Taking World Bank as an example, the share of funds for education going into civil works has fallen from almost 100% in the 1960s to about 45% (1995–1998) (Theunynck, 2002; Zhao, 2010).

8.2 China's Education Aid: "Hardware" and "Software" Go Hand in Hand

For China, education aid plays an important role in enhancing national soft power, reflecting international social responsibility and shaping a good image of an emerging power. Compared with the obvious decline in "hardware" investment from traditional donors, China's education aid is also beginning to focus more on "software" enhancement. However, it has not ceased in school construction.

China offers education aid majorly in three forms: providing educational loans and scholarships (financial aid), sending teachers and developing teaching and management capacity (professional aid), building schools and donating facilities (material and technical aid). Among them, complete sets of projects (refer to construction of productive or civil projects) is the most important manner, accounting for 40% of China's foreign aid expenditure. The proportion of educational facilities in the total number of complete sets of projects has increased from 6% by 2009 to more than 20% by 2018 (The State Council Information Office of the People's Republic of China, 2011, 2014, 2021) (Table 8.1).

China-aided school construction is government-led and adopts a "turn-key" mode. First of all, the Ministry of Commerce of the People's Republic of China (MOFCOM) signs a framework agreement with the recipient country for the school construction. Next, the aid recipient negotiates and communicates on specific matters such as the site selection, construction scale and design requirements, and then delivers a specific plan to the Chinese side. After that, MOFCOM will invite qualified institutes and companies for biding and determining winning designers and contractors who shall undertake the site investigation, school design and construction within the schedule specified in the contract (the recipient country may or may not be involved in decision-making). Finally, the Economic and Commercial Office of local Chinese embassy shall take the lead in organizing local reputable companies to participate in the acceptance testing before officially handing over the project to the recipient governments (Man, 2008; Niu, 2014; Wang, 2013) (Fig. 8.1).

Table 8.1 Sectoral distribution of China's complete sets of projects overseas (*Source:* White paper "China's Foreign Aid" released in 2011, 2014 and 2021)

Sector	By 2009		2013–2018	
	Quantity	% of Total	Quantity	% of Total
Public facilities	***670***	***33.09***	***306***	***74.63***
Schools	130	6.42	86	20.98
Health care	106	5.23	58	14.15
Civil construction	143	7.06	19	4.63
Well and water supply	72	3.56	20	4.88
Municipal infrastructure	37	1.83	60	14.63
Others	182	8.99	63	15.37
Economic infrastructure	***390***	***19.26***	***80***	***19.51***
Transport	201	9.93	56	13.66
Broadcast and telecommunications	92	4.54	13	3.17
Electricity	97	4.79	6	1.46
Others	–	–	5	1.22
Agriculture	***215***	***10.62***	***19***	***4.63***
Agricultural processing	168	8.30	6	1.46
Agricultural pilot centers	–	–	5	1.22
Farmland water conservancy	47	2.32	2	0.49
Others	–	–	6	1.46
Industry	***635***	***31.36***	***5***	***1.22***
Light industry	320	15.80	–	–
Textiles	74	3.65	–	–
Machinery industry	66	3.26	–	–
Chemical industry	48	2.37	–	–
Building materials processing	42	2.07	–	–
Geological prospecting and mineral exploration	38	1.88	–	–
Others	47	1.23	–	–
Others	***115***	***5.68***	–	–
TOTAL	**2025**	**100**	**410**	**100**

8.3 Major Types of China's Foreign-Aided Schools

8.3.1 Schools for Deprived Groups: To Promote Education Equality

Accounting for the largest proportion of China's education aid (>40%), schools for deprived groups are the ones that have achieved the most recognized results. The

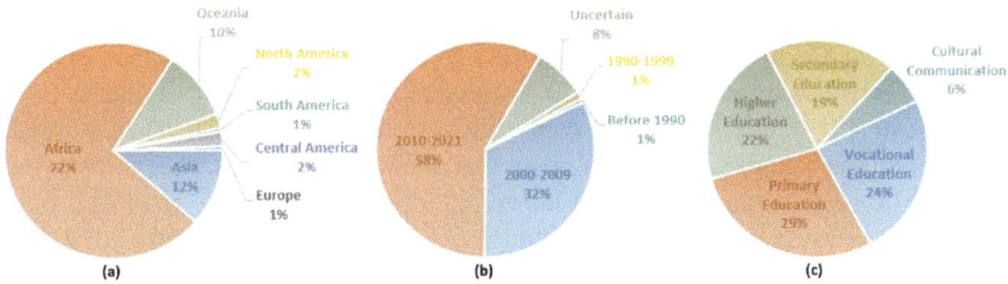

Fig. 8.1 Distribution of China-aided construction of educational facilities by 2021. **a** Location distribution. **b** Period distribution. **c** Type distribution. (*Source:* Drawn by the author based on the database of 182 projects)

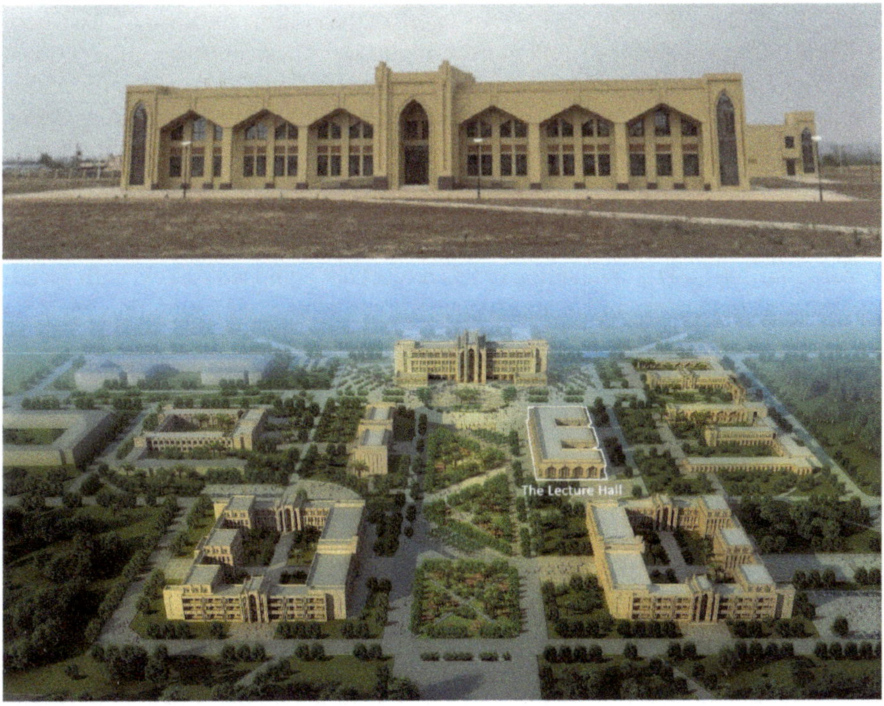

Fig. 8.2 The bird's eye view and lecture hall of the Kabala Campus of the University of Bamako in Mali (*Source:* Provided by the SIPPR Engineering Group, adapted by the author)

distinguishing feature lies in the fundamental purpose of their design to meet the educational needs of the recipient countries, aiming to mitigate the "vacancy" and "shortage" of educational resources.

• *Complementing the Infrastructure and Basic Education System*

Admittedly, as mentioned above, while quantity has become less of a concern, it is now time to shift our focus to improve the quality of education. However, despite more than 60 years of international aid for education, most recipient countries have not yet been able to provide adequate education on their own, and their most urgent needs remain on school access, enrollment and retention. In Africa, for example, the World Bank's 2018 report shows that the completion rate of primary schools is only 67%, and the enrollment rate of higher education is only 5% (Klees et al., 2019; The World Bank, 2017).

Therefore, unlike traditional donors, such as Japan, whose contribution of the number of schools in different recipient countries varies greatly according to the educational development plan, it is not accident to find China-aided schools less dramatic but more functional, and are basically intended to be evenly distributed with the primary aim of filling gaps in infrastructure and basic educational services (Niu, 2014). For example, under the framework of the Forum on China-Africa Cooperation (FOCAC), China put forward the Eight Measures for Africa in 2006 and 2009, committing to build 100 rural primary schools and 50 China-Africa friendship schools across the continent, which have achieved initial results as expected (Wang, 2013). In 2007, for instance, the Ministry of Education of Angola commissioned the East China Architectural Design and Research Institute (ECADI) to design 28 schools, including 15 middle schools, 13 technical colleges, 7 administrative colleges, and the restoration of an agricultural college (China National Complete Engineering Corporation, 2007). The completion of this project has equipped Angola with a well-established system of secondary and higher schools in all major cities, thus enabling the Angolan government to carry out post-war reconstruction in the field of education (China National Machinery Industry Corporation, 2007).

- *Coping with Teacher Shortage and Guaranteeing Gender Parity*

Affected by multiple factors such as the shortage of educational resources, local culture, and colonial history, the education mode of recipient countries is quite different from that of China. Apart from materials and supplies, the most obvious problem is the shortage of teachers. The teacher-student ratio is as low as 1:60 while the world average is around 1:20.[1] The SIPPR Engineering Group encountered one of the most severe cases of this issue in the design of the Kabala Campus of the University of Bamako in Mali (2016).

Mali is the eighth largest country, and the third largest producer of gold in Africa, but the sixth lowest in economic income (The World Factbook, 2021). As the only comprehensive university in Mali, one teacher at the University of Bamako often has to face 800–1,000 students. To accommodate such demand, Chinese designers designed three large terraced lecture halls, one in the middle with a capacity of 500 students, and two on both sides for 300 students each. Although function comes first, the designers raised the height of the room to about 10 m, which mitigates the sense of constriction caused by the thick wall structure stems from climate and religious

[1] Data from the Global Economy. https://www.theglobaleconomy.com/rankings/student_teacher_ratio_primary_school/Africa/

influences.[2] Layered space, large scale and light changes make these lecture halls, which originally meant to make up for shortcomings, become the most attractive crown jewels (Fig. 8.2). President Keïta called the university "an important milestone in the development of higher education in Mali," believing that it will produce positive impact on sub-urban and rural areas and "promote further development of trade and cooperation between the two countries." (Chinese Embassy in Mali, 2018).

Apart from "hardware" provision and design adaptation, tremendous effort has also been devoted to gender equality which is the most urgent, yet persistent, obstacle in the quest towards an equal education for all. The recent report *Building Bridges for Gender Equality* shows that in the past 20 years, 55% of G7[3] aid to education goes to achieving gender equality, but results lag (UNESCO, 2019). The number of illiterate adult women in low-income countries has grown by 20 million since 2000, one third of countries have not achieved gender parity in primary education, while over a quarter of people still believe that it is more important for boys to go to university than girls (The Global Education Monitoring Report Team, 2019). "We can improve education systems as much as we want but real change is unlikely to happen unless we also tackle negative gender norms and attitudes in society," cautioned Manos Antoninis, Director of the Global Education Monitoring Report. "We have to empower girls, educate boys and men and identify new role models to challenge the status quo successfully" (UNESCO, 2019).

In respect to this issue, Eritrea sets an example. Before 2005, Eritrea had only one university—the University of Asmara (UoA), originally established in 1958 by Italy with the highest capacity of 1,200 students. In just 12 years, seven institutions of higher education had been established (Temesghen, 2015). Among them, the Eritrea Institute of Technology funded by China is the largest, located in Mai Nefhi (25 km southwest of the capital city, Asmara), embracing three colleges: College of Education, College of Engineering and Technology, and College of Science. As a national key project and China's largest construction aid to Eritrea, the College of Science consists of seven departments with an area of 18,453 m^2, expected to accommodate 6,000 students, and currently has 141 staff members and 953 students among which 40% are females (Seid, 2017). This is an exciting number in technical and scientific programs which are usually male bastions.

China conducted the first feasibility investigation in November 2011, and completed in June 2017 after two and a half years of construction by workers from both countries. The "courtyards and corridors" layout organically combines the teaching units, the administrative units and the sharing units, enables each area interact with the others while maintaining its functional independence and completeness. Brick-red natural stone paint is applied to the exterior façade, together with basic deformation of Platonic solid, highlighting the integrity and sculptural sense of the building (Sohu News, 2019). Domestically and internationally, this kind of coating

[2] Information from the interview of Guanghui Ding with the foreign aid project design team of the SIPPR Engineering Group on May 27, 2021.

[3] The Group of Seven (G7) is an inter-governmental political forum consisting of Canada, France, Germany, Italy, Japan, the United Kingdom and the United States

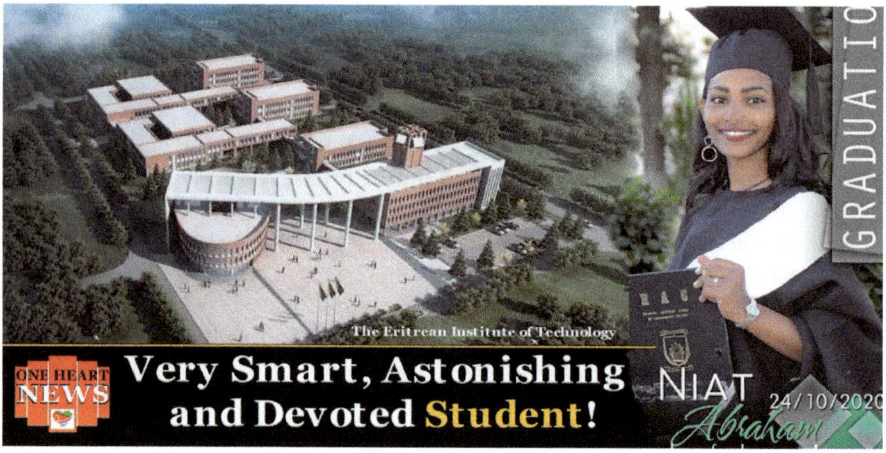

Fig. 8.3 Graduate with distinction, Niat Abraham, and the College of Science of Eritrea Institute of Technology (*Source:* https://www.65tes-habeshamusic.com/very-smart-astonishing-and-devoted-student/)

and techniques are commonly seen in China's campus design. The concept is simplifying complexity and adapting to changing educational needs and local culture with concise appearance.

In 2020, the College of Science conferred first degrees to 291 and diplomas to 61 graduates (Ministry of Information Eritrea, 2020), and the distinct graduate award went to Niat Abraham, "a very smart, astonishing and devoted female student who participates in extracurricular activities, especially in organizations that empower women and fellow students" (Teklom, 2020). The image of Abraham appears on the university poster together with the college building (Fig. 8.3), showcasing the university's progress in promoting women's development, and persistent endeavor on instigating principal essence of equity and quality education.

- *The "Double-Edged Sword" of Quantity-Oriented Design*

According to the white papers "China's Foreign Aid" released in 2011, 2014 and 2021, it is estimated that more than 300 educational facilities have been built so far, covering over 120 countries in Africa, ASEAN, Oceania, Europe, Latin America and the Caribbean, with the number and scale of projects keep expanding (The State Council Information Office of the People's Republic of China, 2021). This achievement is due in part to China's reputation for the incredible speed of construction, which has consistently performed well in foreign-aided projects, especially schools for deprived groups that are in great demand. On the other hand, China is also working hard with its own issue of universal access to equal education, providing a wealth of ready-made methods, techniques and experience to draw upon.

But quantity-oriented design is usually a double-edged sword. The design of construction-aid projects is highly influenced by the procedures enacted by the

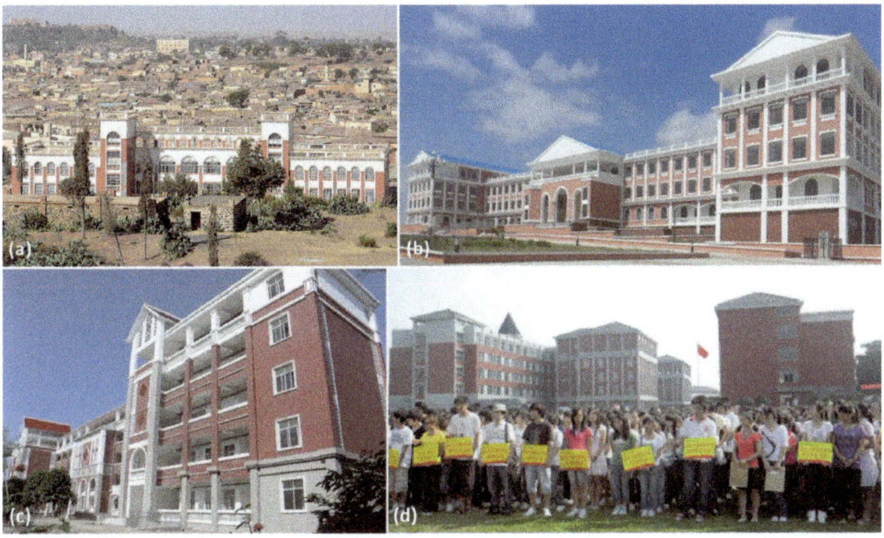

Fig. 8.4 **a** Elementary school in Arbate-Asmara district of Asmara, Eritrea (2014). **b** Malawi University of Science and Technology, Thyolo, Malawi (2013). **c** Putian Huaqiao High School, Fujian, China. **d** Zhejiang International Studies University, Zhejiang, China (2010). (*Source:* **a** purchased from ISTOCK, **b** provided by Tianjie Zhang, **c** and **d** from Google Image[4])

Chinese government with inadequate local input in most cases. The designers have no chance to be on site when they bid the design. This has to be said a deficiency in architectural design. And the bidding timeframe is terribly short. For example, in order to implement the promise made at the FOCAC to build 100 primary schools, architects from Beijing Institute of Architectural Design (BIAD) were required to submit 10 proposals within 20 days, which is incredibly tight. When BOT mode is adopted, architects are working under the construction contractors. The designers have even shorter time to do design scheme, sometimes just a weekend. What even worse, restricted by economic and technological limitations, the Chinese side compresses the design and construction schedule and applies low-grade materials and techniques, while the recipients themselves are only concerned about the "on-time free delivery" of schools.

Although recent multi-story courtyard-style schools have improved significantly in terms of design, functionality and user experience compared to the earlier design of "a row of huts surrounding an open playground", most of the aided schools for deprived groups are similar to that of China's domestic ones from layout, form to techniques as stated in the case of College of Science of EIT. Some of them can even be considered as a direct "transplantation" or "duplication" with few innovative examples (Fig. 8.4).

[4] **c**https://www.zhonzhuan.com/pthq.
dhttps://edu.jobui.com/college/zisu/.

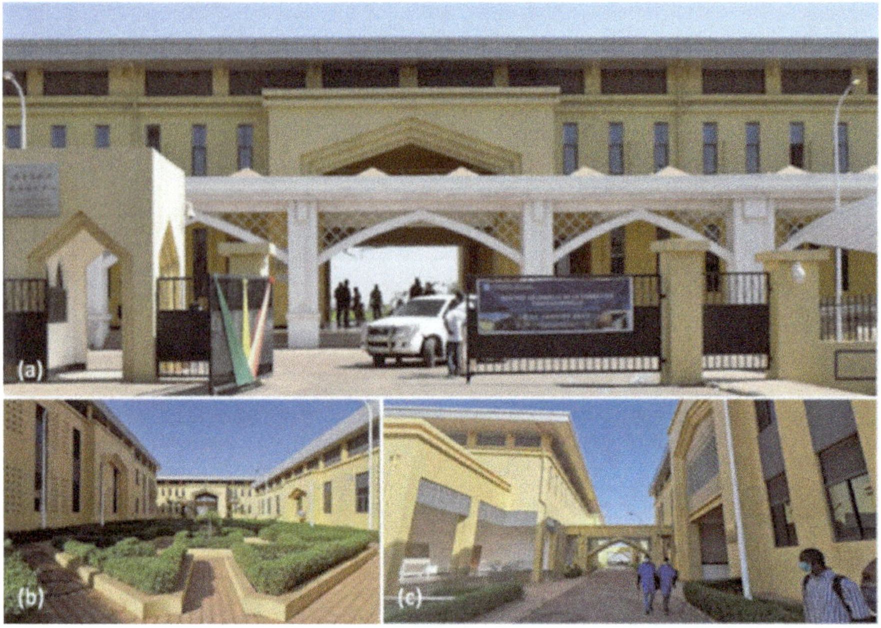

Fig. 8.5 The Sénou Vocational Training Center, 2018. **a** The main entrance. **b** The parterre courtyard. **c** The passage and corridor (*Source:* MarliChine. https://malichine.com/)

8.3.2 Schools of Vocational and Police Training: To Promote Employment, Eliminate Poverty and Improve Social Security

Of all interventions, vocational education and professional training that help students develop marketable skills have been proved to be the most effective and efficient assistance, leading directly to higher incomes, economic stability, and better health (Morgenstern, 2021). In addition to the purpose of employment, the police academies also shoulder the important task of cultivating social security defenders.

Such schools are often located in remote areas due to the need for training venues and equipment, but they are far more significant than building a fancy school in downtown. Construction aid in developing countries often faces economic and technological limitations, and the shortage of resources, especially electricity and water, is even more pronounced in non-urban areas. Therefore, the natural environment, specifically climate and topographical conditions, is usually the primary challenge faced by Chinese architects. China-aided school projects are mainly distributed between the Tropics of Cancer and Capricorn. Inspired by the local architectural response to the climate, and adopt Chinese modern Lingnan tropical architectural techniques

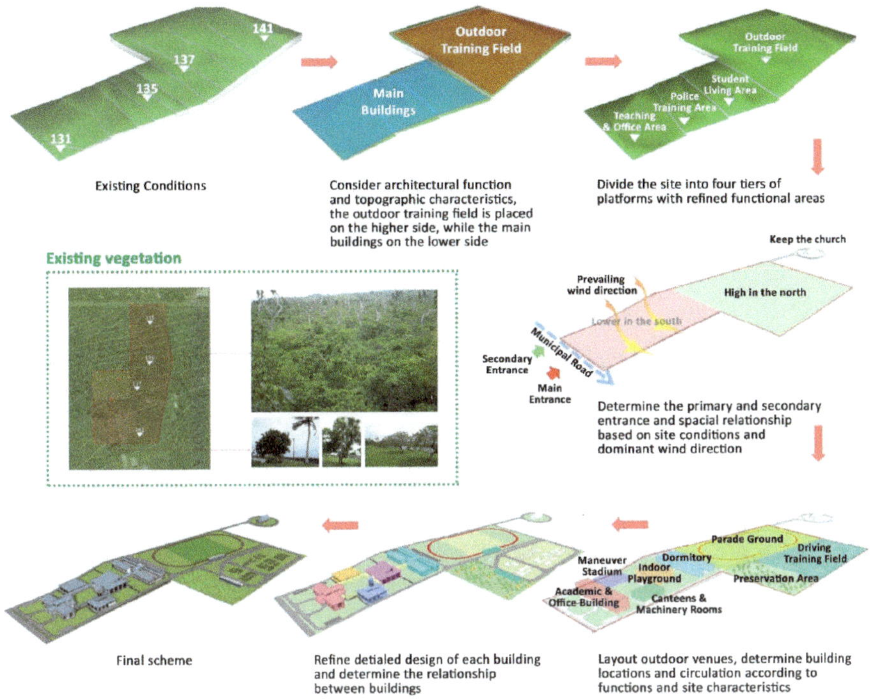

Fig. 8.6 Samoa Police Training Academy, 2019. Design strategies adapt to terrain and context conditions (*Source:* The Arcplus Group design package[6], adapted by the author)

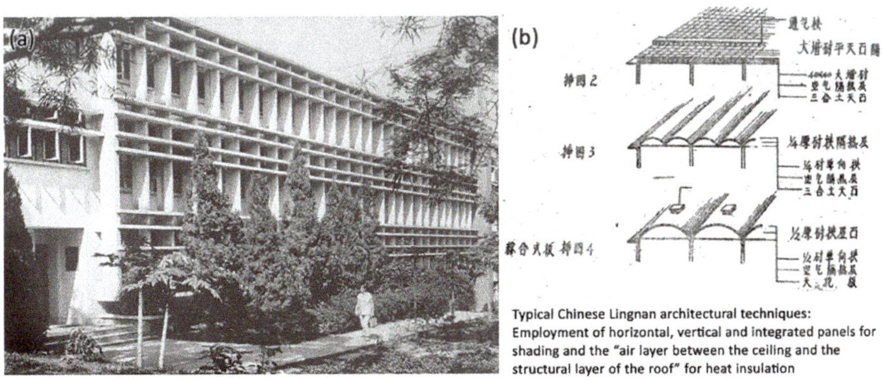

Fig. 8.7 Typical Chinese Lingnan architectural techniques. (*Source:* **a** from Architecture in New China, 1976; **b** from China Academy of Building Research. The Proceedings of Building Climate Zoning Conference, 1958)

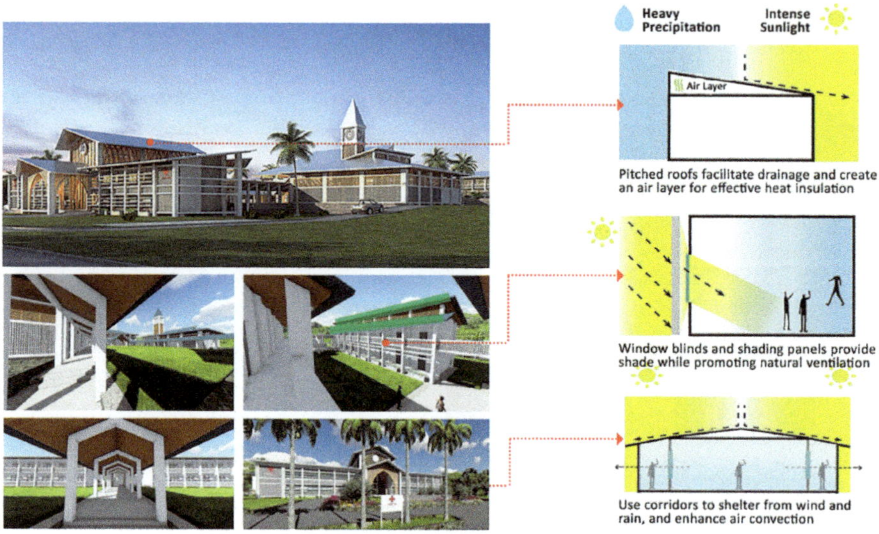

Fig. 8.8 Design strategies adapt to climate conditions of Samoa Police Training Academy, 2019. (*Source:* The Arcplus Group design package,[5] adapted by the author)

which focus on heat insulation, natural ventilation, and sun shading, Chinese architects have created very typical tropical regionalism buildings with natural factors as the fundamental determinant (Table 8.2).

- *Tropical Regionalism Techniques—Inspiration from Local Context*

The Ségou Vocational Training Center by the SIPPR Engineering Group is one of the three vocational training centers (located in Gao, Mopti and Ségou) built under Mali's Education III Project signed in December 1997. Besides of being a strategic action in the fight against poverty, the value added resides in its decentralization of access to high-level vocational training supply, thereby contributing to social equity (AfDB, 2006).

It is a typical case in a remote area designed according to climatic characteristics of Bamako, Mali. Bamako is located in a tropical desert with a hot, dry climate. Under such natural conditions, the temperature of an open room with flowing hot air is significantly higher than that of a closed room, that is why small windows with thick walls are commonly adopted. However, due to the lack of electricity, natural ventilation is still necessary. Fully open auxiliary spaces such as atriums and parterre courtyards are introduced, different functional areas are connected by semi-open corridors, and classrooms are equipped with ceiling fans to facilitate natural ventilation for indoor cooling. Different shading measures are adopted in different

[5] Information from the Arcplus Group design package of Samoa Police Training Academy. https://112.74.51.184/forum.php?mod=viewthread&tid=406884&extra=page%3D1&page=1&_dsign=e213cf5f&mobile=no.

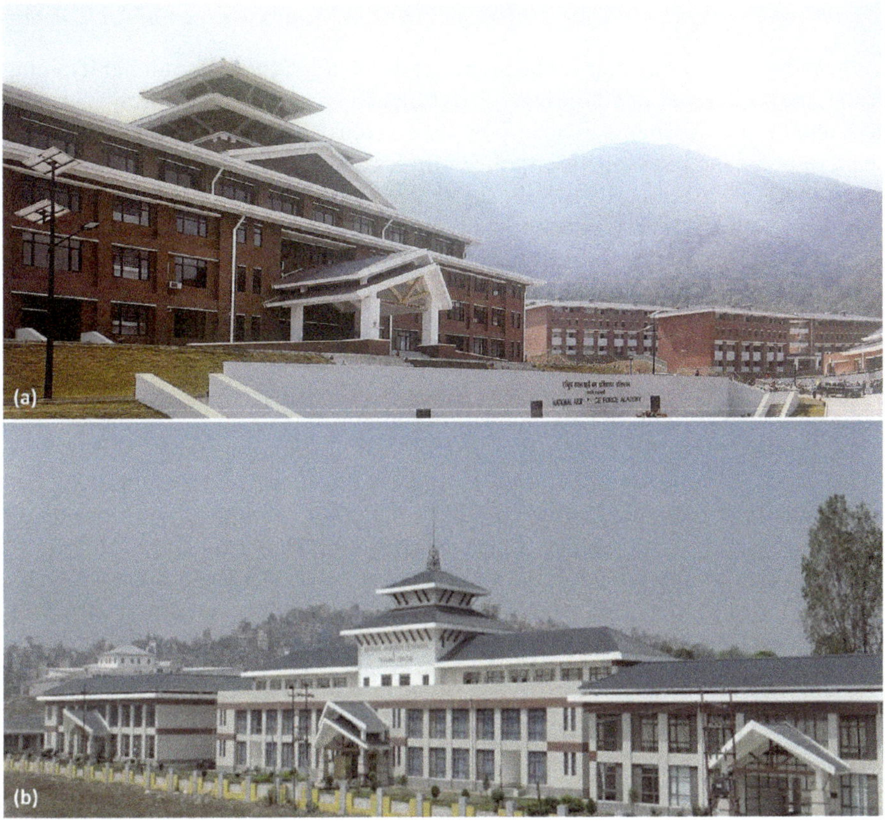

Fig. 8.9 **a** The National Armed Police Force Academy of Nepal (2017). **b** National Ayurveda Research and Training Center of Nepal (2011). (*Source:* **a** provided by China State Construction Engineering Corporation, **b** from the institute's official website https://nartc.org.np/)

functional zones: large overhanging roofs and colonnades minimize direct sunlight through their own structure; the elongated windows are equipped with terra-cotta blinds; corridors are shaded with metal perforated panels and lattice frames, which make full use of local materials, abstract local cultural symbols, and then express as shading structures in a modern way (Fig 8.5).

The training center's opening was delayed until January 2021 due to the COVID-19 pandemic. However, this accident has evoked awareness of the importance for young people to undergo vocational trainings especially with regards to the dynamic change of global environment. In the post-epidemic era, in addition to the original functions, Mali is actively exploring with China to promote on-line technical training and other innovative ways, so as to better leverage the advantages of the vocational education and benefit more Malians (Embassy of the People's Republic of China in Mali, 2020).

- *Tropical Regionalism Techniques—reference from Chinese Lingnan Architecture*

Compared to the vernacular architectural style of the Sénou Vocational Training Center, the techniques of Chinese modern Lingnan architecture are more evident in the Samoa Police Training Academy by the Arcplus Group. While the academy is meant to boost the recruitment of police officers and making the induction process more robust, Fuiavailiili Egon Keil, the Police Commissioner, says the goal is to go beyond further. "The first of its kind in Samoa, the Samoa Police Academy is envisioned as a multi-agency training center, with a view towards a regional center of excellence for policing in the Pacific region," Keil said. "This academy will be hub for law enforcement and the courses will be available to tackle the needs of the Pacific Islands." (Loop Pacific, 2020; Feagaimaali'i, 2020) Such a vision towards overseas employment opportunities determines a better acceptance of foreign cultures and an unintentional weakening of local cultural expression.

The project is located on the south-west side of the Samoan capital city of Apia, about 7 km from the government office building in downtown, close to the Tafa'igata prison. The total site area is approximately 56,000 m^2 with a gross floor area of approximately 5,770 m^2 (Liu, 2018). The lower south side is a relatively flat grass training ground (slope 3%), while the higher north side has a large elevation difference (slope 5%). Respecting to such topographical conditions and combining with actual function needs, the site was divided into four tiers of platforms with outdoor training field on the higher side, and main buildings on the lower side. The architects also tried to retain the vegetation resources as much as possible, gave full emphasis to the tradition and continuity of original context (Fig. 8.6).[6]

Chinese architects, on one hand, protected and utilized the existing environmental conditions; on the other hand, responded to adverse factors such as intense sunlight, heavy rainstorm, and frequent earthquake. All buildings on the campus adopt pitched roofs, with simple and concise modern facade design. Walls are made of hollow blocks covered by anti-corrosion paint. Some windows are equipped with blinds and panels for shading and natural ventilation. External corridors are attached to every single building, which not only enriches the appearance, offers the function of shading and sheltering, but also facilitate resting and social activities (Yang, 2021) (Figs. 8.7 and 8.8).

- *The Realization of Regionalism by "Bricolage"*

While being function-oriented, the recipient countries also place high expectation on culture inheritance and nourishment of aided schools. And the architects respond to this demand through "regionalism".

The introduction, reinterpretation and reorganization of local architectural culture is the most commonly-used manner, which can be called the "bricolage" technique. Chinese architects delve deep into local architectural context, discover the most

---

[6] Information from the Arcplus Group design package of Samoa Police Training Academy. https://112.74.51.184/forum.php?mod=viewthread&tid=406884&extra=page%3D1&page=1&_dsign=e213cf5f&mobile=no.

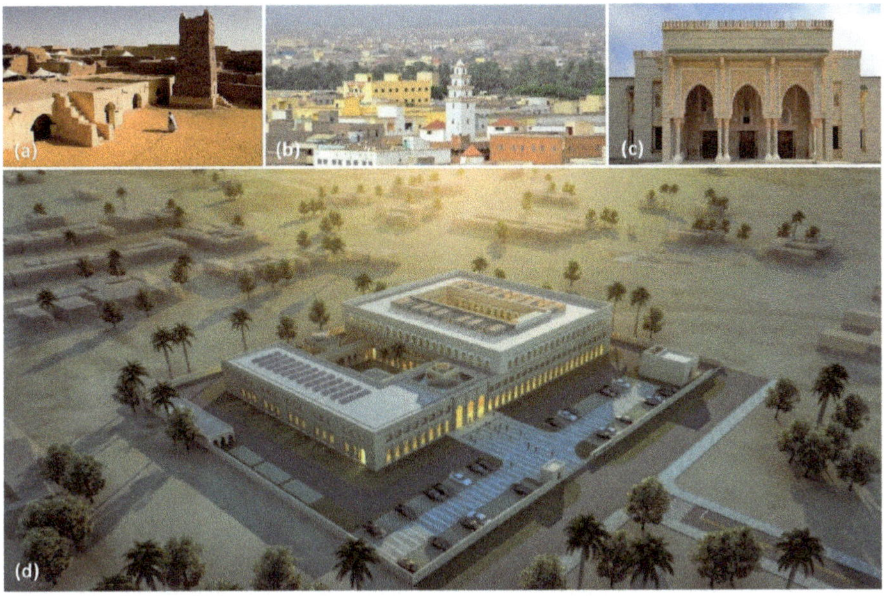

Fig. 8.10 The National Institute of Public Health in Mauritania, 2020. **a** and **b** Local houses in Mauritania. **c** The Nouakchott Grand Mosque. **d** Bird's-eye view rendering (*Source:* **a** and **b** from Google Image[7]; **c** and **d** from Ge, 2020)

unique and representative cultural symbols, and then generalize, abstract, and transform the familiar components or symbols with modern materials and new techniques, thus to stamp the architecture with strong local cultural characteristic.

Such "bricolage" technique abounds in China's foreign-aided schools. Local traditional dwelling, especially religious architecture with distinctive features, are usually sources of inspiration. The National Armed Police Force Academy of Nepal (2017) and the Traditional Medicine Research and Training Center of Nepal (2011) (Fig. 8.9) are such examples where the concept of design is apparent that even those with no architectural expertise or design background can recognize at one glance.

"Bricolage" is not in itself pejorative, but why most of the "bricolage" examples seem awkward and contrived? The reason might be that, although the local architectural and cultural elements are widely applied, they are essentially a repetition of basic units of the same nature, resulting in a homogeneous and superficial representation. The architectural symbols float over the surface of physical structure, disconnecting historical memory and spontaneous associations. In contrast, a more effective practice is the use of groups of basic units with hierarchical relationships, such as the National Institute of Public Health in Mauritania by China Aviation Planning and Design Institute (Ge, 2020) (Fig. 8.10).

[7] a https://www.telesurtv.net/opinion/Mauritania-libre-del-azote-muyahidin-20200629-0020.html. b https://anamusafer.com/tag/%D8%A7%D9%8A%D9%86/.

On the base of various application of arch, brick art and geometric patterns of Islamic architecture, the spatial organization is closely related to local urban texture. The classical principles of spatial organization are combined with elements that can be referenced from the traditional architecture. The whole building resembles a mini-Islamic city, with domes, window groups, corridors and courtyards as the spatial forms of mosques, dwellings, streets and plazas. The poetic complexity, rhythms of arched colonnade, combined with light and shadow in the sun, endow the building with a sense of sculpture, reflecting the stately elegance of Islamic architecture.

The original material for the "Throughout the project, the Tunisianbricolage" technique is the architectural culture derived from natural environment or cultural customs in the historical conditions at that time. Architecture that conveys cultural significance cannot be realized unless one understands how to effectively translate the existing culture in architectural creation. From the Renaissance to Le Corbusier's "Five Principles" of modern architecture and the transnational architectural practice under the trend of globalization, how to transform traditional forms into modern new architectural forms that inherit culture has been a long-lasting topic that deserves further discussion.

Table 8.2 Main climate types and corresponding architectural characteristics of the recipient countries (*Source:* summarized by the author)

Climate type	Climate characteristics	Architectural characteristics
Tropical desert region		
	High sunlight intensity High temperature Distinct wet and dry season (tropical wet-dry climate)	Reflecting heat radiation Cooling, shading Rainwater collection system
Tropical rainforest region		
	High temperature High humidity Heavy precipitation	Cooling, shading Ventilation Rainproof, sheltering, drainage
Tropical Island region		
	Strong sea wind High temperature High humidity Heavy precipitation High salt concentration in air	Windproof Cooling, shading Ventilation Rainproof, sheltering, drainage Corrosion resistant material

8.3.3 Schools of Politics and Diplomacy: To Nurture and Cultivate the Next Generation of Leaders and Managers

While China's foreign aid has attracted much attention, it has also been controversial. As noted above, President Keïta called the University of Bamako aided by China "an important milestone in the development of higher education in Mali," believing that it will produce impact beyond education itself and "promote further development of trade and cooperation between the two countries." (Chinese Embassy in Mali, 2018) This added value, in most aid realms, is often accused by some western governments, academics and media as "Neo-colonialism in Africa" and "China's increasing influence in Africa is at the expense of the wellbeing of local people" (Mitchell & McKee, 2018). In contrast, the education aid is universally admired and pursued due to its internationalism and humanitarian. As a far-reaching public welfare undertaking, it is much less likely to trigger anti-sentiment and antipathy in recipient countries, and easier to win respect and praise internationally even if it is cross-regional, cross-national, cross-political, cross-cultural and cross-ideological.

Interestingly, more than just high acceptance and recognition, the recipient countries are heartily willing to invite Chinese architects to design educational institutions that train their own political talents and public servants. Such as the Diplomatic Academy of Angola (2018), the Diplomacy Training Academy of Tunisia (2019), Ethiopia Meles Leadership Academy (2021), The National Intelligence Service Training Institute of Angola (2020), etc. These special schools, usually located in capital cities, are highly concerned by the government and have the highest design level and techniques among aided schools.

- *The Carrier of Political Metaphors with Emphasis on Modernity and Technology*

Schools of politics and diplomacy are a symbol of alliance to convey support from China and aspiration of the recipient countries, which often carry political meaning and metaphors. The Diplomacy Training Academy of Tunisia (2019) by the Arcplus Group is built on the basis of active communication and cooperation between China and Tunisia. Throughout the project, the Tunisian side had an unprecedented level of involvement, not only in every step of the decision-making process, sending commissioners to China for design and supply inspection, but also Mondher Dhraief, the director general of this academy, was personally participated in the design because of his childhood love for diplomacy and the dream of building the first Tunisian diplomatic academy with international standards (Xinhua News, 2019).

The first proposal was a low-rise courtyard-style building emphasizing Tunisian architectural tradition. The scheme was developed with the Arabian courtyard as the basic element. Multiple courtyards correspond to different functional zones, connecting by a primary corridor with strong Islamic features for culture display and communication (Fig. 8.11).[8]

[8] Information from the Arcplus Group design package of Diplomacy Training Academy of Tunisia.

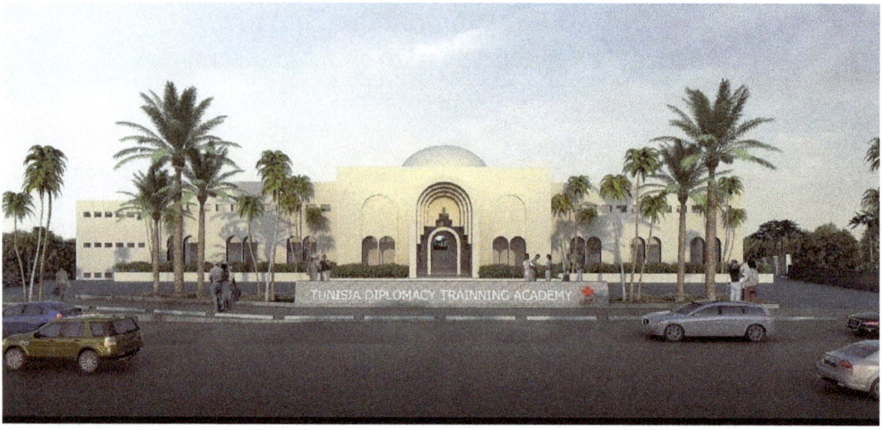

Fig. 8.11 The first proposal for Diplomacy Training Academy of Tunisia. (*Source:* Provided by The Arcplus Group)

However, the Tunisian side rejected this traditional proposal, preferring a modern and future-oriented design. Furthermore, this scheme still made the mistake that often happens in political architecture. Due to the convention of "being grand" accepted by both the architect and the client, the massive structure is roughly embedded into the urban texture, failing to respond to the context and the public where the building is located. Dhraief did a sketch overnight, highlighting the sense of sculpture and volume, as well as the attitude of open and welcoming (Fig. 8.12), hoping that the most important academic lecture hall would be "grand" and "towering" with easy access to the public. "Tunisia is working on the development of its foreign policy and the promotion of its diplomatic skills," said Dhraief. "The major aim of this diplomatic academy is to strengthen the influence of Tunisian diplomacy in the world." (Xinhua) (Xinhua News, 2019).

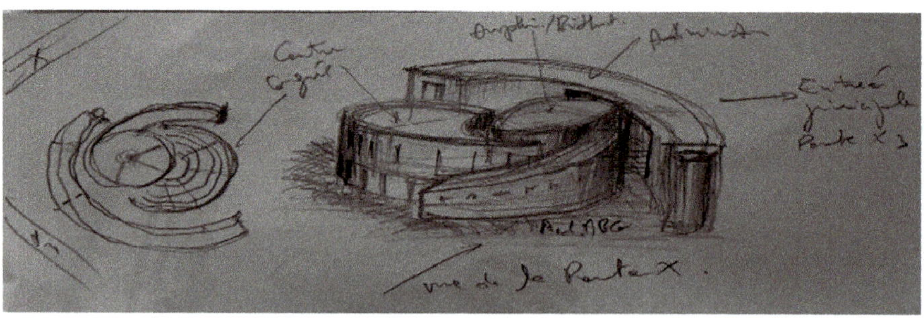

Fig. 8.12 The sketch from Mondher Dhraief, the director general of the Diplomacy Training Academy of Tunisia, for design communication. (*Source:* Provided by The Arcplus Group)

---

https://112.74.51.184/thread-406880-1-1.html.

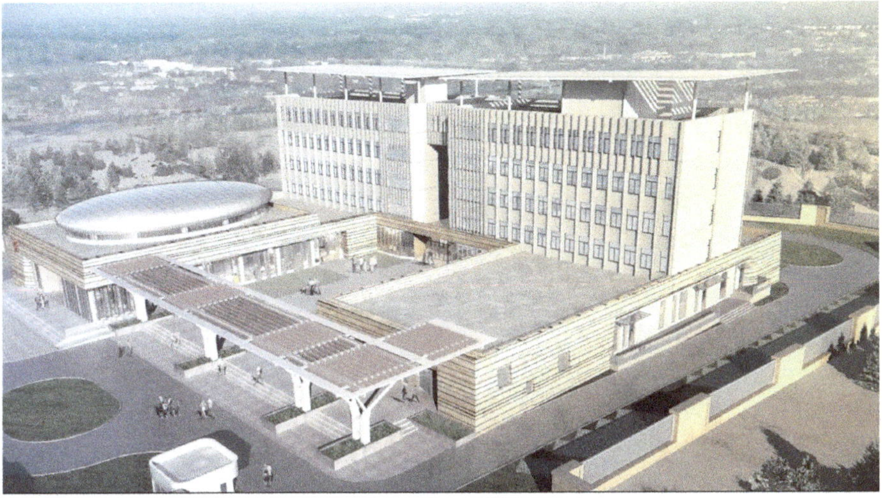

Fig. 8.13 The Diplomacy Training Academy of Tunisia (2019). (*Source:* Provided by The Arcplus Group)

After several rounds of discussions, a five-story building with an underground parking lot was finally determined, located near the headquarters of Tunisian Ministry of Foreign Affairs, north of the capital Tunis (Xinhua News, 2019). This scheme goes in the opposite direction from the first proposal, showing an exploration of space and the content rather than the appearance of traditional elements, transforming them into a modern form that responds to the client's "futuristic" requirements. While the building as a whole does not appear to have an apparent vernacular look, details such as the dome, corridors and overhead structures are subtly localized with Islamic characteristics. The most important lecture hall was placed at a prominent position on the ground level, introducing an Islamic-style dome and vast open front yard reinterpreted through modern techniques. The entrance directly faces the municipal road, reflecting an open and welcoming attitude. The tower was divided into two parts, eliminating the sense of dullness and heaviness and presenting a lighter image of a connecting bridge (Xinhua News, 2019). The design achieves a balance and harmony between tradition and modern, with an understandable expression of Tunisia's aspiration to the world and the future (Fig. 8.13).

8.3.4 The Confucius Institutes: To Promote Cultural Communication

Foreign-aid architecture is influenced not only by local culture of the recipient country, but also by that of the donor country. Local culture itself is constantly changing and developing, absorbing foreign cultures in a relatively stable system.

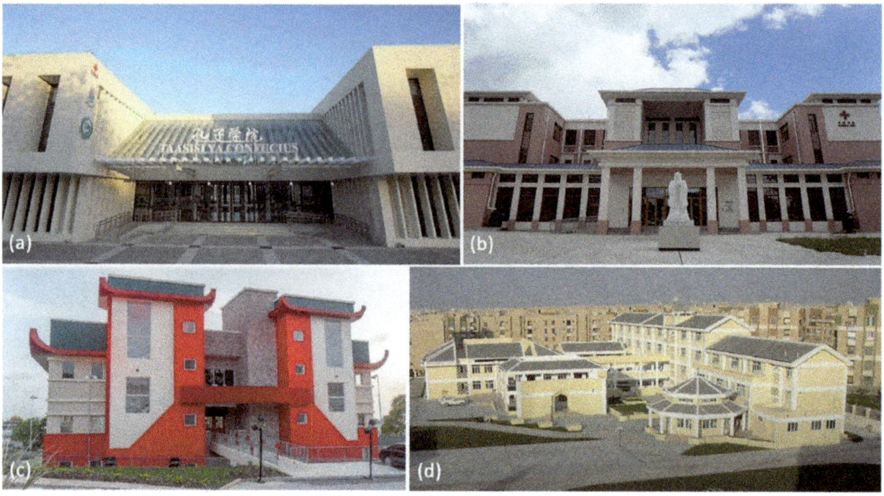

Fig. 8.14 **a** Confucius Institute at the University of Dar es Salaam, Tanzania (2018). **b** Confucius Institute at the University of West Indies, Mona Campus (2009). **c** Confucius Institute at the University of West Indies, Cave Hill Campus (2017). **d** Cairo Chinese School in Egypt (2008). (*Source:* Google Image[9])

The constant communication and integration between transnational cultures is an inevitable result of globalization. Foreign architects bring their understanding of the land from different perspectives, injecting fresh cultural concept into the recipient country. In this regard, there is no better example than the Confucius Institute to demonstrate the active promotion of bilateral cultural communication and integration.

Confucius Institutes are usually operated in cooperation with foreign universities through renting classrooms or constructing their own academic buildings. By December 2018, China had constructed 548 Confucius Institutes in 154 countries and regions around the world (Xinhua News, 2018). Since the first Confucius Institute in Africa was established in Kenya in 2005, Africa has witnessed the birth of 46 Confucius Institutes in 32 countries within 10 years, making it the most rapidly growing and dynamic region for Confucius Institutes (International Communication, 2016; Qin, 2017).

- *The Dilemma of Confucius Institutes*

Unfortunately, the overseas Confucius Institutes have suffered significant setbacks in recent years. As of 2020, the United States has closed 13 Confucius Institutes,

[9] a https://www.udsm.ac.tz/web/index.php/institutes/ci
b https://www.facebook.com/permalink.php?story_fbid=4090363230985288&id=146430592045258
c https://www.cavehill.uwi.edu/News-Events/News/?release_id=20917
d http://design.citic/portal/article/project_detail/id/2614/cid/24.html

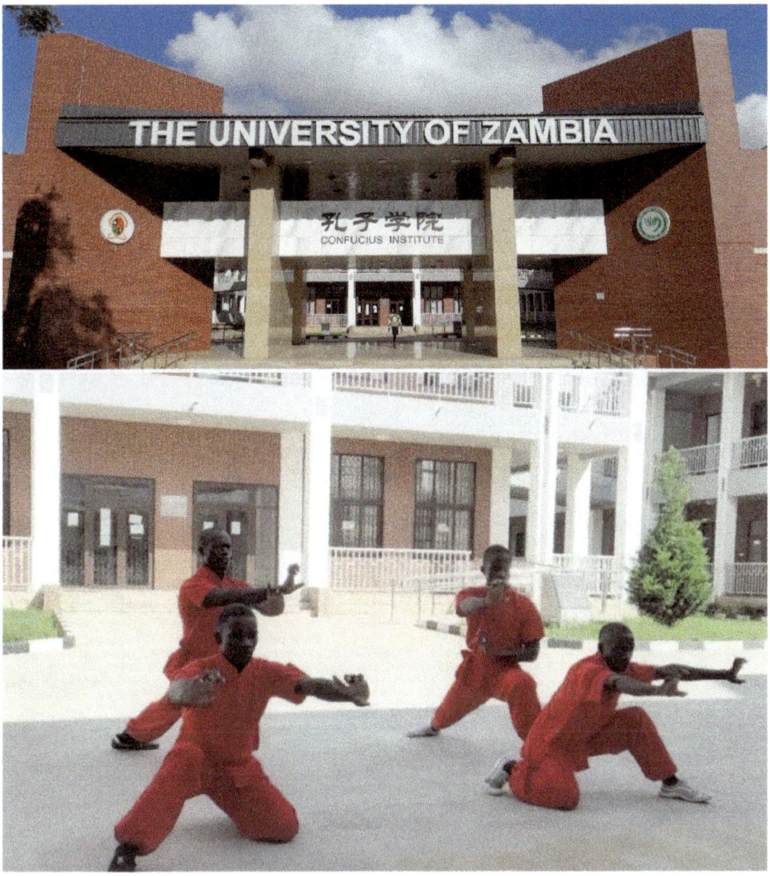

Fig. 8.15 Students performing Chinese martial arts at the Confucius Institute at the University of Zambia. (*Source:* provided by the Confucius Institute at the University of Zambia)

accounting for one-third of the total in its territory; in April, the last Confucius Institute in Sweden announced the closure; in June, Germany launched an investigation into Confucius Institutes; according to Google Search, 91 out of 105 (86.7%) western media reports on Confucius Institute have a negative tone (Zhang, 2021).

In contrast, among the 357 mainstream newspapers, online media and academic literatures in Africa, the number of reports on Confucius Institutes is increasing year by year, and the proportion of positive (30%) or neutral reports (60%) is much higher than that of negative reports or comments (10%) (Zhang, 2021). However, this positive image is largely due to economic values and diplomatic meaning, meeting the local needs of language skills training for employment and investment, rather than higher needs at the cultural level.

Due to the long history of colonization, many recipient countries have retained a high degree of cultural identity with the colonized countries, making it difficult

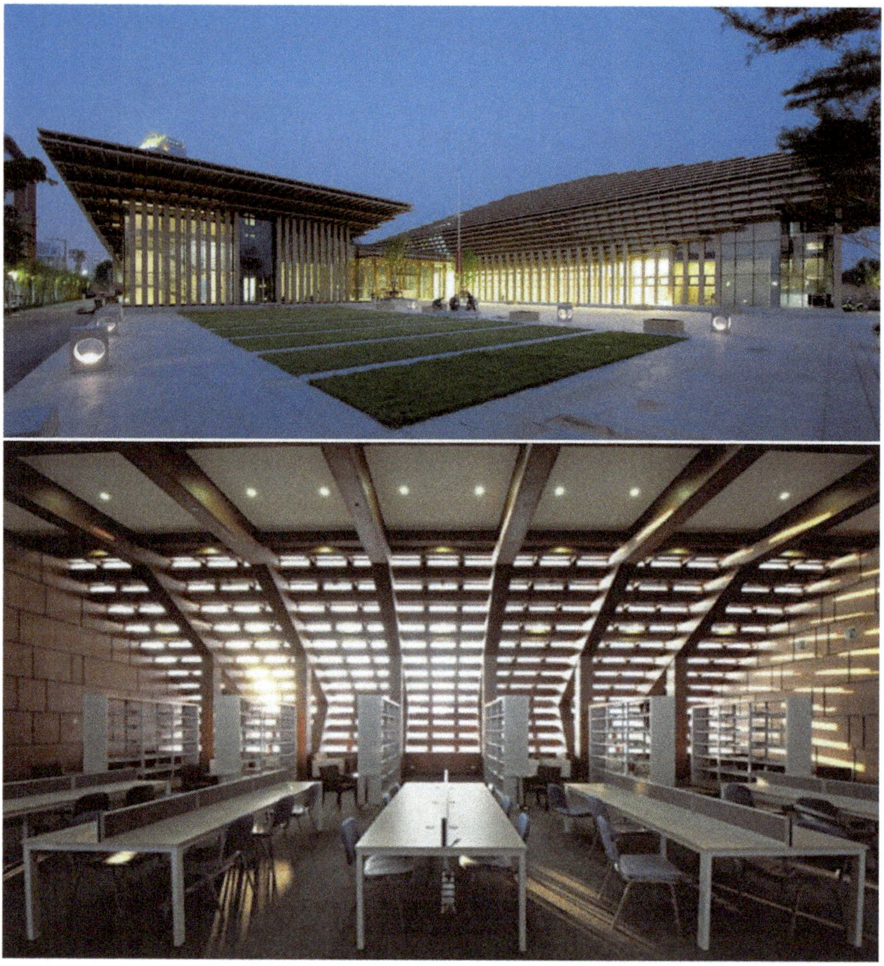

Fig. 8.16 The exterior and interior structure of Chinese Cultural Center in Bangkok. (*Source:* Provided by Cui Tong)

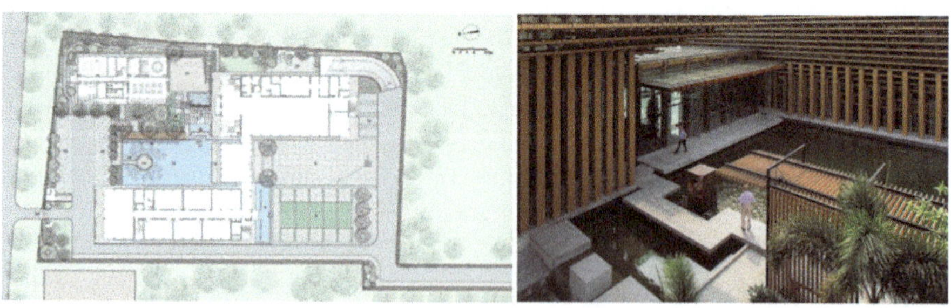

Fig. 8.17 The master plan and "enclosed" back yard of Chinese Cultural Center in Bangkok. (*Source:* Provided by Cui Tong)

for the concept of "multiculturalism" to be established. The "software" restriction of low cultural acceptance, coupled with the severe shortage of "hardware" such as teachers, teaching materials and equipment, have made architectural design the first victim for cost control. At the cultural representation level, the architectural products are only Chinese pitched roofs and simple facade decorations, while at the cultural integration level are only replicates of vernacular architectural components and the use of local materials. The final result is either indistinguishable from the surrounding buildings, lacking in recognition; or standing abruptly outside of the context, lacking in communication (Fig 8.14).

- *Exploration of Spreading Culture by Architectural Form*

As an awarded global model and "The Confucius Institute of Excellence" for outstanding teaching achievement (The Office of Foreign Affairs of Hebei University of Economics and Business, 2012), the Confucius Institute at the University of Zambia (CIUNZA) is a typical example worth discussing. Founded in 2010 by Hebei University of Economics and Business in collaboration with the University of Zambia, it is the first built Confucius institute building by China. The total area is 5,873 m^2 (4,523 m^2 for academic building and 1,350 m^2 for accommodation building), including Chinese culture rooms, language labs, multimedia rooms, offices, meeting rooms and teachers' apartments.

By 2020, the teaching sites have been spreading across ten provinces in Zambia, forming a pattern of "one center, sixteen teaching sites and four Confucius classes" with nearly 30,000 registered students. It offers Chinese courses covering all levels of primary and secondary schools, universities and short-term training, as well as popular events like Chinese martial arts, singing and dancing, festival custom teaching, annual "Chinese Bridge" Chinese Proficiency Competition and summer/autumn camps (CIUNZA, 2020) (Fig. 8.15). In recent years, hundreds of Chinese enterprises have opened in Zambia, which is in great demand for employees across language and cultural barriers, providing vast employment opportunities. The Confucius Institute also encourages outstanding Chinese language learners to continue their studies by offering scholarships to study in China. "More and more ordinary Zambian students like me are getting out of the boundary and changing our lives by learning Chinese." Said Luyako, a Zambian exchange student graduated in 2020 from Renmin University of China (Zhang, 2020).

It is understandable that at this stage, the construction and development of foreign Confucius Institutes should respond to local practical needs, with Chinese language and skills training as the main focus to attract more participants, and only then be in a position to consider expansion and quality improvement. However, as a place for overseas language teaching and cultural exchange, creating an environment with the atmosphere of Chinese culture is an integral part of successful education and communication. Despite varied external appearance, the internal key lies not in designing a building that meets functional requirements, nor in coping Chinese architectural elements, but in how to root the spirit of traditional Chinese culture in a new foreign environment, while achieving a harmonious symbiosis with local context and environment. The 13th Confucius Institute Conference (2018) specifically discussed "shaping and presenting the public image of Confucius Institutes" as one of the eight main topics, including both the cultural image and the physical architectural image (China Today, 2018). In this regard, the two techniques adopted by CIUNZA are examples worth discussing.

Firstly, the spatial expression of metaphorical spirit. Traditional Chinese academy buildings usually apply central axis courtyard-style layout with a strong sense of ritual. Main entrance is often marked by symmetrical, tall and exquisite gate. Inner space consists of courtyards and corridors of different scales as transitions and connections between various functional areas. The largest courtyard often stands as a symbol of "genius loci"[10] (Curl, 2006), represented by a preserved hundred-year-old tree, or a stone monument with slogans, or a sculpture of special significance, etc., which is a transformation of the ritual space in traditional academies. The end of the axis is usually where the library or the most important building located, indicating the precious "bibliotheca (藏书阁)" where knowledge is collected, spread and communicated (Guo, 2012). The clear and neat axis relationship not only expresses traditional Chinese philosophy, but also produces a kind of ritual—the form of order, which regulates the layout of buildings, as well as the patterns of human activities on site.

Secondly, the architectural and landscape details that integrate local and Chinese features. The most common Chinese elements are large pitched roofs, wooden doors, gable walls and Chinese patterns used in railings, windows, shelters, pavings, etc. The materials and forms are localized to suit regional climate, environment and culture. The Confucius Institute at the University of Zambia adopted the same brutalist fair-faced concrete, red brick walls and brick columns as the campus buildings (Guo, 2012). Landscape is another realm that designers played hard with. The process of transplanting Chinese courtyards into foreign Confucius Institutes is not a direct reference to Chinese components such as pavilion, tower, gallery, etc., but rather a simplification and abstraction approach and a detailed design language consistent with the context. In order to achieve the effect of changing sceneries in traditional Chinese garden, the courtyard design breaks the symmetrical layout and distinguishes a series of courtyards with corridors, walls and height differences to create a diverse and variable spatial effect. Permeable brick walls facilitate shading and ventilation while block part of the view, resulting in a classic vague beauty (Guo, 2012).

Unfortunately, this kind of eclecticism is still not fully convincing, partly because Chinese culture has not yet succeeded in finding a self-defining ideology within the values of the recipient country, and partly because the "historical" traditional style does not resonate with the facts of the recipient country's pursuit of advanced technology and modernity. On these two issues, the Chinese Cultural Center in Bangkok (2012) has made a better answer as an attempt to create an alternative overseas cultural communication venue other than the Confucius Institute.

---

[10] The Latin term "genius loci" means 'the genius of the place', referring to the presiding deity or spirit. Every place has its own unique qualities, not only in terms of its physical makeup, but of how it is perceived. In contemporary usage, it can refer to a place's distinctive atmosphere (Curl, 2006).

Firstly, how does the broad and diverse Chinese culture position itself in local values in order to be well understood and recognized? Thai cities are filled with temples, whose cultural dominance is unshakeable even by modern civilization. This unique "spiritual world" is the foundation of Thai urban atmosphere and public personality. In order to fit into local values, the cultural center positions itself as a temple-like "spiritual place" (Cui et al., 2013). At the same time, the mystery and majesty of the temple architecture are removed, leaving only its peaceful character and natural taste (Anonymous, 2017; Cui, 2015). This important translation also reflects the humanistic and naturalistic spirit of Chinese Confucianism and Taoism.

The architectural form seeks the relevance of classical Chinese architecture through the densely-layered eaves, while the correlation with Thai temple architecture reflects in the magnificent horizontal extension of the front, and the vertical overlap of the sides. In addition, inspired by the natural rhythms of the Thai rainforest, the free release and diffusion of the building mimics the spreading form of trees in advanced modern techniques, with dense forest-like columns and horizontal beams woven together to form a striking network-like space. The bifurcation of the building borders and transition from solid wood to translucent glass and membrane resembles the fractal logic of moving from tree trunk to branches and leaves (Anonymous, 2017; Cui et al., 2013) (Fig. 8.16).

Secondly, how to interpret bilateral traditional style into an architectural carrier that responds to modern pursuits while inheriting the culture? The designer replaced the Chinese traditional stereotyped impression of "winding path accompanied by varying views" with keywords of "classical and profound, bright and broad", to emphasize that China and Thailand are both "ancient countries" with glorious history and "grand countries" with openness and advancement. Thus, the layout and atmosphere of the two courtyard spaces—one "open" and one "enclosed"—formed by the Z-shaped buildings are defined (Anonymous, 2017; Cui et al., 2013; Fang, 2013) (Fig. 8.17). The "open" front yard is bright and broad, while the "enclosed" backyard is serene and calm, presenting dual cultural attributes of "grand and ritual" as well as "tranquil and private". Through the resonance between visitors and the environment, people's feeling and consciousness in the space are activated and sublimated. The environment influences people and educates people, thus generating interest in further exploration of Chinese culture.

8.4 Conclusion: Building a New Humanistic Hope

This chapter briefly reviews China's endeavor in education aid and campus building in the past decades. The technical schools and training facilities of Chinese aid first appeared in Asia and Africa in the 1970s. Large-scale exportd school buildings blossom in the twenty-first century, 300 various kinds of schools scattered in more than 120 countries of five continents. They timely alleviate the severe shortage of education facilities in developing and underdeveloped countries, and give opportunities to millions of young people to receive basic, higher and vocational education. Some buildings are located in remote areas, lacking electricity, running water and road access. Chinese aid schools stand there, and are indeed oasis in the physical, psychological and cultural desert. Although there are misunderstanding or ill-conceived criticism on Chinese aid, the school buildings donated by the Chinese people won applaud as they reflect mankind's common hope of progress and envisaging a better tomorrow. This continuous and long-lasting efforts are partly paid. Some countries start to embark on the road of development, new generation of professionals and technicians appear in Asia, Africa, Oceania and Latin America. Some Chinese trained people step into the management, and even president of the nation.

In terms of the campus design, they are the results of design competition among Chinese state-owned design institutes. Facing the challenge of functional requirements and an unfamiliar environment, the designers try to fulfill the tasks from various angles—climatic, topographical, environmental and cultural. Most of the designs provide classrooms, laboratories, lecture halls and other school facilities. Some buildings shoulder ritual requirements, and they are designed with more symbolic and cultural flavor. These works enrich the typological study of school (and public) buildings. Most of these buildings may not be fabulous, but they faithfully serve the teaching and learning in the campus, and may reside in the heart of thousands of students throughout their lives.

Admittedly, the design of China-aided schools remains conspicuously flawed. Most Chinese designers thank foreign-aided projects for giving them more freedom to play with fewer restrictions. However, due to cost control, tight schedule, inadequate local input and insufficient cognition, some school buildings fall to the modular, homogeneous products of industrial assembly line. This contradictory mentality is evident in the design of aided schools. "Born in China and adapted overseas" is a fundamental principle for the implication of foreign-aided architecture. Although Chinese architects racked their brains to achieve localization, the design techniques are less innovative than homogeneous. Most school designs are still confined to the "square box style" similar to Chinese local schools with variations only appearing in roofs and façade decorations, far from being an outstanding work of architecture. While localization is insufficient, cultural integration is also weakened by immature use of Chinese and local symbols, reduced to metaphorical stacking and superficial expression.

Restricted by economic conditions, some recipient countries have been struggling in poverty and war, failing to form their own architectural culture; some others have lost their architectural and cultural uniqueness after long-term colonial control or war. And the rush of aid to quick success and instant benefits can only make it worse, leaving the recipient countries on the modernized road out of poverty, but losing their vitality and sense of identity, filling with the machinery and apathy of industrial society.

The nature of foreign aid is, in general, humanitarian—a compassion for human beings, a belief in progress, and a desire to contribute for this great cause. Whereas humanitarian emphasizes the breadth of knowledge and compassion, humanism is more interested in the perfection of the individuals than in the improvement of mankind as a whole. As Rifkin says in *The European Dream* (2013), the two major spiritual currents prevailing in today: one is the desire to pursue higher personal meaning in an increasingly materialized world; another is the need to find some sense of commonality in a progressively alienated and apathetic society.

If the enlightenment of the 18th century was centered on "self-liberation" and the pursuit of world universality, then the new humanism of the 21st century advocates respect for others, resilience for differences and multi-cultural complementarity in an increasingly interconnected world. This commonality and diversity are reshaping an advanced humanism of the new era, which is the future that education aid is dedicated to build. The tangible and intangible accomplishments achieved by the next generation is infinite.

Acknowledgement The authors heartily thank the kind help and support from architect Su Yuan and engineer Sun Zhiwei from the SIPPR Engineering Group Co., Ltd. This chapter is part of a research supported by the National Natural Science Foundation of China, Project No. 51878584.

References

AfDB. (2006). *Mali: Education III project*. Retrieved December 20, 2021, from https://reliefweb.int/report/mali/mali-education-iii-project.

Anonymous. (2017). The Chinese Cultural Center in Bankok. *Architectural Knowledge* (15), 54–59. 佚名. (2017). 曼谷中国文化中心. *建筑知识* (15), 54–59. CNKI:SUN:JZZS.0.2017–15–012.

Birchler, K., & Michaelowa, K. (2016). Making aid work for education in developing countries: An analysis of aid effectiveness for primary education coverage and quality. *International Journal of Educational Development, 48*, 37–52.

CIUNZA. (2020). *An Interview with Qiu Guangmin, the teacher of the Confucius Institute at the University of Zambia*. Retrieved December 20, 2021, from https://mp.weixin.qq.com/s/Z30dcPUfyN5hNa0nbXA4-w CIUNZA 赞大孔院. (2020). *赞比亚大学专访孔院教师邱广民*. 网址.

China National Complete Engineering Corporation. (2007). *The Project Commissioned by the Ministry of Education of Angola*. Retrieved September 27, 2021, from http://www.cmcec.com/ywly/csjcss/201703/t20170307_141605.html 中国成套工程有限公司. (2007). *安哥拉教育部项目*.网址.

China National Machinery Industry Corporation. (2007). *The Completion of Eleven Schools Commissioned by the Ministry of Education of Angola*. Retrieved October 7, 2021, from http://www.sasac.gov.cn/n2588025/n2588124/c3843196/content.html 中国机械工业集团公司. (2007). *国机集团"安哥拉教育部11所学校建设项目"竣工*.网址.

China Today. (2018). *The 13th Confucius Institute Conference*. Retrieved Oct 7, 2021, from http://www.chinatoday.com.cn/zw2018/rdzt/kzdh/index.html. (2018). *第十三届孔子学院大会*

Chinese Embassy in Mali. (2018). *The Kabala Campus of the University of Bamako in Mali was completed and handed over*. Retrieved December 16, 2021, from http://invest.afrindex.com/dynamic/detail_109/ 中国驻马里大使馆. (2018). *中国援马里卡巴拉大学城项目竣工移交*. 网址.

Cui, T. (2015). Chinese Cultural Center, Bankok, Thailand, 2012. *World Architecture* (01), 102–105. 崔彤. (2015). 中国文化中心,曼谷,泰国. *世界建筑*(01),102–105. https://doi.org/10.16414/j.wa.2015.01.019.

Cui, T., Chen, X., & Wang, Y. (2013). Order of growth: Thinking on Thailand Bangkok Chinese Culture Center Design. *Architectural Journal* (03), 105+100–104. 崔彤,陈希 & 王一

钧. (2013). 生长的秩序——泰国曼谷·中国文化中心设计思考. *建筑学报* (03),105+100–104. CNKI:SUN:JZXB.0.2013–03–023.

Curl, J. S. (2006). *A dictionary of architecture and landscape architecture* (2nd ed.). Oxford University Press. https://doi.org/10.1093/acref/9780198606789.001.0001.

Embassy of the People's Republic of China in Mali. (2020). *Ambassador Zhu Liying in Mali meets with the Minister of Employment and Vocational Training of Mali.* Retrieved December 20, 2021, from http://ml.china-embassy.org/chn/sbgx/202010/t20201028_5931076.htm. 中华人民共和国驻马里共和国大使馆. (2020). 驻马里大使朱立英会见就业和职业培训部长杜尔. 网址.

Fang, M. (2013). Broadness and Serenity, Allegro with Adagio—Landscape Design of China Cultural Center, Bangkok, Thailan. *Chinese Landscape Architecture* (04), 24–29. 房木生. (2013). 敞阔深幽,张弛有度——曼谷中国文化中心景观设计. *中国园林* (04),24–29. CNKI:SUN:ZGYL.0.2013–04–009.

Feagaimaali'I, J. (2020). *Police Academy plan on the move.* Retrieved December 20, 2021, from https://www.samoaobserver.ws/category/article/55545.

Ge, Z. (2020). Local expression in foreign aid architectural creation: The design of National Institute of Public Health in Mauritamnia. *Architecture Technique* (S02), 20–23. 戈珍平. (2020). 援外建筑创作中的在地性表达——毛里塔尼亚国家公共卫生研究院方案设计. *建筑技艺*(S2),20–23. CNKI:SUN:JZJY.0.2020-S2–007.

Guo, L. (2012). *The exotic rebirth of the spirit of place—Reflections on the architectural design methods of confucius institute.* The Central Academy of Fine Arts, Beijing. 郭龙.(2012).*场所精神的异域重生——孔子学院建筑设计方法思考*(硕士学位论文, 中央美术学院).

International Communication. (2016). *Construction and development of confucius institutes in Africa in the new era.* Retrieved November 12, 2021, from https://read01.com/gaO4J7.html#. YYeezp5BxPY 对外传播. (2017). *新时期非洲孔子学院的建设与发展.* 网址.

Klees, S. J., Stromquist, N. P., Samoff, J., & Vally, S. (2019). The 2018 world development report on education: A critical analysis. *Development and Change, 50*(2), 603–620.

Liu, G. (2006). Education, equality, and national citizenship. *Yale LJ, 116*, 330.

Liu, L. (2018). *Beijing Institute of Geological and Prospecting Engineering undertakes the geotechnical engineering suevey for Samoa Police Academy supported by the Ministry of Commerce of China.* Retrieved December 20, 2021, from http://www.bjdky.com/c/cn/news/2018-05/07/news_546.html 刘璐. (2018). *我院承担商务部援萨摩亚警察学院岩土工程勘察项目.* 网址.

Loop Pacific. (2020). *Samoa Police Academy to capitalise on potential overseas employment op[portunities.* Retrieved Decemeber 20, 2021, from https://www.loopsamoa.com/samoa-news/samoa-police-academy-capitalise-potential-overseas-employment-opportunities-93882.

Man, C. (2008). Discussion on creative experience of foreign aid building design. *Shanxi Architecture, 34*(24), 53–54. https://doi.org/10.13719/j.cnki.cn14-1279/tu.2008.24.200 满春红.(2008). 援外建筑设计创作经验刍议. *山西建筑* (24),53–54. CNKI:SUN:JZSX.0.2008–24–032.

Ministry of Information Eritrea. (2020). *Mai Nefhi College of Science graduates 280 students.* Retrieved Decemeber 15, 2021, from https://shabait.com/2020/10/22/mai-nefhi-college-of-science-graduates-280-students/.

Mitchell, I., Caitlin, M. (2018). *How do you measure aid quality and who ranks highest?*. Center for Global Development. https://www.cgdev.org/blog/how-do-you-measure-aid-quality-and-who-ranks-highest.

Morgenstern, E. M. (2021). *Foreign assistance and the education sector: Programs and priorities.* Congressional Research Service.

Niu, C. (2014). Education aid and international social responsibility: A comparative study on school construction projects in Africa between China and Japan. *Comparative Education Review, 36*(5), 6–11. CNKI:SUN:BJJY.0.2014-05-002. 牛长松.(2014).教育援助与国际社会责任——中日在非援建学校项目的案例比较. *比较教育研究*(05),6–11.

Qin, S. (2017). Confucius Institutes in Africa. *South Reviews,* (11). Rereived November 12, 2021, from https://www.nfcmag.com/article/7270.html 覃胜勇. (2017). 孔子学院在非洲. *南风窗* (11). 网址.

Rifkin, J. (2013). *The European dream: How Europe's vision of the future is quietly eclipsing the American dream.* Wiley.

Seid, S. (2017). *Eritrea: College of science educational renaissance.* Retrieved Decemeber 15, 2021, from http://www.madote.com/2017/07/eritrea-college-of-science-educational.html.

Song, J. (2019). Architectural design for foreign aid projects. *Shanxi Architecture* (9), 40–42, 82. https://doi.org/10.16330/j.cnki.1007-7359.2019.09.016 宋建华. (2019). 援外工程建筑设计有感. *安徽建筑*(09), 40–42+82.

Sohu News. (2019). *Award-winning project|College of Science in the first phase of the Eritrea Institute of Technology.* Retrieved Decemeber 15, 2021, from https://www.sohu.com/a/338891790_297098 搜狐新闻. (2019). 获奖项目| 援厄立特里亚科技学院项目一期工程中的科学学院. 网址.

The Office of Foreign Affairs of Hebei University of Economics and Business. (2012). *The Confucius Institute at the University of Zambia signs building construction agreement.* Retrieved Decemeber 20, 2021, from https://ofa.heuet.edu.cn/info/1012/1241.htm 河北经贸大学国际交流与合作处. (2012). *赞比亚大学孔子学院签署建设大楼.* 网址.

The Global Education Monitoring Report Team. (2019). *Gender Report: Building Bridges for Gender Equality.* Retrieved December 15, 2021, from https://cerlalc.org/wp-content/uploads/2020/01/91_Gender_report_building_bridges.pdf.

The State Council Information Office of the People's Republic of China. (2011). *China's Foreign Aid.* Retrieved September 27, 2021, from http://english.www.gov.cn/archive/white_paper/2014/09/09/content_281474986284620.htm.

The State Council Information Office of the People's Republic of China. (2014). *China's Foreign Aid.* Retrieved Septemeber 27, 2021, from http://english.www.gov.cn/archive/white_paper/2014/08/23/content_281474982986592.htm.

The State Council Information Office of the People's Republic of China. (2021). *China's International Development Cooperation in the New Era.* Retrieved Septemebr 27, 2021, from http://english.scio.gov.cn/node_8021417.html.

The World Bank. (2017). World Development Report 2018.

The World Factbook. (2021). *Explore All Countries—Mali.* Retrieved September 27, 2021, from https://www.cia.gov/the-world-factbook/countries/mali.

Teklom, M. (2020). *Very smart, astonishing and devoted student! Niat Abraham 2020.* Retrieved Decemeber 15, 2021, from https://www.65tes-habeshamusic.com/very-smart-astonishing-and-devoted-student/.

Temesghen, B. (2015). *A future abundant of intellectuals: Eritrean institutions of higher education.* Retrieved December 15, 2021, from http://www.madote.com/2016/06/a-future-abundant-of-intellectuals.html.

Theunynck, S. (2002). *School construction in developing countries: What do we know.* World Bank.

UNESCO. (2019). *While recognizing progress on parity in access to education, UNESCO calls for increased efforts on quality and completion to ensure equal opportunities for girls and boys.* Retrieved Decemeber 15, 2021, from https://en.unesco.org/news/while-recognizing-progress-parity-access-education-unesco-calls-increased-efforts-quality-and.

Wang, X. (2013). Education aid and cultivating national soft power: A comparative case study on aided primary schools by China and Japan in Nigeria. *Comparative Education Review, 35*(3), 75–79. CNKI:SUN:BJJY.0.2013-03-014. 王学军.(2013).教育援助与国家软实力培育——中日在尼日利亚小学援建项目的案例比较. *比较教育研究*(03),75–79.

Xinhua News. (2018). *There have been 548 Confucius Institutes around the world.* Retrieved October 7, 2021, from https://web.archive.org/web/20210310084159/, http://www.xinhuanet.com/world/2018-12/05/c_1210009045.htm 新华网. (2018). *世界各地已有548所孔子学院.*网址.

Xinhua News. (2019). *A China-made cradle for Tunisian diplomats.* Retrieved October 7, 2021, from http://xinhua-rss.zhongguowangshi.com/233/-4067403128630087850/6037062.html 新华网. (2019). *通讯：突尼斯外交官摇篮中国造.*网址.

Xu, Z. (2007). Electrical design of primary and secondary schools for foreign aid projects. *Construction Science and Technology, 20*, 58–59. https://doi.org/10.16116/j.cnki.jskj.2007.20.001 许茁. (2007). 援外工程中小学校的电气设计. *建设科技*(20),58–59.

Yang, C. (2021). Thoughts on the design practice of China aid projects under the background of "One Belt One Road". *Shanxi Architecture, 47*(12), 28–30. https://doi.org/10.13719/j.cnki.1009-6825.2021.12.011 杨成钢. (2021). "一带一路"背景下援外项目设计实践思考. 山西建筑 (12),28–30.

Zhang, H. (2020). "Learning Chinese has changed my destiny—Remembering my student Luyako. Retrieced Oct 7, 2021 from https://mp.weixin.qq.com/s/1ysIb4iYRXq4c7qe08UvHw. (2020). *学汉语改变了我的命运——记我的学生路亚克.*

Zhang, W. (2021). The Public Opinion Predicament of Confucius Institutes in the New Situation: Characteristics, Causes and Countermeasures. *Modern Communication (Journal of Communication University of China),* (03), 20–26. 张未然. (2021). 新形势下孔子学院的舆情困境:特征、原因与对策. *现代传播(中国传媒大学学报)* (03), 20–26.

Zhao, Y. (2010). *A Study on educational aid*. Doctoral dissertation, Southwest University. 赵玉池. (2010). *国际教育援助研究* (博士学位论文,西南大学).

Yingting Chen is a PhD candidate at the City University of Hong Kong, with 5-year practice experience in the context of urban design, landscape architecture and architecture in the US and China. Her research interest lies on human-nature relationship, impact of design on health and wellbeing, and international design exchange and cooperation. Current research focuses on China's importation of American architecture and China's foreign aid architecture.

Charlie Qiuli Xue has taught architecture at Shanghai Jiaotong University, University of Texas and City University of Hong Kong. An award-winning architect and writer, he has published 15 books, including '*Building a Revolution: Chinese Architecture since 1980*' (HKU Press, 2006), '*Hong Kong Architecture 1945–2015: From Colonial to Global*' (Springer, 2016), '*A History of Design Institutes in China: from Mao to Market*' (with G. Ding, Routledge, 2018) and '*Grand Theater Urbanism: Chinese cities in the 21st century*' (Springer, 2019, ed.). He has published more than 160 research papers in professional and international refereed journals and 40 book chapters. His papers are published in such journals as *Cities, Habitat International, Urban Design International, Journal of Architecture, Journal of Urban Design, Architectural Research Quarterly Journal of Urban History Planning Perspective Architecture + Urbanism Domus* and Chinese journals like *Architectural Journal Architect New Architecture Time + Architecture World Architecture* and *Taiwan Architect*. His book on Hong Kong was awarded by the International Committee of Architectural Critics (CICA) in 2017. Xue's research interests are in Chinese architecture, transnational design and high-density environment. Xue is also extensively involved in design and consultant practice in Hong Kong, Chinese mainland and the US.

Guanghui Ding is Associate Professor of Architecture at the Beijing University of Civil Engineering and Architecture in China. He completed his Ph.D. in architecture from the University of Nottingham, United Kingdom in 2013 and later worked as a Postdoctoral Research Fellow at City University of Hong Kong. His research focuses on modern and contemporary Chinese architecture, including many subjects in critical architecture, architectural criticism and periodicals, design institutes and China's architectural aid in the Global South. He is the author of *Constructing a Place of Critical Architecture in China: Intermediate Criticality in the Journal* Time + Architecture (London and New York: Routledge, 2016) (Chinese edition,《建筑批评的一朵浪花实验性建筑》Beijing: China Architecture and Building Press, 2018) and co-author of *A History of Design Institutes in China: From Mao to Market* (London and New York: Routledge, 2018, with Charlie Qiuli Xue) (expanded Chinese edition,《中国设计院价值与挑战》Beijing: China Architecture and Building Press, 2022). His scholarly articles have been published by *Architecture* *and Culture, Architectural Research Quarterly ARENA Journal of Architectural Research, Domus, Habitat International Histories of Post-War Architecture, Journal of Architecture, Journal of the Society of Architectural Historians Jianzhushi/The Architect, Shidai jianzhu/Time + Architecture, Shijie jianzhu/World Architecture, Xin jianzhu/New Architecture* and other edited volumes.

Yizhuo Gao is a Ph.D. Candidate at Huazhong University of Science and Technology and City University of Hong Kong. He has a keen interest in Modern Chinese Architecture in Mao's China and Cold War architecture, with particular attention to cases related to the Third Front Construction (sanxian jianshe) and Chinese foreign aid architecture.

Chapter 9
Embedded Support: Chinese Aid Projects in the Horn of Africa—Case Studies of Djibouti City and Addis Ababa

Lujia Zhang, Yan Wan, Xinyu Liu, and Charlie Qiuli Xue

Abstract Lacking resources and still under the shadow of their colonial past, the countries in the Horn of Africa have struggled over past decades with low urbanization rates and high poverty rates. Since the 1970s, China has provided aid projects to these countries in the form of public buildings, educational projects, and infrastructure. Such projects, which aim to support local economic development, have been embedded in the countries' urban life and have furthered the indigenous urbanization process. This chapter is based on research combining documentary collection with on-site investigation and observation of urban space and development, and interviews that were conducted with scholars, managers, and building end-users to examine Chinese aid projects and their roles. Taking Djibouti City and Addis Ababa as examples, this chapter analyzes how Chinese aid projects in the Horn of Africa have been embedded in urban space and have supported urban development. It aims to provide a realistic view of Chinese aid projects overseas, rethinking the process of design, construction, implementation, and subsequent operation and maintenance.

After gaining independence, East African countries experienced a long period of political instability. Urbanization remained slow and incomplete due to regional conflicts, limited financial resources, and lack of government control. However, in the era of rapid globalization, no country is willing to fall behind. Since the turn of the millennium, African countries have entered a period of rapid economic growth and urban development, especially in east Africa (African Development Bank, OECD and UN Development Program, 2016). Aid projects are an internationally recognized way to help economically backward countries and accelerate their economic growth. During the urbanization process, a large number of projects have been

L. Zhang (✉) · X. Liu · C. Q. Xue
Department of Architecture and Civil Engineering, City University of Hong Kong, Kowloon, Hong Kong
e-mail: luj.zhang1989@foxmail.com

Y. Wan
University of Hong Kong, Pokfulam, Hong Kong
e-mail: successc_w@163.com

C. Q. Xue and G. Ding (eds.), *Exporting Chinese Architecture*,
https://doi.org/10.1007/978-981-19-2786-7_9

constructed in Africa with international aid. Such projects, in the short term, provide the equivalent of a blood transfusion; but whether they will ensure the continued health of African countries with fragile economies is another question.

During its early stages of industrialization in the 1950s, China received significant financial support and aid from the Soviet Union and Eastern European countries. To break through the blockade of superpowers led by the US and USSR, China started to align itself with developing countries in Asia and Africa by providing aid in the form of construction projects like factories and military facilities. In 1973, at the end of the Cultural Revolution, expenditure on foreign aid projects accounted for 7% of China's national expenditure. After the announcement of the Reform and Opening-Up policy, the central government adjusted its policies of ideology-only recognition to achieve mutual benefits with recipient countries. The number of foreign aid projects received by China gradually decreased, and as China's economic strength improved, the total amount of foreign aid from China to other countries increased year by year. In 2001, China and Africa established the Forum on China–Africa Cooperation, and "going global" was the direction of many state-owned and private enterprises (Xue, Ding, Chang, Zhang, 2018; Ding & Xue, 2015). In 2013, overseas economic activities were further encouraged by the Belt and Road Initiative and foreign aid projects; investments and construction projects in Africa by China's state-owned and private enterprises have become a notable trend.

Chinese aid projects and policies in Africa have been criticized for many years as forms of "debt trap" diplomacy and "infrastructural violence." However, China's long-term pragmatism and low-key behavior have helped to mollify these criticisms. The American scholar Deborah Brautigam in her book (Brautigam, 2011) commended the opportunities that Chinese aid projects brought to Africa, and criticized biased "debt trap" news in the media (Brautigam, 2020).

In the 1980s, the paradigm of architectural research shifted due to the development of urban history, a field that was transformed by trends in social thought in the previous decade. Since then, formal and aesthetic issues have no longer had dominant discursive power in architectural history. Architecture is instead examined within its social, cultural, and economic contexts. This chapter takes Djibouti City and Addis Ababa in the Horn of Africa as examples to examine how Chinese architectural aid projects have been embedded in urban life and have supported the urbanization of African cities over the past 40 years. Djibouti and Addis Ababa have unique geographical locations and close historical and economic ties. The two cities are currently vibrant areas of construction and economic activity in the Horn of Africa region. The research team made on-site investigations of Chinese aid projects and the urban space of both cities, and conducted interviews with scholars, managers, and users.

9.1 Urban Development and International Aid Projects in the Horn of Africa

Africa is the last region of the world to urbanize, also known as the "Last Development Frontier". After the turn of the millennium, Africa entered a stage of high-speed urbanization. In 2015, Africa's urban population reached 472 million, while its total population exceeded 1.2 billion in 2016, including 9.5 million displaced people. In recent years, the urbanization of countries in the Horn of Africa has grown at the high rate of 4.68%, and the urban population has increased significantly (World Bank, 2016). However, the urbanization levels of these countries are still comparatively low, and they face practical challenges such as unbalanced urban development and reliance on an informal economy. The instability of the political environment has affected sustainable urban development. Urban planning and policies have met with many obstacles, and a cycle "from planning to failure" has often occurred (Fig. 9.1).

The development of African countries cannot be separated from the history of colonialism and post-colonialism. After the Second World War, a succession of African countries gained independence. However, poverty is the reality in Africa. There are 33 African countries on the UN list of "least developed countries," including all of those in the Horn of Africa except for Kenya. Underdevelopment has led to weak public order: government control over public facilities and resources are limited; public order is insecurely established; and transportation systems are not standardized (Collier, 2007). Due to limited economic strength and a shortage of manpower and material resources, these countries initially had to rely heavily on the aid and support of their former colonizers. The continuation of urban policies,

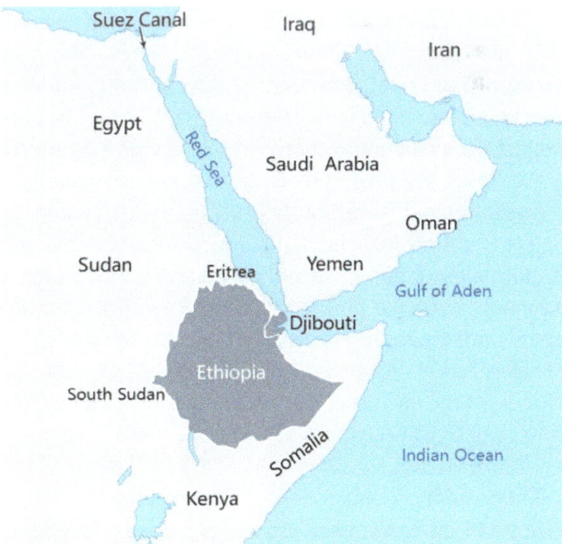

Fig. 9.1 Map of Horn of Africa (drawn by Lujia Zhang)

systems, and patterns from the period of colonial rule also had a profound impact on their political systems, economic structure, and urbanization after independence.

The external forces needed for architectural production, including funding, technology, materials, machinery, and skilled manpower, mean that Africa's urban development has relied on alternative urban experiences (Levin, 2015). In the 1960s, China began to fund building construction through aid projects in African countries, even in difficult economic times. Most of these buildings were factories to help these countries become more self-reliant. Along with China's increase in economic strength and international influence, the number and scale of Chinese aid projects has grown. In recent years, Chinese aid projects have involved both project construction and materials and a variety of building types and infrastructure, such as roads, railways, and municipal water supply (Information Office of the State Council of the PRC, 2014). These projects focus on urban construction and economic development to promote modern city life. Chinese aid projects at present rarely involve the design and construction of a whole street block, but instead focus on landmark buildings. These buildings contribute to urban public life and the urbanization process (Amoah, 2016).

Britain and France have funded numerous aid projects in their former East African colonies, including military, political, economic, and social aid. After Djibouti's independence in 1977, France offered financial support to the government in military and state affairs, sent consultants to government departments, and established military bases. These policies were largely efforts to promote France's ideological and political interests and have not brought substantial changes to Djibouti's urban development (Cohen, 2013).

U.S. aid projects in Africa also have a close relationship with the U.S.'s national interests. They promote a policy of "America First, Economy First," and cover areas such as education, healthcare, agriculture, infrastructure, and social management. After the Cold War, Ethiopia entered a new phase of urban development. Having been a proxy country for Africa during the Cold War, Ethiopia became one of the first recipients of the U.S. "Power Africa" program, receiving technical and financial support for sustainable energy (Ministry of Commerce of the PRC, 2018).

As the second largest foreign aid donor in the world currently, Japan has expanded its economic aid from Southeast Asia to Africa and South America since the 1970s. Japanese aid projects in Africa now represent 15% of all Japanese foreign aid on an annual basis. Japan's aid policy has followed Japan's own stages of development. In recent years, the policy has shifted to infrastructure projects, designed to expand Japan's influence in response to the growing scale of Chinese aid projects in Africa (Mercer, 2017). For example, the Northern Corridor project involves building roads, bridges, ports, and other infrastructure between Nairobi (Kenya's second largest city) and Kigali (Rwanda's capital), with the goal of creating a broader urban transportation network in Africa.

These aid projects, combined with materials and human assistance from the United Nations High Commissioner for Refugees, UN-Habitat, and numerous NGOs in education, health, medical care, humanitarian relief, and disease control, have created a large aid system in Africa. These have partially contributed to the urbanization process in Africa (Fowler, 2019).

9.2 Chinese Aid Projects in a Post-Colonial City: A Case Study of Djibouti City

9.2.1 Characteristics of Djibouti's Urban Space

Djibouti has been an important trade hub since the Suez Canal was opened in 1869. Once a French colony, it gained independence in 1977, and at present has a total population of less than one million, with more than 75% concentrated in Djibouti City. As it has limited resources, the country relies on imports for more than 90% of its supplies. The three ports (the old port, the container terminal, and the port of Doha Ray) are therefore considered the mainstay of the country's economy and the symbol of the capital city. Located in a key area of the Gulf of Aden, Djibouti City accommodates several national military bases and the only overseas navy supply base of the Chinese People's Liberation Army. The income from leasing these military bases accounts for more than 40% of the country's annual economic income (Sun and Zonbir, 2021).

In the 1960s, the French colonial authorities took advantage of ethnic tensions in Djibouti and created a closed zone with military barrage. The colonial core and the old port were on the eastern side, and the Balbala District, the "shady town," was on the western side. They are artificially separated. The government of Djibouti followed colonial policies in the early years of independence, with France providing military, economic, and human assistance. The barrage border was dismantled in the early 1980s, but it continues to influence the city center of Djibouti. The Balbala region, however, remains marginalized and underdeveloped (Bisaillon and Mohammed, 2005).

The architecture of Djibouti City presents a mixture of French and Arabic styles, and the urban space, influenced by colonial architecture, shows an obvious dual structure, with a clear development gap between the former colonial zone and the other residential zones. The former colonial zone is divided into the European Quartier and the African Quartier. The European Quartier, located in the northern part of the peninsula connected to the port, is the core urban area, with a relatively regular arrangement of buildings, including government offices and financial institutions, and some high-end residential areas. The African Quartier, located to the south of the European Quartier, has seven subdivisions and mainly features residential buildings of no more than three stories; there is a serious lack of infrastructure and extremely poor sanitary conditions (Imbert-Vier, 2012).

The Djibouti government has had limited control over urban development since independence. Tangible and intangible borders have fragmented the urban space, which is characterized by uneven urban development, inadequate municipal facilities, and a huge gap between rich and poor (Brass, 2008) (Figs. 9.2 and 9.3).

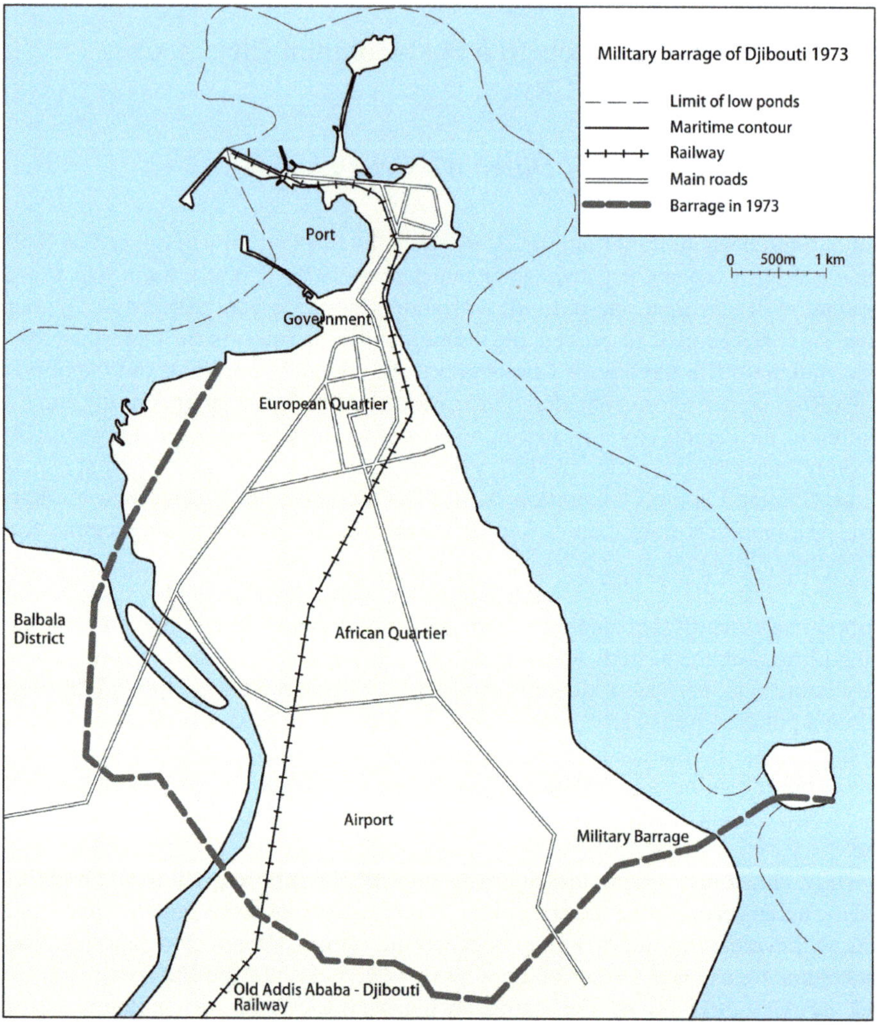

Fig. 9.2 Military border during the French colonial period. (*Source*: S. Imbert-Vier, *The Barrage de Djibouti? From migration barrier to identity building*, adapted by the authors)

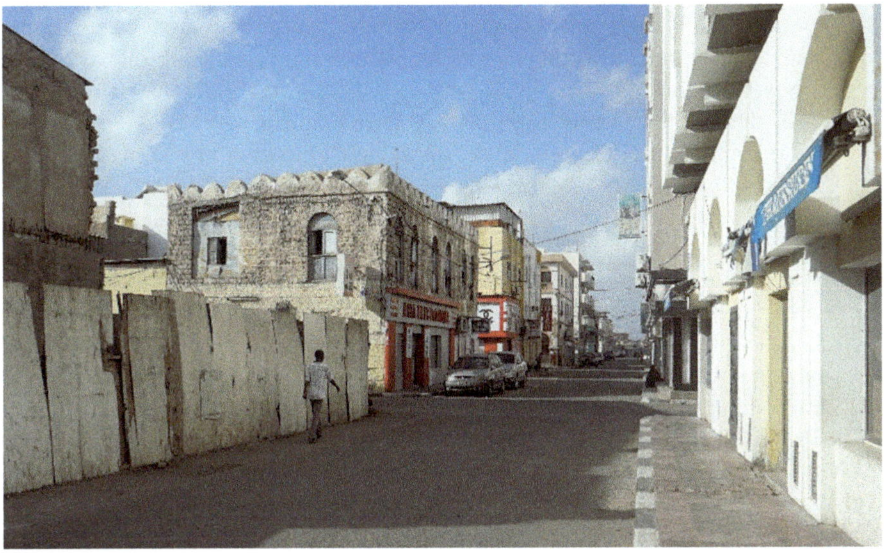

Fig. 9.3 Street in City Center of Djibouti (shot by Yan Wan)

9.2.2 *Aid Projects and Urban Spaces*

China established diplomatic relations with Djibouti in 1979, and it has organized aid projects there ever since. Djibouti is a small country with a fragile economy and a complex mixture of ethnicities. Eighty percent of its economic investment comes from other countries, and most aid projects originate from France, Japan, the United States, Saudi Arabia, China, and Italy. China has become one of its largest sources of aid in recent years, especially in infrastructure development, which has involved construction, manpower, technical support, and materials. By the end of 2017, China had completed 29 aid projects, including the People's Palace, the National Stadium, the National Library and Archives, the administrative building of the Foreign Affairs and International Trade Administration, the building of the Committee on the Elimination of Racial Discrimination, a new hospital in Arta, a rural elementary school, and the dialysis unit of the General Hospital in Peltier (Wan et al., 2020).

Under the Reform and Opening-Up policy, China's aid policies went beyond the goal of ideological consistency at the national level and pursued the new goal of mutual benefit and cooperation. With more state-owned design institutes involved, project designs became more diverse and flexible. Due to a limited amount of aid investment, early projects followed the domestic design principles of "practical, economical, and beautiful if possible" and made use of scale, cultural characteristics, and spatial approaches appropriate to the local conditions. After the turn of the millennium, with more experience with foreign aid projects, China was able to obtain better results through improved design, materials, and construction techniques. China has also sent technical teams and consultants for maintenance of completed buildings; some projects have been maintained by Chinese personnel for more than 30 years since their completion.

In 1983, the construction of the People's Palace and the bronze Monument to the Warriors on the west beach of the downtown area began with a foreign aid loan from China. Designed by the former Hubei Industrial Building Design Institute, the building features a symmetrical façade intended to convey gravitas and a free plan layout to improve the spatial experience (Zheng, 1983). The façade applies a simple Islamic style with a triangular folding arcade, and the layout features courtyards of different sizes. The total ground floor area (GFA) of this conference building is 9,100 m^2, including an 800-seat auditorium, a 200-seat conference hall, banquet halls, and small meeting rooms. The project was completed in February 1985, as the first Chinese foreign aid building in Djibouti.

The People's Palace has now been in use for more than 35 years. After completion, the Chinese government sent teams of technicians every two years to maintain the building and equipment, and gave technical training to Djiboutian personnel. The People's Palace was closed in 2010 for two years due to a fire, after which China undertook the restoration. As the country's only national performance venue and conference center, the People's Palace is an important landmark in Djibouti City and an integral part of the city's image. Major festivals, national performances, receptions for foreign guests, and national conferences are held there on a regular basis (Fig. 9.4).

"Stadium diplomacy" has been a major element of Chinese aid projects to Africa over the years. This "policy" has never been set forth in any document, but more than 70 stadiums have been built in Africa. Stadiums play a vital role in urban life in many African countries. The National Stadium was built in the 1990s with the aid of the Chinese government and named Gouled Stadium after the then president. The stadium is located on the west side of the African Quartier, next to the main road. It has a standard eight-track athletic field and a capacity of 10,000 seats. The groundbreaking ceremony was held in June 1991 and the stadium was completed in June 1993. Since then, the venue has been maintained by Chinese technician teams, and the current team is from the same institution that designed the People's Palace. Soccer is an enormously popular sport in Africa, and it could be called the "national ballgame" in Djibouti. In 2005, the Chinese government helped Djibouti to build two more small stadiums in the small towns of Tadjourah and Dikhil. The national stadium is a simple, functional, and modern venue for national sporting events and ceremonies, and for daily games and athletic training (Xue et al., 2019) (Fig. 9.5).

Following the launch of the Belt and Road Initiative in 2013, many Chinese investment projects sprouted up in Djibouti. The port operated by China Merchants Group is one of the most notable projects, and the large port facility has become a landmark on the city coastline.

In May 2013, China and Djibouti signed a contract in Beijing for the construction of a national library in Djibouti. The National Library and Archive is located in the southeast of the Balbala district of Djibouti City, adjacent to the University of Djibouti. The building was designed by the Domestic Trade Engineering Design and Research Institute (formerly known as the Design Institute of the Ministry of

Fig. 9.4 People's Palace, Djibouti

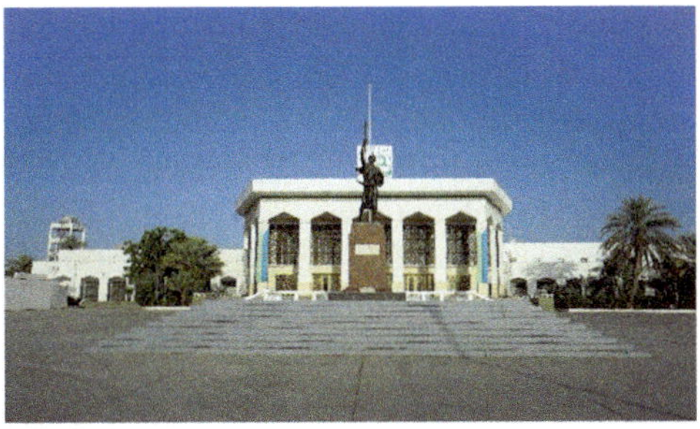

(a) People's Palace (Shot by Lujia Zhang)

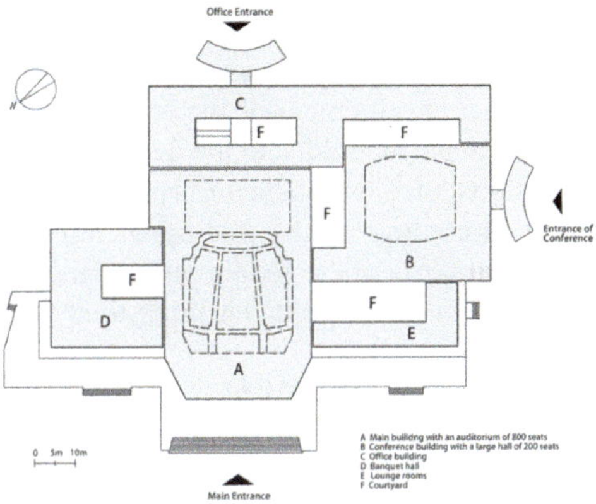

(b) Ground floor plan, People's Palace (Source: Zheng Jingwei. People's Palace, Republic of Djibouti. In *Huazhong architecture*, 1983.)

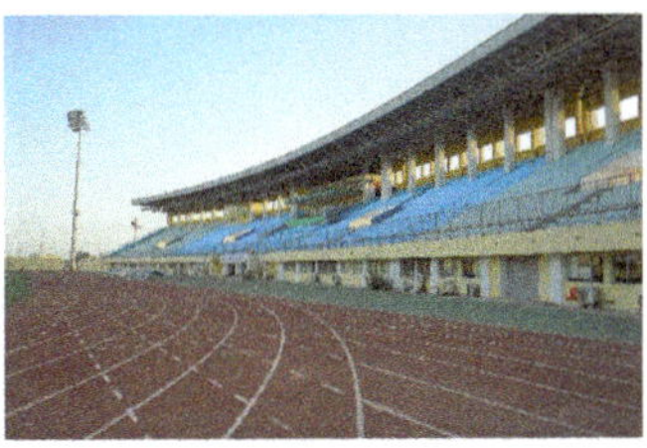

(a) National Stadium

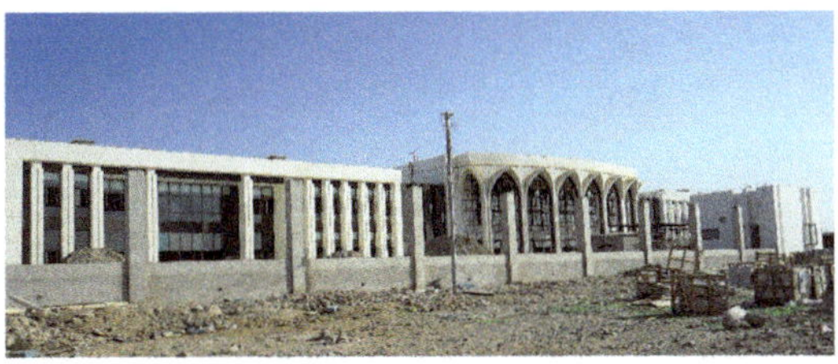

(b) National Library and Archive, at the end of construction

Fig. 9.5 Chinese aid buildings in Djibouti (shot by Lujia Zhang)

Commerce, now renamed Huashang International Engineering. 华商国际工程有限公司), and the construction was completed by Yunnan Construction and Investment Group, with a total GFA of 16,600 m^2. Construction began at the end of 2015 and was completed in July 2019 (Wang, 2016). The building currently shares some of the conference functions of the original People's Palace. Djibouti's current President Guelleh commented at the opening that the building "will contribute to our cultural impact, our social and political memory."

These three important public buildings are all iconic projects in Djibouti, located along the city's main roads and gradually extending from the city center to the western side of the Balbala District. They are functional, on a moderate scale, and located close to residential areas to ensure that they are accessible to ordinary people. Both the location of public projects and the relocation of the old port show the government's willingness to expand the city center, transcend the original boundaries, and address the uneven development of the city; however, most buildings in Djibouti City are still traditional and old, and the public buildings designed by Chinese architects and institutions have established only fragmented "new city" images within the urban space. In contrast to the traditional informal architectural spaces and façades in residential areas, these iconic public buildings introduce modern architectural and urban design into the city, ensuring they will have a long-term impact on urban life (Fig. 9.6).

According the World Bank, in 2018, 23% of Djibouti's population lived in extreme poverty, and the country hosted nearly 30,000 refugees from neighboring countries. Despite annual economic growth reaching 8% in recent years, the country's total GDP in 2018 was less than \$2 billion, and industrial and economic limitations have

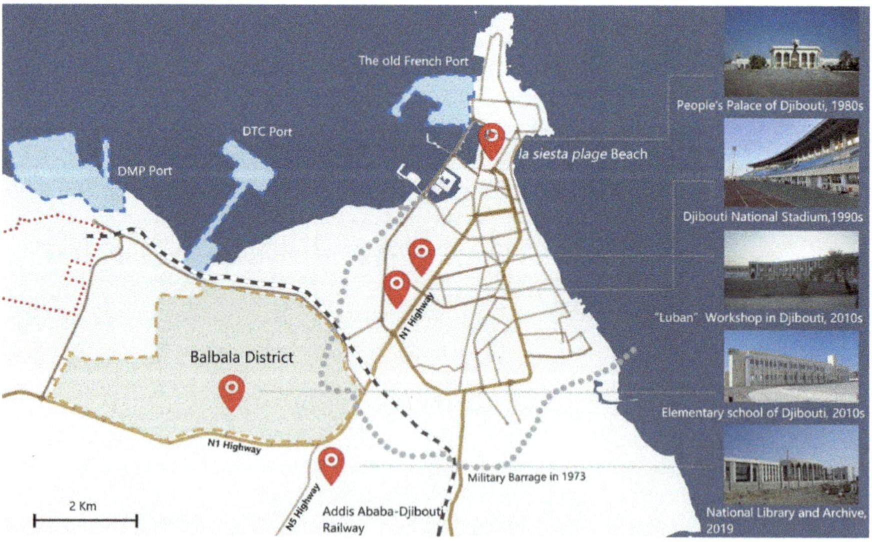

Fig. 9.6 The distribution of Chinese aid projects in Djibouti (drawn by Lujia Zhang)

made urbanization a difficult, lopsided, and slow process. There is a huge developmental tension between the desire of the powerful and elite for modern urban life and the construction of infrastructure for generally low-income populations. Djibouti's compulsory education includes only elementary school, and only around 60% of its population have a primary education. The country relies on educational foreign aid projects every year from countries such as France, Japan, and China, as well as NGOs. In September 2017, a primary school designed and constructed by CCCC First Highway Engineering Group was opened in the Balbala district, about 12 km from the city center. With a total GFA of 6,000 m^2, the school accommodates teaching buildings, administrative office buildings, sports fields, and outdoor facilities. In addition to aid projects for elementary schools, China also opened the first Luban Workshop (鲁班工坊, a vocational education aid and cooperation project) in the Industrial and Business College of Djibouti to develop educational cooperation between schools, government, and enterprises. China built teaching spaces and provided equipment and technical support for this project. The Luban Workshop project will provide technical training for the operation and maintenance of the new Addis Ababa–Djibouti Railway.

9.3 Chinese Aid Projects in a Self-Developed Urban Space: A Case Study of Addis Ababa

9.3.1 Characteristics of Addis Ababa's Urban Space

Ethiopia has the second largest population in Africa, and its capital city, Addis Ababa, is the headquarters of the African Union (AU), and is thus known as the "political heart of Africa." Addis Ababa, however, has been constantly influenced by European countries in the midst of strife.

After World War II, Addis Ababa underwent several rounds of master planning, but none of them were effective in guiding and controlling the city's development. During the period of Italian control in the 1930s, the first round of urban planning was embarked on by Le Corbusier at the behest of the Italian government and refined by two Italian architects. These designs were semi-colonial in style and left their traces on the urban environment even after the Italian regime left. Going through several changes in the post-war period of economic recovery and influenced by the planning of Greater London and the USSR's urban–rural planning, Addis Ababa initially developed an urban structure combining circular and radial road networks. Haile Selassie (1892–1975), the emperor of Ethiopia, was determined to lead Africa and held up Addis Ababa as a model of "imperial" modernization without changing the political system. Under his leadership, notable buildings designed by architects from Italy, France, Israel, Britain, and Yugoslavia were constructed in the 1950s and 1960s. Construction companies were also hired from overseas (Levin, 2016). However, these efforts were only local despite the city's sprawl. However, after the

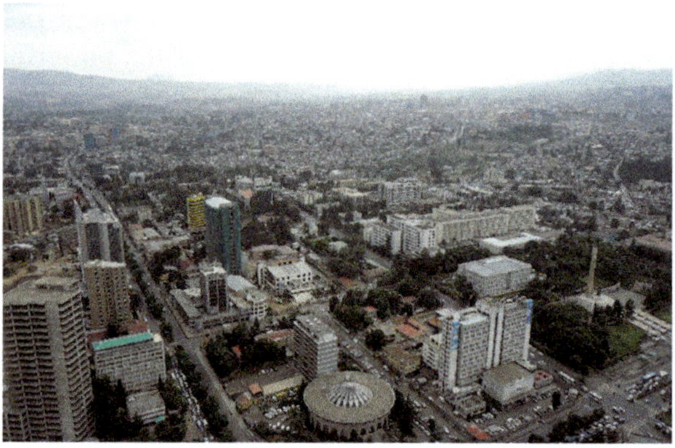

Fig. 9.7 Planning and existing cityscape of Addis Ababa. Spontaneous development reaching the foot of the mountain. (Shot by Lujia Zhang)

end of the Cold War and the collapse of the military government, Addis Ababa experienced massive urban development in a newly free economy. Following the flows of capital, the development has been poorly controlled and sprawling (Xu, Joachim, Wang, and Xu, 2018).

In 2019, Ethiopia's population reached 110 million. With urbanization at less than 30%, around half of its residents still live below the UN's poverty line. Addis Ababa keeps growing, with an urbanization rate above 5%, and adds around 120,000 new residents each year. At present the city's urban population is nearly 5 million, and urban development has been explosive. In contrast with these impressive numbers, in reality the government has limited financial capacity and is unable to control urban development. The quality of facilities in the old city areas is inadequate, while the new districts are expanding chaotically with blurred boundaries. Therefore, urban conditions are highly complex. As South African scholar Vanessa Watson noted, after years of rapid expansion, it is unclear "whether the beautiful urban planning for African cities is dreams or nightmares" (Watson, 2014) (Fig. 9.7).

9.3.2 Aid Projects and Urban Spaces

China has been the largest contributor of aid investment in Ethiopia in recent years. More than 300 construction projects have been completed, including the Bank of Ethiopia headquarters, currently the tallest building in East Africa with 48 floors. Large numbers of aid projects are active in Ethiopia, mainly in the area of infrastructure, and it represents a fast-growing volume of trade. In the 2018 Forum on China–Africa Cooperation, the Chinese government promised a future aid amount of $15 billion, consisting of non-reimbursable foreign aid projects, interest-free loans, and concessional loans. Aid projects in Addis Ababa include the light rail, the AU headquarters and power plant construction (BBC, 2019).

The AU headquarters, fully funded by China, is a landmark building in Addis Ababa, and a masterpiece of aid project architecture in Africa. The building was designed by the architect Ren Lizhi and his team at Tongji University Architectural Design and Research Institute, and built by China Construction Group (CSCEC) for Phase I and Anhui Foreign Economic Construction (Group) for auxiliary facilities, which is also in charge of maintenance and technical training after completion. The AU headquarters is located in the downtown area of Addis Ababa, where the old and infamous Alem Bekagn prison once stood. The prison was built around the time the Italian army captured Addis Ababa during World War II, and represented Ethiopia's humiliating history of invasion and semi-colonization. The prison was closed in 2004, and with the completion of the new building, no trace of the original structure remains, except for a small monument on the north side of the building in memory of the national wars (International Business Daily, 2016).

The AU headquarters was completed in December 2011 with a total investment of approximately RMB 800 million (USD 140 million). The main office building is 99.9 m high, making it the tallest building in the city at the time of its construction. The radially shaped conference center not only represents the cohesiveness of the AU countries and their friendly relations with China, but also reflects the Chinese architects' understanding of symbolism, local traditions, and modernity. The circular conference hall connects with the hundred-meter-high office building, soaring to the sky. The design highlights the vertical line of the tower. As with many aid projects, most of the construction materials had to be shipped from China. The art and decoration were designed and made by Chinese and African artists. The design team visited the site frequently, flying from Shanghai to Addis Ababa. Several young architects and engineers stayed on site for three years. The contrast in living conditions between Africa and China posed challenges for the designers and construction workers.

The completion of the AU headquarters put an end to the previous embarrassing situation, in which the AU countries had to borrow spaces for their meetings. The magnificent mansion adds value to Addis Ababa. Former Ethiopian President Meles once praised the building as "a symbol of Africa's rise." The AU headquarters epitomizes the impact of Addis Ababa's fast-growing urban development. The building offers new possibilities and a sense of place and renewal, reinforcing Addis Ababa's image as a political center. However, the interaction between the building and urban life is very limited due to the building's specific function. Ordinary citizens have little access to the building.

One project that has significantly changed the urban environment is the light rail in Addis Ababa. The project, constructed by China Railway Corporation, officially opened in September 2015 and became the first modern light rail on the African continent. After completion, it was operated by a team of technicians from China Railway Second Bureau and Shenzhen Metro Operating Company. Local technical staff were provided with training and guidance, and most of the rail's operations have now been handed over to the local management team. The light rail provides Addis Ababa with modern public transportation and has greatly improved traffic conditions in a short time. The light rail is currently 37 km long, with 39 stations, and has an average daily traffic of 104,500 passengers. It was once called "the beautiful scenery on the roof of Africa" by the media. However, with the growing urban population, the light rail is no longer capable of dealing with the increasing traffic congestion.

To relieve the pressure of urban traffic requires long-term investment and a complex transportation system. Without assistance, such investment is beyond the capacity of the local government (Figs. 9.8 and 9.9).

The complexity of urbanization in Addis Ababa is a common issue for African cities. Aid projects from a single state cannot make a profound difference to the urban development of such a large city. However, landmark public buildings and infrastructure establish the image of a fragmented, modern city, offering directions for future development. These buildings act as flagships to guide development in the surrounding area.

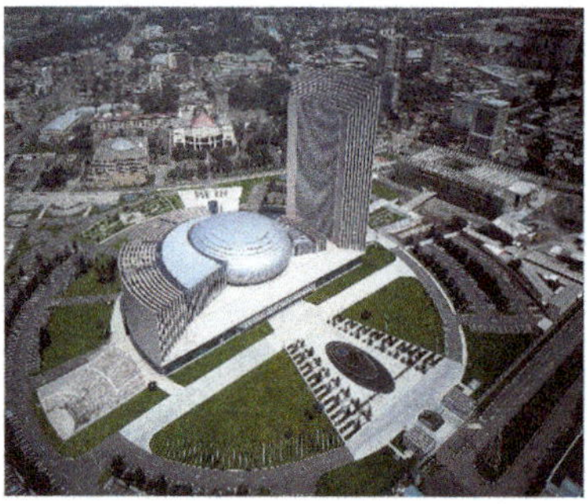

(a) African Union headquarters (courtesy of Ren Lizhi)

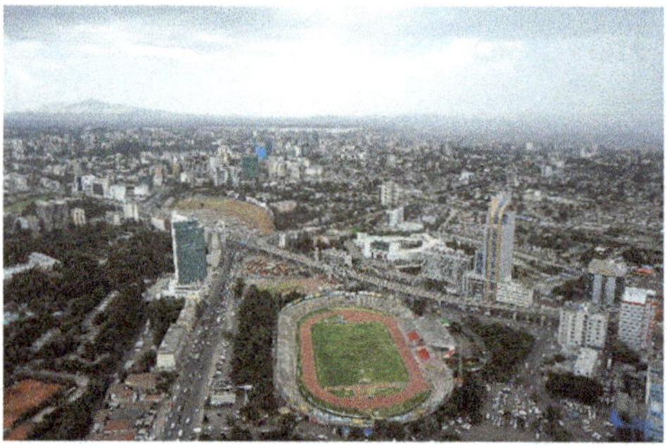

(b) Plaza in city center and the light rail (shot by Lujia Zhang)

Fig. 9.8 Addis Ababa and Chinese aid projects

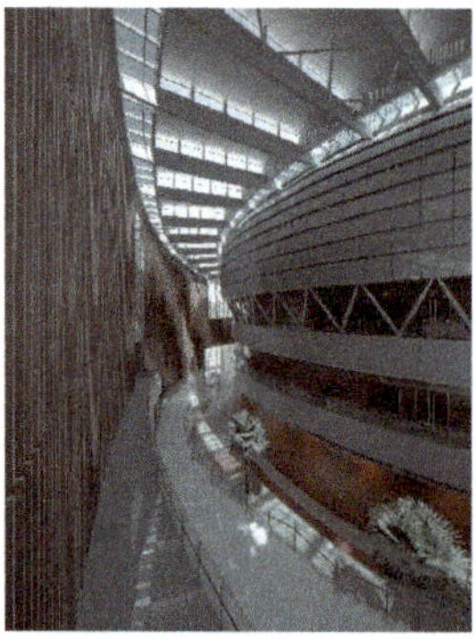

(a) Interior of Afican Union Headquarters

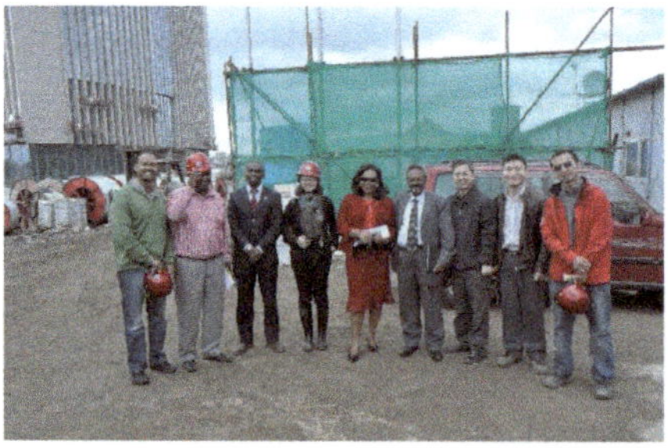

(b) Interior designer Wu Jie (No.4 from left hand side) and construction team on site, 2011

Fig. 9.9 African Union Headquarters in Addis Ababa (courtesy of Wu Jie)

9.4 Discussion and Conclusion

In recent years, Chinese aid projects have been accused of "infrastructural violence"—construction that takes place too quickly. This can be seen as a positive comment on China's capacity for rapid infrastructure construction, which is essential for establishing public order. However, considering the economic situation of African countries, aid projects are required to fit local economic and technological development and take employment issues into account. It is also necessary to have reasonable expectations for the future growth of urban space and the population (Huang, 2019). Successful implementation and maintenance of foreign aid projects requires effort and cooperation from the donor and recipient countries. The principle of aid projects is to maximize their influence despite limited investment. Recipient countries are usually weak in the industrial sector; some countries may not be able to produce even a nail. Because of the long-distance shipping of construction materials, the cost and construction period of a building in Africa are much greater than in China. Because many African countries do not have a unified construction standard, construction quality varies. One major issue is thus how to ensure the quality of the aid project and take advantage of efficient construction processes without burdening the local economy.

The need for continuous maintenance and technical support is also a special feature of foreign aid projects. Lacking a team of technicians for independent operations, the recipient country may confront huge economic burdens if the project is not fully utilized. Through the bidding process conducted every two years by China's Ministry of Commerce, the maintenance and training of the local technical workforce will continue in the future. However, this training will also need constant adjustment to reflect local conditions, so that use and maintenance can keep pace with development. In recent years, technical exchange activities have been organized by government departments in China, which can be an effective way to ensure sustainable development. Of course, the donor country takes on a large responsibility and financial burden in this situation (Xue & Ding, 2018).

The complicated urban space of the Horn of Africa is a microcosm of the urbanization process in Africa. The process and quality of urbanization are very different from previous development experiences of Chinese cities due to the large number of citizens living in poverty and the government's constraints and ineffective management. In aid projects, these countries confront challenges from the mismatch between expectations and ability in urban development. As the South African scholar Vanessa Watso has pointed out, behind the "beautiful urbanization data," the illusion of urban development and blind planning do not lead to real modernization and urbanization (Watson, 2014). Aspiring in the long run to the status of developed cities like Singapore or Dubai is worthwhile, but this is unrealistic for the short term. Rapid development and the pursuit of commercial interests may lead to speculative urbanism; as the American scholar Michael Goldman notes, uneven urban development may lead to disorder (Goldman, 2011).

In modern life, people's experiences and attitudes need to be promoted by the city. In the Horn of Africa, urbanization is still progressing slowly. The global experience of modernization has been "parachuted" into cities with the help of donor countries. As Dominic Sachsenmaier notes, the Western form of modernity is not the only one; other cultural traditions and social forms can also develop their own modernity. Modern architecture from Western countries or even China may not fit the demands of the African context. Architecture concerns places for living; the question of how the modern life fostered by aid projects can be integrated into the urban experience is a major issue in design, implementation, and operation.

The iconic public buildings in Djibouti and Addis Ababa quickly established the cities' image. They also performed practical public functions. However, these aid projects have only created a fragmented picture of the modern city, and the impact on urban life is limited. The construction of stadiums in Africa has benefited many residents, while public buildings such as conference centers have fewer users due to their function. The architects and design institutions from the donor country need feedback from the aid projects and must think about how these buildings can be better implemented. How these aid projects continue to serve the people, by changing urban space and lifestyle, requires long-term research; it is necessary to explore the positive interaction between the space and the residents.

This chapter has briefly reviewed some important Chinese aid projects in the Horn of Africa. In response to the Belt and Road Initiative, aid projects and economic cooperation with African cities will become more extensive. Donors' support is always limited. While individual projects currently only have a limited impact on urbanization in Africa, in the future, more projects will be deeply involved in urban development. These "flagship" buildings can lead to more positive interaction in development. This goes back to the issue of "transfusion" discussed in the beginning of this chapter. Chinese architects and design institutions are already engaging in large-scale architectural and urban design projects and exporting their design and operational concepts for modern cities to Africa.

While Chinese aid projects are exerting influence in Africa, countries such as the United States and Japan, as major international aid donors, are also adjusting their aid policies. Africa has become a site accommodating multiple international economic powers, and the complex situation will undoubtedly affect the future development of African cities. Ensuring the impact of Chinese aid projects on social development and urban life in Africa is a challenge that government agencies, architects, and design institutions must consider in future projects and competitions.

(The authors are grateful to the kind help and guidance of Pan Xiaobo and manager Wu Zhimin from China Merchants Group (招商集团) in Djibouti, Tang Yongcheng and the engineers of China State Construction Engineering Group (中国中建) and China Railway Group (中国中铁) in Ethiopia with the on-site investigation and interviews, and Dr. Huang Zhengli for the whole trip in Africa and generous advice in the following academic discussions. This chapter is part of a research supported by the National Natural Science Foundation of China, Project No. 51878584.)

References

African Development Bank, OECD and United Nations Development Program. (2016). *African economic outlook 2016: Sustainable cities and structural transformation.* OECD Publishing.

Amoah, L. G. A. (2016). China, architecture and Ghana's spaces: Concrete signs of a soft Chinese imperium? *Journal of Asian and African Studies, 51*(2), 238–255.

Bisaillon, L. M., & Mohammed, A. R. (2005). Djibouti the two faces of the city: Modern and traditional forms. *Urbanistica, 2005*(40), 30–40.

Brass, J. (2008). Djibouti's unusual resource curse. *The Journal of Modern African Studies, 46*(4), 523–545.

Brautigam, D. (2011). *The dragon's gift : The real story of China in Africa.* Oxford University Press.

Brautigam, D. (2020). A critical look at Chinese "debt-trap diplomacy": The rise of a meme. *Area Development and Policy, 5*(1), 1–14.

British Broadcasting Corporation (2019) Dongfei "Xiao Zhongguo'" Aisaiebiya: Weiji Gaige Bingbian he Zhongguo Yuan. [East Africa's "Little China" Ethiopia: Crisis, Reform, Mutiny and the Relation with China]. Retrieved February 2, 2021 from https://www.bbc.com/zhongwen/simp/world-48749888 英国广播公司. 东非"小中国"埃塞俄比亚: 危机、改革、兵变和中国缘.网址 https://www.bbc.com/zhongwen/simp/world-48749888

Cohen, M. A. (2013). Giving to developing countries, controversies and paradoxes of international aid. *Social Research: An International Quarterly, 80*(2), 591–606.

Collier, P. (2007). *The bottom billion : Why the poorest countries are failing and what can be done about it.* Oxford University Press.

Ding, G., & Xue, C. (2015). China's architectural aid: Exporting a transformational modernism. *Habitat International, 47*, 136–147.

Fowler, C. (2019). French foreign policy in East Africa: Not without challenges, but promising signs exist. Retrieved December 20, 2019 from http://www.futuredirections.org.au/publication/french-foreign-policy-in-east-africa-not-without-challenges-but-promising-signs-exist/

Goldman, M. (2011). Speculative urbanism and the making of the next world city. *International Journal of Urban and Regional Research, 35*(3), 555–581.

Huang, Z. (2019). Yaoxiangfu Xianxiulu- Zhongguo Jijian yu Feizhou Chengshi Fazhan.[To Become Rich, Should People Build Roads First": Infrastructure Construction in China and Urban Development in Africa].Renlei juzhu.[Human Settlements].(02), 10–11. 黄正骊.要想富,先修路—中国基建与非洲城市发展.人类居住. (02), 10–11.

Imbert-Vier, S. (2012). The barrage de Djibouti: From migration barrier to identity building. *Northeast African Journal of Social Sciences and Humanities, 02*, 89–107.

International Business Daily. (2016). Cong Aisai Yangben Kan Zhongguo Duiwai Yuanzhu Zouxiang[The Trend of China's Foreign Aid from the Ethiopian Sample]. Retrieved February 2, 2021 from http://finance.china.com.cn/roll/20160313/3624591.shtml 国际商报.从埃塞样本看中国对外援助走向.网址 http://finance.china.com.cn/roll/20160313/3624591.shtml

Levin, A. (2015). Beyond global versus local: Tipping the scales of architectural historiography. *ABE Journal, 8*, 1–7.

Levin, A. (2016). Haile selassie's imperial modernity. *Journal of the Society of Architectural Historians, 75*(4), 447–468.

Mercer, M. (2021) How Japan is helping Africa achieve 'inclusive and dynamic' develop-ment. Retrieved February 2, 2021 from https://www.centreforpublicimpact.org/japan-africa-inclusive-development/

Ministry of Commerce of the PRC.(2018). Report on Development of China's Outward Investment. Retrieved February 2,2021 from http://fec.mofcom.gov.cn/article/tzhzcj/tzhz/ 中华人民共和国商务部. (2018).中国对外投资发展报告.网址 http://fec.mofcom.gov.cn/article/tzhzcj/tzhz/

Sun, D., & Zoubir, Y. (2021). Securing China's "latent power": The dragon's anchorage in Djibouti. *The Journal of Contemporary China, 30*(130), 677–692.

The State Council Information Office of the PRC. (2014). China's Foreign Aid. Retrieved February 2, 2021 from http://www.scio.gov.cn/zfbps/ndhf/2014/document/1375014/1375014.htm. 中华人民共和国国务院新闻办公室.中国的对外援助 (2014).网址 http://www.scio.gov.cn/zfbps/ndhf/2014/document/1375014/1375014.htm

Wan, Y., Zhang, L., Xue, C. Q., & Xiao, Y. (2020). Djibouti: From a colonial fabrication to the deviation of the "Shekou model." *Cities, 97*, 102488.

Wang G. P. (2016). Yuan Jibuti Guojia Tushu DanganGuan Kongtiao Xitong Sheji.[HVAC system design for Djibouti National Library and Archives].Jianzhu jieneng.[Journal of Building Energy Efficiency]. (07), 6–8. 王鸽鹏.援吉布提国家图书档案馆空调系统设计.建筑节能, (07), 6–8.

Watson, V. (2014). African urban fantasies: Dreams or nightmares? *Environment and Urbanization, 26*(1), 215–231.

World bank.(2016). Horn of Africa: World Bank $175 million financing supports regional initiative on communities hosting refugees. Retrieved February 2, 2021 from https://www.worldbank.org/en/news/press-release/2016/05/31/horn-of-africa-world-bank-175-million-financing-supports-regional-initiative-on-communities-hosting-refugees

Xu, W., Joachim, D., Wang, X., & Xu, J. (2018). Yadisiya Jinxiandai Chengshi Guihua Lishi Yanjiu. [Research on Modern Urban Planning History of Addis Ababa in the Last Century]. Guoji chengshi guihua.[*Urban Planning International*].(05), 86–92.许闻博,乔基姆·迪特尔,王兴平,徐嘉勃.亚的斯亚贝巴近现代城市规划历史研究.国际城市规划 (05), 86–92.

Xue, C. Q. L., & Ding, G. (2018). *A history of design institutes in China : From Mao to market*. Routledge.

Xue, C. Q. L., Ding, G., Chang W., & Zhang, L. (2018).Yuanwau Jianzhu-Zhongguo Shejiyuan Zai Haiwai de Licheng. [Construction Aid Modern Chinese Architecture in Overseas Projects]. Shidai jianzhu [*Time + Architecture*] (05), 42–49. 薛求理, 丁光辉, 常威, 张璐嘉. 援外建筑—中国设计院在海外的历程.时代建筑 (05), 42–49.

Xue, C., Ding, G., Chang, W., & Wan, Y. (2019). Architecture of "Stadium diplomacy"-China-aid sport buildings in Africa. *Habitat International, 90*, 101985.

Zheng J. W.(1983). Jibuti Gongheguo Renmin Gong.[People's Palace of the Republic of Djibouti].Huazhong jianzhu.[Huazhong Architecture] (01), 15–18. 郑经纬. 吉布提共和国人民宫.华中建筑 1983(01), 15–18.

Lujia Zhang is a Ph.D. candidate at City University of Hong Kong. She received her master degree of architecture in the South China University of Technology. She is interested in the contemporary Chinese architecture practice and Chinese aid architecture under the globalization. She has published research articles in journals such as *Cities, New Architecture, Time + Architecture, Journal of Architecture and Urbanism and Journal of Asian Architecture and Building Engineering.*

Yan Wan is a Ph.D. candidate in the architecture department, the University of Hong Kong, where her dissertation focuses on the dialectical urban history of Shenzhen and Hong Kong. She has professional experience with various non-profit-making organizations and design companies. Her interests include port cities, urban development, and transnational urbanism, including the urbanization process stimulated by Chinese state-owned enterprise versus that of villages.

Xinyu Liu is currently a joint Ph. D. candidate from both the City University of Hong Kong and Southeast University, Nanjing. In 2017, he obtained a master degree in urban design from Chinese University of Hong Kong where he started his interest on landscape and architectural history and theory. His papers mainly focus on landscape history and are published in journals such as *Chinese Landscape Architecture, Landscape Architecture Journal*. Before engaged in academic career, he also practiced for years as a landscape architect in both Shanghai and Hong Kong.

Charlie Qiuli Xue has taught architecture at Shanghai Jiaotong University, University of Texas and City University of Hong Kong. An award-winning architect and writer, he has published 15 books, including '*Building a Revolution: Chinese Architecture since 1980*' (HKU Press, 2006), '*Hong Kong Architecture 1945–2015: From Colonial to Global*' (Springer, 2016), '*A History of Design Institutes in China: from Mao to Market*' (with G. Ding, Routledge, 2018) and '*Grand Theater Urbanism: Chinese cities in the 21st century*' (Springer, 2019, ed.). He has published more than 160 research papers in professional and international refereed journals and 40 book chapters. His papers are published in such journals as *Cities, Habitat International, Urban Design International, Journal of Architecture, Journal of Urban Design, Architectural Research Quarterly, Journal of Urban History, Planning Perspective, Architecture + Urbanism, Domus and Chinese journals like Architectural Journal, Architect, New Architecture, Time + Architecture, World Architecture and Taiwan Architect*. His book on Hong Kong was awarded by the International Committee of Architectural Critics (CICA) in 2017. Xue's research interests are in Chinese architecture, transnational design and high-density environment. Xue is also extensively involved in design and consultant practice in Hong Kong, Chinese mainland and the US.

Part III
One Belt One Road

Chapter 10
Architecture of Eclecticism: China's Architectural Projects in Pakistan (2001–2019)

Sohrab Ahmed Marri

Abstract This chapter discusses two Chinese built cases in the situation of Belt and Road Initiative. Since the beginning of the twenty-first century, China has radically increased its development aids, cooperation, and investment with less developed countries. These development programs comprise of many architectural projects. The aim of this China's international development program is to strengthen bilateral relations and cooperate in mutual economic development projects. BRI is China's latest form of international economic cooperation. Pakistan has close ties with China and become an important partner of China in the Belt and Road Initiative (BRI). In such a development scheme, the designers of architectural projects are mainly from Chinese state-owned design institutes. In a few cases, they collaborates with local architectural firms. This chapter investigates the cross-cultural architecture exchanges between China and Pakistan. It has established a "contact zone" between two state expertise, where new eclectic architecture evolved by a collaboration of complex actors from both sides. The process finds a "third space" that syncretizes the similar architectural features of both cultures in a modern way. This study challenges the western way of globalization and broaden our epistemological understanding of south-south architecture exchanges.

10.1 Introduction

Since the Mao era, China is providing development aid to less developed countries to strengthen the bilateral relationship and cooperating in mutual economic developments. In the early 2000s, Beijing launched its "Going Global" strategy to encourage its biggest companies to invest abroad in widespread areas by supporting it with bilateral diplomatic ties and creating a favorable environment (Gonzalez-Vicente, 2011). The policy of "Going Global" augmented the development aids, which includes exported architectural projects in less developed countries. It intended to enhance

S. A. Marri (✉)
Department of Architecture, Balochistan University of Information Technology, Engineering and Management Science, Quetta, Pakistan
e-mail: sohrab.ahmed@buitms.edu.pk

C. Q. Xue and G. Ding (eds.), *Exporting Chinese Architecture*,
https://doi.org/10.1007/978-981-19-2786-7_10

its soft power, to increase trade and mutual economic development (King, 2013; Zhao & Jing, 2019). Recently, this complex cooperation is rebranded into China's Belt and Road Initiative which is inspired from old silk road (Williams et al., 2020). BRI is a massive scale twenty-first century globalization backed by Beijing. It calls for inclusive globalization that is a vision of co-existence, Win–Win Cooperation, People to People relation, boosting trade, regional economic development and prosperity for mankind by ensuring poverty eradication (Liu & Dunford, 2016). Beside these abstract ideas, words, ambitions, slogans, the most visible part of any development aid is perhaps the gift of architecture projects. It is particularly interesting to decipher the production of architectural project that is a concrete object and its influences from these abstract ideas (Levin, 2015, 1–4) and exchanges of ideas from established "contact zone" (Pratt, 1991)[1] between two countries.

Since 1950, China and Pakistan relations commenced when Pakistan was among the first countries who recognized the People's Republic of China and ended the diplomatic ties with the Republic of China. Since then both countries on regular basis strengthen their bilateral relations (Khan, 1961). Pakistan has received substantial development aid projects including some architecture projects from China. In the Belt and Road Initiative, China has invested billions of dollars in Pakistan on infrastructure development, energy pipeline, its infrastructure, port, airports, industrial parks, etc. It consists of numerous architectural projects, some are constructed, and others are in the designing and planning phase. These architecture projects are designed and built by China state-owned design and construction companies and sometimes it collaborated with local architectural companies (Butt, 2019b). Although Chinese architectural projects surging in Pakistan, since last two decades, within the specific context from development aid collaboration to BRI, no particular attention is being paid by scholars either from receiving side or donor side. This chaper is an attempt to fill this gap by investigating the Chinese architectural projects in Pakistan. It discusses the established "contact zone" (Pratt, 1991) between two state expertise that leads to a "Third space" (Bhabha, 1994; Bhabha & Rutherford, 2006; Borch, 2002; Lefebvre, 1991).[2] It exposes a new way of doing critical regionalism in a non-western context, which is slightly different that is practiced by western architects. There are a few relevant Chinese research articles, design institute catalogues and news articles.

[1] See in "Arts of the Contact Zone" by Mary Louise Pratt. She introduced the concept of a "contact zone". She stated that "This term refers to the social space in today's world that refers to the social space in which cultures meet, collide, and work with each other, often in the context of very asymmetric power relations, such as colonialism, slavery, or its aftermath". Tom Avermeate and Maristela Casciato recently adopted this concept in order to explain the phenomenon of architectures exchanges in their research.

[2] Third space concept introduced by Homi Bhabha; Edward Soja; Henri Lefebvre. According to Homi Bhabha, first space is of native space, second space is the foreigner's space who brought with them and third space is intermixing of first and second space, it is ambivalent or hybrid space. According to Soja who inspired from Lefebvre trialectics of spatiality; first space is "things in space" that is of native, second space is of "thoughts about space" or "mental space" and third space fall between these two spaces which Henri Lefebvre called "lived space" or "real space". Along with "contact zone" the "third space" is equally interesting concepts to know the transcultural processes in architecture.

The other research source is retrieving feasibility report documents from Pakistan government offices, interviewing Pakistani stakeholders and field observation of the projects.

This chapter presents two case studies emerged in a different context but shares many commonalities. One is Pakistan China Friendship Center which is realized within the setting of Chinese "going global" policy while other case is Gwadar Business Center, which is recently constructed in the framework of Belt and Road initiative. These two diverse cases are exemplifying an architecture of eclecticism that is fusion of similar local architectural elements with Chinese architecture features in modern way. Chinese construction experts are exporting up-to-date construction technologies, following a path of austerity and keeping sustainability goals in line.

The use of the term "eclecticism" in this chapter is not presenting the revivalism of historical styles but this transcultural architecture praxis represents a creative syncretizing of architecture features of two nations in the modernist critical approach. Something that is original, progressive and pragmatic that conform the broad definition of eclecticism in architecture (Épron, 1997) and slightly differs with the idea of critical regionalism. The "Critical regionalism" introduced by Alexander Tzonis and Liane Lefaivre (1981) and Kenneth Frampton (1983). According to these authors, critical regionalism emphasizes the placeness by considering contextual elements like scenery and historical references without falling into imitation and traditionalism. It does not aim to reinstall vernacular architecture but attempts to vernacularize the modern architecture. Critical regionalism is linked to the western enlightenment tradition a fact can be beneficial as well as problematic when it is applied in non-western context (Botz-Bornstein, 2016, 1–2). This research expands the western concept of critical regionalism in global south. The repercussion of this transcultural eclectic architecture is resulted from "contact zone" where interaction of various actors in a specific socio-political context.

10.2 Locating the Research in Export–Import Architecture Criticism

Much of the research has been done since last two decades about the exportation of architecture in post war period from western countries either from socialist or capitalist countries to developing countries and generated many debates. For instance, the confrontation between west and east, modernism versus traditionalism, multiple form of collaboration between various actors, from individual architects to teamwork of architects in large construction, government institution and international aid agencies (Stanek, 2012, 299–300). One of weak spots of architecture and urban models in the post-war era is presenting the motivation and consideration of donor side and neglecting the contribution of so-called receiving sides (Avermaete, 2012, 476). Much of our epistemology of exported and imported architecture model on less developed countries are originated from and based on western perspectives and lacks critical stance from so-called receiving side scholars (Akcan, 2016).[3] Less research has been done about China exportation of architecture and urban model to global south (Chang, Xue & Ding, 2019; Ding & Xue, 2015; Roskam, 2015). In the early time of PRC, China received substantial urban models from the Soviet Union, which influenced its architecture culture for decades and became an example of its architectural exports (Li, 2012; Roskam, 2015). Since the Mao era, many State-owned design institutes were formed and served the state strategic socialist construction and urbanization and exported score of architecture aid projects mainly in developing countries. This exportation of architecture become the main driver of China's diplomatic mission (Chang et al. 2019; Xue & Ding, 2018). The Chinese architectural aid projects detaching itself away from dominating ideologies and finding its own path in disseminating modern architecture that could integrate the local architectural features (Lu, 2010; Roskam, 2015). The chapter presents a two way of critical architectural dialogues between China and Pakistan and situates it in an international debate.

There are few researches on it which are mostly situated in post war era. This research attempts to go beyond the post war context and map out recent export architecture interventions with case study of Chinese architectural projects in Pakistan. Since the separation of Pakistan from India based on ideology of Islamic state that embodying Muslim aspiration, during post war period Pakistan sought western architects to design public buildings in Modern Islamic architectural styles especially in Islamabad city which was planned by Greek architect Doxiadis with a concept of modern Islamic city. The aim of the architectural projects in newly so called modern Islamic city Islamabad was to represent Pakistan as modernizing country with its Islamic values. For instance, Supreme court of Pakistan in Islamabad designed by Kenzo Tange, Islamabad parliament house by Edward Durrell Stone, Pakistan secretariat by Gio Ponti and many other notable architects translated the modern Islamic concepts in architecture (Daechsel, 2015; Mumtaz, 1985). While some dominating western architects were unsuccessful to convince the local authorities like Louis Kahn. These architectural designs for Pakistan by western architects have had a lasting impact on Pakistan's architectural culture for decades (Rehman, 2013). In case of Pakistan and China "export and import architecture", both are non-western countries, it could be interesting to understand how Chinese architects re-interpret modern Islamic architecture or specific local requirements or propagate its own architectural influences? The author is particularly interested in the cross-cultural architecture negotiations in "third space" i.e., in terms of architecture representations and specificity through a process of collaborations in a "contact zone" between the different complex network of actors.

[3] See the post-colonial critiques presented by Esra Ackan.

10.3 Architecture of "Common Space" in Case of Pakistan China Friendship Center

In the early twenty-first century, there were many momentous events occurred which intensified the relation between Pakistan and China. Following the China "going global strategy" and becoming a member of WTO (China Policy, 2017),it has exported many architectural projects as an aid, comprised of mainly culture-related centers to its partner countries to present a positive image of China and enhance its soft power. The term soft power is originated from the west and attribute with an ideology of cultural imperialism (Antonescu, 2014). Chinese soft power differs slightly from western ones. Soft power, along with development aid of Chinese interventions are based on more equal south-south transactions. These are culture exchanges, not political influences (King, 2013). Architectural gifts are meant to increase cultural exchanges between the two countries. In the first decade of twenty-first century, there are many projects emerged for examples National Opera House of Algiers, Bangladesh China Friendship Center, Senegal National Grand Theater, etc. signifying Chinese "go out" policy and new role in the global order.

In December 2004 Prime Minister Shaukat Aziz made an important visit to China, where they discussed the bilateral trade, defense cooperation, technical assistance in some project and many economic developments between two countries (Rajan 2017). During his visit, the decision was also made that China aid to construct Sino-Pakistan Friendship Center which will be a gift from China to people of Pakistan (*Dawn* News, 2009). In 2005, Chinese Premier Wen Jiabao visited first time in Pakistan. He has signed many major agreements and most prominent was initiating the free trade agreement between two countries. In this trip, he laid the foundation of China Pakistan friendship cultural center. Perhaps, a friendly business environment needs people to people relations by cultural exchanges and other familiar activities. The motivation behind the construction of the center was to expand the people-to-people cultural exchanges and to set up the China Cultural Center to promote Chinese culture in Pakistan. The project is financially and technically assisted by China (News sina, 2010). The Pakistani government was asked to provide the land for the project. Later on, CDA Islamabad provided 12-acre land. The friendship center was planned to build on 12-acre land with an approximate cost of Rs 3.128 billion PKR out of which the Chinese government will provide 2.12 billion, and the construction period will take two years. All other necessary matters regarding the complete execution of the project are decided to be carried out by Chinese state-owned design and construction companies (*Dawn* News, 2009).

China state owned construction companies along with Chinese government have set principle guideline for foreign construction project, which are to respect local culture, environment, local construction by laws while also ensuring best up to date modern technology and expertise (*Social* Responsibility, 2017). In this context, the Chinese State Design Institute exported architecture that respects local architecture, complies with local environmental laws, and also promotes Chinese culture abroad. According to Ding Jian, President of China International Engineering Corporation

IPPR, in the past, foreigners spread culture through missionaries, but how do we Chinese today spread Chinese culture? He believes that Chinese architects going abroad to do architectural design, building a house is "preaching" and spreading Chinese culture. This is great mission, because it will make China better to integrate into the world (Huang et al. 2008).

There are many possible architectural trajectories that can be followed in such a context. One of these avenues is to find a "common space" between two different cultures that highlights the hybridization of similar architectural features of both nations and excludes the contrasting architectural features. In such a way harmony can be established in architecture. This architecture trajectory is consolidated in case of Pak–China Friendship Center located in Islamabad, constructed in 2010. In a bid the Zhongyuan International Design Co., Ltd. (IPPR) was nominated to design this culture center and constructed by Shanghai Engineering construction group, both are Chinese state-owned enterprises (News sina, 2010). The architects of IPPR sought two peculiar common features of Islamic and traditional Chinese architecture that is inward courtyard and the perforated design features of windows and walls. Therefore, the overall design is derived from coalescing of these two common features of two cultures. According to deputy chief architect of project:

> China has assisted Pakistan for decades in many projects but not many buildings that reflect their common architectural features, thus we proposed a concept to integrate their common architectural features in a critical modernist way to symbolize friendship between two countries (News sina, 2010).

The architect quest to syncretize the architecture features of two different cultures is an adroit choice because not only it will connote the idea of representing friendship between two countries but also promote the Chinese architecture features abroad.

The Pakistan China Friendship center is located in one of prime locations of Islamabad city. The site is surrounded by green landscape, museums, China previously aided sport complex and many notable monumental buildings. The Chinese previously aided sport complex has gained a much respect among Pakistan local architects. According to Divisional Head at National Engineering Services Pakistan, the architect Muhammad Arif Changezi:

> The sport complex exemplifies a dedication and a great engineering work of that time by Chinese experts. The modern architecture masses and space of Liaqat gymnasium depict its monumentality which is noteworthy gift from China. It has facilitated many local and international sport events in Islamabad (Changezi, 2018).

While, in other case few of Pakistani scholars like Abdul Rehman criticized that Liaqat gymnasium as typical modern box lacking local contextual features (Rehman, 2013). The prime location of Pakistan China Friendship Center exerts the monumental character in Fig. 10.1.

The center comprised of three buildings: conference—exhibition center, banquet hall, art and dance center, lounge for various ceremonies and service rooms. The three volumes encased in rectangular perforated shell and eclectically employs architecture elements that ranges from contemporary vocabulary to traditional Chinese and Islamic architecture. The entrance gate has three Islamic architecture pointing arches,

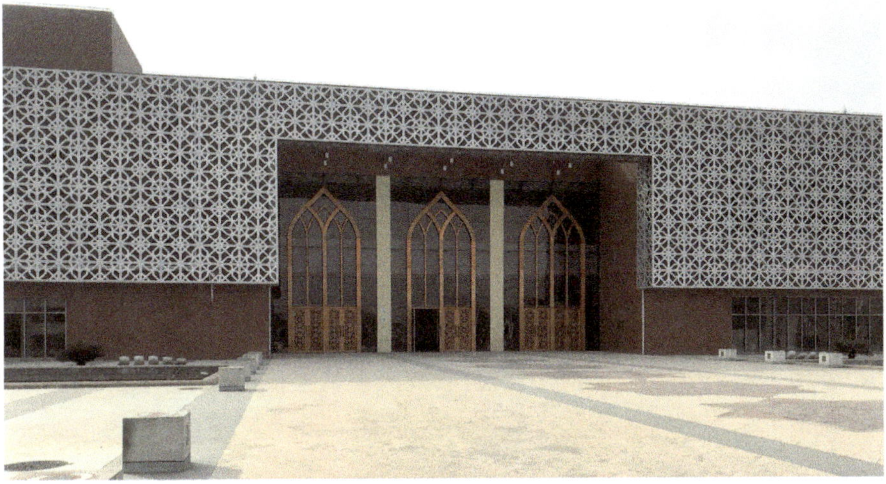

Fig. 10.1 Pakistan–China Friendship Center (Photo by the author)

probably IPPR architects got inspired from Bangladesh China Conference Center's three arches that was constructed earlier than it. These arches are notable feature of culture center that has pop up from modern rectangular shell to welcome the visitors. The outer rectangular shell of center is inspired form Islamic Mashrabiya or "Jali".[4] The design pattern also resembles to Chinese plum blossom, a common traditional architectural element that used in windows. According to deputy designer:

> The façade is to highlight common features of both Chinese and Islamic architecture. The façade is composed of aluminum plates, each plate is one-meter square a successful molding and high-pressure water cutting. This is art style of Chinese paper cut and it is deformation of Chinese plum blossoms (News sina, 2010).

The designers then prescribed it as also functional element used as shade from burning sun of Islamabad in summertime (Huang et al. 2008). This creativity is apparently an Islamic feature but has a spirit of Chinese art.

In between the ballroom is the Islamic courtyard, comprised of a fountain and planters surrounded by colonnades of Islamic style—the architect probably got inspired by Alhambra Moorish architecture (Fig. 10.2). The molding of arches is done in a modern way with the usage of frugal material. To balance this thematic Islamic Garden, the architect deliberately injected Chinese traditional garden element opposite to it—the garden itself contrasting each other articulation and displaying two cultures in front of each other. In an interview with the resident engineer of Pakistan China Friendship Center, Islamabad:

[4] Jali is local language word means "perforated wall" This word specifically originated from Mughal architecture.

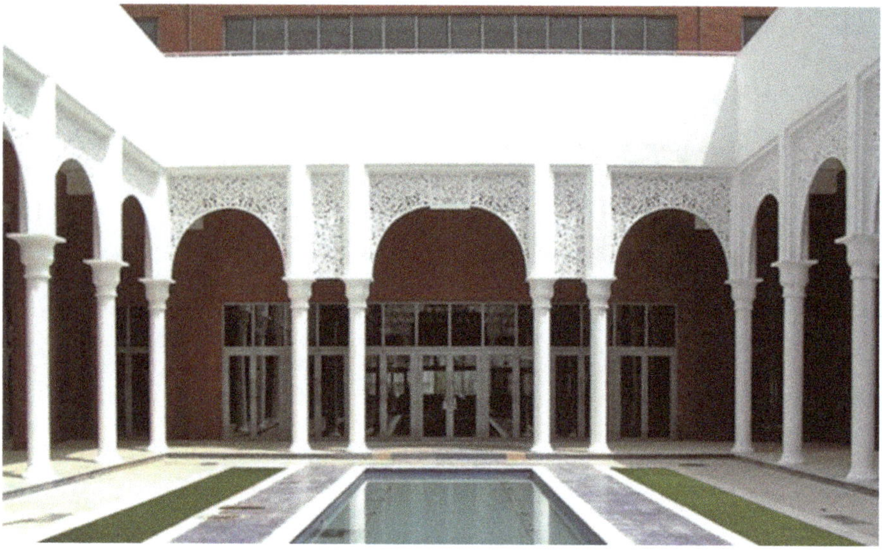

Fig. 10.2 Islamic garden (Courtesy China IPPR.com.cn)

> There is Islamic Garden, and the other side is Chinese garden, but this space is not much in use, but with lightings, it displays a unique environment during the events (Resident Engineer, 2019).

The selected color of the facade as white and background as red is aimed to expose the tripled volume, a metaphor of ancient Chinese tripod (Huang et al. 2008); this superficial fabrication is again architect's agenda of dismantling and unifying the two cultures.

This complex articulation of design elements also has sophisticated facilities that is office rooms, conference halls to guest rooms, banquet hall, exhibition hall, etc. The president chamber is designed and intended to accommodate both presidents of state meeting. According to management officer of Pakistan China Friendship Center, Islamabad:

> it was never used by two state presidents to hold a meeting (Management Officer, 2019) (Fig. 10.3).

The interior design again presents amalgamation of both cultures. In this architecture complex, the architect adopted a critical approach by using indirect or sensual Chinese architecture element while exposing understandable Islamic architecture.

The decoration of high-quality and almost all construction materials and construction machineries are exported from China, except some locally available construction materials were used like cement bags and steel bars (Huang et al. 2008). At start it has organized many joint cultural and trade events of China and Pakistan. Since the launch of BRI it becomes vital avenue for two cultures to organize many events here. According to the event manager of Pakistan China Friendship Center:

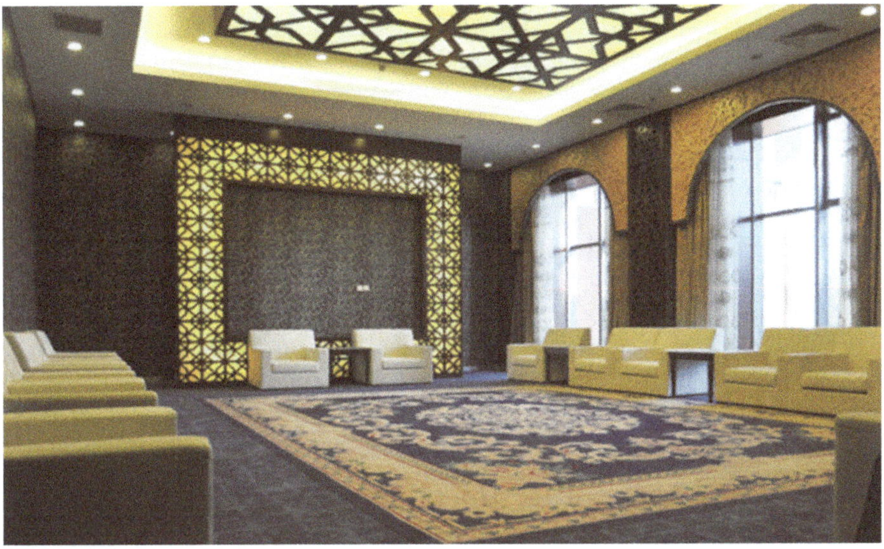

Fig. 10.3 Conference room, all decorations are imported from China (Courtesy China IPPR.com.cn)

The rent of Pak-China Friend Center has contributed almost 1 million USD annually to Pakistan government and has created many jobs (Event Manager, 2019).

10.3.1 Architecture for Other? Gwadar Free Zone

Gwadar is a least developed coastal city of Pakistan. The population is around 0.1 million and their livelihood rely on fishing and boat making business. The ethnic people are Balochs and possess cultural influence of Omani Arabs who ruled Gwadar for almost two hundred years. In 1958 Pakistani government purchased the Gwadar peninsula from Oman and ended its rule on Gwadar. It has traces of old silk route. According to British gazetteer, in the nineteenth century to early twentieth century, the Gwadar generated much of its revenue from trade of spices, sea food and slaves. Since last century, the Gwadar trade activities has been halted due to negligence of Pakistan government and construction of new modern port such as Karachi port. Due to its strategic location, Pakistan government sought China government to develop Gwadar port. In 2007, the initial phase of Gwadar port is being constructed by China Communication and Construction Company. The Government of Pakistan in a bid awarded concession agreement (CA) of Gwadar port to Singapore port authority on BOT basis (Marri et al.2019).

In 2013, with the establishment of CPEC (China Pakistan Economic Corridor) the flagship project of BRI, The Gwadar port and free zone were transferred from Singapore port company to Pakistan China overseas port holding company (derived from three parental companies that is CCCC, COSCO and CM Port). According to long term contract Gwadar port and free zone will be leased to COPHC for 40 years. During this duration the COPHC Pakistan will manage, upgrade the port and develop the Free Zone and retain almost 90 percent of revenues generated from it while rest goes to Pakistan government port authority. COPHC developed master plan of Free zone in which the south of free zone is designated as trade and logistic zone while north as an industrial zone (Marri et al.2019). The south part of Free zone in which the most prominent building is Gwadar business center, which is recently constructed by CCCC and operational while north part also includes central business district which is in planning and design phase. The COPHC is almost free in planning and designing of free zone but according to agreement, they have to review it to GPA and planning commission of Pakistan prior to execution of projects (Marri et al.2019). The BRI differs slightly from the previous China aid and cooperation beside geopolitical aims, it proffers free trade, culture exchanges, development projects, mutual beneficial cooperation in organized framework. The framework of BRI involved many stakeholders in different stages as compared to previous cooperation one. The author has drawn Gwadar project as example in this framework (Fig. 10.4). CPEC comprised of joint cooperation committee (JCC) which meets bi-annually and discusses new prospects of project and also reviews undergoing projects. It consists of multi-disciplinary researchers from both sides that are called

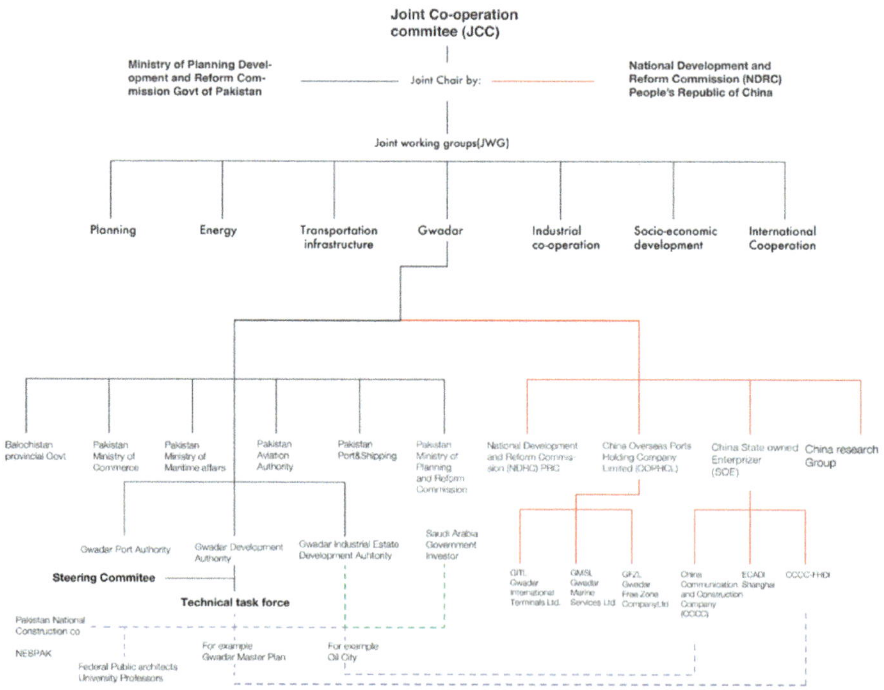

Fig. 10.4 The United cooperation committee (Drawn by the author)

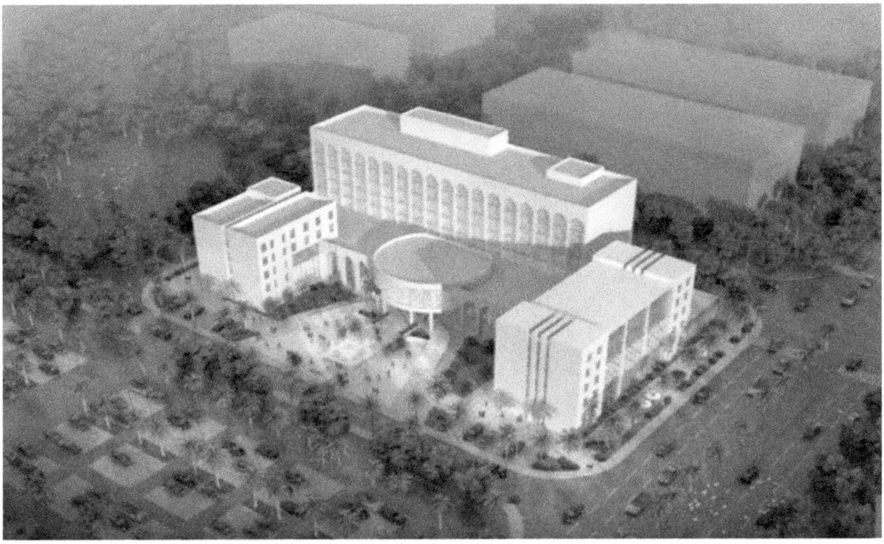

Fig. 10.5 Gwadar Free Trade Zone, design scheme 1 (Courtesy Wang Qian)

Joint Working Group (JWG). It is deemed to provide equal weightage in decision making process from both sides that conforms the slogan of BRI—inclusive and "Win–Win situation". The main aim is to make their research contribution in making this project sustainable (Fig. 10.5).[5]

The site of south Free Zone consists of some reclaimed land from sea. The Gwadar Business Center is part of initial phase of South Free Zone. It is mainly about the development of the industries such as merchandise exhibition, warehousing logistics, cold chain logistics, international transit/distribution, business/life services, etc., and gradually develops it into an important commercial logistics zone. The Business Center is a comprehensive service center integrating office, accommodation, catering, leisure and security. The target customer groups are Chinese customers going to Gwadar for business but it also facilitates the international and Pakistani customers (Figs. 10.6 and 10.7).

Many design proposals were made for GBC (Gwadar Business Center) to review with the local technical committee. The local technical committee comprised of project managers, politicians, CPEC officials, economist, planners and architects. According to D. Director of CPEC authority:

> the CCCC's initial design proposal of GBC was more or less modern box with Chinese characteristics. It was recommended by Pakistan technical committee members to modify it to local architectural style which has both Arabic and Persian influences (Butt, 2019a).

[5] Discussion with CPEC center members and analyzing its research documents. CPEC center is research group working under Pakistan planning commission their task is to do research on CPEC projects and made their contribution in sustainability of these projects. Author visited several times to this office in Islamabad.

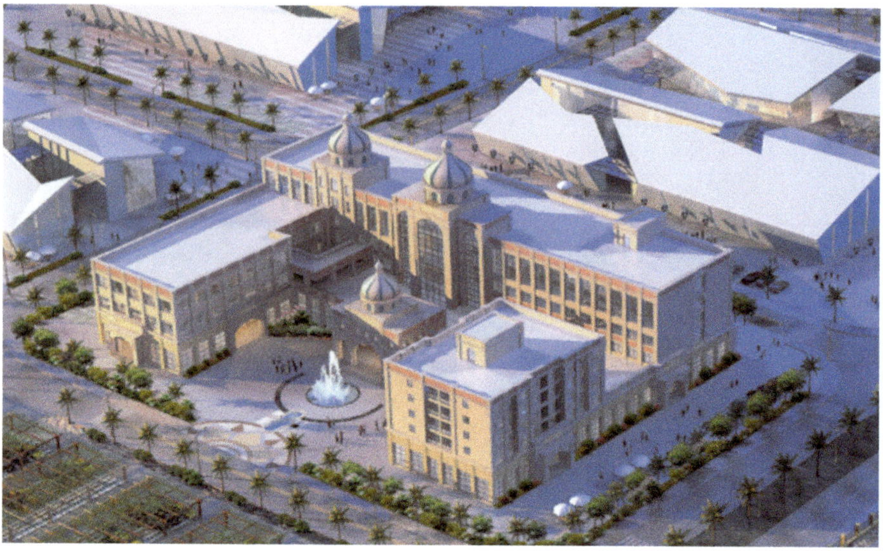

Fig. 10.6 Gwadar Business Center, showing the eclectic domes (Courtesy COPHC. Ltd. Gwadar)

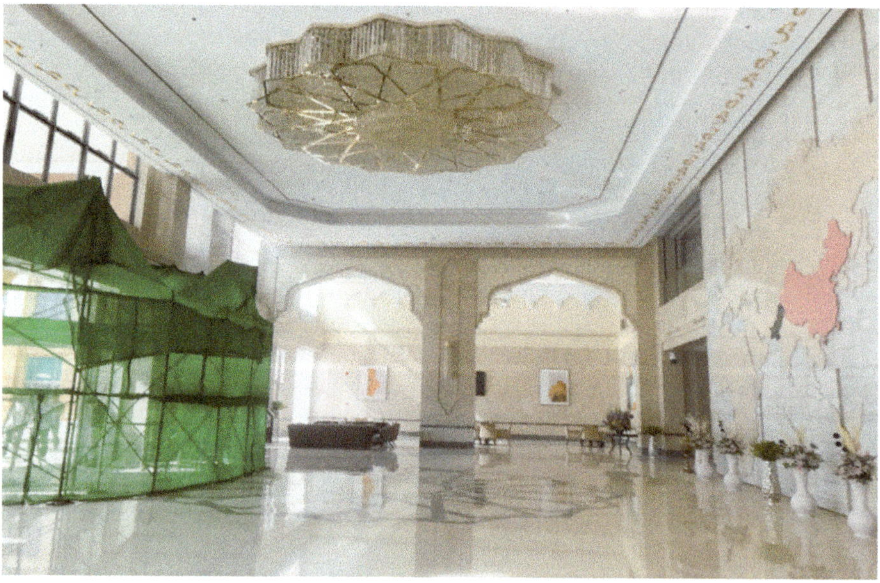

Fig. 10.7 The inspiration comes from Islamic patterns of Xinjiang and Chinese painting (Photo by the author)

The details of the earliest design proposal were not available on the Internet or in the offices of Pakistani local authorities. However, the author found some reasonable sources for other two design proposals, one made in 2016 other in 2017.

A Chinese research article authored by Wang Qian explained the 2016 design proposal for GBC. In this design proposal the main building and auxiliary buildings form a U-shaped layout. The main building is comprised of conference halls and tourism facilities for ships crews stopping at Gwadar port. The auxiliary buildings are offices and apartments, and service area such as kitchens and some catering and entertainment functions. The proposed design of GBC presents the bold Islamic architecture feature, the Arabic lattice windows and pointed arches are integrated into the building. The lattice windows were used to provide a certain shading effect on sunlight. The main idea was designing whole building with strong Islamic style (Wang 2016). This design proposal resembles the orientalist praxis of Western architects. The screen patterns of the windows or walls and the pointed arches reflect a generalization of Islamic architecture. It is ill practice. Despite the Muslim country, each place has its own architectural characteristics.

This design of GBC was revised. In an interview with Coordinator and Deputy Project Director Hassan Daud Butt in August 2019, he said;

> The Gwadar has unique Persian and Arabic culture and Pakistan has many Indo Gothic architecture heritages we asked the China construction company to see such examples. In next design proposal, they presented us the new design which is inspired from Xinjiang Islamic architecture and also Pakistan local Islamic architecture. This design proposal represents central Asian and Anglo-Asian architecture and the committee applauded it. (Butt, 2019a).

The final design of GBC is consecutively improved by discussion with local experts. For instance, one proposal consists of more arches, more domes and domes colored green- the green color domes represent specific sects of Muslim in Pakistan and is mostly used in mosque. This green-colored dome is omitted and arches were reduced in final design proposal to give it a modern outlook. The final design of GBC is much altered. It includes only three domes, and it is colored with white beige and brown color. The beige and brown color scheme is inspired from the Gwadar vernacular mud architecture. This proposal consists of round arches contrary to the previous design proposal, which were point arches. It is a smart move by the designer of GBC because Gwadar local mud architecture has mostly round arches. The domes are similar to Indo gothic architecture. Other features are contemporary Chinese architecture which blend harmoniously. The interior also consists of mixed Xinjiang decorative with Islamic point arches and Chinese paintings. The ground floor comprised of grand lobby with large marble sculpture displaying the Belt and Road Initiative map and has other facilities like restaurants, offices and supermarket. The first floor has gym, shops, restroom and one stop service. While, in top floor there is apartments for guest.

This superficial structure is manifested or reinforced the local architectural characters of Gwadar city. The Business Center architecture is much accordance with local characteristic and harmonizing with local identities. A field survey of structured questions was asked by author from Gwadar native art historian, intellectuals and architectural students. Almost 90 percent agrees that it has the quality to represent local identity and national identity of Pakistan and also it will contribute to the city image of Gwadar (Marri, 2021).

The Gwadar Business Center is constructed in less than one year which is commenced in early 2017 and completed in January 2018. The construction is entirely made of prefabricated material exported from China and assembled here. All other decorative materials, appliances etc. are also imported from China (Baloch, 2019). It is just similar to Pakistan China Friendship Center case as discussed earlier. For instance, the importation of construction and decorative materials from China and using Chinese construction methods and standards. However, the GBC designers emphasized the local architectural elements rather than finding the common architectural features of two cultures. The construction is carried out by both Chinese engineers and local construction workers. The utilization of high-tech construction techniques, structural design with Chinese standards and functional requirement of center was passed without any objection from local technical staff except the architectural style (Butt, 2019a; Khan, 2019a, b).

GBC is again representing architecture of new eclecticism which had derived inspiration from British colonial Indo-Gothic architecture, Xinjiang Islamic architecture, and local architectural features with contemporary Chinese architecture. The domes resemble the Xinjiang middle eastern, the color scheme of Indo-Gothic with round arches of local mud architecture. All of which are adorned in contemporary Chinese architectural box. This complex structure is not easy to comprehend, Fig. 10.8.

Other reason of this eclectic architecture is the constant criticism of "Gwadar is turning out to China's new colony" (Khan, 2015; Pauley & Shad, 2018) emanating from international media. It has persuaded Chinese designers by following a soft trajectory that speak of local architecture to contend such criticism. As the chairman of COPHC said many times:

> we are here to develop Gwadar for others not for self (Khan, 2019a, b).

GBC strives to speculate architecture for other not for the self. Similarly, the same architectural principles and design strategies can be seen in other BRI Free trade zone, for instance the Djibouti international free trade zone. This is developed and coordinated by both the same CCCC company and IPPR. The entrance gate arcade and the landmark consist of repetitive pointing arches symbolizing Islamic architecture in modern way. However, this eclectic architecture of GBC is well regarded by local Gwadar people as it will enhance the image of Gwadar and bring prosperity.

10.4 Transcultural Architecture, "Contact Zone" and "Third Space"

Transcultural or cross-cultural architecture is process of engagement of different cultures. Ortiz discusses; in transculturation, different process of transition occurs

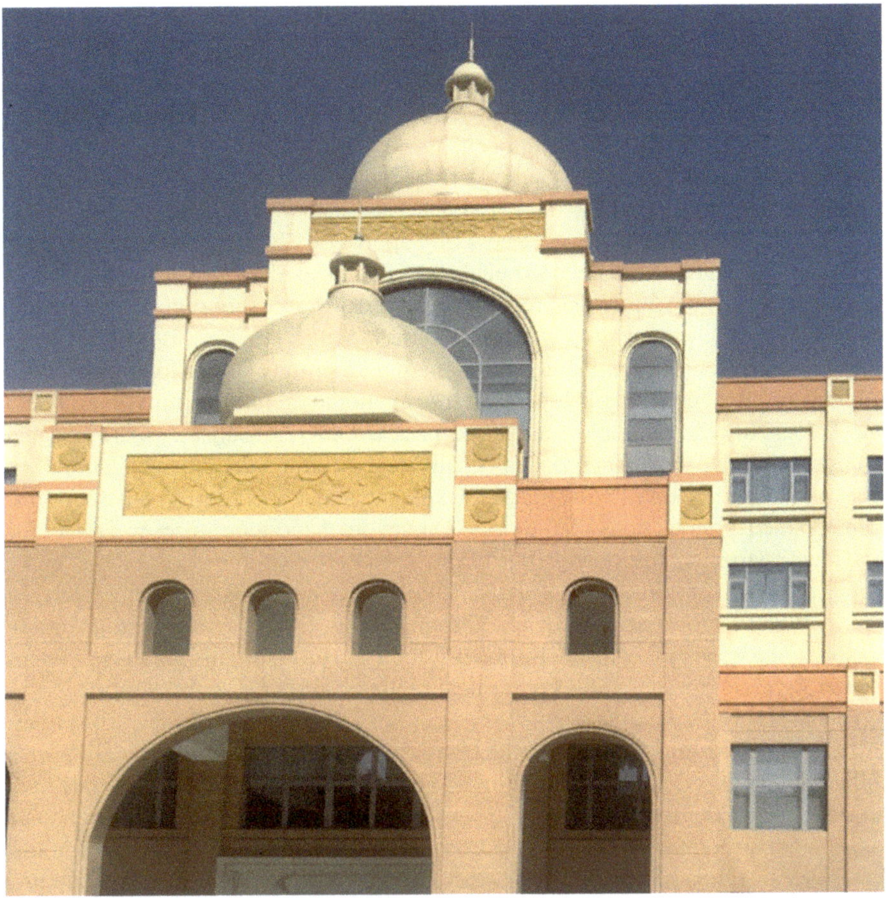

Fig. 10.8 Gwadar Business Center, eclecticism formed by arch and dome (Photo by the author)

from one culture to another. It may acquire other culture that process is called "acculturation", also may be uprooting previous culture i.e., "deculturation". In addition, it may also carry the idea of consequently creation of new cultural phenomenon called neo culturation (Ortiz and Fernández 1995, 102–3). Chinese architectural projects in Pakistan represent eclectic architecture of both cultures. It does not necessarily be called as Islamic architecture or Chinese architecture or a meta culture but something creative or new. In similar way, Tom Avermeate in an architecture issue on "Cold War Transfer: architecture and planning from socialist countries in the Third World" argues that the transcultural architecture process facilitates "contact zone" between different cultural knowledge and interest and it rearticulates the very character of architectural design. As a result, architectural design models in global south are not in adequate copies or distortions of developments in the North but had their own logics and can be considered as unique and creative articulations (Avermaete, 2012).

In transcultural architecture, there is a constant tension between what is critical and what is not? Bornstein believes that some of today's critical inputs are more important than ever in any architecture, because the multicultural world we live in is constantly challenging our critical and self-critical analytical capacities (Bornstein 2016). The Western understanding of the critical architectural approach requires a particular philosophical understanding of the relationship between history and the present that has developed in Western intellectual history. The problem is that such historical understanding does not necessarily apply equally in all cultures. Although the aim of critical regionalism is to help establish a local identity that counters westernized globalization, but critical regionalism itself a western concept that will not be necessarily be interpreted by no western cultures in same way (Botz-Bornstein, 2016, 1–2). In post-colonial situation, the modernizing ambitions of developing countries and their political concerns behind search for national cultural identity in architecture (Vale 2014) obscure the western concept of critical regionalism.[6] Keith Eggener argues, Critical Regionalism is optimistically designed for colonialism or a modified version of imperialist nostalgia. Further, he explains that, it is itself a construct came from outside from positions of authority. On the one hand it promises to protect the local identity from western globalization, on the other hand it comes from same source (Eggener 2002, 228). Further Bornstein agrees with Eggener but not completely, he argues critical regionalism is beneficial in some cases. But, in some cases, it is problematic in the non-west context (Botz-Bornstein, 2016, 1–5). This premise provides ample room for experimenting new critical regionalism in the global south.

The concept of center and periphery is useless to discuss in these case studies. China is not a western country, nor its transnational architecture models are purely Chinese. China itself adopted many Soviet and Euro-American modern architecture models (Cody, 2003; Li, 2012; Lu, 2010). Thus, the exchanges between China and Pakistan occurred in a highly saturated transnational environment. The transculturation process gives rise to a "third spaces" that not only speaks of local architecture, Chinese architecture but also multiple international architectural influences. In the above case studies the emphases, however, placed on the direct representation of local vocabularies or some time infusing with Chinese architecture features that are harmonious, indirect and phenomenological spaces. It can be said a critical regionalist approach by Chinese architects within their capacity. This point of view complicates the western definition of critical regionalism, but it presents a successful execution in the global south, for example, GBC building is well regarded by locals.

The non-western cultures interpret critical regionalism in their way contrary to that is practiced in the west. One of the famous architects in Pakistan Nayyar Ali Dada could be said as Pakistani critical regionalist who has designed many notable buildings in Pakistan. One of his masterpieces is Alhambra art council Lahore that was the recipient of Aga Khan award in 1998. In Alhambra art council the architect Nayyar Ali articulated modern geometrical architecture masses and spaces. It is dressed with red brick- a typical building material of many historical buildings in

[6] Lawrence Vale discussions hints that the western concept of critical regionalism is ambivalent in nonwestern context.

Lahore. Nayyar Ali Dada argues that there is no creativity if you directly imitate from local traditional architecture, but the spirit of the past is important that can be recreated in a modern way to make something interesting and creative (Dada, 2019). However, in his other major work, for instance, in Lahore expo and convention center, he deliberately used arches in a modern way to ensure the national identity and local brickwork to create an environment that possesses a spirit of locality. According to Prakash, it is difficult for the non-west architects to escape from national identity burden while there is no such requirement for the western architects. Therefore the western architects without any restriction can follow a western self-critical approach (Prakash 1997, 51–2.).

The Pakistan China Friendship Center Islamabad followed much similar architectural approach of Nayyar Ali Dada architecture approach to inject subtle meaning of both cultures. It played modern architectural masses and spaces with harmoniously including some direct representative local architectural elements like Islamic pointing arches in main entrance. Can we say it critical regionalist approach in expressing Chinese cultural features and a post-modernist approach in defining local cultural features? Whether it is western or eastern culture but to translate the other's language is extremely difficult and needs an expert knowledge and experience. Therefore, local expert opinions are valuable, comparatively GBC is much influenced from local actors. In case of GBC the local technical members tried to pursue Chinese designers to put forward architecture that represents the local context, national identity of Pakistan but at same time be a modern architecture. Thus, GBC ends up in eclecticism of various local characters.

The western critical regionalist definitions of involving only critically indirect imitation of local architecture and contextual factors which might be unacceptable to local Pakistan because it is difficult for them to comprehend. Pakistani scholar Abdul Rehman in his book "Islamabad master planning and architecture of dynapolis" discusses that Louis Kahn was invited in the 1960s by Pakistan officials to design President estate at Islamabad house. He proposed three consecutive design proposals for president estate but he was unsuccessful to convince the local authorities as the Pakistani officials urged him to introduce some Islamic domes and arches, which he has omitted in his design proposals (Rehman, 2013, 137). The flexible design work of Chinese state-owned design institutes demonstrates a team work of architects rather than dominated individual architect.

China is on a wage to emerging new global power and exporting architecture to promote positive Chinese image outside China. At the same time, Pakistan hopes to modernize its country without compromising its national identity. In such a context, the architects of both sides distinguished their architectural approach from the west but also striving to satisfy the international architectural disciplinary demands. This transnational architectural model exchanges are not merely the business of Chinese and Pakistan architects, but it involves many other professionals, actors, their interests and ambitions. The critical architecture here offers an economical, sustainable and culture-specific by inclusion of both physical and spiritual architectural features of both cultures rather than relying only on indirect expression to refrain from confusion.

This eclectic cross-cultural architecture could be said a non-western critical regionalist approach set up by Chinese and Pakistani experts within a specific socio-political context.

10.5 Conclusion

The creation of friendship environment, a mutual beneficial and equal base cooperation between two states. This has produced an abstract space which in words of Henry Lefebvre the production of abstraction, a mental space (Lefebvre and Nicholson-Smith 1991). It has pushed the Chinese architects to research on local vernacular architecture and understand local culture and produce a critical architecture that is to symbolize the friendship between two nations. Thus, for perusing such mission, the architects utilized a new pragmatic, eclectic approach with minimum expenditures. The aim is to allure the local subjective dimensions and bulge out positive image of China. The "contact zone" between the experts of two countries and its consequences in "third space" which differs slightly from the west and non-west exchange of models. The premise of center (west) and periphery (non-west) could not apply in non-western globalization. Critical regionalism and other international critical modernist architectural approach, however, originated mostly from the west but non-west interprets or appropriate in their own way. Chinese designers are flexible and refraining itself from dominated ideologies. Beside these criticisms, this chapter clearly maps out how architectural projects get shaped in this complex context. The end product of architecture in "third space" itself becomes complex that what author points out as architecture of new eclecticism.

References

Akcan, E. (2016). Global conict and global glitter: Architecture of West Asia (1960–2010). In *A Critical History of Contemporary Architecture*. Routledge, pp. 339–366.

Antonescu, M. V. (2014). Imperialismul cultural sau „puterea imperială soft" în ordinea globală a secolului XXI. *Polis Journal of Political Science, 2*(05), 194–219.

Avermaete, T. (2012). Coda: The reflexivity of Cold War architectural modernism. *The Journal of Architecture, 17*(3), 475–477.

Baloch, D. (2019) 'Gwadar Port and Free Zone Development Process'.

Bhabha, H. K. (1994). Introduction: Locations of culture. *The Location of Culture, 2*, 1–27.

Bhabha, H. K., & Rutherford, J. (2006). Third space. *Multitudes, 3*, 95–107.

Borch, C. (2002). Interview with Edward W. Soja: Thirdspace, postmetropolis, and social theory. *Distinktion: Scandinavian Journal of Social Theory, 3*(1), 113–120.

Botz-Bornstein, T. (2016). *Transcultural architecture: The limits and opportunities of critical regionalism*. Routledge.

Butt, D. (2019a). Construction of Gwadar Business Centre.

Butt, D. (2019b). General information about CPEC architecture project processes.

Chang, W., Xue, C., & Ding, G. (2019). Architecture of diplomacy: Chinese construction aid in Asia, 1950–1976. *ARENA Journal of Architectural Research, 4*(1).

Changezi, A. (2018). Foreign architects contribution in Pakistan.

China Policy. (2017). *China Going Global between ambition and capacity*. Research report. https://policycn.com/wp-content/uploads/2017/05/2017-Chinas-going-global-strategy.pdf.

Cody, J. W. (2003). *Exporting American Architecture, 1870–2000*. Psychology Press.

Dada, N. A. (2019). Does tradition and modernity exist separately in architecture? https://www.youtube.com/watch?v=eAIAopnGlYU&t=623s.

Daechsel, M. (2015). *Islamabad and the politics of international development in Pakistan*. Cambridge University Press.

Dawn News. (2009). Pak-China Friendship Center, Islamabad. A gift from China to Pakistani People.', 7 September. Retrieved November 15, 2018, from https://www.dawn.com/Pak-China Friendship Center, Islamabad. A gift from China to Pakistani People 09/07/2009.

Ding, G., & Xue, C. Q. (2015). China's architectural aid: Exporting a transformational modernism. *Habitat International, 47*, 136–147.

Eggener, K. L. (2002). Placing resistance: A critique of critical regionalism. *Journal of Architectural Education, 55*(4), 228–237.

Épron, J. -P. (1997). *Comprendre l'éclectisme*. Éditions Norma.

Event Manager. (2019). Pakistan China Friendship Centre Events.

Frampton, K. (1983). Prospects for a critical regionalism. *Perspecta: The Yale Architectural Journal, 20*(20), 147–162.

Gonzalez-Vicente, R. (2011). The internationalization of the Chinese state. *Political Geography, 30*(7), 402–411.

Huang, W., Ri, Z., & Xiaoming, L. (2008). Pak-China Friendship Center in Pakistan', *Architectural Creation 雅昌艺术网*. Retrieved May 23, 2021, from http://ebook.artron.net/book.php?bookid=113442.

Khan, A. (2019a). Local building codes and Chinese codes.

Khan, H.-R. (1961). Pakistan's relations with the People's Republic of China. *Pakistan Horizon, 14*(3), 212–232.

Khan, L. (2015). *Is Pakistan turning into China's colony?* Retrieved April 1, 2019, from https://www.marxist.com/is-pakistan-turning-into-chinas-colony.htm.

Khan, Y. H. (2019b). COPHC makes a difference, 8 May. Retrieved September 3, 2019b, from https://nation.com.pk/08-May-2019b/gwadar-cophc-makes-a-difference?show=preview.

King, K. (2013). China's aid and soft power in Africa. *The Case of Education and Training. Woodbridge: James Currey* [Preprint].

Lefaivre, L., & Tzonis, A. (1981). The Grid and the Pathway. *Architecture in Greece, 15*, 167–178.

Lefebvre, H. (1991). The social production of space, translated by Donald Nicholson-Smith, Malden MA: Blackwell [Preprint].

Levin, A. (2015). Exporting Zionism: Architectural modernism in Israeli-African Technical Cooperation, 1958–1973.

Li, Y. (2012). In search of a socialist modernity: the Chinese introduction of Soviet culture.

Liu, W., & Dunford, M. (2016). Inclusive globalization: Unpacking China's belt and road initiative. *Area Development and Policy, 1*(3), 323–340.

Lu, D. (2010). *Third world modernism: Architecture, development and identity*. Routledge.

Management Officer. (2019). Discussion about their Experiences.

Marri, S. A. et al. (2019). Fondazione Italia Cina. *Mondo Cinese*, 155–175.

Marri, S. A. (2021). Transnational global infrastructure spaces and their impact on historical places: Resistance, negotiation and alternatives in the case of Gwadar. In *Cities' Vocabularies: The Influences and Formations*. Springer, pp. 325–339.

Mumtaz, K. K. (1985). *Architecture in Pakistan*.

News sina. (2010). Pakistan China friendship centres become new landmark of Pakistan China friendship', 18 December 2010. Pakistan-China Friendship Centre becomes new landmark of Pakistan-China. http://news.sina.com.cn/c/p/2010-12-18/154621666254.shtml.

Pauley, L., & Shad, H. (2018). *Gwadar: Emerging Port City or Chinese Colony?* Retrieved May 24, 2021, from https://thediplomat.com/2018/10/gwadar-emerging-port-city-or-chinese-colony/.
Prakash, V. (1997). Identity production in postcolonial Indian architecture: Re-covering what we never had. *Postcolonial Space (s)*, pp. 39–52.
Pratt, M. L. (1991). Arts of the contact zone. *Profession*, 33–40.
Rajan, D. S. (2017). Visit of Pakistan Prime Minister to China—An Assessment | ORF', *Observer Research Foundation*, 27 December. Retrieved May 23, 2021, from https://www.orfonline.org/research/visit-of-pakistan-prime-minister-to-china-an-assessment/.
Rehman, A. (2013). *Islamabad: Master Planning and Architecture of Dynapolis*. Lap Lambert Academic Publishing GmbH KG. https://books.google.com.pk/books?id=3J_cnQEACAAJ.
Resident Engineer. (2019). Discussion about their experiences.
Roskam, C. (2015). Non-aligned architecture: China's designs on and in Ghana and Guinea, 1955–92. *Architectural History, 58*, 261–291.
Social Responsibility. (2017). Company achievements. China Communication Construction Company. Retrieved November 15, 2018, from http://en.ccccltd.cn/corporateculture/socialresponsibilityrepc/201805/P020180528558025899463.pdf.
Stanek, Ł. (2012). Introduction: The "Second World's" architecture and planning in the "Third World." *The Journal of Architecture, 17*(3), 299–307.
Vale, L. (2014). *Architecture, power and national identity*. Routledge.
Williams, J., Robinson, C., & Bouzarovski, S. (2020). China's belt and road initiative and the emerging geographies of global urbanisation. *The Geographical Journal, 186*(1), 128–140.
Wang, Q.王倩. (2016). 瓜达尔自由区商务中心——巴基斯坦项目设计 (Gwadar Free Zone Business Center-Pakistan Project Design)', *建筑与文化 (Architecture and Culture)*, 0(4), pp. 48–51.
Xue, C. Q., & Ding, G. (2018). *A history of design institutes in China: From Mao to market*. Routledge.
Zhao, J., & Jing, Y. (2019). The governance of China's foreign aid system: Evolution and path dependence. *Public Administration and Development, 39*(4–5), 182–192.

Sohrab Ahmed Marri received his Ph.D. from Politecnico di Turin in 2021. He has held the position of assistant professor of architecture at Balochistan University of Information Technology, Engineering and Management Science, Pakistan. He collaborated with the China Room research group, where he actively participated in research activities on the Chinese context. He has published research articles both in Italian and international research journals such as Mondo Cinese, Urbannext and Springer book chapters. He has a research interest in transnational architectural practice.

Chapter 11
18 Years of Overseas Design Practice of CCDI Group as a Complex Journey

Xia Ai

Abstract CCDI Group is one of the first private design institutes to advance business out of China. This article reviews the 3 types of international projects undertaken by CCDI. The first one is the work as technical supporting for Chinese construction companies, such as the role in the project of Doha Tower; the second mode is acquiring corporation or founding new design brand in international market, such as Archilier Architects and PTW Architects; the third mode is to follow the investing pace of Chinese developers into the Middle East and South-east Asia market. These 3 kinds of strategy articulate a clear process on how to be deeply involved into international competition over the past 18 years.

11.1 From "Foreign Aid Project" to "International Integration"

Architectural design is closely related to the site where its project is located. When talking about the boundaries of a site, one may think of artificial or natural boundaries such as streets, walls, waters, red lines and slopes, but actually the biggest "boundary" is the "border". It is obviously a dual practical challenge of "sense of accomplishment" and "freshness" for architects and their organizations who aim to provide explorative and innovative design services in a brand-new context with different languages, political environments as well as historical and cultural traditions.

In the early 1960s, Chinese architects practiced oversea architectural design, but they generally used a more contemporary term: foreign aid design (*yuanwai sheji*). From the beginning of the reform and opening up to the end of the twentieth century, foreign aid construction projects can be understood as China's important political and economic instruments on the international stage. However, design institutes hardly appealed to enhance their technical level and to improve industry reputation through overseas performance. Consider, for example, Bandaranaike Memorial International

X. Ai (✉)
CCDI Group, Shanghai, China
e-mail: ai.xia@ccdi.com.cn

C. Q. Xue and G. Ding (eds.), *Exporting Chinese Architecture*,
https://doi.org/10.1007/978-981-19-2786-7_11

Convention Hall, Colombo of Sri Lanka (designed by the architect Dai Nianci from Beijing Industrial Architectural Design Institute in 1964) and Ghana National Performance Center (designed by the architect Cheng Taining from Hangzhou Architectural Design Institute in 1986). These classic buildings show that Chinese architects had innovated architectural language across borders, expressing some forms that are not easily shown in domestic projects.

In the first two decades of the twenty-first century, a series of events point to a more integrated international opportunity: in 2001, China officially joined the World Trade Organization, and the construction projects as "fixed asset commodities" in a broad sense are indirectly affected by such openness. Since 2005, China has strengthened multilateral cooperation through BRICS (Brazil, Russia, India, China and South Africa) and Shanghai Cooperation Organization, which has led to increased cross-border demand. In the 2008 Beijing Summer Olympics and the Expo 2010 Shanghai, China, by interpreting these two international events only from the field of architecture, one can see that the social attention to and curiosity for the built environment have been raised to a highest degree, thus enhancing the social status of architects. In 2013, President Xi Jinping put forward the strategic idea of "Belt and Road Initiative", which re-promoted the thinking of internationalization in the new era different from previous experiences.

In this context, many international firms carried out subversive innovative designs in China, while Chinese architectural design firms also strived for overseas business in response to rising international competitiveness, thus forming a certain competition and balance between Chinese and overseas design firms. The overseas design practice of Chinese architects is transforming from a "loving care project" emphasizing assistance to "compound output" realizing win–win value.

Nowadays, the vagaries of the global epidemic have affected the internationalization of Chinese design, but also give us a precious opportunity to reflect on and sort out all kinds of experience in this process, so as to re-examine the practical feasibility in the future.

The excitement that European and American architectural firms found an "experimental site" in China 20 years ago is now reversely being replaced by the mission of Chinese design firms in another way. A prepositional topic of this article is: given China's huge and growing domestic market, what does overseas property mean to a design firm. After a considerable number of "outbound" attempts, we come back to our "motivation" and "original intention". Our intentions include testifying our strength, exporting technology and carrying on international cooperation. There are of course other complicated factors to motivate overseas projects. This is the starting point of this chapter.

11.2 Direct Output: Design Firms Wining Overseas Projects by Providing Technical Support for the General Contractor of Construction

CCDI (formerly known as China Construction Design International, founded in 1994), a large-scale design firm starting in Shenzhen, has gradually stepped into the national and overseas market after 27 years of unremitting efforts, with its number of staff growing from a few dozen to 6,000 in 2021. The cultural spirit of Shenzhen is deeply implanted in the organization of CCDI, which can be construed as the pursuit of technical effectiveness and service quality, as well as friendliness to new things and the environment.

Among large private design groups in China, CCDI is the first to have the ability to “practice in overseas”. When CCDI tried its first overseas operation in 2003 (Fig. 11.1), it employed just over 200 people. In that time, many Chinese people had never been abroad before, and probably did not even have passports, so people were curious and eager to “go abroad”, even to Africa. As long as frontline staff heard about overseas projects, they actively cooperated even if they worked overtime. In retrospect, the reason why we have such “international initiative” may be that we have had sufficient “experience in international cooperation” before carrying out design business abroad.

In 2003, CCDI took the initiative to invite PTW, an architectural firm based in Sydney, Australia, to jointly design and bid for the Beijing Olympics project (National Aquatics Center) in China (Zheng & Zhang, 2008). They eventually won the project, which laid a firm foundation for the company’s rapid development of sports architecture. In that year, a team of architects working in Sydney for two months created the “Water Cube” scheme that combined the spirit of the times, technology, and traditional Chinese philosophical overtone. This “foreign-related” process had given some CCDI architects a completely different insight and experience although the site of this project was in Beijing. Then, shortly after CCDI submitted the competition plan

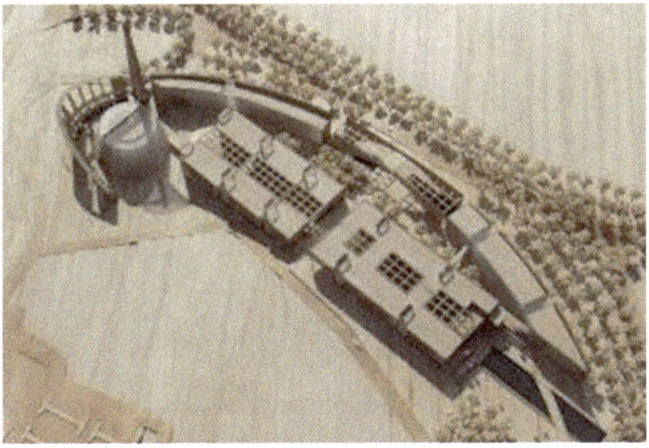

Fig. 11.1 The design of the Algerian Ministry of Foreign Affairs building

for the Olympics project, CCDI Shenzhen embarked on a real overseas "adventure": the Chinese embassy in Algeria invited us to design a brand-new building through China State Construction Engineering Corporation. Located in North Africa, Algeria was once a French colony, so their design briefs and scheme texts are all written in French, which adds a lot of difficulties to Chinese architects. Zhu Yiyou, a principal architect and now the chief architect of CCDI, completed the scheme in one round. At the same time, he also elaborated the model and many details, and studied the basic requirements of French codes for architectural technology. But unfortunately, it had not been really implemented due to various reasons of the project itself.

Five years later, in 2007, still in Algeria, CCDI won another opportunity to build an important exhibition building "Oran Convention Center" through China State Construction Engineering Corporation (Fig. 11.2) (Ai, 2010). The project was built

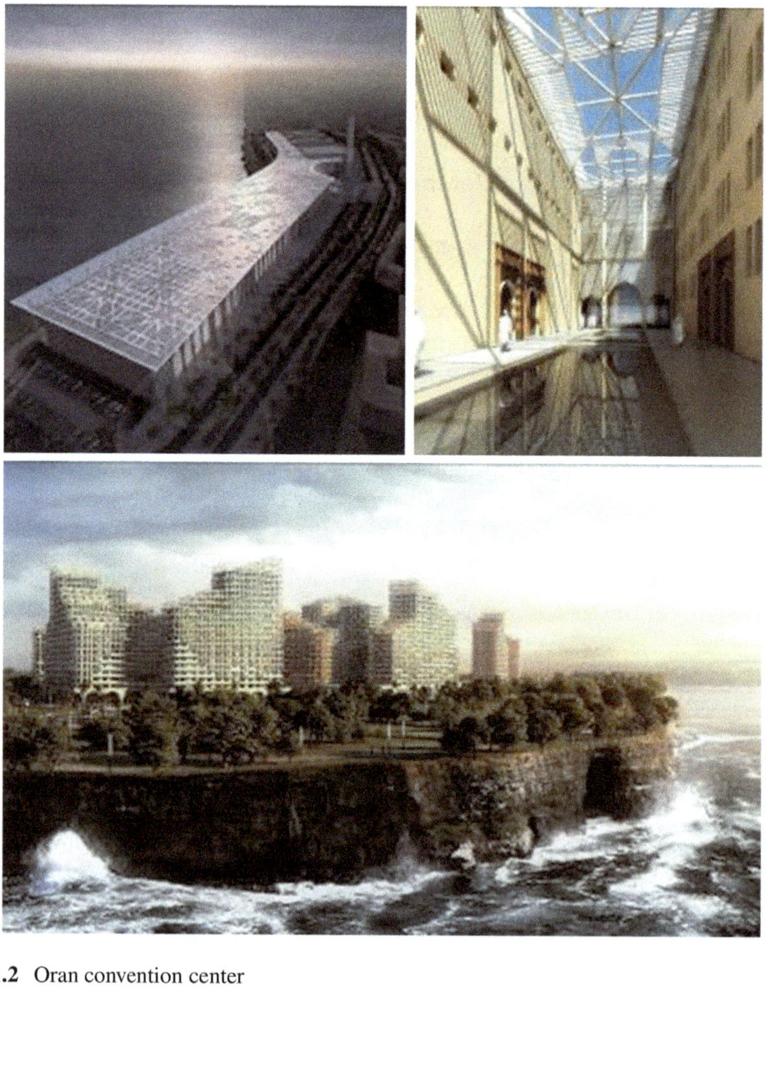

Fig. 11.2 Oran convention center

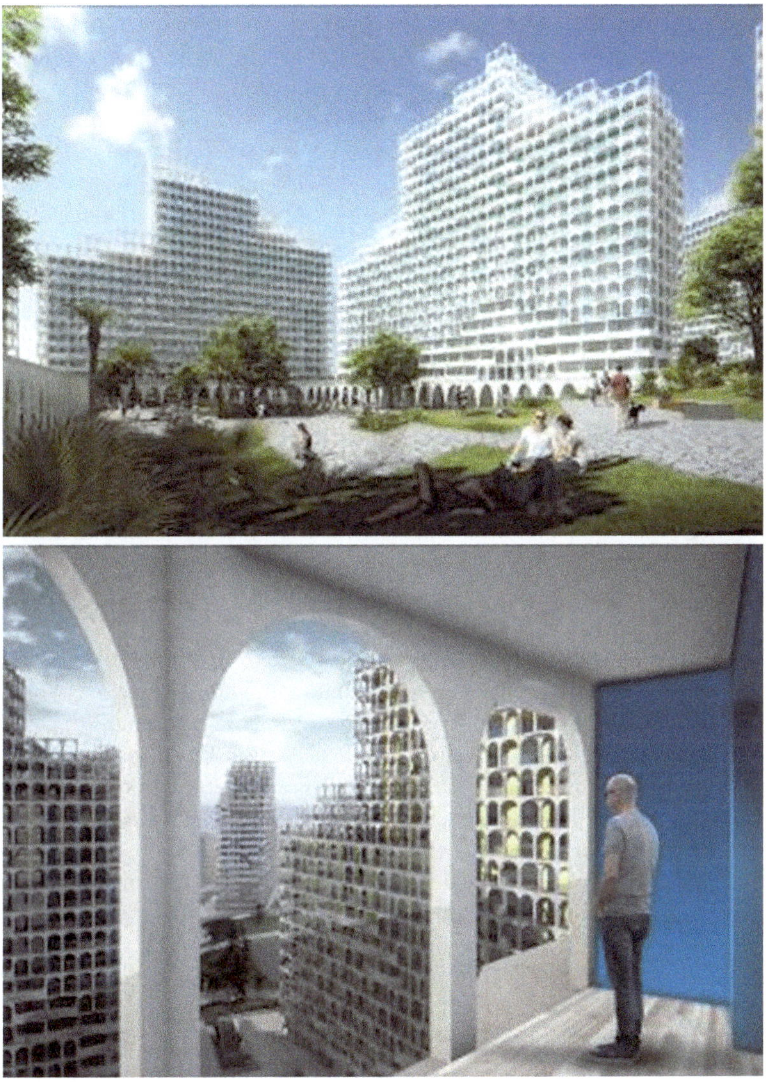

Fig. 11.2 (continued)

as the main venue of the 16th International Conference & Exhibition on Liquefied Natural Gas four years later (2010). Wang Hai, an architect who just returned from America and joined CCDI paid tribute to classical Islamic culture with modern characteristics. His design was highly praised (published in the first issue of *Time + Architecture* in 2010). In the process of design development, in order to interpret the design to the local government departments and the public, CCDI invested a lot of energy to make 3D animation, and dispatched many professionals in charge of architecture, structure and M&E for field exploration. The preparation of construction drawing almost started. However, local government changed the site and construction conditions. China State Construction Engineering Corporation withdrew from the bid for general contracting and CCDI's scheme still did not escape of being suspended.

CCDI's second overseas architectural scheme was more regional with symbolic languages and elements: an octagonal plan with Arabic Moorish style and modern sense. Architects enlarged and extended the building to form a roof system which became a unique space grid structure, and then added functional spaces such as exhibitions, conferences and hotels. For the long and narrow buffer between multiple functional modules, the designers used the traditional Arab gardening concept to create an interesting, quiet, clear and peaceful intermediary space. Although colonized by France for many years, Algerians still have a strong sense of national pride. Walking through the Oran, one could see the historical Arabian Moorish architecture blended with the European classical architecture. The design of this brand-new convention center is undoubtedly a big step forward in the modernization of Algeria.

From these two experiences, it can be seen that when China State Construction Engineering Corporation undertook the general contracting project overseas and invited CCDI to design, the architect's identity had a "dependency" (on general contractor) from the beginning. Once the constructor fails to get the contract smoothly, the design scheme will be aborted.

Aware of this problem, CCDI wondered how to successfully launch its first overseas brand project. Perhaps the cooperative design with international masters is more likely to win. The ensuing opportunity came from a super high-rise building designed by Jean Nouvel in Doha, and China State Construction Engineering Corporation undertook part of the construction. The building is structured with unique concrete cross inclined columns. Because local design firm in Qatar made some mistakes in structure design, Fu Xueyi, chief engineer of CCDI's structural consultant, led a team to complete the difficult structural calculation. Especially for the joint reinforcement scheme of giant inclined columns, they submitted a more economical, reasonable and easy-to-construct detailed design, and successfully signed two contracts for architecture and structure design. After eight years of completion, this building has become the most striking landmark of Doha Bay skyline, and it also lays a certain foundation for CCDI's technical cooperation ability to meet the requirements of international professionalism (Fig. 11.3).

11.3 Indirect Output: Design Firms Set up or Acquiring Design Firms Abroad to Indirectly Carry Out Overseas Practice

After learning a series of experiences and lessons, CCDI has made a real design breakthrough overseas in sports architecture. In the five or six years after the 2008 Beijing Olympic Games, a large number of stadiums and gymnasiums were built

Fig. 11.3 Doha tower

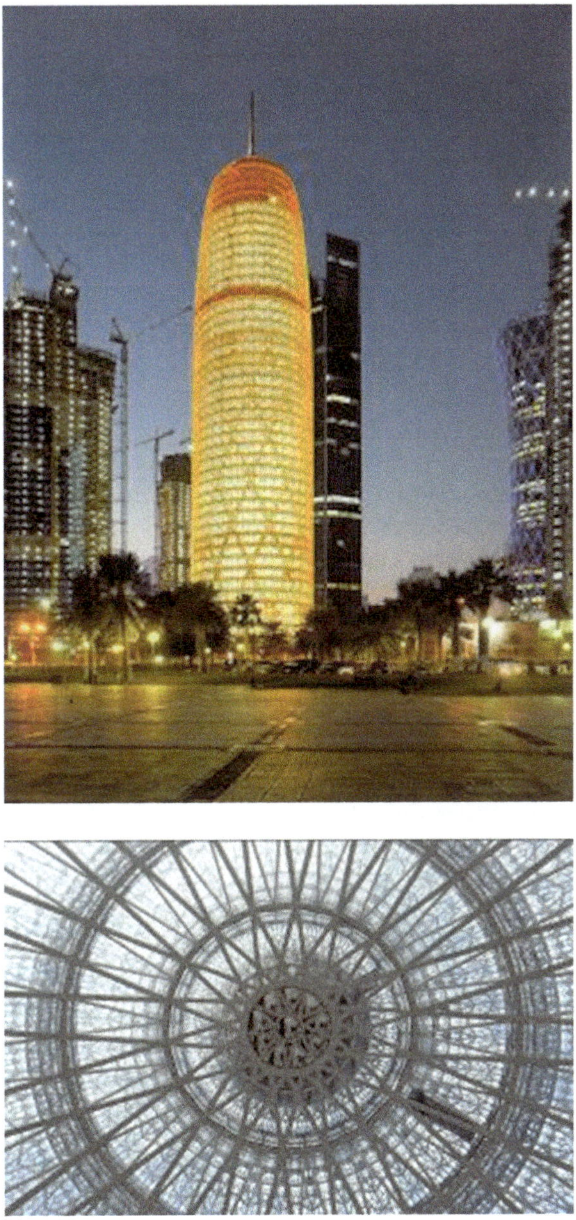

in major cities in China, and CCDI's sports business has gained rapid technology accumulation. But at the same time, more and more international leading design firms began to bid in China, making the competition even more intense. Therefore, the Group's leaders and sports design team began to study a new strategy to go abroad to win international major projects, and then leverage international reputation to "crack" the domestic market. Since many large and well-established design groups had considered the "international + domestic" two-way brand strategy, it seemed that it is not enough to rely on the "single brand" operation of domestic and local design to succeed in this strategy.

In 2012, China Architecture Design & Research Group wholly acquired Singaporean-based CPG Design Group, which was also the first overseas acquisition by a Chinese survey and design enterprise. Soon after that, in 2013, CCDI wholly acquired PTW, a time-honored Australian-based architectural firm. In 2014, Shanghai Xian Dai Architectural Design (Group) Co., Ltd. (predecessor of East China Architectural Design & Research Institute) acquired Wilson Associates, a famous American-based interior design firm. For the construction industry, these acquisitions are almost as significant as the acquisition of foreign brands by Chinese automobile brands. From this moment on, what goes abroad is no longer "Chinese design" in a narrow sense, but a much closer and more diversified relationship between "China and the world". The acquisition of overseas companies not only enables Chinese design firms to directly connect with international business platforms, but also indirectly extends and improves the industrial chain of Chinese-based design enterprises in the world construction engineering market, rapidly promoting the internationalization of Chinese design organizations and talents.

As early as 2002, the successful cooperation between CCDI and PTW of Sydney on the Water Cube laid a firm foundation for further alliance between the two firms. "Ten years after that cooperation, the Chinese name of CCDI is changed from "中建国际" to "悉地国际", and one of the words "悉(Xi)" subtly echoes with the partnership in Sydney (悉尼) many years ago, even now many old employees quipped.

In 2013, PTW officially became a wholly-owned company of CCDI. Both sides have a good correlation in design concepts and business types, and express great sincerity for future cooperation. The mutual penetration of the two sides has also opened up new avenues for overseas markets. In the first year after CCDI acquired PTW, the two sides as a consortium won the international design competition for The All-Africa Games (a three-hall sports center in Brazzaville, Congo) (Fig. 11.4) (Shi, 2016). This complex was completed in just three years with "China Speed", and has successfully hosted many events. This is also the first time for Chinese design firm to complete large-scale international sports facilities at the level of "continental sports games" overseas, which is of far-reaching significance.

Although most of Chinese designed projects in Africa adhered to the simple principle of "economy, practicality and moderate aesthetics", the Congo Brazzaville Sports Center had put forward a higher standard of "international level": it must be fully invested by the State and built for hosting the 11th All-Africa Games, and excellent schemes must be solicited through public bidding. Congo, as one of the most

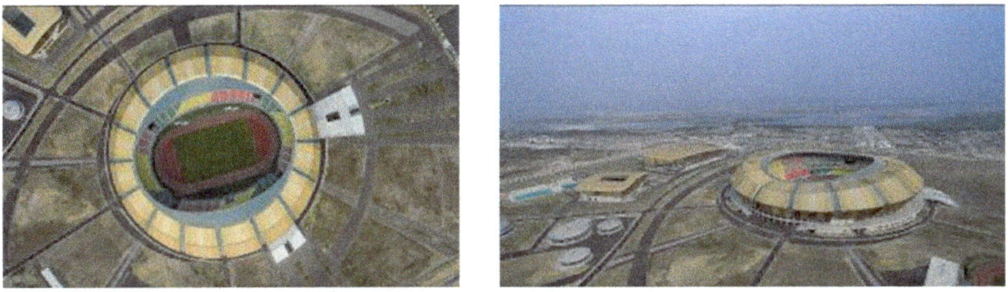

Fig. 11.4 Congo Brazzaville sports center

underdeveloped countries and regions in the world, was still backward in economic strength, infrastructure and social development, so it required our design works not only to bear the national political ideas, but also to fully consider the carrying capacity of economy and technology. As Shi Shaofeng and Meng Ke, the main architects of CCDI on the project, said: "if it was designed according to the usual "Olympic standards" or "international standards", it would definitely exceed the local cost and craft boundaries. Therefore, we must find a simpler, concise, direct and powerful configuration to accurately formulate conceptual schemes."

The main stadium acts as the core of the sports center. Once the design language of this building is established, the rest of the venues will emerge as the times require. The collective creation of CCDI's architects envisages a "sun-cut boulder" as a form clue, with 16 huge sections spreading out from the stadium as the axis of the layout. The Torch Tower engraved with Congo was planned on the south side, implying welcoming guests, and the audience could overlook the Congo River from the Torch Tower. The main theme color of the facade was the golden yellow of African land, implying its history and glory. In tropical climatic conditions, in order to improve the lighting and ventilation conditions of the inner ring road, the architects designed a large number of openings at the top of the inner ring road to the outside. The facade design adopted multi-angle grilles to offer shading and ventilation for the audience's rest platform and to introduce air into the infield through the entrance, thus improving the comfort of the audience (Ai, 2018).

Subsequently, CCDI + PTW won the bid for the African Cup of Nations Football Stadium (Football Stadium in Port-Gentil, Gabon) (Fig. 11.5) and Constantine Theater in Algeria (Fig. 11.6), which were also built in 2017–2018. Meanwhile, CCDI had gained a lot of knowledge in international contract management and overseas tax law, established overseas business units, and successively joined "China International Contractors Association", "China Association of International Engineering Consultants" and "Council on Tall Buildings and Urban Habitat (CTBUH)". These institutions broaden their horizons at the information level and play an indirect role in international business and cooperation.

While planning to acquire international design brands, as for hotels and commercial buildings, CCDI also invested in the establishment of a new design brand Archilier Architects in 2011, a high-end design brand headquartered in New York

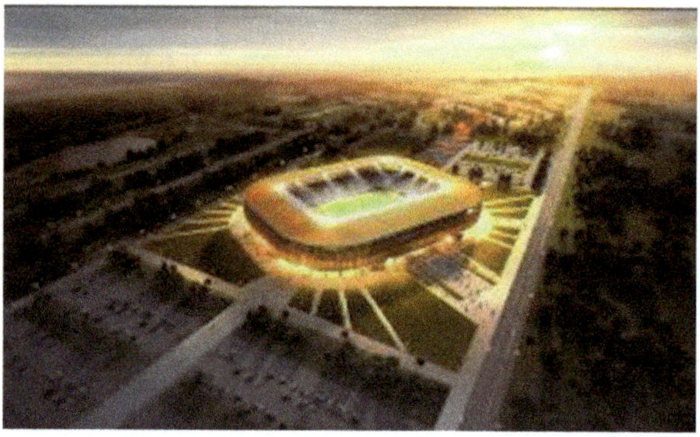

Fig. 11.5 Gabon stadium

City (its predecessor was CCDI New York Office). The founder Sheng Kai had important international five-star hotel design experience, and led the team to make breakthroughs in hotel, business, TOD and other comprehensive fields. Archilier's affiliation with the CCDI Group was relatively kept confidential for the first few years, and many customers only knew that a brand-new design firm was born in New York City, but they didn't know that Chinese enterprises were behind it. After ten years' accumulation, Archilier has won many international competitions, such as the high-end serviced apartment complex in Hudson Park (Fig. 11.7), New York, and the overall renovation of Manhattan transportation hub (Fig. 11.8), and has become an emerging force of CCDI in overseas markets.

11.4 Compound Output: Following the Overseas Investment of Chinese Developers to Realize Full Professional Compound Design Output

In recent years, a business trend has been evident in overseas market: Chinese large enterprises' investment in overseas construction will directly bring in design business. For example, a Chinese developer directly participated in overseas investment in Kuala Lumpur People's Square (designed by CCDI) (Fig. 11.9), Christie Street 88 project of Sydney (designed by PTW) (Fig. 11.10), and headquarters building invested by China Railway Construction Engineering in Papua New Guinea (jointly designed by CCDI and Vector). China is transforming from "construction export" to "investment export", which is entirely consistent with the current national strategy of "Belt and Road Initiative". The overseas role of Chinese architects is also very likely to shift from "design relying on construction and development" to "design relying on rich professional value to realize compound output".

From the perspective of market positioning, which places are the easiest for Chinese architectural design firms to get overseas business? Emerging cities and events in developing countries in Oceania, Africa, South America and Asia are the

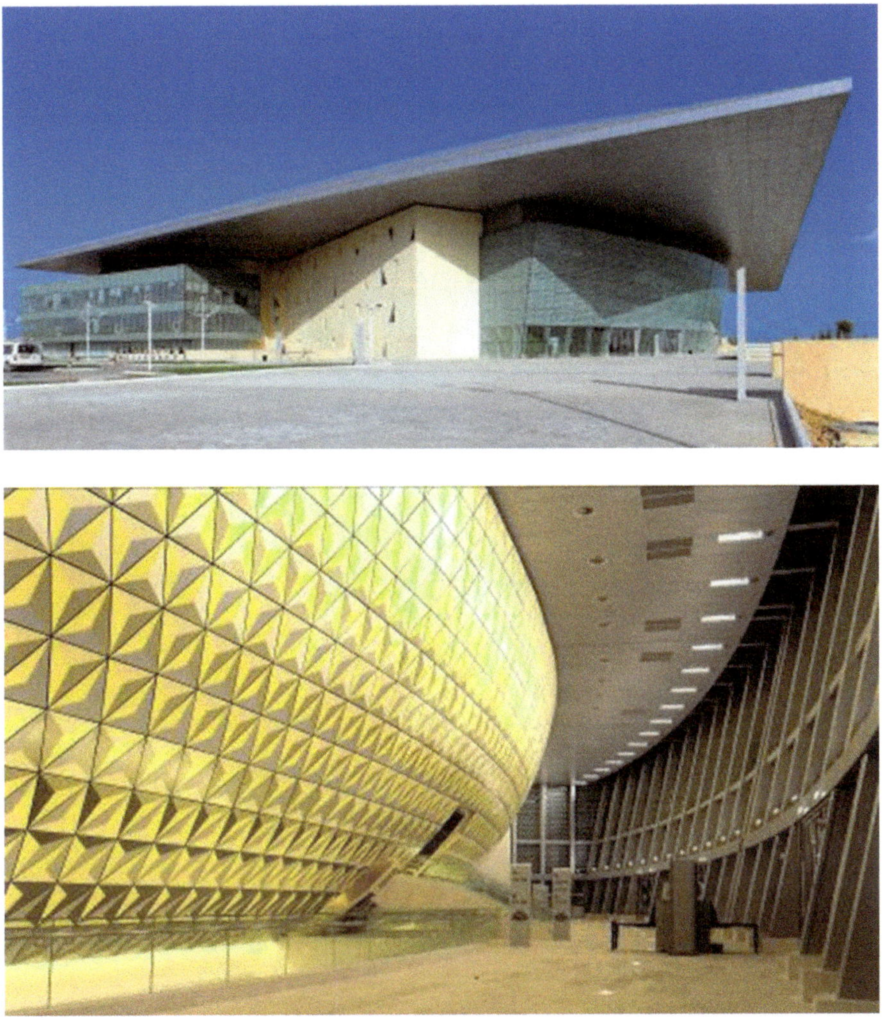

Fig. 11.6 Constantine theater in Algeria

main sources of CCDI's overseas markets. Having experienced the process from backwardness to economic growth, China, as compared with European and American countries, we can well understand some pain points in this process. Chinese architects have also developed flexible and adaptable way of working at home, which are down-to-earth, and good at predicting and suggesting the progress of projects in a complex environment lack of external conditions.

Opportunities are always accompanied by challenges. If someone asks, "what are the biggest difficulties that China faces in developing design business in overseas developing countries? The answer may have two parts:

Fig. 11.7 The high-end serviced apartment complex in Hudson Park, New York

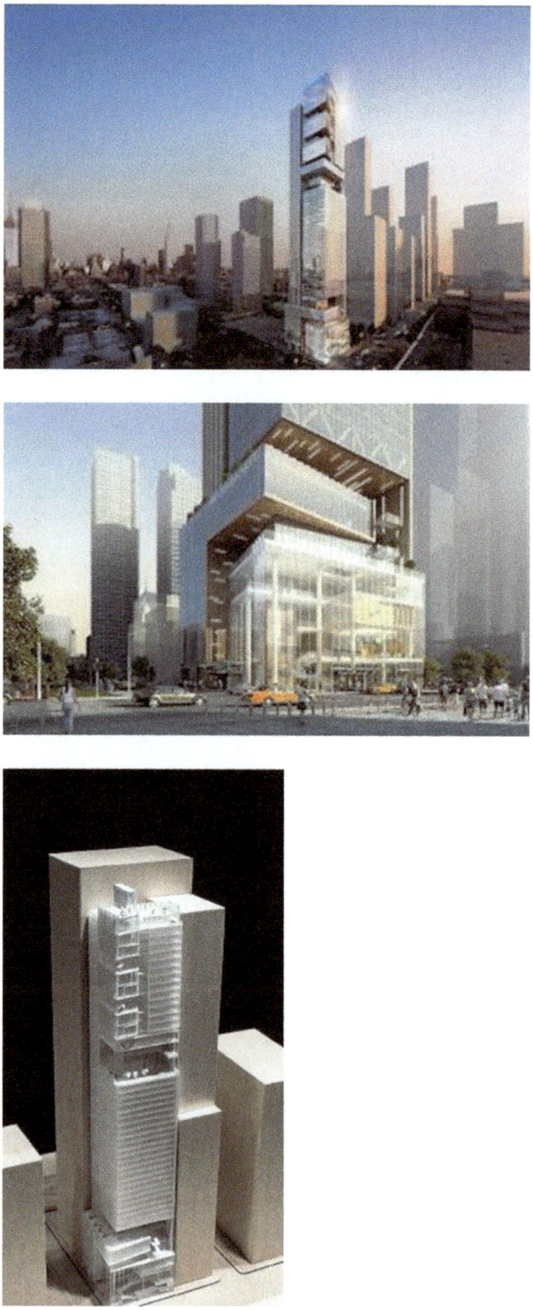

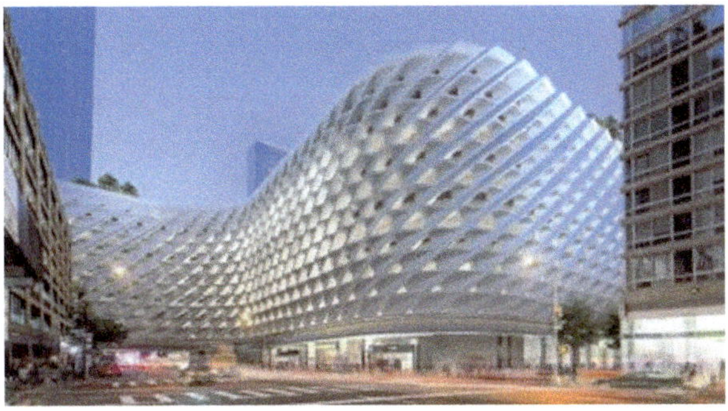

Fig. 11.8 Manhattan transportation hub, New York

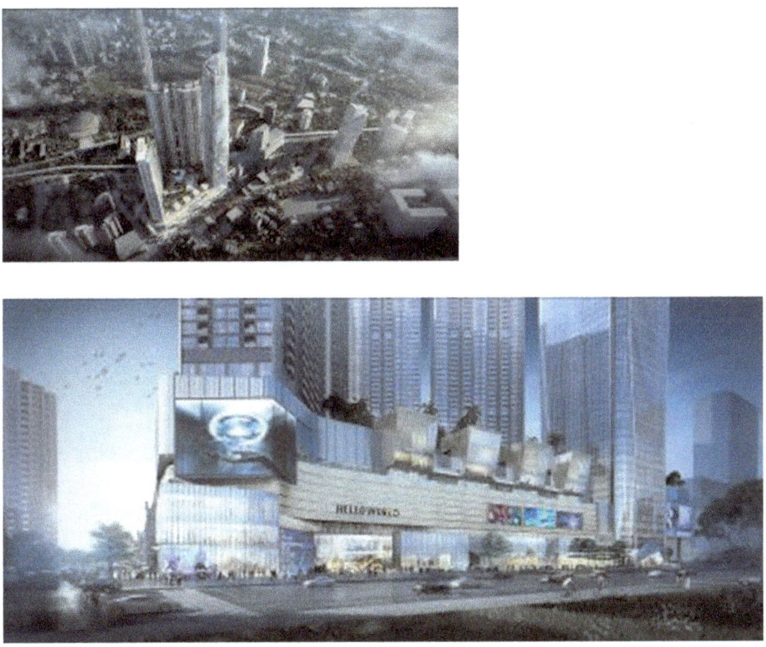

Fig. 11.9 Kuala Lumpur people's square

On the one hand, such challenge is no longer a linguistic and technical barrier, but a consensus from an international perspective. For Chinese architects, the question used to be "can we go", but now it is "why". This is not only a matter of business needs, but of taking architects' professional mission and international win–win results as the start of work. In any case, when our design project is completed, it may probably be a national landmark. The 100-m high-rises that have become common in China may be the tallest buildings in some overseas cities. In overseas projects, the impact of a project on a country is sometimes more evident than that of domestic

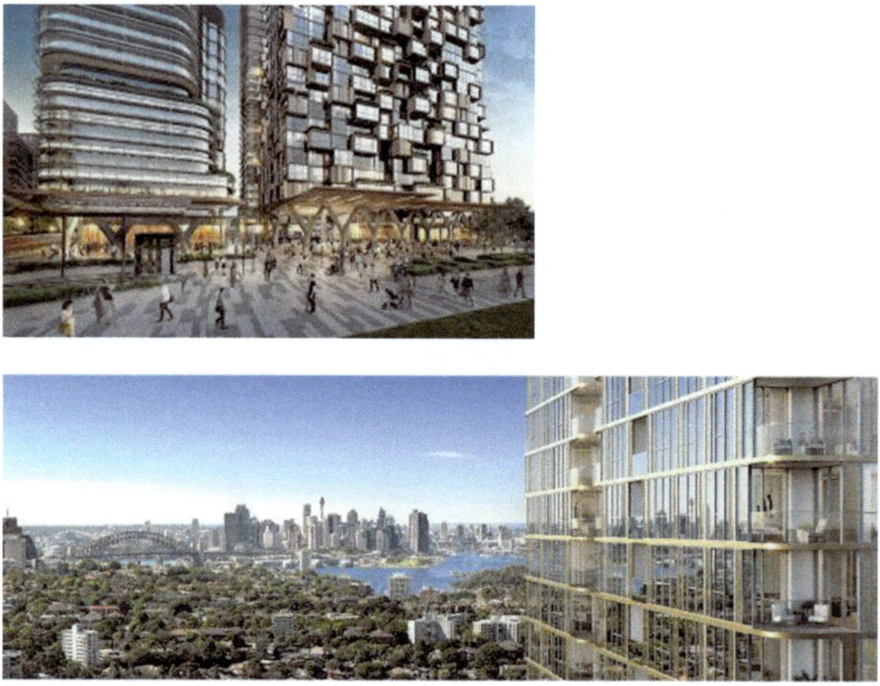

Fig. 11.10 Christie street 88 project of Sydney

landmarks. Nowadays, everyone chooses to travel to the United States, Japan and Europe, but I believe few people apply for tourist visas to Congo, Bangladesh, Gabon and Papua New Guinea. Although these countries are not well developed, they are not as backward as we used to think. They have their own national personality and cultural charm, and deserve a place in the global village of common prosperity.

On the other hand, the real difficulty also comes from the understanding of international professionalism and design norms. Some Africa and South America countries were colonized by Europeans earlier. Some of their institutions and systems, such as architect accountability system, are actually closer to European standards than those in China. On this point, China appears to be "backward", and there are certain thresholds for technology output. Others seek CCDI's services because of China's strength. However, many of CCDI's projects in recent years are exploring all the way in an extremely non-standard process. We should make up a missed lesson in the degree of professionalism. When designing building in any country, tradition and modernity are always in conflict. Chinese architects need to spend a lot of time understanding the policies, norms, cultural intentions and form preferences of foreign countries, so as to obtain a value judgment that is recognized in a cross-cultural context and finally realize a broad "world culture", and then to combine the common environmental value standard of mankind with the differentiated development path adhered to different regions. This standpoint of respect, civilization, fraternity and sharing is actually a contemporary portrayal of ancient Chinese wisdom.

Nowadays, the design business of CCDI is distributed in China, Southeast Asia, the Middle East, Africa, Australia, North America and other regions. Its 6,000 employees are distributed in many brand entities of different sizes and with different positions, such as CCDI, Tengyuan Design, PTW, Archilier and Link-Arc, in an attempt to jointly contribute design services of different dimensions to the world. Looking at the whole industry, even if the current pandemic has "slowed down" the world economy to a certain extent, we still have sufficient reasons to predict the future multilateral mechanism between China and developing countries, and the general policy trend of a country that actively develops cooperative partnerships. As an unfathomable "blue ocean", the overseas business of large Chinese design firms is still worthy of further research and exploration.

References

Ai, X. (2018). Hot & honor: Architectural review of the Brazzaville Sports Center. *Time + Architecture*, (02), 132–135. 艾侠.酷热与荣耀 布拉柴维尔体育中心设计评述.时代建筑, 2018(02), 132–135.

Ai, X. (2010). Breeze of the sea—Oran convention center, Algeria. *Time + Architecture*, (01), 84–87. 艾侠. 凭海临风 阿尔及利亚奥兰会展文化中心[J]. 时代建筑, 2010 (01), 84–87.

Shi, S. (2016). Golden glory—Congo Brazzaville stadium. *Architectural Practice*, *36*(03), 36–41. 石少峰.金色荣耀—刚果布拉柴维尔体育场.建筑知识, 2016, 36(03), 36–41.

Zheng, F., Zhang, X. (2008). Water cube—National aquatics center. *Architectural Journal*, (06), 36–47. 郑方,张欣.水立方—国家游泳中心.建筑学报, 2008 (06), 36–47.

Xia Ai is a research-oriented expert of design and knowledge management who has brought 12 publications and over 40 articles into fruition. Graduated from Tongji University (Bachelor 2000, Master 2004), he leads a research team to explore an interaction between technical and commercial value and he is also Associate of Architectural Critics Committee, China.

Chapter 12
Architects' Foreign Aid Design Practice: The National Stadium of Cambodia and China-Cambodian Friendship Hospital

Yang Li and Qingnan Fan

Abstract The design elements of modern architecture in Cambodia are characterized with the integration of structure and decoration and the combination of lines and symbolic patterns into building forms, and the emphasis on natural ventilation and shading. Taking the Cambodian National Stadium and the China-Cambodian Friendship Hospital as examples, this chapter explores the issues of cultural expression and design mode in China's foreign aid architecture. Both projects aim to achieve low maintenance cost and low energy consumption while meeting cultural and functional requirements. This chapter also discusses the signification of technical specifications in overseas design practice.

12.1 China's Aid to Cambodia

Since 1950, China has provided material support to neighboring friendly countries. From then on, China has provided aid to more than 160 countries and international organizations. After the Cambodian Prince Norodom Sihanouk (1922–2012) alienated the United States, the diplomatic relations between China and Cambodia gradually deepened. The Chinese aid history to Cambodia could be divided into three phases.

The first phase was the Kingdom of Cambodia (1953–1989). Cambodia was witnessing economy deficit of income and experiencing internal and external troubles after its independence in 1953. Based on internationalism and responsibilities, China began to provide free military and financial aid to Cambodia especially during its war in the 1970s.

Y. Li (✉)
China Electronics Engineering Design Institute Co., Ltd., Beijing, China
e-mail: 502317@qq.com

Q. Fan
Beijing University of Civil Engineering and Architecture, Beijing, China

C. Q. Xue and G. Ding (eds.), *Exporting Chinese Architecture*,
https://doi.org/10.1007/978-981-19-2786-7_12

The second phase was a period of political stability and progress (1990–2009). China focused on infrastructure construction in Cambodia, such as bridges, roads, water, electricity, and manufacturing plants. The aid funds have shifted from gift to preferential loan with consideration of economic cooperation and mutual benefit.

From 2010 to 2021, Cambodia joined the framework agreement of "the Belt and Road Initiatives," and the two countries have established a comprehensive strategic cooperative partnership. The rapid development of bilateral trade has achieved the goal of economic cooperation and mutual benefit. At the same time, China has become Cambodia's largest aider and assisted many large-scale livelihood projects with local influence, such as the Cambodian National Stadium and the China-Cambodian Friendship Hospital.

12.2 A Brief Introduction of Cambodian Modern Architecture

12.2.1 History of Modern Architecture in Cambodia

Cambodia is located at the southern tip of the Indochina Peninsula and thus maintains an important strategic position. It was not until 1953 that Cambodia enjoyed a short and rare period of peaceful development. The country adhered to the basic principle of the trinity of state, religion and king after independence, which also affected the decision-making of the national architectural style. Architects who returned from abroad in the 1950s and 1960s began to combine Cambodian elements with modern principles and have created a series of modernist buildings with Cambodian regional characteristics. The architectural achievements during this period were defined as New Khmer Architecture by historians.

Architect Vann Molyvann (1926–2017) who studied in France in 1946 not only became a leader of the new Khmer architecture school, but also was considered as the founder of modern Cambodian architecture. After returning home in 1955, he served as chairman of the Cambodian Architectural Association during Sihanouk's regime.

In recent years, with the rapid development of Cambodia's economy, real estate development projects based on modernist style and design techniques, in particular, super high-rise buildings have begun to emerge. Local people are gradually appreciating modernist styles.

12.2.2 Features of Cambodian Modern Architecture

The New Khmer architecture explicitly reflected Cambodia's political self-confidence, economic openness, and cultural identity. While stubbornly expressing national culture, Cambodian architects also made corresponding adjustments in formal and technological innovations. The specific manifestations are as follows:

(1) Overall consideration on building function and indoor-outdoor decoration. Architects tended to use durable concrete structure to achieve the integrity of form, structure, space and indoor-outdoor decoration, while reducing construction and maintenance costs;
(2) The organic integration of architectural style and national culture. The appearance of buildings emphasizes simple and clear line forms and decoration with luxurious and complex patterns, such as medallion shields, Angkor Buddhism and others, which reflect Cambodian national image;
(3) Effective use of building technology and responding to regional climate. Because of its tropical location, Cambodian architecture pays attention to natural ventilation and sun-shading. Architects adapts to local climate through technical measures such as waterscapes, ventilation, and sun-shading components.

12.2.3 Cambodian National Sports Complex

The National Sports Complex, located in Phnom Penh and designed by Molyvann, is well known by Cambodians as a representative work of the new Khmer architecture (Fig. 12.1). This 190,000 square-meter sports complex, built by a Chinese company in 1964, consists of three parts arranged symmetrically along the axis: an indoor

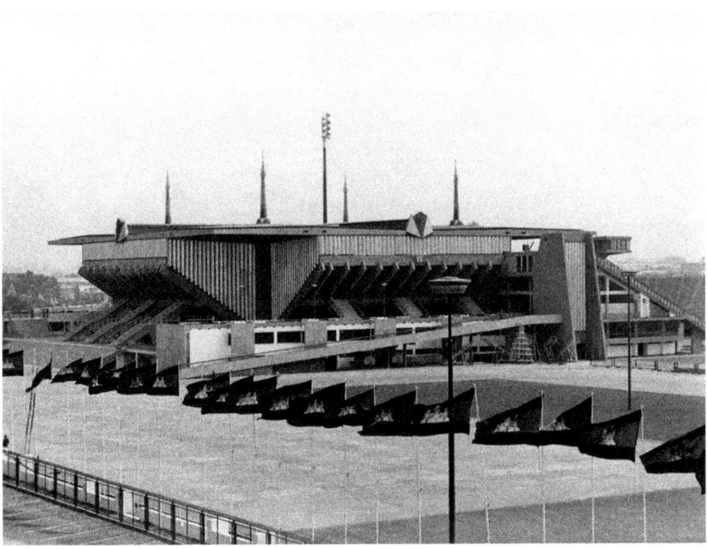

Fig. 12.1 Cambodian national sports complex. *Source* https://www.wmf.org/project/national-sports-complex-cambodia

stadium, an outdoor stadium and a swimming pool. The roof of the indoor stadium was designed with a remarkably splendid shield decoration, which reflects the royal tradition of Khmer architecture.

The gymnasium is constructed by concrete and supported by four 40 m-span columns and 1.5 m-high two-way beams. The overhanging stands, steps and platforms outside form the semi-outdoor space with shade and ventilation at the lower part, which is convenient for the passage of spectators during the game and can be used as public fitness space on weekdays.

The gymnasium adopted measures such as natural ventilation and lighting. For example, the concrete stand slabs under the indoor seats were designed to be hollow, and the facade surface adopted L-shaped aluminum alloy components to interlock and install each other, creating a building form that combines natural ventilation and sun-shading (Fig. 12.2). The whole stadium was shimmering with little light in the morning and welcomed a large number of exercisers.

The west stand of the open-air stadium is arranged at the lower part of the east stand of the gymnasium. The south, north, and east sides of the stadium use the terrain height difference to form a soil slope to be used as a spectator stand.

Waterscape is the main feature of Cambodian Buddhist temples. Molyvann designed four rectangular pools around the four main columns. The pools are not only used for decoration, but also as storage tanks for draining rainwater in the rainy season, and for cooling in the dry season. As a functional, artistic, economical, and

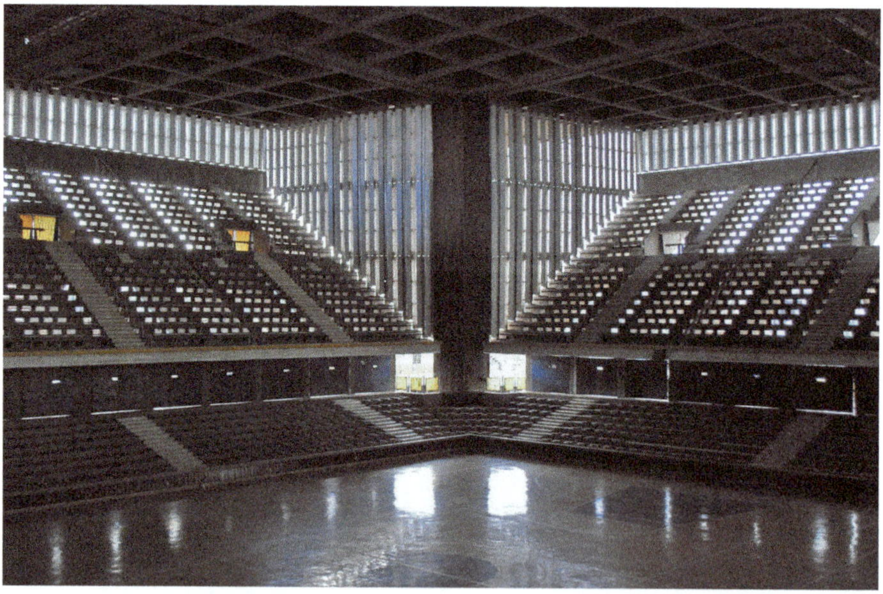

Fig. 12.2 Interior of the Cambodian national sports complex, *Source* https://www.wmf.org/project/national-sports-complex-cambodia

maintainable stadium, it has become a nationally iconic historical building, and an inspiration for the design of the Cambodia National Stadium.

12.3 Cambodia National Stadium

The newly planned sports center in Cambodia is located in the north Phnom Penh. Designed and built by the Chinese, the 82,400 square-meter, 60,000 seats main stadium of the sports center was a comprehensive multi-functional venue for sports competitions, gatherings, performances, catering, accommodation, exhibitions and conferences (Fig. 12.3). The stadium proposal was selected by Cambodian Prime Minister Hun Sen and constructed for 2023 Southeast Asian Games and will be used as a civic fitness center for Phnom Penh citizens.

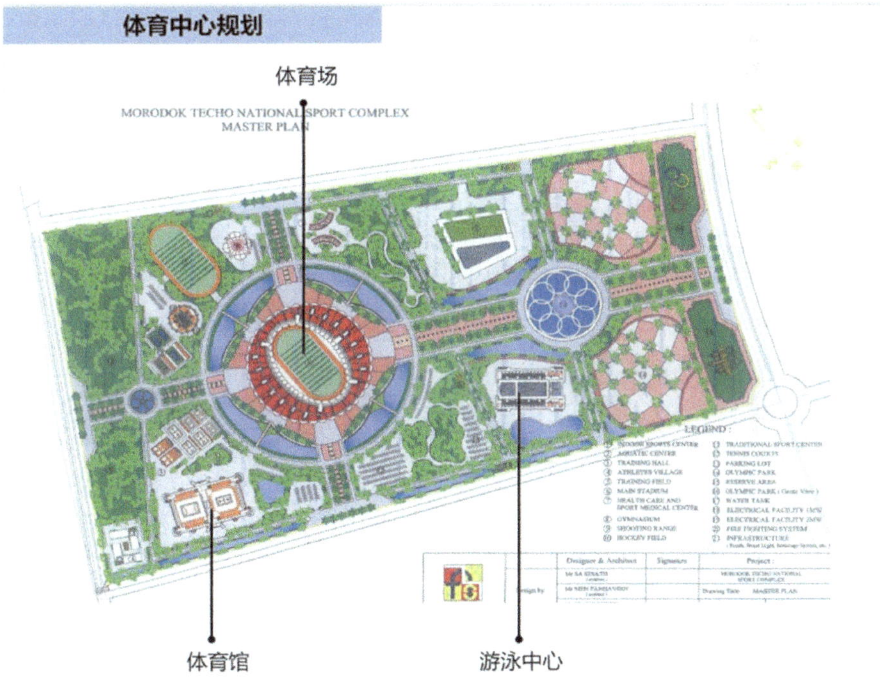

Fig. 12.3 Master plan of the sports center

12.3.1 Cultural Authenticity

As the symbol of the friendship between the two countries, the National Stadium design should not only provide reasonable functional configuration, but also reflect Cambodian cultural and regional characteristics and respect the local ethnic beliefs and cultural symbols (Figs. 12.4 and 12.5).

Based on this principle, the architects extracted representative elements from Cambodian cultural traditions (Buddhist Namaste, Dragon Boat Race, Angkor Wat Sculpture, and rumdul flower) to formulate the concept of "Cambodian Boat" (Fig. 12.6).

Cambodian Boat

The first issue to be considered in the design of the Cambodian National Stadium is how to reflect the friendship between the two countries. As the project is located between the Tonle Sap and Mekong rivers, "water" had become a design inspiration. The Water Delivery Festival (Bon Om Touk), also known as the Dragon Boat Festival, as the most important traditional festival in Cambodia was created to express gratitude for the Tonle Sap and Mekong Rivers for their upbringing. The dragon boat races during the Water Delivery Festival and the Chinese Dragon Boat Festival had similar cultural origins. Therefore, the concept of "Cambodian boat" implies the strong friendship between the two countries.

In the design refinement stage, the building form is composed of four parts with comprehensive functional and structural consideration: the complete "hull", the raised "mast", the inclined "ropes", and the propped white "sail". A cable-stayed membrane structure was adopted after close collaboration between architects and

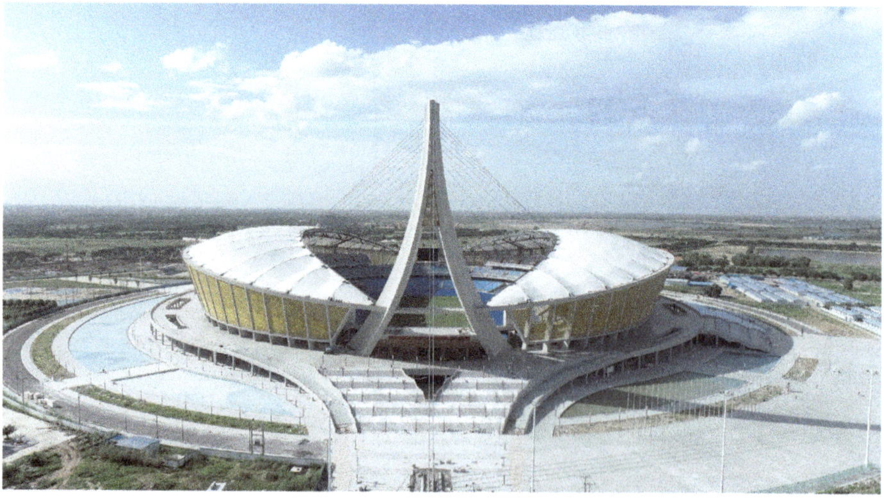

Fig. 12.4 The Cambodia national stadium

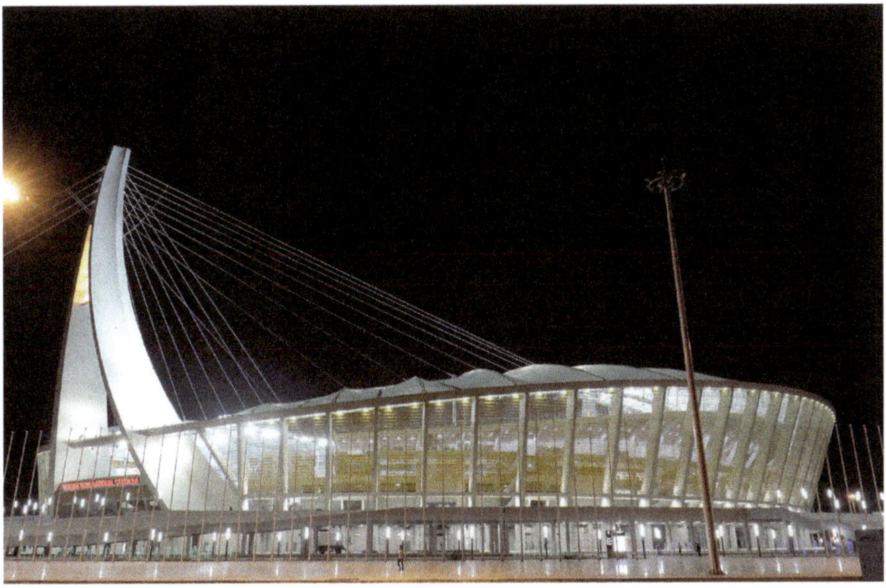

Fig. 12.5 Night view of the Cambodia national stadium

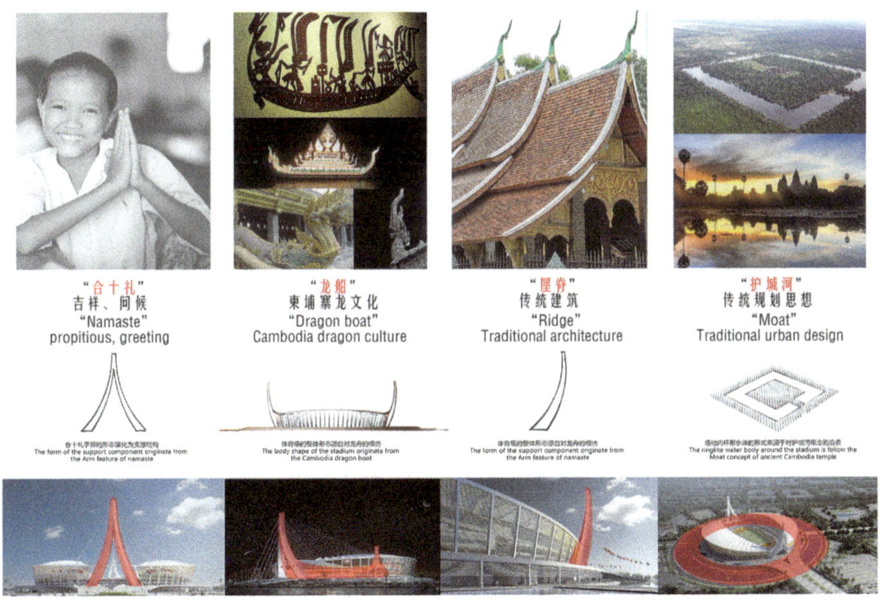

Fig. 12.6 The concept of culture

structural engineers, as the latter offered innovative technical solutions through model calculations, simulation analysis, and wind experiments.

Buddhist Namaste

The "Buddhist Namaste" that originated from Indian Buddhism referring to being auspicious later developed into a nationwide etiquette in Cambodia. Inspired by this greeting gesture, the 99-m-high structural suspension towers at both ends of the stadium were designed into a stable herringbone shape. The towers were made of plain concrete and functioned as water tank rooms and included inside steel ladders for maintenance purpose. The hyperbola-shaped structure closes up to form a graceful herringbone tower. Together with the building's ring beams and columns, and the steel cables, they form an integrated structure which supported the membrane structure canopy. The structure itself became a building landmark as well.

Longdu Flower

The surface design of sports buildings had to satisfy the function of ventilation and shading while paying particular attention to aesthetics. First of all, the outer skin, inspired by the patterns of Longdu flower elements, was fixed to the inverted conical colonnade with a height of 12–29 m. In the absence of a mature case, the architects made a 1:1 physical model, and finally selected a 1.2 mm thick aluminum-magnesium-manganese alloy plate with better toughness, and realized the semi-permeable effect of ventilation and sun-shading through punching. Perforated standing seam 360 panels were fixed with the flexible cable net point-supporting curtain wall system (Fig. 12.7).

Besides, in an attempt to reflect the Cambodian national flower pattern on the outer skin, Chinese architects collaborated with Cambodian colleagues to choose gold color that is more in line with local favorites. The flower pattern was simplified to

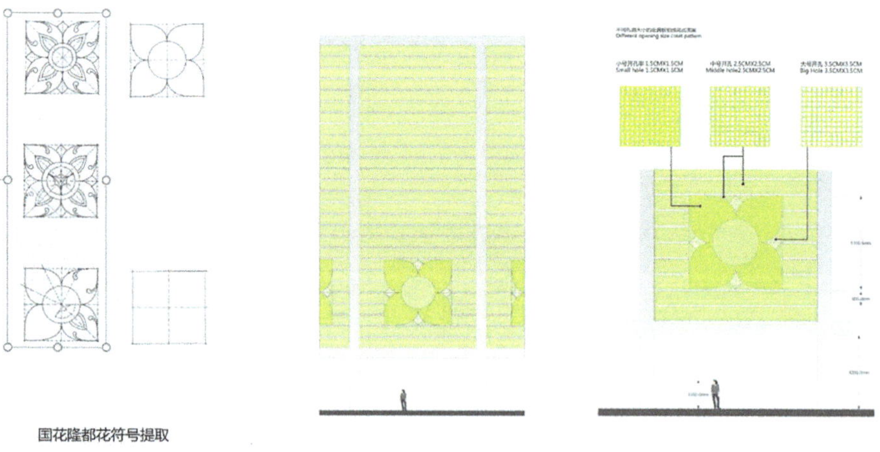

Fig. 12.7 Building skin design of the stadium

suit industrial processing and production. At the same time, the architects adjusted the scale and size of the pattern, experimented with various effects by changing different perforation rates and finally realized a gauze-like facade, which also conformed to the national image of Cambodia (Fig. 12.8).

Angkor Moat

The Angkor Wat, a holy land in Cambodia, is surrounded by water and only maintains access in the east–west direction. The moat of Angkor Wat not only plays a role of decoration and defense against foreign enemies, but also stores rainwater during the rainy season and regulates the environment during the dry season.

The master plan design draws on the concept of "moat". The stadium is surrounded by water and only maintains access in the north–south direction, which reflects

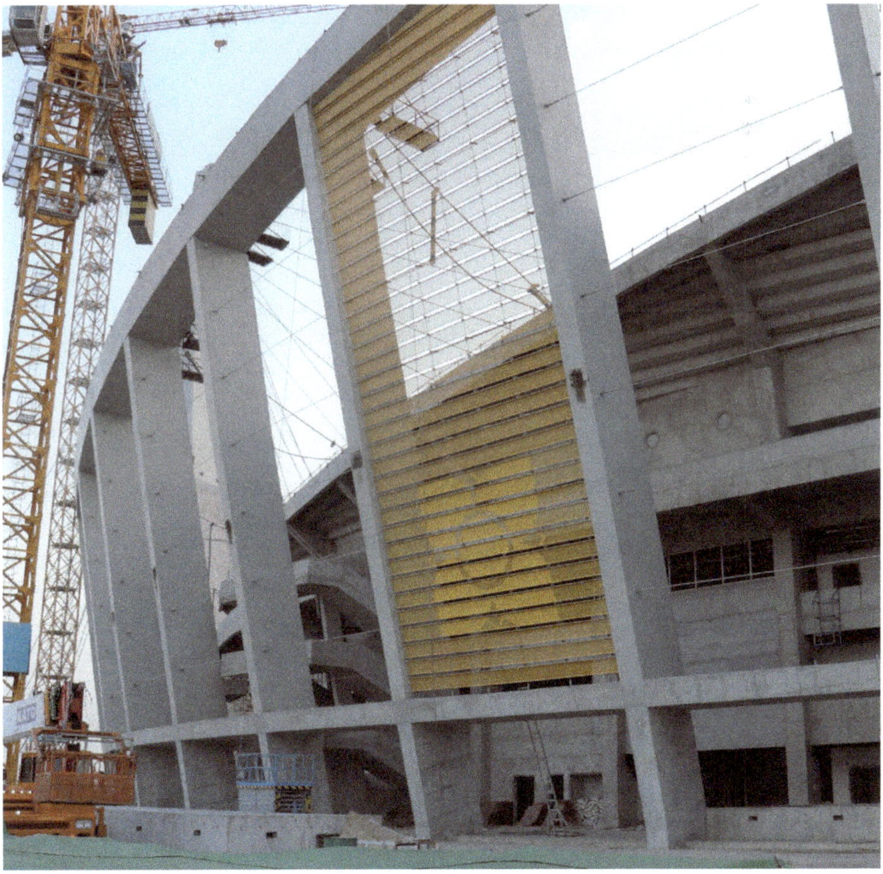

Fig. 12.8 Aluminum magnesium manganese pressure plate and cable curtain wall construction status

Cambodian traditional culture. The circular pool not only became part of the landscape, but also served for drainage and storage, even played a role in improving the microclimate of the site in the dry season.

The pool is 25 m wide and 0.6 m deep with a hardened ground which meet the need of the children to play. The pool's depth ensures the safe use of the stadium.

12.3.2 Design Principles

Sports Technology Design

The stadium field is arranged with the north–south direction, which meets the needs of field, track and football games. The 400-m track includes 10 straight and 9 curve lanes. The plastic poly track is designed in a blue color to be more suitable for use in tropical climate and the natural turf football field meets FIFA standards.

Functional Layout

The stands are arranged in a saddle shape around the circle of the competition venue, with a total of 60,000 spectator seats, including a platform reserved for 5,000 temporary seats on the north and south sides. The stands consist of three parts of: low, middle and high areas. The low area is located on the first floor with 22,000 seats for ordinary and disabled spectators. The middle stand is located on the third floor with a total of 13,000 seats, including VIP, media, and athlete seats. The high stand is located on the fifth floor, and the seats here are provided for the ordinary spectators (Fig. 12.9).

The first floor is arranged for functional rooms: VIPs, athletes, event management, and news media rooms on the west; Athlete training halls, sports equipment warehouses, and equipment rooms on the north; Venue management, security, and equipment rooms on the south; External commercial houses are arranged on the east (Fig. 12.10).

The second floor is the audience entrance layer, including audience evacuation platforms, bathrooms and service facilities.

The third floor is the mezzanine for VIPs. The VIP lounge, media and athlete lounge are arranged under the west stand, and the hotel rooms are arranged under the east stand.

The fourth floor is the box floor. The west side is equipped with VIP and sponsor boxes, and competition technology rooms, and the east side is equipped with guest rooms and restaurants.

The fifth floor is an evacuation platform leading to the high stands, consisting of toilets, service and equipment rooms.

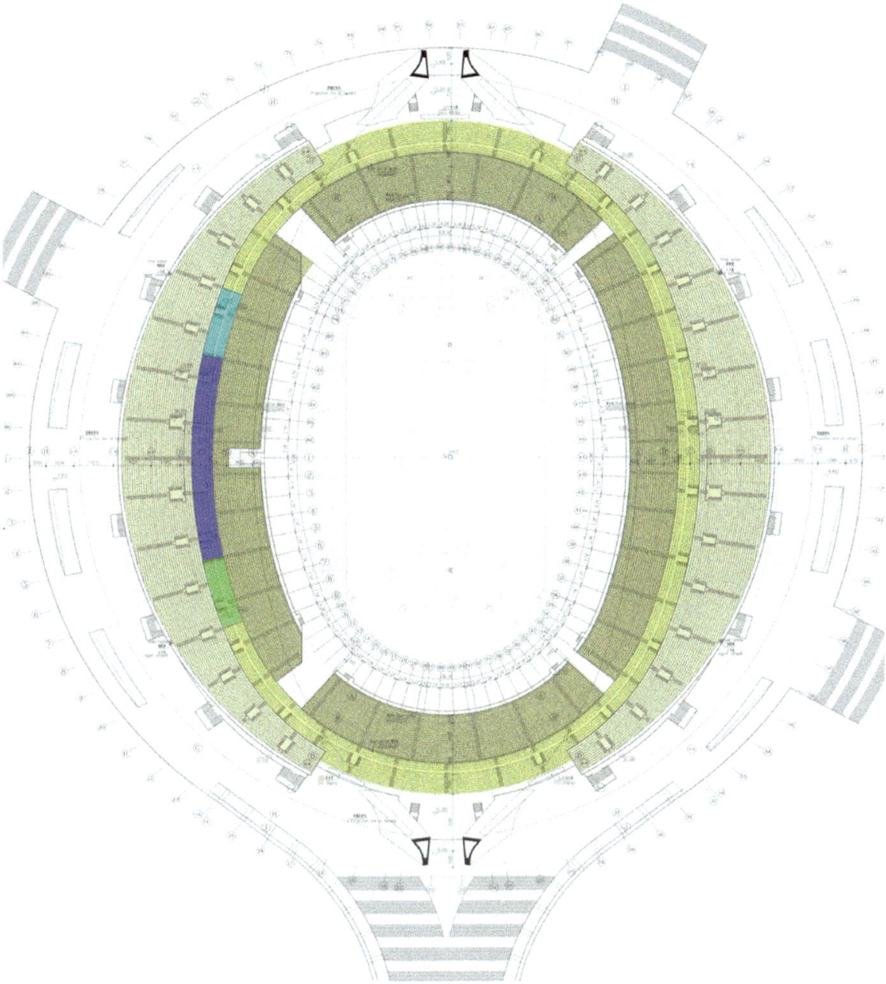

Fig. 12.9 Grandstand floor plan of the stadium

Multi-functional Architecture

The maintenance cost of large stadiums during the operation phase is huge, and the design needs to consider multi-functional use to reduce operation and maintenance costs.

On the first floor of the west stand, a large space is arranged to facilitate flexible conversion during and after the game. Independent external commercial spaces on the first floor of the east stand were open to residents, including gymnasium, boxing club, rock climbing club, exhibition hall, and VIPs, hotels, restaurants on the third and fourth floors.

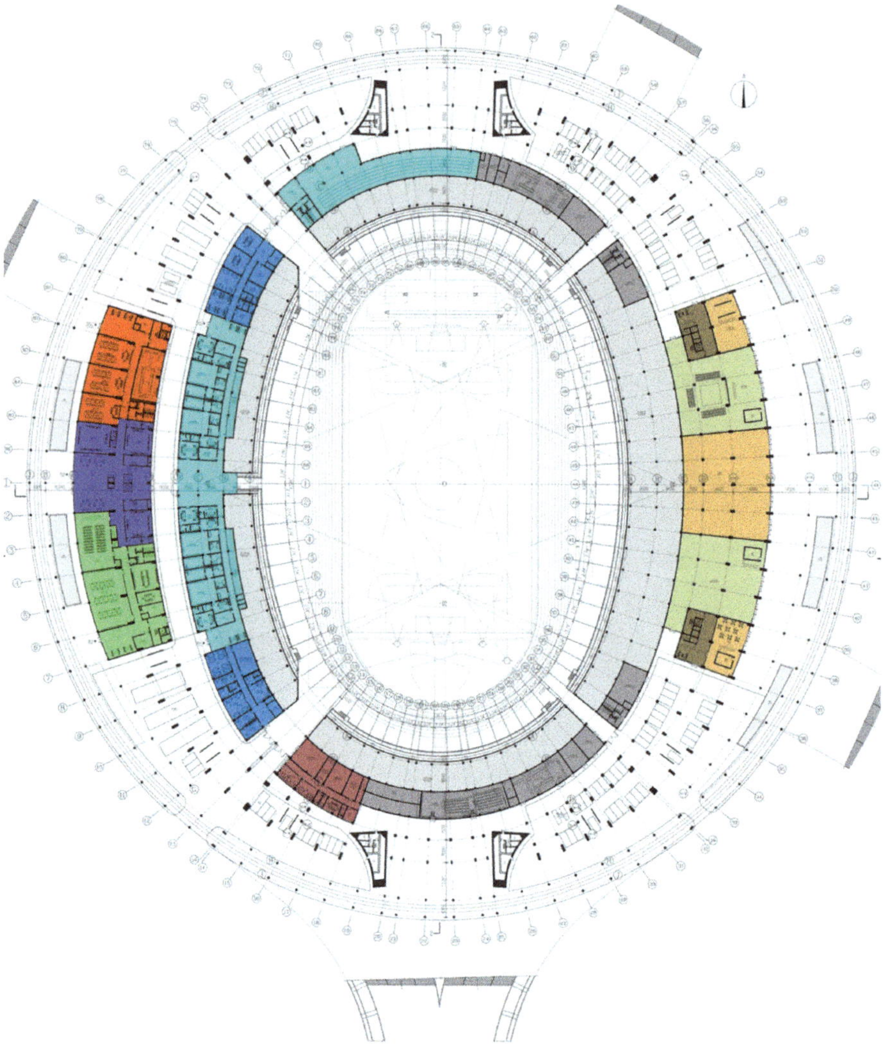

Fig. 12.10 Ground floor of the stadium

Besides, the setting of closed rooms is reduced, and the semi-open space with higher utilization rate is increased, such as the fitness track under the platform on the first floor, which provides a fitness field opened to the public (Figs. 12.11 and 12.12).

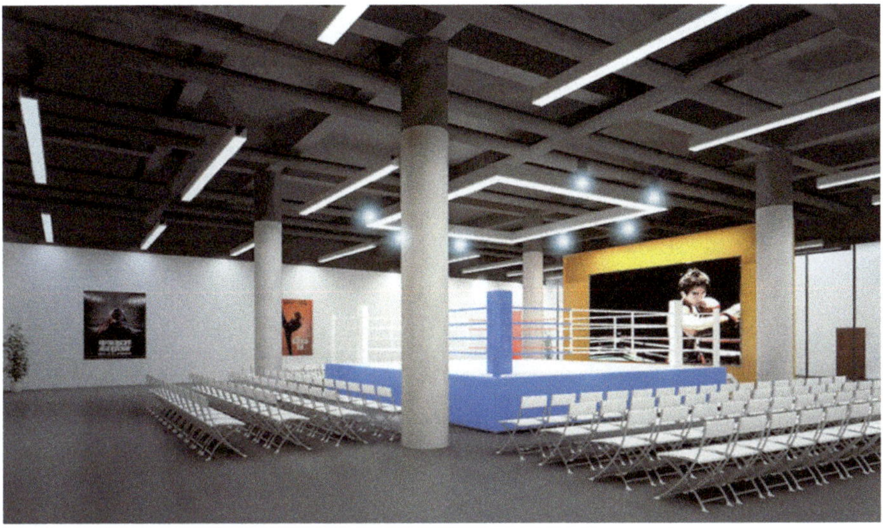

Fig. 12.11 Boxing club

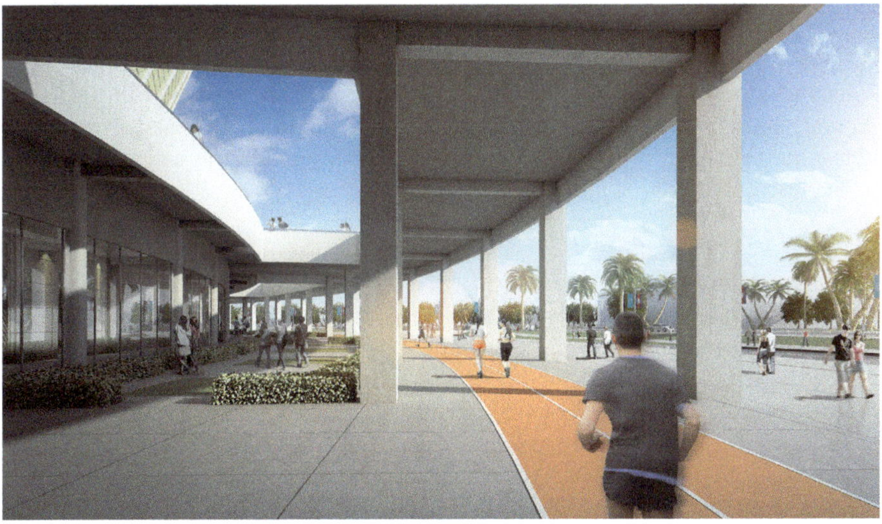

Fig. 12.12 Rendering of the fitness track

12.3.3 Low Maintenance Construction Practices

Prefabricated Stand System

The common stadium stand system is divided into prefabricated and cast-in-place stands. The former which is prefabricated in factory and installed on site has high

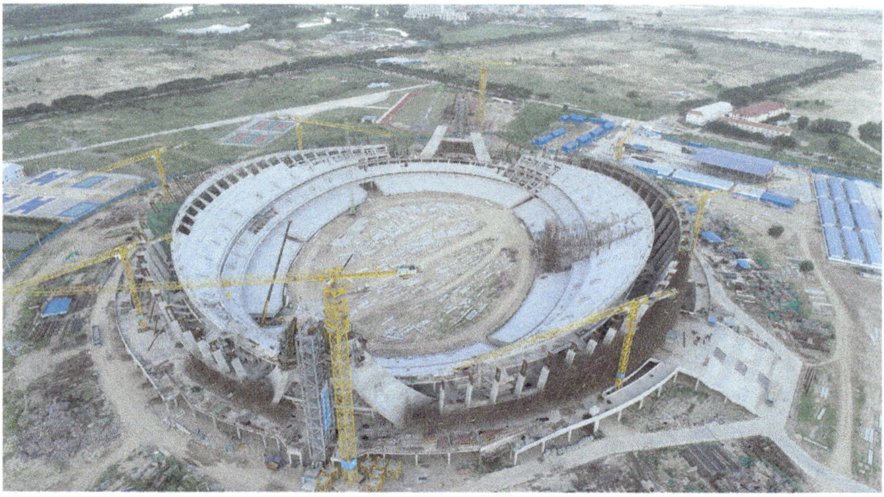

Fig. 12.13 Construction process

construction efficiency, controllable quality and high mechanical cost. The latter is cast on site with low construction efficiency, high labor cost, poor durability and additional waterproof surface.

Given the project's large scale and sufficient construction sites, to establish a temporary prefabricated component factory on site could achieve better durability and low maintenance costs (Fig. 12.13). The Cambodian side was satisfied with the construction quality of the prefabricated stands (Fig. 12.14).

Fair-Faced Concrete

The structural columns, beams and suspension towers are made of fair-faced concrete for convenient maintenance. The prepared technical specification required construction company to adopt customized formwork, one-time pouring of structure without external decoration and using sealing and protecting agent of fair-faced concrete, etc., and provided reference photos to clarify the design content and purpose.

Fair-faced concrete structure has high design and construction requirements, and it is necessary to strictly control the construction quality of concrete pouring, and to pour it in one time, avoid repairing through building decoration, and achieve the purpose of building durability and low maintenance.

Polished Concrete Floor

Outdoor square floors commonly used permeable concrete or stone paving. The permeable concrete floor is environmentally friendly, but has low density and poor durability, while the stone paving is costly and not environmentally friendly. By searching for similar cases, the architects found that the square design of Durban Stadium in South Africa took into account durability, environmental protection, economy and beauty. The project's polished concrete floor which had been built for

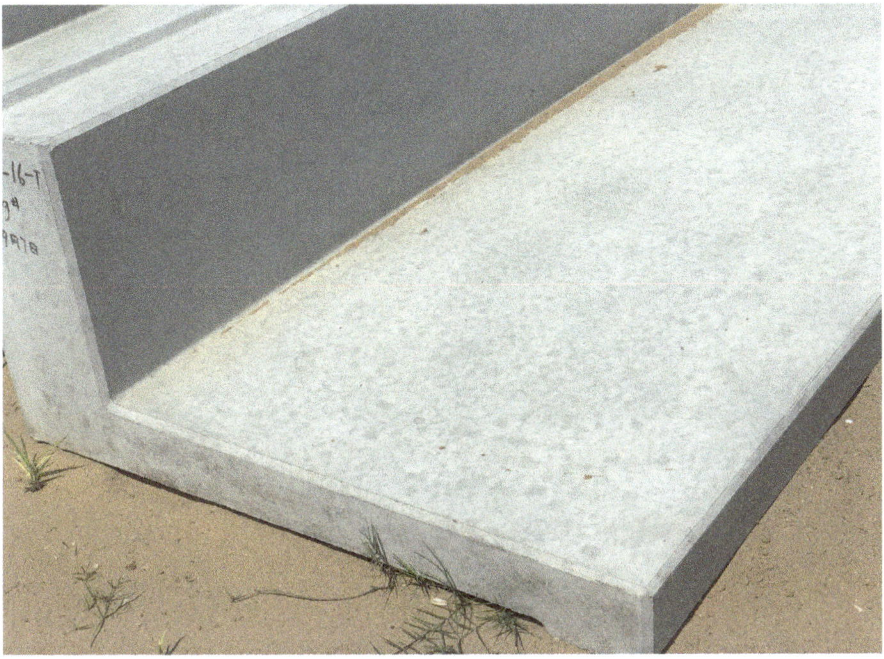

Fig. 12.14 Prefabricated stand

nearly 10 years with excellent effect and durability was realized with the technology and equipment of the Swedish HTC company.

The architects have given clear design requirements in the technical specifications in order to better ensure the effect of the polished concrete floor. The construction method of the concrete floor includes: to pour a 180 mm thick ordinary C30 concrete surface, and then mechanically polish it with professional equipment, and add chemical sealing curing agent to produce dense and bright concrete surface. The polished concrete floor is used in outdoor squares, so adding anti-slip property is also very important (Fig. 12.15). The method is to control the polishing anti-slip effect, and balance both usability and decorative effect.

12.4 The China–Cambodia Friendship Hospital

With the deeper understanding of Cambodia, the design team undertook the design and management of the China-Cambodia Friendship Hospital project in early 2017.

Preah Kossamak Hospital is known as the "Monk Hospital" where located in the center of Phnom Penh. The core object of this project is to provide high-level medical services to meet the medical needs of people from all walks of life through reconstruction and extension a General Medical Building which around 400 beds.

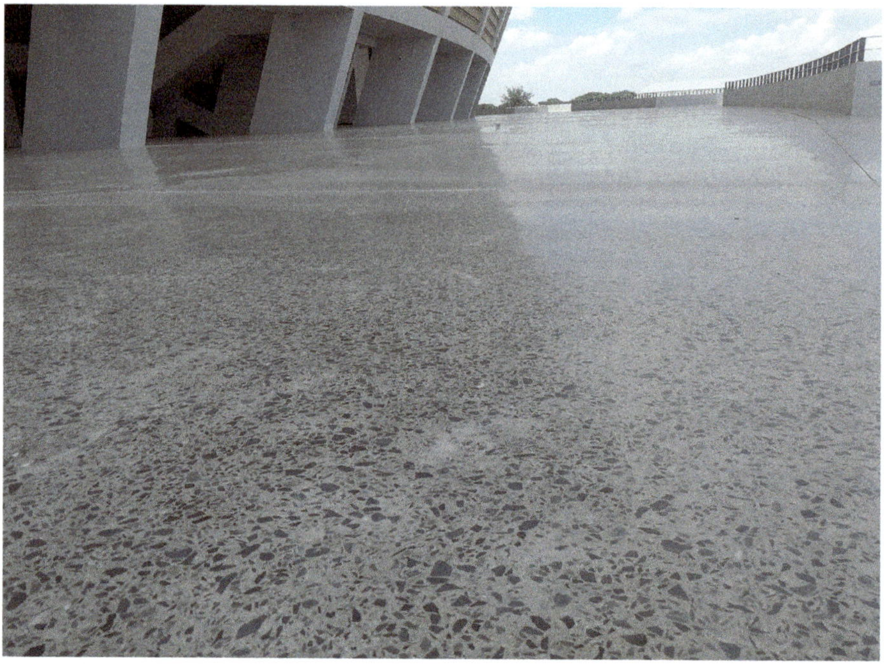

Fig. 12.15 The polished concrete floor

In addition to meeting the modern medical process and reflecting the iconic architectural image, the design has also done in-depth research on green buildings suitable for Cambodia (Figs. 12.16, 12.17 and 12.18).

12.4.1 The Goal of Low Energy Consumption and High Quality

The current medical situation in Cambodia is divided into public and private hospitals, showing a trend of polarization. Represented by Cosma Hospital and Royal Phnom Penh Hospital, the local public hospitals have poor medical conditions and the rooms are mainly open, and the operation and maintenance costs are low (low energy consumption and low quality). But the rooms of local private hospitals are mainly air-conditioning, and their operation and maintenance are high cost (high energy consumption and high quality). The China–Cambodia Friendship Hospital is positioned as a national public hospital, and the primary design goal is to create a high-quality medical experience on the basis of low energy consumption.

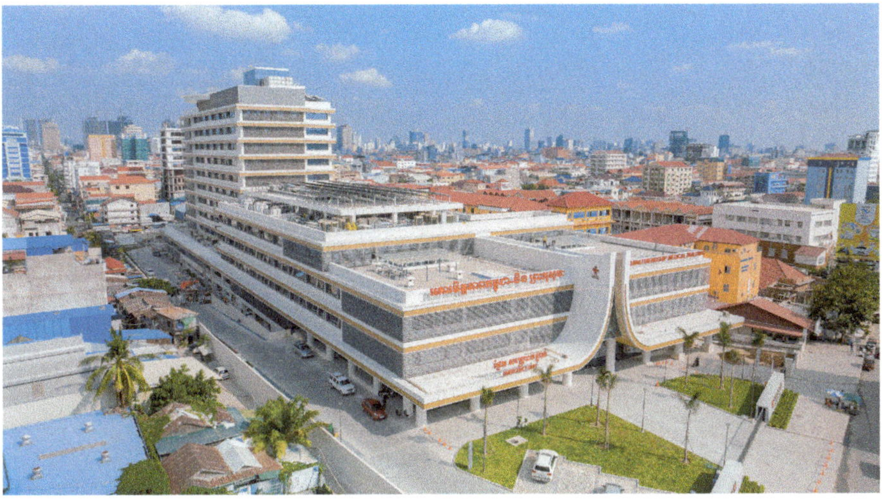

Fig. 12.16 The China–Cambodia friendship hospital

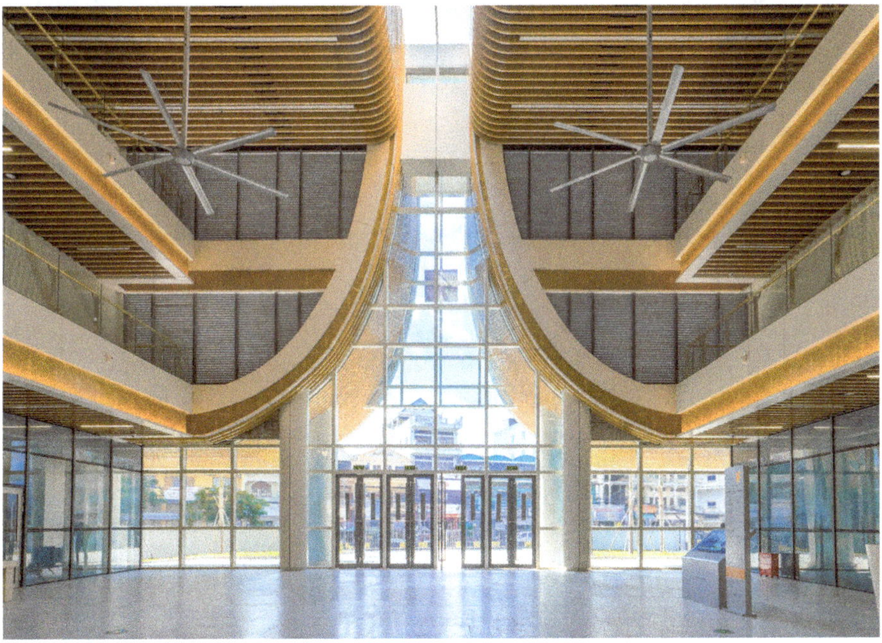

Fig. 12.17 The lobby of the China–Cambodia friendship hospital

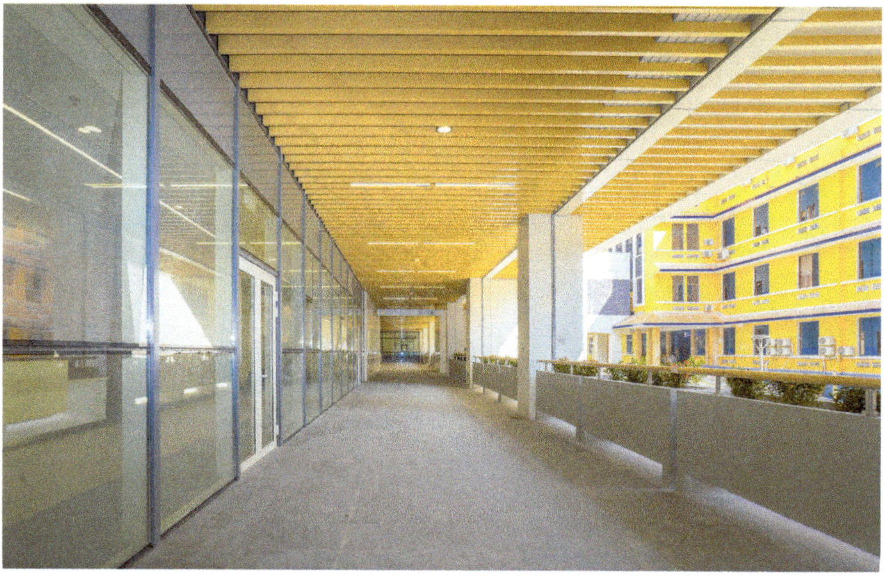

Fig. 12.18 The corridor of the China–Cambodia friendship hospital

12.4.2 Green Building Design Standards Suitable for Cambodia

Being restricted by geographical conditions Singapore has carried out active exploration and practice in advocating green buildings and environmental sustainability. Aiming to create safe, efficient, and recycling-friendly building environment, Singapore's Green Mark evaluation system emphasizes the importance of energy conservation and natural ventilation. Cambodia's resource-poor geographical conditions and hot-humid climate characteristics are highly similar to that of Singapore. The use of the Singapore Green Mark evaluation system is more in line with the project's design characteristics, compared with the US LEED design standard and China's Green Building Design standard.

12.4.3 Low Energy Consumption Design

(1) In order to reduce energy consumption, the building space is divided into air-conditioned and non-air-conditioned areas. Public areas such as halls, main streets are designed as semi-open spaces with ceiling fans to enhance natural ventilation. Air conditioning systems are installed in functional spaces such as patient waiting areas, medical rooms and wards. The open space accounts for 40% of the total building area (Fig. 12.19).

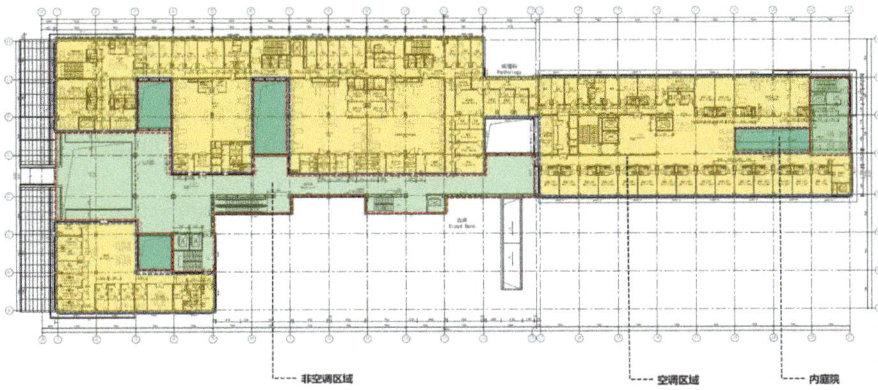

Fig. 12.19 Division of air-conditioned and non-air-conditioned areas

(2) The photovoltaic power generation systems and solar hot water systems were installed on the roofs to reduce building power consumption.
(3) The building envelope's thermal performance is improved through adding thermal insulation materials on the external wall and roof and using broken bridge aluminum windows, so that the ETTV value is less than 45 W/m^2.

12.4.4 Realize High-Quality Methods

(1) No-step site design and eye-catching park sign system were adopted to improve the comfort of disadvantaged groups.
(2) The inner courtyards and flower ponds are introduced to create a green corridor, and the open public space is equipped with leisure seats to improve the use quality of the hospital's semi-open public spaces.
(3) Cambodia's medical resources are relatively backward and there is no complete medical information system. In order to improve the medical process and experience, the project design refers to the standards of China's second-class hospitals.
(4) The core connotation of medical buildings is reasonable functions and scientific processes, and the design adopted medical main street concepts. The functions are divided into doctor office module, medical function module and medical main street module. The circulation design took into account the flow of doctors and patients in each function. The users and logistics circulations are separated to create an efficient and safe hospital.
(5) The project was equipped with advanced medical equipment.
(6) The energy consumption of this project is 70% of similar hospitals in China by referring to the evaluation standard of Singapore Green Mark.

12.5 The Practice of Refined Design

Foreign aid projects acting on international convention earlier. In 2015, the requirement of compiling the design-technical specification was put forward. The above two projects achieved the purpose of fine design and high completion through the compilation of the specification.

As a supplement and refinement of the in-depth design documents, specifications can be used for defining equipment material specifications, performance parameters, applicable technical standards, use position and appearance requirements. It can also be used by general construction contractors to select and purchase the main equipment and materials to realize specify grade and design effect.

The design-technical specification shall cover all engineering design contents of the project as far as possible. Meanwhile, the content of it shall include technical specifications of the main equipment and materials, technical requirements, design pictures and reference examples. The main contents are as follows (Fig. 12.20):

(1) Technical specification: The description of dimensions, approaches, materials, specifications, models and colors of the main equipment and materials.
(2) Technical requirement: The description of the technical parameters and the key parameters that affect the performance and appearance of the equipment and materials.
(3) Design pictures: Product, effect and real pictures of main equipment materials.
(4) Reference examples: 3–5 reference brands to illustrate the grade requirements and reference prices of equipment and materials

The design-technical specification is a tool to achieve design effectiveness and the implementation of "Integrated Design Documents for Drawings, Materials, Quantity and Price". The project management mode based on general contract strengthens the connection between design, procurement and construction. Architects are involved in the construction and achieve high quality construction by specifications.

12.6 Conclusion

The exploration on regional culture and design mode of foreign-aided architecture, as represented in the Cambodian National Stadium and the China–Cambodia Friendship Hospital, can provide useful references for future foreign-aided project. Within the framework of the "Belt and Road Initiative" and under the background of Chinese architectural design and construction industry in line with international standards, architects will have more opportunities to explore new design modes, and practice the architect's responsibility system abroad.

3. 室外广场铺砌

3.1 抛光混凝土路面

1）技术规格

序号	做法	位置
1	180mm 厚 C30 混凝土，面层先密封固化剂再机械研磨抛光	除外环车行道路及主入口广场外的道路广场。
2	300mm 厚水泥稳定碎石基层（分两层施工）	
3	150 厚级配碎石压实	
5	路基压实（压实系数不小于 0.93）	

2）技术要求

序号	名称	技术要求	标准
1	研磨机	1）采用瑞典进口 HTC 地坪研磨机； 2）金刚石刀具； 3）抛光 500 目； 4）湿态防滑值 60≤BPN<80。	HTC SuperfloorTM 技术标准
2	固化剂	1）固化剂渗透深度 5-8mm； 2）pH 值 8.7； 3）增加耐磨度 8 倍； 4）莫氏硬度 8 级；	
3	混凝土	1）28 天混凝土抗折强度 4.0Mpa； 2）纵缝间距 3~4.5m，横缝间距 4~6m，缝内填充填缝料； 3）横缝设置传力杆，纵缝设置拉杆； 4）水泥稳定碎石层 7 天抗压强度不小 3.0Mpa.	

11

Fig. 12.20 The design-technical specifications

Yang Li graduated from Harbin Institute of Technology, has been engaged in architectural practice for more than 20 years, specializing in sports and medical architecture design. He has participated in the design of the Softball Field and Weightlifting Hall for the 2008 Beijing Olympic Games, and designed many China-aided projects under the "Belt and Road Initiative", including the National Wrestling Arena in Senegal, the National Stadium of Cambodia, and the China-Cambodia Friendship Hospital. He insists that architectural design should not only meet functional requirements, but also reflect regional culture, adapt to local climate characteristics, and facilitate maintenance and sustainable vitality.

Qingnan Fan is a postgraduate architecture student at the Beijing University of Civil Engineering and Architecture. Her recent research topics include China-aided architecture and architectural media.

Chapter 13
Comparison of Chinese-Invested Shopping Malls in Georgia and China

Xiaolei Cai, Charlie Qiuli Xue, and Lara Jaillon

Abstract Increases in economic exchanges between China and other countries have encouraged the international emergence of Chinese-invested shopping malls, and this process has been accelerated by the Belt-and-Road Initiative. This chapter uses detailed case studies to analyse and compare two largest Chinese-invested shopping malls, Hualing Tbilisi Sea Plaza in Tbilisi, Georgia, and Hualing Integrated Market in Urumqi, China. The analysis investigates the reasons these shopping malls were developed and the influences of these malls on urbanisation. The economic and political incentives of the B&R are the initiatives for the Chinese-invested malls, bringing prosperous activities to the B&R cities. This chapter discusses the architectural and urban influences of shopping spaces developed in accordance with the Belt-and-Road Initiative on local urban development. The Chinese design codes and construction efficiency provide good examples to building activities in other B&R related countries, even these prototypes need to be more adapted to local environment. This study will enrich the existing literature on the Belt-and Road-Initiative from a spatial perspective, and on the literature of shopping spaces and urbanisation in China and the South Caucasus region, providing insights for future Chinese-invested building activities in B&R cities and countries.

X. Cai (✉) · C. Q. Xue
Department of Architecture and Civil Engineering, City University of Hong Kong, Kowloon, Hong Kong
e-mail: xiaolei.cai.521@gmail.com

L. Jaillon
Chu Hai College of Higher Education, Hong Kong, China

C. Q. Xue and G. Ding (eds.), *Exporting Chinese Architecture*,
https://doi.org/10.1007/978-981-19-2786-7_13

13.1 Introduction

The emergence of cities has led to an increase urbanisation worldwide. Since the second half of the twentieth century, urbanisation has expanded from developed to developing countries in what is considered the second wave of urbanisation (Dijkstra et al., 2018). Currently, more than half of the global population lives in urban areas.

In China and most developing countries, the spatial distributions of economic development and urbanisation are unbalanced. Production and urbanisation are generally concentrated in large cities, developed provinces and wealthy countries (Zhang, 2016). The same pattern was observed in China when it entered the globalisation process, in which productive elements naturally arose in large coastal cities. However, the Chinese government implemented policies to balance development between cities and provinces. Since approximately 2003, policies have awarded greater benefits to more remote cities and provinces rather than supporting only major seaports (Li & Gibson, 2013). The encouragement of secondary and tertiary industrial development has led to improved urban development in central and western China.

On the other side of Asia, the nation of Georgia has experienced challenges related to economic development since the dissolution of the Soviet Union (Papava, 2013). Georgia has since opened its market to international investors for two main reasons. First, the domestic economy is not well-developed because of political instability due to the national geopolitical history. Consequently, local developers do not have sufficient currency to fund large-scale development. Second, Georgian cities are placed in strategic locations, and Georgia borders nations such as Russia and Turkey and lies on the shore of the Black Sea. Therefore, international investors, including superpowers such as China, United States and Russia, are very willing to invest in Georgia and use its geographic advantages to better communicate with other countries (The Economist, 2013) (Fig. 13.1).

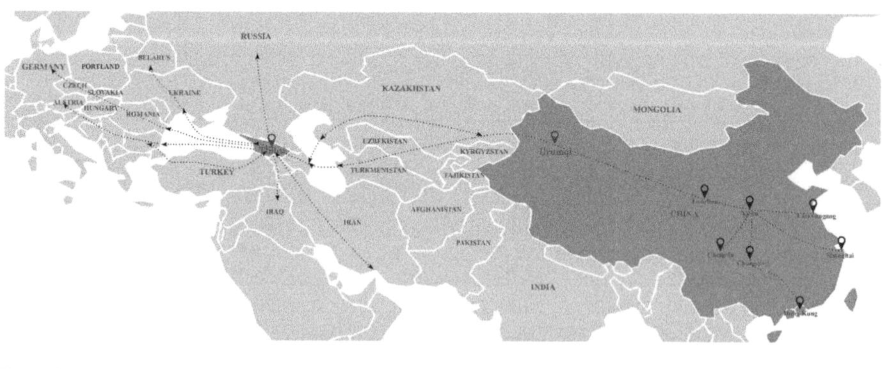

Fig. 13.1 Part of the strategic map of the Belt-and-Road Initiative (B&R), from China to Georgia

The initiation of the Belt and Road Initiative (B&R) has led to rapid, large-scale Chinese investment in Georgia, as demonstrated by projects that include infrastructure, industrial parks, shopping malls and housing. Particularly, the development of shopping malls represents a key step in commercial communication and a keystone in the economic development aims of Georgia and China. The cities of Urumqi (China) and Tbilisi (Georgia) serve as main transit hubs and key inland port cities on the Silk Road Economic Belt (i.e., land belt of the B&R), and both have received large-scale Chinese investment. Economic exchange requires a setting for the transfer of strategic goods. Therefore, shopping malls funded by Chinese investments have been developed quickly in these two cities.

This research aims to identify the influences of the B&R on Georgian people and cities. Specifically, it aims to use two detailed case studies of large shopping malls, Hualing Integrated Market in Urumqi and Hualing Tbilisi Sea Plaza in Tbilisi, to address the following questions: what are the main similarities and differences between shopping malls built by Chinese investors in China and Georgia, and what exciting or unexpected results have these shopping malls brought to the urban environments of the two cities? In addition, this study aims to fill the existing research gap in the English-language literature on urban development in Transcaucasia, as the current paucity of literature is incompatible with the increasing construction wave in that region.

13.2 Literature Review and Theories on Shopping Malls, Urbanisation and the B&R

13.2.1 Shopping Malls and Urbanisation

Urbanisation is a process of population transformation wherein an increase in the urban population is accompanied by a decrease in the rural population. A growing urban population represents the increasing importance placed on secondary (manufacturing) and tertiary (service) industries. During this process, transformation is observed in several fields, including occupational, industrial structural and land and territorial aspects (Li, 2012). Ray (1975) proposed the important "S Curve", or Northam Curve, of urbanisation. According to this proposed curve, an increase in the urbanisation rate to 30%–70% indicates a rapidly growing stage of urbanisation wherein large numbers of people and production elements migrate to urban areas. During this stage of rapid growth according to the S Curve, industrial organisation transforms from primary to secondary and tertiary industries to accommodate and promote increases in demands for consumption and services. Notably, urbanisation rates of 59.6% in China and 58.6% in Georgia have been reported (World Bank, 2018). Consumption has become the primary function of cities (Miles & Miles, 2004). Accelerating urbanisation promotes the agglomeration of commercial activities and thereby transforms cities into commercial hubs (Berghäll & Konvitz, 1997.).

Commercial agglomeration becomes the key link between production, consumption and service and mainly affects shopping spaces.

The agglomeration of spatial elements promotes the aggregation of other productive elements, such as labour forces and investments. Beyond its function as a commercial hub, a shopping space is a key manmade structure in which people can participate in public life and congregate and communicate with each other (Chung et al., 2001; Graham & Marvin, 2002; Xue et al., 2012). In contemporary society, such commercial and social activities are concentrated in shopping malls that include various types of stores (Crawford, 1992). The singular function of the shopping mall has expanded to composite functions that address the various requirements met by shopping activities (e.g., social needs). Buildings that house shopping malls are relatively complete architectural systems and can undergo self-functional modifications to satisfy various types of commercial requirements (Chung et al., 2001; Xue & Sun, 2021).

13.2.2 The Belt & Road Initiative

The B & R was initiated in Kazakhstan by Chinese President Xi Jinping in 2013. This initiative includes two routes, namely the Silk Road Economic Belt and the 21st-century Maritime Silk Road, and holds the main goal of promoting mutual development with the involved countries (Xinhua, 2019). From the Chinese perspective, Georgia has very strategic geographic advantages that will enable China to make better connections with Western countries. From the Georgian perspective, the country aims to shed the influence of the Soviet Union and thus seeks cooperation with superpowers such as China or the European Union. The mutual development goal of the B&R would also bring tremendous opportunities to Georgia, consistent with the national development plan (Zabakhidze & Beradze, 2017). The signing of a memorandum between these two countries in 2017 accelerated the process of cooperation (Xinhua, 2019).

Urumqi and Tbilisi are important cities that serve as the gates of the B&R, through which China can reach countries in Central Asia and Europe. Products produced or sold in China and Georgia under Chinese investment can now reach customers much more rapidly with support from improved land transport infrastructure (Ismailov & Papava, 2018). An Association Agreement was signed by Georgia and the European Union in 2014 (European Commission, 2014). These efforts have drawn the East and West much closer than ever before. The influences of the B&R on architecture and urban areas warrant investigation because they may benefit the development of future cities in countries that participate in the B&R.

13.3 Analytic Model and Research Methods

A shopping mall is a type of building that first emerged in Western countries in the 1970s. The popularity of this building type has been proven through decades of development in different cities and cultures. This article aims to explore how this building type has contributed to the transitions of cities from frugal to consuming societies. The following analytic framework is proposed for this work (Fig. 13.2). First, the complicated geopolitical contexts of Georgia and China are discussed briefly, whereas the B&R is discussed separately from the geopolitical context throughout the article. The relationship between urbanisation and the shopping space is the main focus of this study. Therefore, four aspects of the main comparative targets (i.e., the two shopping malls), including three architectural aspects (site, design and activity) and the urban impact. The latter is studied individually to offer a deep understanding of the rationale for and effects of the association between the shopping mall and urbanisation under the influence of the B&R.

This study strategically compares shopping malls in Urumqi, the most prosperous city in north-western China, and Tbilisi, Georgia, one of the most developed cities in Transcaucasia. Despite their similar urbanisation rates (59.6% and 58.6%, respectively), it may be inappropriate to compare China and Georgia (Table 13.1) because the geopolitical and economic conditions of these two countries differ greatly. China is a socialist nation with a Chinese culture and has the world's second-largest economy. In contrast, Georgia only gained its independence in 1991 and is now a democratic republic whose deep reforms in economic management and governance have earned it a reputation as a "Star Reformer" (World Bank, 2020). However, Urumqi and Tbilisi are reasonably comparable. First, both have similar populations and urbanisation rates (90.2 and 97.3%), which indicate similar production elements in these two cities. Second, the two cities have similar geographical conditions, as both are inland national, regional or even international transit hubs. Finally, the B&R

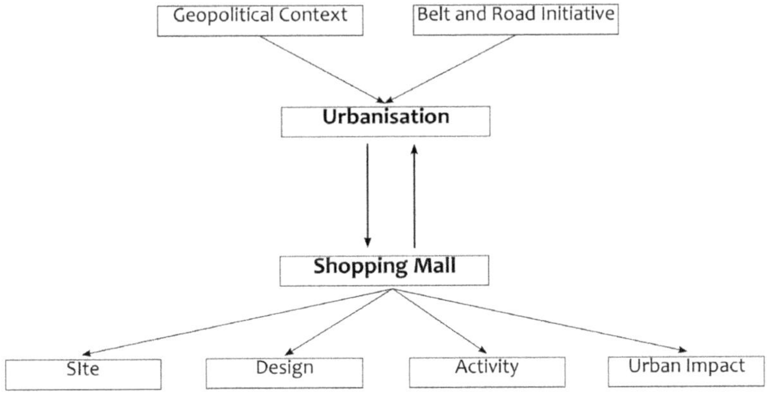

Fig. 13.2 Analytic framework of the study

Table 13.1 Urbanisation Statistics in 2018 (unit: thousands) (Geostat, 2018; Government of Urumqi, 2018; National Bureau of Statistics of China, 2018; World Bank, 2018)

	Urban population	Rural population	Total	Urbanisation rate (%)
China	831,370.0	564,010.0	1,395,380.0	59.6
Georgia	2,174.8	1,554.8	3,729.6	58.6
Urumqi	**2,003.7**	**21.9**	**2,222.6**	**90.2**
Tbilisi	**1,128.4**	**30.3**	**1,158.7**	**97.3**

has linked these cities, and the production and transport of strategic goods through the two cities have had considerable influence.

The same developer, the Hualing group, invested in the development of Hualing Integrated Market in Urumqi and Hualing Tbilisi Sea Plaza, and the same architecture firm, Xinjiang Renkai System City Complex Consultant Corporation Ltd, designed both shopping malls in this study. Therefore, the malls share many common attributes, but also exhibit striking differences due to the influences of different urban environments. The former mall is one of the largest commercial markets in Central and West Asia, while the latter is the largest shopping mall in Transcaucasia (Fehlings, 2017). Accordingly, both shopping malls have non-negligible influences on the surrounding urban environments (Cai et al., 2019). The Hualing Group was initially established in 1988 as a private company in Urumqi in the Xinjiang autonomous region. The company encompasses more than 20 business entities that provide services such as commerce, real estate, international commerce, logistics, livestock industry, heat energy, greenery, finance and education. Since 2007, the company has expanded its international business as an active response to the call of "Going Out" by the Chinese government, and it now participates in the B&R, through which it has attracted high levels of popularity and influence in Central/Western Asia and Eastern Europe. In Georgia, the ventures of the Hualing Group include international commerce, manufacturing, finance and real estate (Hualing, 2018).

This research uses case study as the main research method, and the key measures include a document review, site observations and interviews. For the document review, the authors have collected information from the literature, governmental reports, local magazines, conference papers, company websites and individual blogs to obtain a holistic overview of the previous and contemporary situations of these two shopping malls and cities. For the site observations, the authors visited Tbilisi in November 2017 and Urumqi in December 2019 to collect first-hand data on the projects and cities. For the interviews, the authors conducted in-person semi-structured interviews of the developer, two designers, two management personnel and some shopping mall users to obtain views pertaining to all project stages from design to implementation.

13.4 Case Study 1: Hualing Integrated Market and Urumqi

13.4.1 Hualing Integrated Market, Urumqi and the B&R

Hualing Integrated Market has a history spanning more than 30 years. This research focuses on the second stage of development, which was initiated in 2003 and included Blocks B and C (Hualing Trade Plaza and Hualing Sanitary Ware City, respectively) but excluded Block A (Hualing Trade City). The project was conducted with guidance from the urban planning department of Urumqi because the old Hualing Trade City was unable to satisfy the market demands (Hualing, 2018). The project encompassed a gross floor area of 517,979 m^2, including 290,125 m^2 during phase 1 and 227,852 during phase 2. Phase 1 was opened in 2004 and phase 2 in 2008. The project was initiated to supply the growing commercial requests from people in Urumqi and throughout Xinjiang. Hualing Integrated Market comprises thousands of manufacturers and sellers and is visited by 10,000 customers and vehicles every day. Together with the old Hualing Trade City, the Market has created a Hualing market business zone that serves both the local and regional markets. The developer and chief architect view Hualing Integrated Market as a prototype that they would like to transfer to overseas areas according to their business strategies.

Urumqi serves as the north-western gate of China. It is the most developed city in this region and contains concentrations of both natural resources and high-quality labour. Urumqi is a transit hub and thus is well suited to the goals of the B&R. Chinese capital and commerce are transferred to central Asia and the Middle East through this strategic inland port city (Li et al., 2019).

13.4.2 Site

The project is located in one of the most prosperous districts of Urumqi, the Shuimogou District, which can be accessed directly by three important roads (Fig. 13.3). The district is bordered by the national road G216 on the western side, Nanhu West Road on the northern side and Xihong West Road on the southern side. The convenient traffic pattern has integrated the shopping mall conveniently within the city and regional system, thus providing many options for easy access. However, the potential traffic congestion associated with the shopping mall is an area of concern. Despite the construction of surrounding overpasses and highways, it remains very difficult to arrive in or pass by the district in a vehicle. During peak traffic times, a vehicle might require more than 15 min to travel a distance of less than 1 km along Xihong West Road on the southern side of the shopping mall.

The siting decision was not determined solely by the developer, but was influenced by relevant governmental departments, the geographic environment and business strategies. Urumqui's urban planning department indicated that this district would become a concentrated commercial zone and identified Hualing as a developer with

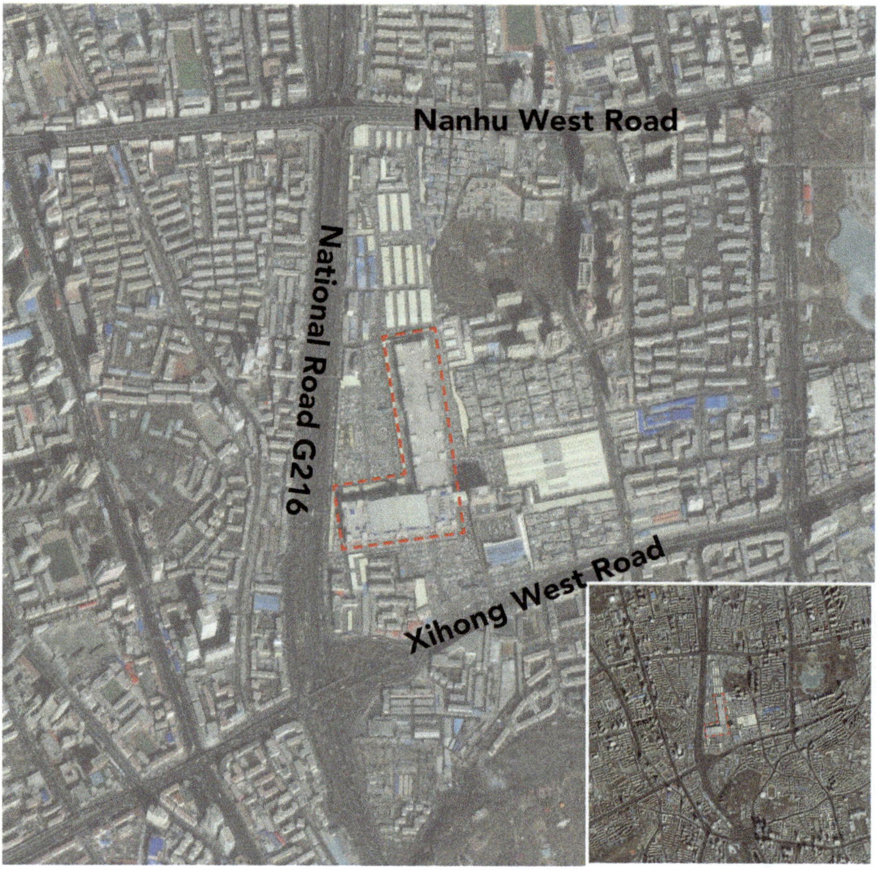

Fig. 13.3 Location of Hualing Integrated Market (Adapted from Google map by the authors)

the ability to implement such a large-scale project. Aside from the issue of traffic convenience, the geographic environment of Hualing Integrated Market is ideal. The location adjacent to other commercial and leisure spaces makes the district even more attractive to local and external visitors. Hualing aims to become an influential business company, and the opportunity to extend the old Hualing Trade City via this project represents a reasonable step in company development.

13.4.3 Design and Activities

The project was designed by Xinjiang Renkai System City Complex Consultant Corporation Ltd. under the leadership of CEO and Chief Architect Renkai Liu. During an interview, Architect Liu emerged as a humble yet determined person

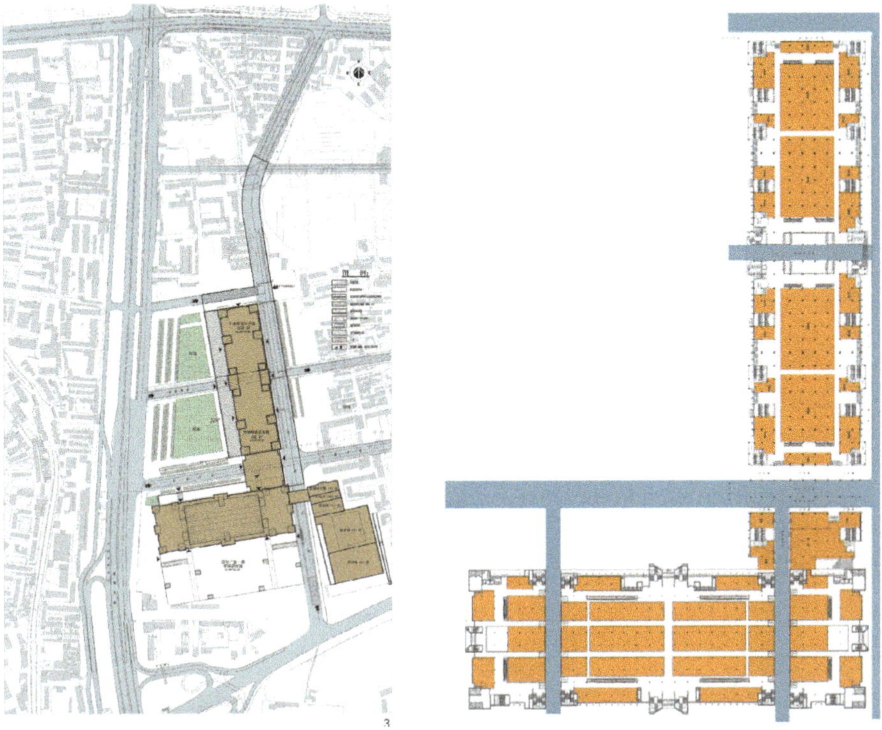

Fig. 13.4 Master plan (left) and ground floor plan (right) of Hualing Market (*Source* Xinjiang Renkai System City Complex Consultant Corporation Ltd.)

whose personality is reflected in his low-profile yet extremely practical designs.[1] For this project, the design embodies the requests of economic effectiveness made by the developer, the functionality required by sellers and visitors and the style and philosophy of the architect. Architect Liu and his team hold an ideology that originated from the Chinese urban development process, which emphasises strong spatial control and pragmatic spatial organisation.

The master plan and floor plan (Fig. 13.4) demonstrate that the floor area is rigidly defined by the fire control requirements. Fire staircases are clearly labelled throughout the project, thus enabling visitors to access the floors using either escalators or staircases. Regarding the shopping space and shopping activities, shop owners can tailor their shop sizes according to their own needs as long as the size conforms to the standard module and the pathways of circulation. A high level of convenience is reflected by the shop owners' ability to select an appropriate shop size and the customers' ability to find their desired goods. Notably, the space on the sixth floor has been totally released to shop owners.

[1] Interview of Architect Liu Renkai, Dec 23, 2019.

A busy market space has been created inside the mall. On the ground floor, a large atrium connects the entrance to the staircases and escalator, and this social space enables visitors to enjoy social interactions and activities. The mall also organises entertainment in this space shared by shop owners and customers, such as a festival to celebrate activities. Architect Liu believes that the social space has become increasingly more important because of the increased number of shopping options. Accordingly, the shopping mall must develop and emphasise a social nature to attract customers, as demonstrated by the bridging space between Block A and Block B where catering is provided on the third floor. People can rest and enjoy food in this transition space. Regarding auxiliary space, the offices of the shopping mall are situated on the seventh floor and can only be accessed via a staircase and office-only elevator, which enable the staff to maintain good control of the mall. Both underground and above-ground parking spaces are available, depending on the duration of the visit. For instance, a customer who wishes to spend 5 hours in the mall would be advised to park in an underground space because of concerns regarding the busy ground floor flow and weather conditions (Fig. 13.5).

The exterior of the shopping mall is perfectly symmetric, and the main entrance is placed at the mid-point (Fig. 13.6). These design features also reflect the designer's ideology of balance and good space management. The arch on the top of the building

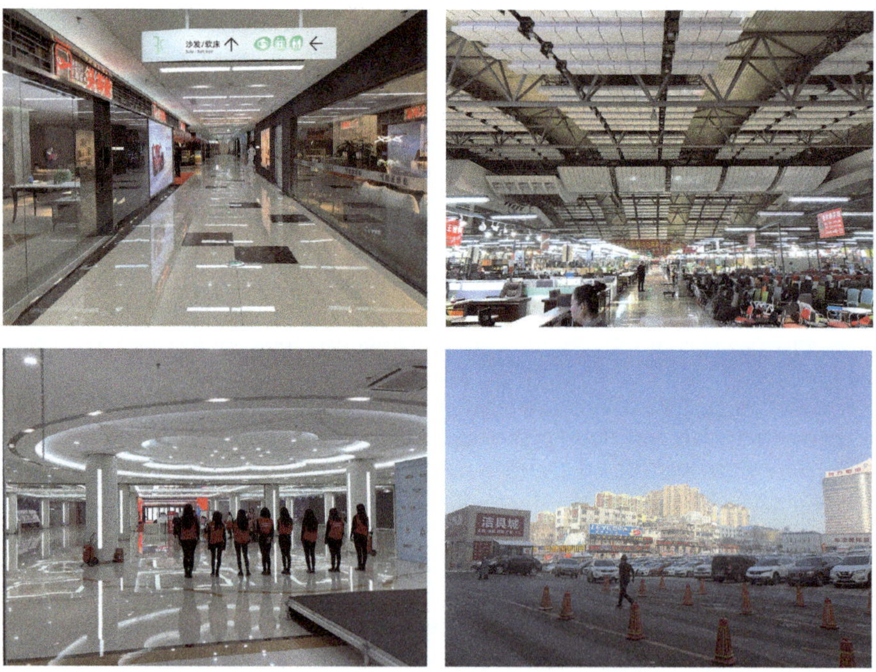

Fig. 13.5 Design and activities of the Hualing Market. Shops (top left); Sixth floor (top right); Atrium (bottom left); Above-ground parking (bottom right). Photos taken by the authors

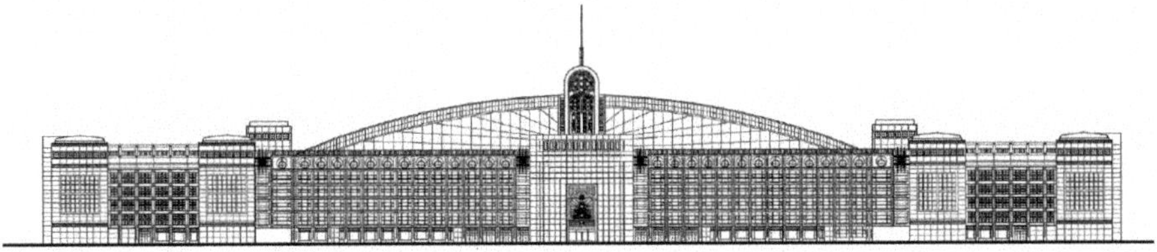

Fig. 13.6 Southern elevation. Xinjiang Renkai System City Complex Consultant Corporation Ltd.

both improves the aesthetics of the appearance and addresses a structural concern by providing support. This allows the use of fewer columns to enable more commercial and social activities. The shopping mall has become a symbol of the district because of its functionality and the grand scale of the buildings (Ke, 2004).

13.4.4 Urban Impact

Spatial impact

The development and agglomeration of a shopping mall promote commercial activities and encourage many aspects of urbanisation. Hualing Integrated Market is located in the development-focused area of the City South District, which was defined by the Urumqi Urban Planning Institute. This district and the City North District will form a powerful economic spine in Urumqi via the primary road G216 (Fig. 13.7). The expansion of common development from this spine to other less developed districts will be promoted. Thus, the prosperity of Hualing Integrated Market will expand to the overall City South District and the entire city. This planning testifies the ability of the rapid urbanisation of Urumqi to stimulate a dense agglomeration of commercial activities, as demonstrated by the accumulation of shopping streets and shopping malls (Wang, 2017). Many notable new developments are arising around the shopping mall. For example, underground and above-ground pedestrian networks have been constructed to facilitate the flow of pedestrians. The main roads have been expanded to reduce traffic congestion. Urban development around the shopping mall is occurring at an accelerated pace.

Other impacts

In addition to spatial development, this large-scale shopping mall promotes the agglomeration of social activities. Urumqi is an ethnically rich city where people from various ethnic groups gather and encourage cultural integration (Han et al., 2005). The housing prices in Shuimogou District underscore the vast urban development in this district. There, the average cost of newly built housing is RMB 9,472 per m^2 floor space (US$ 1 = RMB 6.9 yuan in 2018), compared to RMB 5,984 per m^2 in Midong district (Anjuke, 2020). Hualing Integrated Market has brought

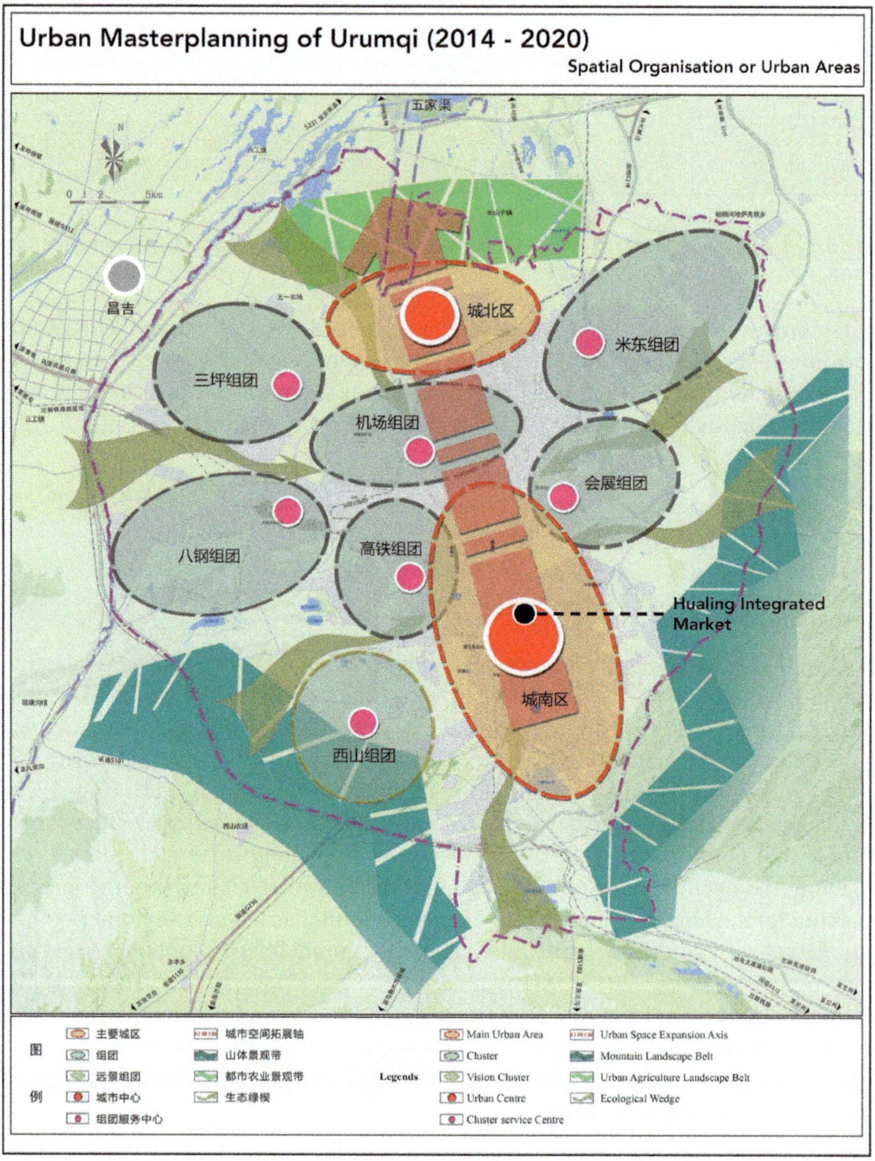

Fig. 13.7 Spatial Organisation of Urumqi, 2015–2020. Urumqi Urban Planning Institute, 2015. Modified and translated by the authors

urbanisation to this region in terms of social infrastructure and housing, but it has also introduced problems such as congestion, pollution and criminal activity. Nevertheless, the commercial success of this shopping mall is a good prototype for B&R investments in shopping spaces overseas.

13.5 Case Study 2: Hualing Tbilisi Sea Plaza and Tbilisi

13.5.1 Hualing Tbilisi Sea Plaza, Tbilisi and the B&R

Hualing Tbilisi Sea Plaza is one of the largest Chinese-invested commercial building projects in the South Caucasus region. The project includes a main building with a gross floor area of 120,000 m^2, building material market groups encompassing 20,000 m^2 of floor space, a bonded warehouse of 100,000 m^2 and a transferring warehouse of 90,000 m^2 (Hualing, 2018). Hualing Tbilisi Sea Plaza is the largest shopping mall in the South Caucasus region and serves as both a logistic and shopping hub and a center for retail, wholesale and international commercial activities. The enormous Chinese investment in this project has attracted not only Chinese merchants, mostly from Xinjiang, but has also interested famous enterprises from Chinese cities such as Shanghai, Guangzhou and Shunde. In addition, the project actively involves more than 200 local Georgian merchants and sellers from Ukraine, Dubai and Turkey. The opening of the shopping mall in 2017 marked the emergence of the most high-profile shopping center in the South Caucasus. This achievement cannot be separated from the efforts of the B&R, which encourages Chinese companies to invest abroad while supporting collaborations between local governments and companies.

Tbilisi is one of the most developed cities in the South Caucasus. It serves as a key regional transport destination by connecting important cities via an enhanced transport infrastructure, including the Baku-Tbilisi-Kar Railway which links Azerbaijan, Georgia and Turkey. The B&R identified the potential of Tbilisi, and investments from China and other influential countries have been offered continuously in recent years.

13.5.2 Site

Hualing Tbilisi Sea Plaza is located in south-eastern Tbilisi, south of the Tbilisi Sea (Fig. 13.8). The primary road, Marshal Joseph Pilsudski Avenue, passes directly northwest of the site. Teopane Davitaia Street and Javakheti Street are located west and southeast of the project, respectively, and are separated by a considerable distance. No public transport options travel directly to this shopping mall. The closest underground station is Varketili, which is more than 2 km away, and no direct route to the station is available. Therefore, visitors to the shopping mall must still

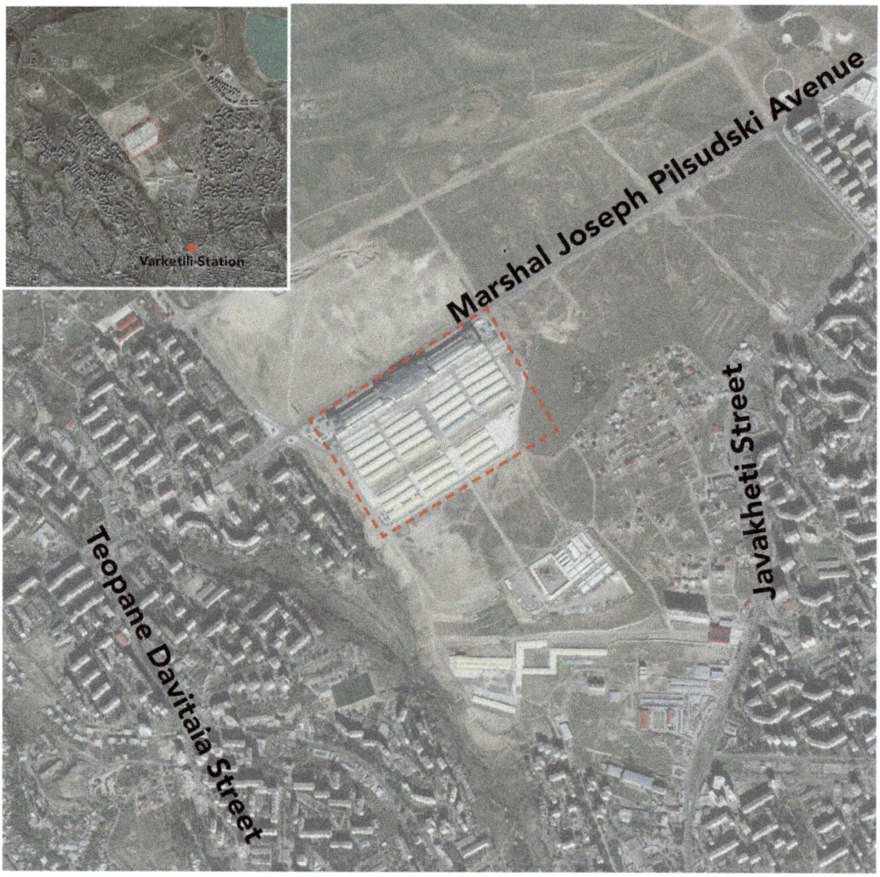

Fig. 13.8 Location of Hualing Tbilisi Sea Plaza. Adapted by the author from the Google map

use a private car or taxi. Few residences surround the project, and the northern side has remained vacant for decades. The distance of the site from the rest of the city and the weak transportation links have relatively isolated the project from city life.

In an interview, the developer stated that they did not really have a choice when selecting the location.[2] Rather, the government of Tbilisi selected the site and offered it to Hualing with policy preference. The land premium was relatively inexpensive because the government sought opportunities associated with this B&R project. On one hand, the site condition could be perceived as a challenge for the developer because of the limited accessibility and low human traffic flows. On the other hand, this could be seen as an opportunity because the city centres are crowded and dilapidated. The development of a vacant new area at a lower price may be more profitable and could create a future sub-city centre.

[2] Interview with Secretary Guo of Hualing Group in Urumqi, Dec 24, 2019.

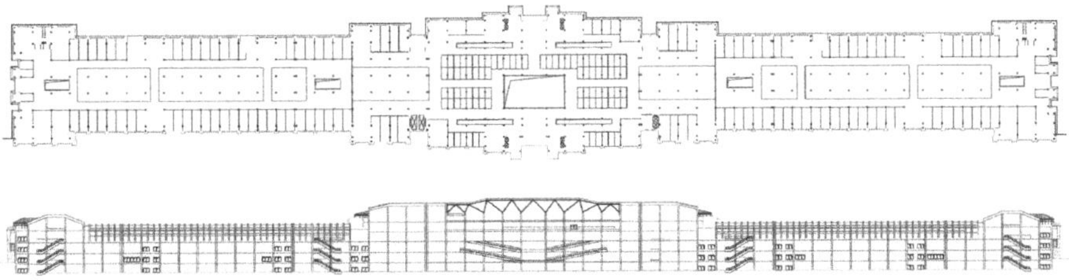

Fig. 13.9 (Top) Plan of Hualing Tbilisi Sea Plaza. (Bottom) Section of Tbilisi Sea Plaza. From Xinjiang Renkai System City Complex Consultant Corporation Ltd

13.5.3 Design and Activities

Architect Liu stated that the design of Hualing Tbilisi Sea Plaza was mostly in accordance with his previous design experiences, although it gave more consideration to the needs of the foreign population with respect to the developer's and shop owners' concerns.[3] The developer required the maximum selling area to maximise profit. As shown in the plan, the design used a grid column system (Fig. 13.9), which enabled a highly compact space. The shopping space occupies most of the area within the building, excluding the necessary circulation routes and auxiliary spaces, and little is left as a social space. The shop owners benefit from flexibility, as they are able to customise their shop size before they move in, as long the size is compliant with the grid system. The developer provides a base shopping module in which the shop owners build individual functional cubes with regard to the systematic and individual requirements. Here, shops close to the main entrance have higher rents, compared to those in the eastern and western ends of the development.

The shopping mall has a horizontal length of 500 m and is encircled by passenger walkways. Consequently, exploration within the mall may be fatiguing (Fig. 13.9). The spatial organisation of the shop arrangement was not planned and involves a mixture of shops selling various products. The grid system is not very effective because visitors cannot find their designated products easily, even though directory signals are provided. Spaces for social activities have also been provided (Fig. 13.10). Five atria next to the vertical circulations reduce the boredom associated with such a long shopping mall and enable people to rest and socialise. However, these atrium spaces are not well used and include no chairs for resting, few catering options and few interesting interior landscapes.

Although the designer stated that the atrium on the ground floor and the arched roof space on the fourth floor would provide horizontal and vertical areas for social life, they admitted that the size restrictions imposed by the developer have limited the functionality of these spaces. The designer was required to make compromises to maximise the commercial benefits. Technically, the building was designed according to Chinese regulations; for instance, two fire engine access points have been built inside the mall, although no such regulations exist in the Georgian building code.

[3] Interview with Architect Liu Renkai in Urumqi, Dec 23, 2019.

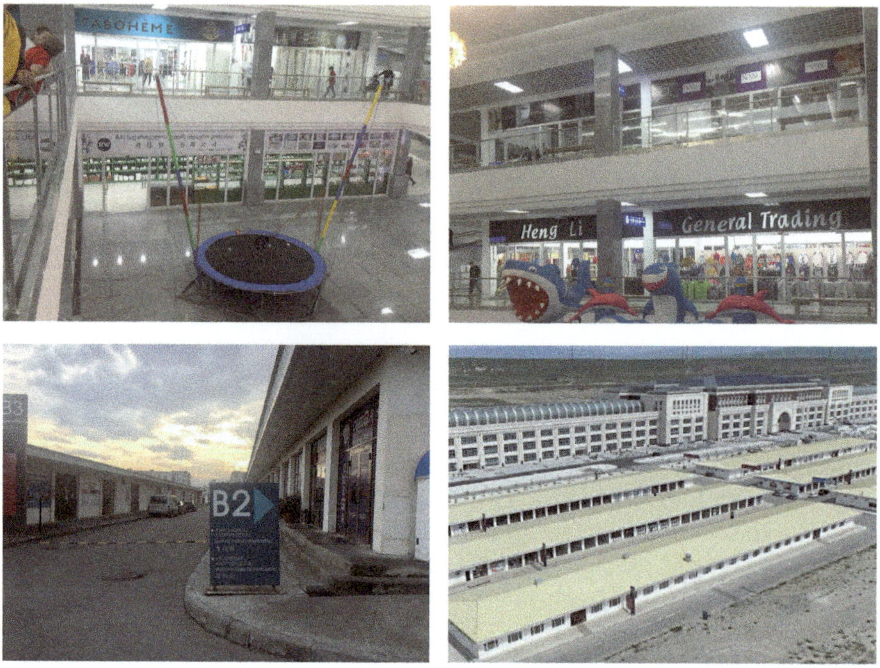

Fig. 13.10 Hualing Tbilisi Sea Plaza. Interior public space (top left); Interior shops (top right); Parking lot and warehouse (bottom). Photo credits: the authors and Hualing Group (bottom right)

There is no precedent example for this construction element in Transcaucasia, and local fire codes lag behind these contemporary requests.

The elevation of the Tbilisi Sea Plaza reflects the designer's preference for classic architectural features (Fig. 13.11). The extremely centric and symmetric architectural style expresses the architect's ideology based on Chinese culture, which includes respect for order. The interior design adheres to the same ideology. Beyond the shopping mall, logistical spaces have been created to fulfil the role of the project as a logistic hub. Warehouses and parking lots have been created in the south area of the shopping mall to facilitate visitors with vehicles and the import and export of wholesalers' products. These efforts have created a well-functioning logistic hub for Western and Eastern economic communication.

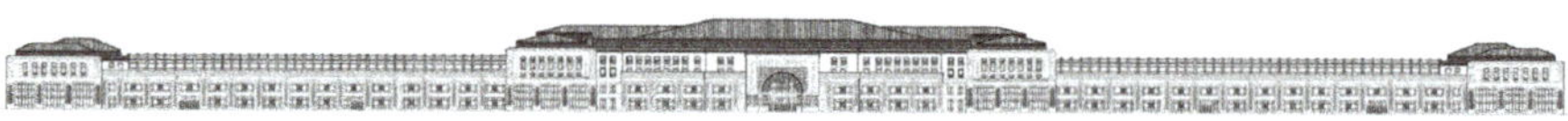

Fig. 13.11 Northern elevation of Hualing Tbilisi Sea Plaza. From Xinjiang Renkai System City Complex Consultant Corporation Ltd

13.5.4 Urban Impact

Spatial impact

Hualing Tbilisi Sea Plaza promotes urban development in south-eastern Tbilisi. Previously, urban development was excessively concentrated in the central old Tbilisi district along the River Mtkvari. The shopping mall represents a pivotal step for foreign investment in Tbilisi and the introduction of a prosperous urban life to a previously vacant urban boundary. Following the success of the Tbilisi Sea Plaza, Hualing gradually introduced other large housing, office and hotel projects in the same district, which have led to rapid expansion and urbanisation. The image of this district has shifted from "vacant space" to "prosperous urban destination". From the perspective of the Tbilisi Polycentric Structure Development, an amendment of the existing 2009 General Land Use Plan, the government of Tbilisi realised that the future of the city future would rely on polycentric development, which would promote common urban development (City of the Future Group, 2015). The district where the Tbilisi Sea Plaza is located will receive new construction, and the surrounding area will be intensively developed. The success of the shopping mall has brought domestic and international investments to this district and has further encouraged construction activity. Because the district was vacant before the initiation of the Tbilisi Sea Plaza, new construction can be implemented effectively, with few disruptions (Sukhiashvili, 2015) (Fig. 13.12).

Other impacts

The shopping mall has provided increased employment opportunities. More than 80% of employees are local residents in both management team or grass-roots positions. Employment is a major social issue in Georgia, which reported an unemployment rate of 11.6% in 2019 (Geostat, 2019). Visitors from other districts, cities or countries are attracted by the scale of the buildings and amounts of available products and visit the shopping mall continuously, as evidenced by the large number of photos posted by visitors on Instagram. The through-traffic and popularity of the shopping mall and the whole district are increasing rapidly. Urbanisation of this district focuses not only on economic development, but also on a modern lifestyle for local residents (Georgian Journal, 2015). This reliance on commerce and industry has led to the creation of developments to improve living and social environments, based on the Hualing Special Economic Zone (SEZ) plan (Fig. 13.13). This project matches the mutual development goal of the B&R.

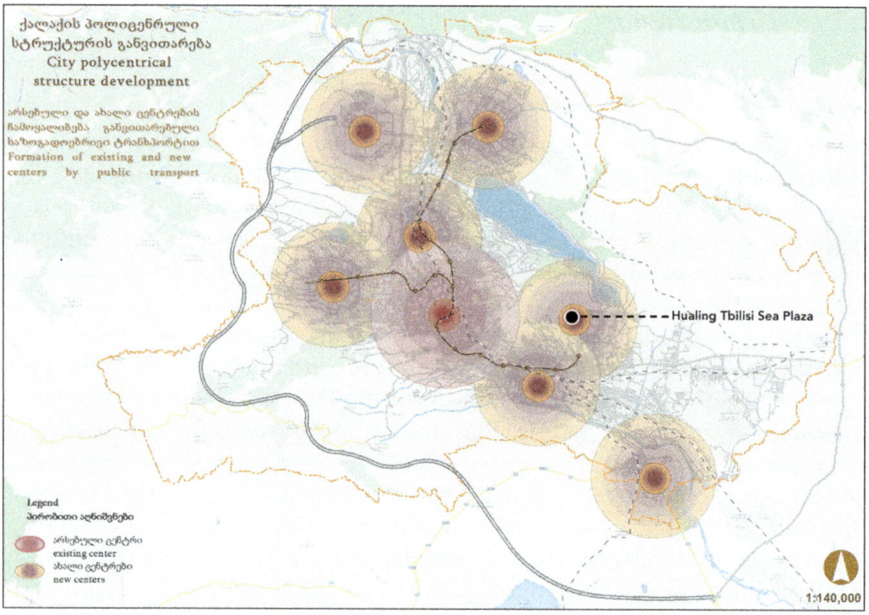

Fig. 13.12 City Polycentric Structure Development (City of the Future Group, 2015). Modified by the authors

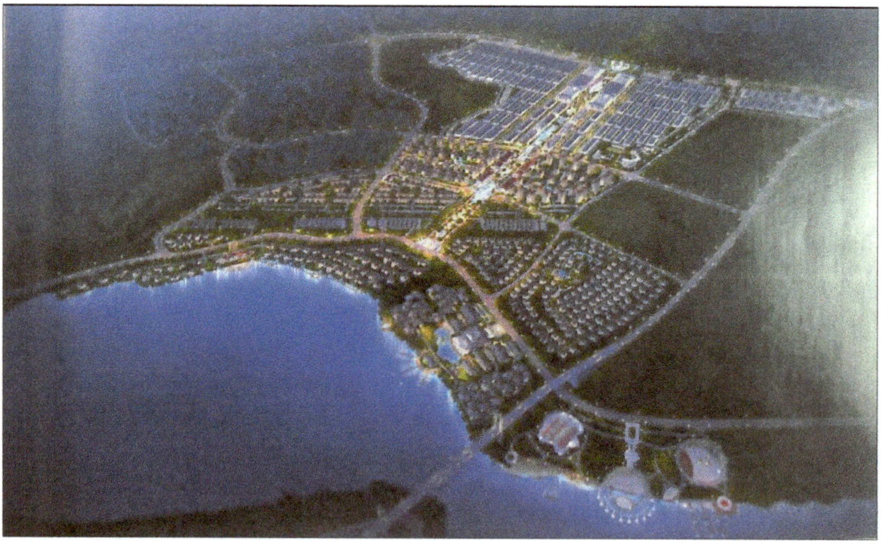

Fig. 13.13 Three-dimensional image of the SEZ plan. From Xinjiang Renkai System City Complex Consultant Corporation Ltd

13.6 Discussion and Conclusion

13.6.1 The Shopping Mall

Hualing Integrated Market, a successful prototype designed by Architect Liu, matched the market demand and economic development. This mall has manifested as a simple yet efficient architectural form with a flexible interior spatial organisation. Hualing Tbilisi Sea Plaza represents an adaptation rather than a replication of the Integrated Market.

Regarding the site context, Hualing Integrated Market was constructed in the city central area in the early 2000s, during a period of rapid urbanisation in China. In Georgia, Tbilisi Sea Plaza opened in the late 2010s, when urbanisation was already expanding from urban centers to suburban areas. However, both shopping malls have direct access from main roads, thus reflecting the heavy dependence of shopping mall development on transport accessibility. Shopping malls at the edges of urban centers focus more on vehicle flows and less on accessibility for pedestrian flows.

From the perspective of design and activities, both shopping malls reflect the architect's preferred ideology of order, which is visible in either the exterior symmetric elevation or the interior shop organisation. This preference for order is associated with the environment in which the architect trained and worked. In other words, the architectural style was cultivated in an urban environment with Chinese features. However, the Integrated Market exhibits a greater focus on social life, as demonstrated by the grand atrium space and catering bridge, whereas the Tbilisi Sea Plaza has sacrificed social space for increased commercial space. Notably, large-scale shopping malls are not as prevalent in Transcaucasia as in China, and therefore in the former region, purchasing and selling are more important than the social aspects within the shopping mall space. The local development status determines the potential success of a shopping mall, even when obvious shortcomings exist. The architectural creativity and techniques may not be avant-garde, but they have been proven to be pragmatic, effective and efficient with respect to the projects in China and Georgia. The design of the two shopping malls may be similar to the "commercial kitsch" seen everywhere in second and third-tier Chinese cities. However, the designs are quite suitable for the development level of cities such as Urumqi and, particularly, Tbilisi. Although the shopping malls are not refined and glamorous, they are greatly welcomed by local residents. These commercial buildings stimulate people's materialistic desires for better lives and futures. Moreover, the Chinese perspectives on regulations and design techniques will promote the development of modern architecture in Georgian cities.

13.6.2 On the Relationship with Urbanisation

Despite the distinctive site selections and urban environments, both shopping malls occupy strategic locations in the respective urban development plans. This commonality reflects the nature of a shopping mall or commercial space development as the core of urbanisation.

The agglomeration of commercial space, particularly shopping space, is closely related to urbanisation because the development of tertiary industries is a key indicator of the level of urbanisation. In Urumqi, the Integrated Market remained in the central city and serves as a magnet for human and vehicle flows, which activate the whole district and the city. In Tbilisi, the Sea Plaza is located along a current city boundary, where plenty of new construction projects are in progress. This new sub-city center will alleviate the heavy burden on the old city center, and the currently less-developed area will embrace future development opportunities.

The urbanisation stimulated by shopping malls will result in fluctuating flows and activities. This dynamic not only provides opportunities for increased employment and a rich social life, but also introduces challenges. For example, traffic congestion is likely during peak times. Issues of safety, comfort and pollution are also evident. These issues of urbanisation problems are observed in the Integrated Market but not in the Tbilisi Sea Plaza, and this reflects the advantages of building in a previously vacant area. The Chinese-invested architecture is highly suitable for the needs of local people in an increasingly urban area. The practicality and efficiency match the needs of urban development in Georgian cities and will promote economic growth and encourage international and regional communication.

13.6.3 On the B&R

The B&R has introduced Chinese companies to an international platform. The support received from the B&R has increased the trust placed in these companies, which then tend to receive local policy support. The harmonious geopolitical relationship between China and Georgia is the foundation for the exports of both Chinese architecture and urbanism.

In Urumqi, the B&R promotes the production and export of Chinese products from this “western gate”. This promotion has stimulated manufacturing and service industries in this provincial capital city and led to rapid urban development. The efficient shopping mall is a typical example of the satisfaction of a request for urbanisation. In Tbilisi, despite criticism of the architecture design skills and lack of social concerns, it is undeniable that this B&R brought new things. Chinese-invested shopping mall has brought urban prosperity to an undeveloped area of Tbilisi and has shifted the image of the city to that of a brand-new, well-functioning regional transit hub.

Practical and efficient shopping malls were proven successful in Chinese cities before Chinese companies' outreach to developing countries such as Georgia. These architectural structures have had tremendous effects on the economic and social lives of locals. Stakeholders should remain aware of the local urban contexts, adhere to urban development plans and adapt their designs to the shopping and living behaviours of locals.

Globalisation represents a simultaneous challenge and opportunity. China uses the B&R in its communications with other involved countries. Chinese investors give emphasis on building efficiency, commercial models, economic benefits and political guidance, while localized social lifestyle should not be neglected absolutely. Policy makers use the B&R to promote urban development, while they should also make rational decisions in its strategic planning to avoid the negative effects of rapid urbanisation. Chinese designers need innovative local adaption when bringing their designs to cities in different countries, acquiring wisdom from local cultures and social behaviours. Local designers can learn from the experiences of the design codes and making techniques from Chinese designers and actively participate in the design and construction process. The concerted efforts of both parties are expected to lead to a new culture of shopping and urbanism.

(The authors heartily thank the generous guidance received from Professor Liu Renkai of Xinjiang Renkai System City Complex Consultant Corporation Ltd., who shared his transnational architectural wisdoms and many architectural drawings of Hualing's projects. Also, the authors want to thank the kind help from Secretary Guo Xiangyang of Hualing Group, who shared Hualing's international developing strategies and visions on The Belt and Road Initiative to us. This chapter is part of a research supported by the National Natural Science Foundation of China, Project No. 51878584.)

References

Anjuke. (2020). Housing Price of Urumqi. Retrieved June 28, 2020, from https://wulumuqi.anjuke.com/market/.

Berghäll, E., & Konvitz, J. (1997). Urbanisation and sustainability. *OECD Policy Approaches for the 21st Century*, 155.

Cai, X., Jaillon, L. C., & Xue, C. Q. (2019). The changing shopping space in Georgia: The influence from the Chinese 'Belt and Road Initiative'. *KnE Social Sciences*, 120–133.

Chung, C. I., Koolhaas, J. R., & Leong, S. (2001). The Harvard Design School guide to shopping.

City of the Future Group. 2015. *From Stability to Sustainability*. Retrieved June 28, 2020, from https://factcheck.ge/wp-content/uploads/2016/04/file0011.pdf.

Crawford, M. (1992). The world in a shopping mall. *The City Cultures Reader*, 125–140.

Dijkstra, L., Florczyk, A., Freire, S., Kemper, T., Pesaresi, M., & Schiavina, M. 2018. Applying the degree of urbanisation to the globe: A new harmonised definition reveals a different picture of global urbanisation. In *Proceedings of the 16th IAOS Conference: Better Statistics for Better Lives, Paris, France* (pp. 19–20).

European Commission. (2014). *The EU's Association Agreements with Georgia, the Republic of Moldova and Ukraine*. Retrieved June 27, 2020, from https://ec.europa.eu/commission/presscorner/detail/en/MEMO_14_430.

Fehlings, S. (2017). The Chinese connection—Informal trade relations between the caucasus and China since the early 1990s. *Caucasus Analytical Digest, 96*, 2–5.

Georgian Journal. (2015). *What Will Tbilisi's New Districts Look Like?—A "City of the Future" Near Tbilisi Sea*. Retrieved June 28, 2020, from https://www.georgianjournal.ge/business/30522-what-will-tbilisis-new-districts-look-like-a-city-of-the-future-near-tbilisi-sea.html.

Geostat. (2018). *National Statistics*. Retrieved June 28, 2020, from https://www.geostat.ge/en.

Geostat. (2019). *National Statistics*. Retrieved June 28, 2020, from https://www.geostat.ge/en.

Government of Urumqi. (2018). *Statistics*. Retrieved June 28, 2020, from http://www.wlmq.gov.cn/DataPublic.htm. (in Chinese).

Graham, S., & Marvin, S. (2002). *Telecommunications and the city: Electronic spaces, urban places*. Routledge.

Han, J. P., Li, X. P., & Yang, D. G. (2005). The characteristics and dynamic mechanisms of urbanization of Urumqi region. *Arid Area Resources and Environment, 2005*(05), 5–10. (in Chinese).

Hualing. (2018). Hualing Group. Retrieved June 28, 2020, from http://www.hualing.cn.

Ismailov, E., & Papava, V. (2018). Caucasian tandem and the belt and road initiative. *Central Asia & the Caucasus (14046091), 19*(2).

Ke, D. (2004). Hualing, building the Eurasian business circle. *China Reform, 2004*(02), 50–51. (in Chinese).

Li, C. H. G. (2012). Trend of" double transfer" and urbanization model transition. *Urban Problems, 2*.

Li, C., & Gibson, J. (2013). Rising regional inequality in China: Fact or artifact? *World Development, 47*, 16–29.

Li, L. Q., Kong, X., Li, Y. M., & Xu, Y. B. W. (2019). The selection of the strategic pivot in China-Central Asia cooperation under the Belt and Road Initiative. *Geographical Research, 38*(07), 1705–1719. (in Chinese).

Miles, S., & Miles, M. (2004). *Consuming cities* (pp. 45–201). Palgrave Macmillan.

National Bureau of Statistics of China. (2018). *Statistics*. Retrieved June 28, 2020, from http://www.stats.gov.cn/english/.

Papava, V. (2013). Reforming of the Post-Soviet Georgia's Economy in 1991–2011. *GFSIS Center for Applied Economic Studies Research Paper—03.2013*.

Ray, M. N. (1975). *Urban geography*. Wiley.

Sukhiashvili, V. (2015). *When will Tbilisi have a general development plan and will it end the chaotic construction in the city?* Grass Fact Check. Retrieved June 28, 2020, from https://www.factcheck.ge/en/story/21558-when-will-tbilisi-have-a-general-development-plan-and-will-it-end-the-chaotic-construction-in-the-city.

The Economist. (2013). *Rising China, sinking Russia; China in Central Asia* 2013, The Economist Intelligence Unit N.A., Incorporated, London.

Wang, Z. Q. (2017). Some considerations of Urumqi urban design. *City Development Research, 24*(03), 143–147. (in Chinese).

World Bank. (2018). *Urban Population*. Retrieved June 28, 2020, from https://data.worldbank.org/indicator/SP.URB.TOTL.IN.ZS.

World Bank. (2020). *The World Bank in Georgia*. Retrieved June 28, 2020a, from https://www.worldbank.org/en/country/georgia/overview.

Xinhua. (2019). *History of the Belt and Road Initiative*. Retrieved June 28, 2020, from http://www.xinhuanet.com/politics/2019-04/26/c_1124418156.htm.

Xue, C. Q. L., Ma, L., & Hui, K. C. (2012). Indoor 'public' space—A study of atrium in MTR complexes of Hong Kong. *Urban Design International, 17*(2), 87–105.

Xue, C. Q. L., & Sun, C. (2021). "Rail villages" in Hong Kong—development ratio and design factors. *Urban Design International., 26*, 97–113. https://doi.org/10.1057/s41289-020-00119-5

Zabakhidze, M., & Beradze, R. (2017). Georgia as a transit hub and its increasing potential in the implementation of the belt and road initiative.

Zhang, X. Q. (2016). The trends, promises and challenges of urbanisation in the world. *Habitat International, 54*, 241–252.

Xiaolei Cai is a designer who have practiced in Beijing, Hong Kong, and London. He received trainings in urban design and city planning from the Bartlett, UCL, and in architecture from Oxford School of Architecture, Oxford Brookes. He has interests on spatial narratives.

Charlie Qiuli Xue has taught architecture at Shanghai Jiaotong University, University of Texas and City University of Hong Kong. An award-winning architect and writer, he has published 15 books, including '*Building a Revolution: Chinese Architecture since 1980*' (HKU Press, 2006), '*Hong Kong Architecture 1945–2015: From Colonial to Global*' (Springer, 2016), '*A History of Design Institutes in China: from Mao to Market*' (with G. Ding, Routledge, 2018) and '*Grand Theater Urbanism: Chinese cities in the 21st century*' (Springer, 2019, ed.). He has published more than 160 research papers in professional and international refereed journals and 40 book chapters. His papers are published in such journals as *Cities, Habitat International, Urban Design International, Journal of Architecture, Journal of Urban Design, Architectural Research Quarterly, Journal of Urban History, Planning Perspective, Architecture + Urbanism, Domus* and Chinese journals like *Architectural Journal, Architect, New Architecture, Time + Architecture, World Architecture* and *Taiwan Architect*. His book on Hong Kong was awarded by the International Committee of Architectural Critics (CICA) in 2017. Xue's research interests are in Chinese architecture, transnational design and high-density environment. Xue is also extensively involved in design and consultant practice in Hong Kong, Chinese mainland and the US.

Lara Jaillon is an architect and researcher. She has over 20 years of experience in teaching and research focusing on sustainability and architecture. She has completed her studies in Architecture in France (Paris Val de Marne) and Canada (McGill University, Montreal), and subsequently joined the Hong Kong Polytechnic University in 2000 where she obtained her PhD. Her PhD research focussed on the evolution of the use of prefabrication techniques in the Hong Kong construction industry. She then joined the City University of Hong Kong in 2011, where she was an Assistant Professor. Her research work focuses on Life Cycle Assessment (LCA) and life cycle design, carbon emissions, prefabrication, construction waste reduction, sustainable construction and design. She has recently completed a research project on comparing carbon emissions of precast and cast-in-situ construction methods, and is currently involved in research projects assessing green building assessment tools, and the circular economy. She has written articles published in both local and international journals, and conferences.

Index

C. Q. Xue and G. Ding (eds.), *Exporting Chinese Architecture*,
https://doi.org/10.1007/978-981-19-2786-7